POLYGAMY

Six Short Stories About Christian Families Who Obeyed The Bible And Wound Up With Multiple Wives

J.D. LANGTON

Copyright © 2024 J.D. Langton. All rights reserved. No part of this book may be used or reproduced without the written consent of the copyright owner.

Scripture quotations taken from the New American Standard Bible® (NASB), Copyright © 1960, 1962, 1963, 1968, 1971, 1972, 1973, 1975, 1977, 1995 by The Lockman Foundation. Used by permission. (www.Lockman.com)

ISBN Hardcover: 979-8-9913155-7-9

ISBN Paperback: 979-8-9913155-8-6

ISBN eBook: 979-8-9913155-9-3

These stories were co-authored by Fatima Abbas. Fatima can be contacted at - fatimaabbas9993@gmail.com

Book Layout by Verve Pages (hello@vervepages.com)

Cover Art: Oladimeji Alaka

Published & Printed by IngramSpark

Visit BiblicalFamily.Church for more information and to contact the author

---

Other Books By J.D. Langton

Marriage, Sex, & Polygamy: It's About To Get Biblical Up In Here

A Christian Defense Of Polygamy Through The Centuries

Available On Amazon

CONTENTS

Introduction i

Story 1 - "Be Warmed And Filled" 1

Story 2 - Reconciled 65

Story 3 - She Shall Become His Wife 135

Story 4 - Called By Your Name 205

Story 5 - Better To Marry Than To Burn 289

Story 6 - A Brother's Duty 391

Epilogue 459

Introduction

This collection of short, fictional stories is meant to serve as somewhat of a companion to the theological work I have published alongside it - *Marriage, Sex, & Polygamy: It's About To Get Biblical Up In Here*.

In each of these stories, you'll meet a Christian (or soon-to-be Christian) family that finds themselves in a unique predicament, yet one which Scripture directly addresses. In each of their cases, practical obedience to clear teaching in Scripture results in a family with more than one wife.

The purpose of these stories is to demystify the nature of multi-wife households by demonstrating practical and relevant implementations of "polygamous" family structures. For the majority of human history, throughout all the world's inhabited continents, families with more than one wife and families with one wife only were morally equal in the eyes of any given society. It is only since the rise of the Greco-Roman empire and subsequent Catholic Church that humans have even sought to differentiate between the two, let alone criminalize one or the other. The modern phenomenon of the Mormon cult has successfully synonymized polygamy with sexual deviancy in the eyes of the Western Church, but God's people—both Old Covenant and New—have embraced the benefits of multi-wife households for thousands of years, long before Mormonism ever existed.

My hope is that these stories will disassociate polygamous family structures from tyranny and perversion in the minds of my readers, as each one demonstrates how easily—and naturally—practical obedience to the Scriptures can lead to multiple wives in one home. Rather than being the preferred family structure of patriarchal brutes and sex-crazed barbarians, these stories show how Biblical Christians, even those in the modern day, can genuinely benefit from a multi-wife household.

In this endeavor, widows are especially dear to my heart, as Western missions have made it impossible for many widows in traditional societies to re-integrate into families, leaving them without hope of finding a husband for themselves and a father for their children.

For those who've read *Marriage, Sex, & Polygamy*, these stories will serve as practical examples of the theology you've learned. For those who haven't read the theological work, my hope is that these stories will pique your interest in the topic enough to drive you to study God's word for yourselves. The other books I've published can aid you in your study, but Scripture Alone must be your ultimate source of truth.

I have never read—let alone written—a fictional story before, but with the help of an interested woman who *does* write, I feel I was able to produce something that can be enjoyed by all, with occasional laughs and tears along the way.

May God bless you and strengthen you in your knowledge of His word as you read these stories.

J.D. Langton

These stories are meant to be read in numerical order.

Story 1 -
"Be Warmed And Filled"

Setting – Northern Norway, Early 20th Century

Lars Holm squinted to avoid the morning sunlight as he stepped out onto the porch of his farmhouse. He had spent most of his forty-five years on the land he tended. His appearance showed clear evidence of his labor, for his face was weathered by the sun and his hands were calloused.

He breathed deeply, his blue eyes scanning his expansive farm. Fields of wheat seemed to stretch on endlessly, swaying with the wind. To the north was a dense forest, its trees a reminder of the wilderness that had once dominated this land. Rolling hills to the east marked the boundary of their property, beyond which lay miles of similar farmland, each as isolated as their own.

"Another day, another blessing," Lars murmured.

The Holm farm had stood for over a century, passed down through generations. It was more than just land and buildings; it was a legacy. The farmhouse itself was a grand old structure, built by Lars' great-grandfather with sturdy oak beams and local stone. Its rooms were spacious, designed to accommodate a large family and farmhands, though now many stood empty, echoing with memories of busier times.

The creak of the door behind him announced his wife's presence before her gentle hand came to rest on his shoulder.

"Good morning, my love," Elsa said softly, her voice still deep with sleep.

Lars turned, his heart swelling with love as it did every morning at the sight of her. At forty-two, Elsa was still as beautiful as the day he'd married her. Her golden hair, now streaked with silver, was braided neatly down her back. Laugh lines crinkled at the corners of her eyes, a map of their shared joys and sorrows over the years.

"You're up early," she observed with concern.

"Couldn't sleep," he admitted, wrapping an arm around her waist and pulling her close. "Got to thinking about the harvest."

Elsa nodded, understanding. "It's been a good year, Lars. The Lord has blessed us abundantly."

"That He has," Lars agreed, pressing a kiss to her forehead. "How's our little Sigrid this morning?"

As if on cue, the patter of small feet echoed from inside the house, and moments later, their eight-year-old daughter burst onto the porch.

"Mama! Papa!" Sigrid cried, her blonde braids bouncing as she threw herself into her father's arms.

Sigrid was their miracle baby, born after years of failed attempts at having children. She was the light of their lives and her presence had filled the big old house with joy since the day of her birth, but as she grew, her parents couldn't help but worry about her isolation, so far from other children her age.

Lars laughed, scooping her up and spinning her around. "There's my sunshine! Ready to help your old papa with the chores today?"

Sigrid nodded eagerly, her blue eyes – a mirror of her father's – twinkling. "Can I milk Bessy today? Please, Papa?"

Elsa chuckled, reaching out to smooth a stray hair from her daughter's forehead. "After breakfast, darling. You need your strength."

The family made their way back into the house, their footsteps echoing in the large kitchen. This room was the heart of their home, warm and inviting with its big cast-iron stove and well-worn wooden table. Shelves lined the walls, filled with preserves from previous harvests.

As Elsa moved to the stove, stoking the fire and setting a pot of porridge to cook, Lars marveled at her efficiency. She was as much a farmer as he was.

"Sigrid, dear, set the table, would you?" Elsa asked, and the little girl eagerly complied, carefully laying out three wooden bowls and spoons.

The table could seat twelve, and Lars felt a pang as he thought of the empty chairs. Once, this kitchen had been filled with the bustle of farmhands and extended family. Now, it was just the three of them.

Lars settled into his chair at the head of the table, unfolding the family Bible that always sat nearby. The book was well-worn, its pages marked with notes and underlined verses – a testament to years of study.

"Shall we have our morning devotion?" he asked, as was their custom.

Elsa and Sigrid joined him at the table, bowing their heads as Lars began to read. "Today's verse is from Proverbs 12:11," he said, his deep voice filling the kitchen. "Whoever works his land will have plenty of bread, but he who follows worthless pursuits lacks sense.'"

He closed the Bible and looked at his family. "What do you think this means, Sigrid?"

The little girl furrowed her brow in concentration. "It means... we should work hard on our farm?"

Lars smiled proudly. "That's right, sunshine. God rewards those who are diligent and work with their hands. It's a reminder of the importance of our daily labor."

Elsa nodded, reaching out to squeeze her daughter's hand. "And it's not just about the work itself, but about being content with what we have and not chasing after things that don't matter."

As they ate their breakfast, the conversation turned to the day's tasks. Afterwards, Lars wiped his mouth with a napkin and said, "I'll need to mend that fence in the north pasture today. Those sheep are crafty creatures."

Elsa nodded. "I'll tend to the vegetable garden and perhaps start on some preserves for winter. The root cellar's looking a bit bare."

"Can I help you, Mama?" Sigrid asked eagerly.

"Of course, my dear. But first, you can help your papa with the milking as you wanted."

After breakfast, the family dispersed to their various tasks. Lars and Sigrid made their way to the barn, a sturdy structure that housed their livestock. The scent of hay and animals filled the air, a smell that Lars found comforting in its familiarity.

"Now remember, Sigrid," Lars cautioned as they approached Bessy, their gentlest cow. "Slow and steady movements. We don't want to startle her."

Sigrid nodded solemnly, her face a picture of concentration as she perched on the small stool beside the cow. Lars guided her hands, showing her how to grip and pull in a smooth, rhythmic motion. These moments of teaching were precious to him, a chance to pass on the knowledge and skills that had been handed down through generations.

5 | POLYGAMY

"That's it, sunshine," he encouraged as the first streams of milk hit the pail. "You're a natural!"

Sigrid beamed with pride. "Papa, do you think I'll be as good a farmer as you someday?"

Lars chuckled, ruffling her hair affectionately. "I've no doubt you'll be even better, my girl. This farm will be yours one day, after all."

As they worked, Lars found himself marveling at how quickly Sigrid was growing up. It seemed like only yesterday she had been a babe in his arms, and now here she was, learning the ways of the farm with an eagerness that warmed his heart. Still, with that joy came a twinge of worry. Sigrid was their only child, and the responsibility of the farm would one day rest solely on her shoulders.

"Papa," Sigrid said suddenly, her voice thoughtful. "Why don't we have more children around? Like in town?"

The question caught Lars off guard, though it wasn't the first time Sigrid had asked about it. He paused, considering how to answer. "Well, sunshine, we live quite far from others. The nearest farm is five miles away, remember?"

"But why don't we have more brothers and sisters for me?" she persisted.

Lars sighed, his heart heavy. This was a question he and Elsa had grappled with for years. The empty rooms in their big house seemed to echo with the absence of the larger family they had once dreamed of.

"Sometimes, Sigrid, God has different plans for different families," he said gently. "Your mama and I... we weren't able to have more children after you. But you know what? That just makes you extra special to us."

Sigrid seemed to ponder this for a moment before nodding. "I love you and Mama too, Papa. But sometimes I wish I had someone to play with."

Lars pulled her into a hug, milk pail forgotten for a moment. "I know, sunshine. But you have us, and we have each other. That's what's most important."

As they finished the milking and moved on to feeding the animals, Lars couldn't shake the lingering sadness from Sigrid's question. He and

Elsa had tried for years to have more children, praying fervently for God to bless them with a larger family, but it wasn't to be, and they had learned to be content with their beautiful, spirited daughter. Still, he wondered if they were doing right by Sigrid, raising her so far from others.

The morning passed quickly, filled with the myriad of tasks that kept the farm running. As Lars worked on mending the fence in the north pasture, he found his mind wandering to their isolated life. The vastness of their land sometimes felt overwhelming, especially when he thought about Sigrid growing up with so little company her own age.

"Lord," he murmured as he worked, driving stakes into the hard ground, "guide us in raising Sigrid to be strong and faithful, even in our solitude. Help us to be enough for her."

As the sun climbed higher in the sky, Lars made his way back to the house for the midday meal. The scent of fresh bread and stew greeted him as he entered the kitchen, finding Elsa and Sigrid already seated at the table.

"How goes the fencing, my love?" Elsa asked as she ladled stew into his bowl.

"Well enough," Lars replied, sinking into his chair with a grateful sigh. "Though I fear those sheep are determined to find every weak spot."

Sigrid giggled. "Maybe they just want to explore, Papa!"

Lars chuckled, reaching out to tweak her nose affectionately. "Perhaps, sunshine. But their exploring could lead them into danger. That's why we must be vigilant."

As they ate, Lars found himself lost in thought, considering their upcoming trip to town. These quarterly journeys were their main connection to the wider world, a chance to attend church, run errands, and socialize with their neighbors.

Finally, he cleared his throat. "Elsa, I've been thinking about our trip to town next month for church. Perhaps we could make a day of it? Take Sigrid to see some of her friends from Sunday school?"

Elsa's eyes lit up at the suggestion. "That's a wonderful idea, Lars. It would be good for her to spend some time with the other children."

Sigrid clapped her hands in excitement. "Oh, yes! Can we, Papa? Can we stay all day?"

Lars smiled, warmed by his daughter's enthusiasm. "We shall, sunshine. It's important to nurture our relationships with our church family, even if we can't see them as often as we'd like."

After they finished their meal, Lars returned to his fencing, while Elsa and Sigrid worked in the vegetable garden, harvesting ripe tomatoes and green beans. The sun beat down mercilessly, but none of them complained. This was the life they knew and loved, hard work and all.

As evening approached, Lars made his way to the edge of their property, surveying the land that stretched out before him. In the distance, he could just make out the steeple of the town church. It was a world that sometimes felt as distant as the stars, yet one they were inextricably tied to through their faith.

"Papa!" Sigrid's voice carried across the field, and he turned to see her running towards him, her golden hair flying behind her.

"Papa, Mama says it's time to come in for supper!"

Lars scooped her up as she reached him, settling her on his hip despite her growing size. "Is that so? And what delicious meal has your mama prepared for us tonight?"

Sigrid wrinkled her nose. "Fish stew. But Mama promised apple pie for dessert if I eat all my stew!"

Laughing, Lars began the walk back to the house, his daughter chattering away in his ear about her day in the garden. As they approached, he saw Elsa standing on the porch, bathed in the golden light of the setting sun. He smiled at her. His heart was ablaze with love, admiring the most beautiful sight in all creation, or at least she was to him.

Later that night, after Sigrid had been tucked into bed with a story and a prayer, Lars and Elsa sat together on the porch.

"She asked about siblings again today," Lars said softly, breaking the comfortable silence.

Elsa sighed, leaning her head on his shoulder. "I know. I overheard you two in the barn this morning."

"Do you ever regret..." Lars began, but Elsa cut him off with a gentle finger to his lips.

"No," she said firmly. "I regret nothing. We have a beautiful daughter, a prosperous farm, and each other. God has blessed us abundantly."

Lars nodded, pulling her closer. "You're right, of course. But sometimes I worry about Sigrid, growing up so alone..."

"She's strong, like her father," Elsa murmured. "She'll be fine."

As the first light of dawn crept through the curtains, Lars Holm stirred from his slumber. He turned to see Elsa still peacefully asleep beside him, her golden hair splayed across the pillow. He smiled softly, marveling at how, even after all these years, the sight of her still made his heart skip a beat.

Carefully, so as not to wake her, Lars slipped out of bed and padded quietly to the window. He drew back the curtains, letting the early morning light flood the room. The farm stretched out before him, fields of wheat swaying gently in the breeze and the dense forest looming in the distance. It was a view he had seen countless times, yet it never failed to fill him with a sense of wonder and gratitude.

"Good morning, my love," Elsa's sleepy voice came from behind him.

Lars turned, his smile widening. "Good morning, beautiful. Did I wake you?"

Elsa shook her head, sitting up and stretching. "No, it's time to get up anyway. We have a big day ahead of us."

Suddenly, as was typical for their mornings, the patter of little feet could be heard running down the hallway. Moments later, their bedroom door burst open, and Sigrid bounded in, her eyes shining with excitement.

"Mama! Papa! It's church day!" she exclaimed, launching herself onto their bed.

Lars chuckled, scooping his daughter into his arms. "Indeed it is, sunshine. Are you excited to see your friends?"

Sigrid nodded enthusiastically. "Yes! Especially Anna. I haven't seen her in so long!"

Elsa smiled, running a hand through Sigrid's tangled blonde hair. "Well then, we better get you cleaned up and looking your best, shouldn't we?"

As Elsa helped Sigrid get ready, Lars made his way to the kitchen to start breakfast. The old farmhouse creaked and groaned around him, a familiar symphony of sounds that he found comforting. He stoked the fire in the stove and began mixing batter for pancakes, Sigrid's favorite.

Soon, the kitchen was filled with the warm scent of coffee and the sizzle of pancakes on the griddle. Elsa and Sigrid joined him, Sigrid now neatly dressed in her Sunday best, her hair braided tidily.

"Smells wonderful, Lars," Elsa said, pressing a kiss to his cheek as she moved to set the table.

They sat down to eat, the morning sunlight streaming through the windows, casting a golden glow over the kitchen. Lars couldn't help but feel a swell of contentment as he looked at his little family.

"Papa," Sigrid said between mouthfuls of pancake, "do you think God lives in the church?"

Lars exchanged an amused glance with Elsa before answering. "Well, sunshine, God is everywhere. But the church is a special place where we go to worship Him and be with our community."

Sigrid nodded seriously, considering this. "Is that why we only go sometimes? Because we can talk to God here too?"

"That's right," Elsa chimed in. "But it's important to gather with others who share our faith. It strengthens us and reminds us that we're part of something bigger than just our family."

Lars nodded in agreement. "And it's a chance for you to see your friends, like Anna. Speaking of which; Sigrid, why don't you tell us what you're looking forward to most about seeing her today?"

Sigrid's face lit up. "Oh! I want to show her the new doll you made me, Papa. And I want to hear all about the baby lambs on her farm."

Lars and Elsa exchanged a look over Sigrid's head, one that silently acknowledged their love of Sigrid's enthusiasm and also their sadness that she couldn't see her friend more often.

As they finished their breakfast, Elsa found her thoughts drifting to Hanna Eriksen, Anna's mother. She couldn't help but worry about how she was managing on her own. Running a farm was hard enough with two people; she couldn't imagine doing it alone, especially with a young child to care for.

"Elsa?" Lars' voice broke through her reverie. "Is everything alright? You seem lost in thought."

Elsa shook her head, offering a small smile. "Just thinking about the Eriksens. I hope Hanna's doing alright."

Lars reached across the table, squeezing her hand. "We'll check on her today."

"Maybe we can invite them for dinner soon?" Elsa asked.

Lars nodded, grateful as always for his wife's compassionate heart. "That's a good idea. We should do what we can to help."

After breakfast, as Elsa and Sigrid cleared the table, Lars retreated to the living room. He picked up the family Bible from its place of honor on the mantelpiece, running his hand over the worn leather cover.

"Sigrid," he called, "come here for a moment, please."

Sigrid bounded into the room, her eyes lighting up at the sight of the Bible. "Are we going to read, Papa?"

"That's right, sunshine. It's important to prepare our hearts before we go to church. Would you like to choose the passage today?"

Sigrid nodded eagerly, climbing onto Lars' lap as he opened the Bible. She flipped through the pages carefully, her small finger tracing the lines of text until she found a familiar story.

"This one, Papa," she said, pointing to the parable of the Good Samaritan.

As Lars began to read, Elsa joined them, sitting close and wrapping an arm around Sigrid. Lars' deep voice filled the room, recounting the story of compassion and neighborly love.

When he finished, he looked at Sigrid. "What do you think this story teaches us, sweetheart?"

Sigrid furrowed her brow in concentration, a familiar expression when she was determined to find a right answer. "That we should help people, even if they're different from us?"

"That's right," Elsa said, smiling proudly. "And why do you think that's important?"

"Because that's what Jesus wants us to do," Sigrid replied confidently. "He wants us to love everyone."

Lars felt a surge of pride at his daughter's understanding. "Exactly, sunshine. And that's something we should always remember, especially when we go to church and see our neighbors."

As they prepared to leave for town, the excitement in the house was palpable. Sigrid could barely contain herself, practically bouncing as she put on her shoes.

"Now remember," Elsa said, kneeling to button up Sigrid's coat, "church is a place of worship. We need to be respectful and quiet during the service."

Sigrid nodded solemnly. "I know, Mama. I'll be good, I promise."

Lars watched this exchange with a smile, marveling at how quickly Sigrid was growing up. It seemed like only yesterday she had been a babe in his arms, and now here she was, understanding the importance of faith and community.

As they stepped out onto the porch, the crisp morning air filled their lungs. The sun had fully risen now, bathing the farm in warm light. Lars took a moment to survey their land, sending up a silent prayer of thanks for their blessings.

"Ready to go?" he asked, turning to his family.

Elsa nodded, taking Sigrid's hand. "Ready. Let's not keep God waiting."

With that, they made their way to the old horse-drawn wagon, the anticipation of the day ahead filling them with a quiet joy. Their horse had become quite the companion, as he had been faithfully pulling them into town for over 15 years now. Their wagon was moderately sized, with a sturdy cover over the top and enough seats to fit the three of them plus two more. As they rode down the long driveway, leaving the farm behind, Lars couldn't shake the feeling that this Sunday might bring more than just the usual worship and fellowship. Something in the air, in the excited chatter of his daughter and the thoughtful silence of his wife, told him that more may have been on the way.

Little did he know just how right he was, or how much their lives were about to be transformed by a simple act of Christian charity.

The sun had barely crested the horizon when Lars and Elsa Holm set out for their trip to town. The family's old wagon tattered down the dirt road, kicking up clouds of dust in its wake. Sigrid bounced excitedly in the back seat, her blue eyes wide with excitement.

"Mama, do you think Anna will be at church today?" Sigrid asked, referring to her friend, the daughter of Elsa's widowed friend.

Elsa turned in her seat, smiling at her daughter. "I'm sure she will be, sweetheart. You two can play together after the service while I have tea with her mother."

Lars' hands tightened imperceptibly on the reins at the mention of their neighbour. Hanna Eriksen had been widowed for just under a year now, and each time he saw her, the weight of her loss seemed to hang heavier on her slender shoulders.

As they rode, the landscape slowly transformed from the familiar fields of their farm to the dense forests that separated their land from the town. The trees loomed on either side of the narrow road, their branches reaching out like grasping fingers.

"The forest seems darker than usual," Elsa remarked, her voice tinged with concern.

Lars nodded, his brow furrowed. "Aye, it does. I hope Hanna made it through alright. These roads can be treacherous, especially for someone driving alone."

They lapsed into silence, each lost in their own thoughts. Lars couldn't help but worry about Hanna. She had been struggling to manage her farm since her husband's passing, and he knew the isolation was taking its toll on her.

As they emerged from the forest, the small town came into view. The white steeple of the church rose above the other buildings, a beacon of faith in their close-knit community. Lars parked the wagon in the grassy lot beside the church, and after setting the horse up with some feed, the family made their way inside.

The interior of the church was cool and dim, sunlight filtering through stained glass windows to cast colorful patterns on the worn wooden pews. As they took their usual seats, Lars scanned the congregation, his eyes falling on Hanna and her daughter Anna, seated a few rows ahead.

Hanna's long, dark red hair was neatly braided, but Lars could see the weight on her shoulders, the way she seemed to curl in on herself. His heart ached for her, and he sent up a silent prayer for God to ease her burden.

The service began, and Lars tried to focus on Pastor Johansen's words, but his mind kept drifting. He found himself looking at Hanna, noting the graceful curve of her neck and the delicate profile of her face. She was a beautiful woman and he found himself worrying about her attracting the wrong sort. A woman like that in need of a husband was sure to catch the attention of every man in town.

As the congregation rose to sing a hymn, Hanna's clear, sweet voice rose above the others. Lars sat straight letting the music wash over him, trying to push away the anxious emotions roiling within him.

After the service, the congregation spilled out into the churchyard. Children ran off to play, their laughter filling the air, while the adults gathered in small groups to chat. Sigrid immediately sought out Anna, the two girls hugging tightly before running off hand in hand.

Elsa touched Lars' arm gently. "I'm going to have tea with Hanna at the café. Will you be alright with Sigrid?"

Lars nodded, forcing a smile. "Of course. You ladies enjoy yourselves. Sigrid and I will find something to do."

As Elsa walked away to join Hanna, Lars couldn't help but watch them go. Hanna's dress was simple a blue cotton affair, but even the plainness of it was not enough to hide her beauty. Once again, he found his mind wandering to thoughts about someone taking advantage of her. His eyes darkened with worry.

The girls interrupted his concern with bubbly laughter, giving each other another big hug. Lars watched them, a bittersweet smile on his face. It was good to see Sigrid so happy, but he couldn't shake the feeling that something was about to change.

Meanwhile, at the small café across from the church, Elsa and Hanna sat at a corner table, steaming cups of tea before them. Hanna's hands trembled slightly as she lifted her cup, and Elsa noticed dark circles under her friend's eyes.

"Hanna," Elsa said gently, reaching out to touch her friend's hand. "How are you really doing?"

Hanna's eyes filled with tears, and she set her cup down with a clatter. "Oh, Elsa," she whispered. "I don't know how much longer I can do this."

Elsa moved her chair closer, wrapping an arm around Hanna's shoulders. "Tell me," she urged softly.

The words tumbled out of Hanna in a rush. "The farm is too much for me to manage alone. I'm up before dawn and working until I collapse into bed, but it's never enough. The fences need mending, the barn roof is leaking, and I can barely keep up with the daily chores. And Anna..." Her voice broke. "She's so lonely out there. I feel like I'm failing her."

Elsa listened, her heart breaking for her friend. "Have you considered selling the farm?" she asked gently.

Hanna shook her head vehemently. "I can't. It's all I have left of Erik. It's Anna's inheritance. But I don't know how I'll manage to keep it running."

Elsa listened as her heart continued to ache. "Have you considered hiring help?" she asked, struggling to hold back her own tears now.

Hanna shook her head, a bitter laugh escaping her lips. "With what money? The farm barely breaks even as it is. And even if I could afford it, who would want to work so far out? There's a reason our farms are the only ones left out there."

Elsa nodded, understanding all too well the challenges of their solitary lives. "We'll think of something," she said, squeezing Hanna's hand. "God won't abandon you, Hanna. He has a plan."

Hanna managed a weak smile. "I hope you're right, Elsa. I really do."

As the women talked, Lars found himself wandering the small town with Sigrid and Anna in tow. The girls skipped ahead, pointing out shop windows and chattering excitedly. Lars' mind, however, was elsewhere.

He couldn't shake the image of Hanna's sad eyes.

"Papa, look!" Sigrid's voice broke through his thoughts. She was pointing at a display of colorful hair ribbons in a shop window. "Can we get one for Anna? Her birthday is coming up."

Lars smiled, grateful for the distraction. "That's very thoughtful of you, sunshine. Of course we can."

As they entered the shop, the bell above the door tinkling merrily, Lars found himself relaxing. This was what mattered – his daughter's kind heart, the simple joy of choosing a gift for a friend.

The girls spent several minutes debating the merits of various ribbons before settling on a deep purple one that complemented Anna's dark hair. As Lars paid for the ribbon, he overheard a conversation between two women at the counter.

"Did you hear about the Eriksen farm?" one woman was saying. "Such a shame. I give it another year before she has to sell."

"Poor dear," the other replied. "But what can you expect? A woman can't run a farm that size on her own. She needs a man."

Lars felt a surge of anger at their callous words. He wanted to defend Hanna, to tell them how hard she was working, but he bit his tongue. It wasn't his place to speak for her.

As they left the shop, Lars found himself looking at Hanna in a new light. Yes, she was beautiful—he couldn't deny that—but more than that, she was strong. To keep going in the face of such adversity, to fight so hard for her daughter's future... It was admirable.

The rest of the afternoon passed quickly. Lars treated the girls to ice cream, watching with a smile as they giggled and whispered together. He saw so much of Sigrid in Anna—the same joy, the same innocence.

The thought of that light dimming under the weight of their isolation and struggles made his heart ache.

As the sun began to dip towards the horizon, Lars gathered the girls and headed back to the church, where they had arranged to meet Elsa and Hanna. He found the women standing near the wagon, their heads bent close in conversation.

As they approached, Hanna looked up, and Lars felt his breath catch in his throat. The setting sun caught her hair, causing its red tones to glow. Her eyes, though red-rimmed from crying, shone with a quiet determination that made her even more beautiful.

"Lars," Hanna said softly, a small smile gracing her lips. "Thank you for looking after Anna today."

"It was my pleasure," Lars replied, his voice gruffer than he intended. "She's a wonderful girl. You should be proud."

A flush crept up Hanna's neck, and she ducked her head. "Thank you," she murmured.

As they said their goodbyes, Lars found himself lingering, reluctant to end the moment. It was Elsa who finally broke the spell, gently touching his arm.

"We should get going, love," she said. "It'll be dark soon."

The ride home was quiet, each lost in their own thoughts. As they pulled up to their farmhouse, the sky ablaze with the last light of day, Lars couldn't shake the feeling that something new and strange had entered his heart.

That night, after Sigrid had been tucked into bed, Lars and Elsa sat on the porch, as was their custom. The night was clear, stars twinkling overhead like scattered diamonds.

"Hanna's not doing well," Elsa said softly, breaking the silence.

Lars nodded, unsurprised. "I overheard some gossip in town. They're saying she won't last the year."

Elsa sighed, leaning her head against Lars' shoulder. "She's so alone out there, Lars. It's killing her spirit. And little Anna... she needs more than Hanna can give her right now."

Lars wrapped an arm around his wife, pulling her close. "We should pray for her."

Elsa smiled, nodding. "That's true. I wish I could do something for her."

They dozed off together, both filled with a mixture of gratitude for their family and concern for their friend. They often fell asleep while sitting whenever something important was on their minds. Elsa found a unique comfort in being held by her husband beneath the stars, and Lars never had the heart to move when his beloved had fallen asleep so content.

On the Friday morning of the next week, the Holm farm stirred to life as Elsa moved with practiced efficiency in the kitchen, preparing breakfast for her family. Lars stood at the edge of the field, wiping sweat from his brow as he surveyed the day's work ahead. Inside, the scent of freshly baked bread and sizzling bacon filled the air.

"Sigrid," Elsa called up the stairs, "Breakfast is nearly ready. Come down and help set the table, please."

Moments later, the patter of small feet echoed through the house as Sigrid descended the stairs, her blonde braids bouncing with each step. Despite the early hour, her blue eyes were bright and alert.

"Good morning, Mama," Sigrid said, reaching for the plates in the cupboard.

Elsa smiled, noticing a hint of melancholy in her daughter's voice. "Good morning, sunshine. Did you sleep well?"

Sigrid nodded, but her usual cheerfulness seemed subdued. As she laid out the plates and cutlery, she kept glancing out the window towards the fields where her father worked.

"Mama," Sigrid said, her voice hesitant, "I miss Anna."

Elsa paused where she stood, looking at her daughter. "I know, sweetheart. It's hard being so far from your friends."

Sigrid nodded, her small face scrunched up in concentration as she sat on the table, placing her napkin on her lap. "Anna told me her mama is sad a lot. She said sometimes she hears her crying at night."

Elsa's heart clenched at this revelation. She had suspected Hanna was struggling this much, but hearing it confirmed, especially through the innocent words of a child, made it all the more real.

"That must be very hard for both of them," Elsa said softly. "Losing Anna's papa has been very difficult."

Sigrid looked up at her mother, her blue eyes wide and serious. "Anna said she misses her papa all the time. She said sometimes she forgets what his voice sounded like, and that makes her cry too."

Elsa sat down at the table next to Sigrid and moved to wrap her arms around her. The little girl leaned into her mother's embrace, sniffling slightly.

"Oh, my darling," Elsa murmured, stroking Sigrid's hair. "It's okay to feel sad for your friend. And it's okay to miss her too."

Sigrid nodded against her mother's chest. "I wish we could help them, Mama. Anna said her mama is lonely."

Elsa pulled back slightly, looking into her daughter's eyes. "You have such a kind heart, Sigrid. We'll think of a way to help them, I promise."

As they sat there, locked in their embrace, Lars entered the kitchen, bringing with him the earthy scent of the fields. He paused in the doorway, taking in the scene before him. The sight of his wife and daughter, bathed in the soft morning light, filled him with a warmth that pushed away the distress of Hannah he'd been grappling with.

"Is everything alright?" he asked softly, not wanting to intrude on the moment.

Elsa looked up, offering him a small smile. "Sigrid's just missing her friend Anna. And we were talking about how hard things have been for the Eriksens."

Lars nodded, moving to join his family. He placed a gentle hand on Sigrid's back. "It's good that you care so much about your friend, sunshine. That's what being a good neighbour is all about."

He planted a kiss on Elsa's cheek before washing up at the sink. "Something smells delicious," he said, his eyes twinkling as he looked at his wife.

The family sat down to breakfast, the mood lighter now as they shared the meal. Sigrid chattered about her plans for the day, her earlier melancholy forgotten in the warmth of her parents' presence.

As they ate, Elsa caught Lars' eye over Sigrid's head. "I think we need to talk later," she mouthed silently. Lars nodded, a flicker of concern crossing his face.

After breakfast, the family dispersed to their daily tasks. Sigrid helped Elsa in the vegetable garden, while Lars returned to the fields. As they worked side by side, pulling weeds and tending to the young plants, Elsa noticed Sigrid growing quiet again.

"What's on your mind, sunshine?" Elsa asked gently.

Sigrid bit her lip, hesitating before speaking. "Mama, do you think God is mad at Anna and her mama? Is that why He took Anna's papa away?"

Elsa's heart broke at the innocent question. She set down her trowel and turned to face her daughter fully. "Oh, Sigrid, no. God isn't mad at them. Sometimes, sad things happen in this world, and we don't always understand why. But God loves Anna and her mama very much, just like He loves us."

"Then why did He let Anna's papa die?" Sigrid persisted, her young face scrunched in confusion.

Elsa took a deep breath, searching for the right words. "God doesn't cause bad things to happen, Sigrid. But He is there to comfort us when they do. And He gives us each other to help and support one another through hard times. That's why it's so important for us to be there for Anna and her mama now."

Sigrid nodded slowly, seeming to process this information. Then, without warning, she threw her arms around Elsa, hugging her tightly. "I love you, Mama. I'm glad God gave me you and Papa."

Elsa felt tears prick her eyes as she hugged her daughter back. "I love you too, sunshine. So very much."

They stayed like that for a moment, the warm sun on their backs, surrounded by the gentle rustling of the garden. When they finally pulled apart, Elsa wiped her eyes and smiled. "What do you say we take a break and make some cookies? I think we could all use a treat today."

Sigrid's face lit up. "Snickerdoodles?"

Elsa laughed, getting to her feet and brushing the dirt from her skirt. "Snickerdoodles it is."

As they made their way back to the house, Lars watched from the edge of the field. His heart swelled with love at the sight of his wife and daughter, arm in arm, heads turned towards each other in conversation. Despite the hard work and isolation of their life, moments like these made it all worthwhile.

The afternoon passed quickly, filled with the comforting routines of farm life. The scent of cinnamon and sugar wafted from the kitchen as Elsa and Sigrid baked, their laughter carrying out to where Lars worked.

As evening approached, the family gathered once more in the kitchen for dinner. Elsa had prepared Sigrid's favorite meal—chicken pot pie with a golden, flaky crust. As they ate, Lars couldn't help but notice the looks Elsa kept sending his way, reminding him of their need to talk.

After Sigrid had been tucked into bed with a story and a prayer, Lars and Elsa retreated to the porch, as was their custom. The night was clear, a canopy of stars stretching endlessly above them. For a long moment, they sat in comfortable silence, each gathering their thoughts.

Finally, Lars spoke, his voice low and hesitant. "Elsa, I... I need to tell you something."

Elsa turned to him, her face calm but her eyes alert. "What is it, love?"

Lars took a deep breath, his hands clasped tightly in his lap. "It's about Hanna. I... I've been having thoughts. Concerns. She's alone with her daughter, and with how..." He paused for a moment, as if looking for the right way to say something. "Well, you know..." he continued, a hesitant chuckle escaping his mouth. "A blind man could see it." He paused again.

Elsa knew he was trying to politely reference her physical beauty. She softly nodded in agreement. Lars put a hand on his knee, and taking a deep breath, said, "I'm afraid the wrong man might make advances. What if she accepts them out of desperation?"

He paused again, waiting for Elsa's reaction, but she remained silent, her face unreadable in the dim light. Encouraged by her silence, Lars continued, the words tumbling out in a rush.

"Even I can't deny that I've noticed her. Her beauty, her strength in the face of all she's endured, and I'm in love with you, my wife, the love of my life. She needs to find a husband to provide for her, to protect her."

Lars fell silent, his heart pounding as he waited for Elsa's response. To his surprise, he felt her hand cover his, her touch gentle and reassuring.

"Oh, Lars," Elsa said softly, "I share your concern. Anyone can see that she's beautiful. She told me no man has bothered her yet, but I fear it might only be a matter of time."

Lars looked up, sighing. "It makes me feel guilty, as if I'd be complicit if something bad happened to her."

Elsa shook her head, a sad expression on her mouth. "Truth be told. I'm glad you shared this with me. I am feeling quite the same, but I wasn't sure how to tell you. Hanna is alone and she's going through a terribly difficult time. I'm afraid we're not doing much to help her."

Lars felt a wave of relief wash over him. He pulled Elsa close, burying his face in her hair. "I do love you, Elsa. You're a wonderful woman. We must figure out something soon."

Elsa held him tightly, her voice muffled against his chest. "I know, my love. And I love you."

As they sat there, wrapped in each other's arms under the starry sky, Lars felt as if a great weight had been lifted from his shoulders. The anxiousness that had been plaguing him began to dissipate, replaced by a love for his wife's compassion.

The night grew cooler, and eventually, they made their way back inside. As Lars closed the door behind them, he sent up a silent prayer of thanks for Elsa's understanding heart.

The sun rose early the next church Sunday, painting the sky in hues of pink and gold. The Holm family bustled about their farmhouse, preparing for their quarterly trip to town for church. Sigrid practically bounced with excitement as she donned her best dress.

"Mama, do you think Anna will like the ribbon I made for her?" Sigrid asked, holding up a carefully braided friendship bracelet.

Elsa smiled warmly at her daughter. "I'm sure she'll love it, sweetheart. It's very thoughtful of you."

As they piled into the old wagon, Lars couldn't help but notice the worry lines creasing Elsa's forehead. "Everything alright, love?" he asked softly.

Elsa nodded, forcing a smile. "Just thinking about Hanna. I hope she's doing better."

The ride to town was filled with Sigrid's chatter about Sunday school and her plans to play with Anna after the service. Lars and Elsa exchanged fond glances, grateful for their daughter's innocence and joy.

As they pulled into the church lot, Lars spotted Hanna's weathered wagon already there. He felt a twinge of concern, noting how the once-pristine wagon now sported cracks in the wood and a loose wheel in the rear.

Inside the church, the congregation greeted each other warmly. Sigrid immediately sought out Anna, the two girls hugging tightly before taking their seats. Hanna sat alone in a pew, her shoulders slumped and her eyes weary.

Throughout the service, Elsa found her gaze continually drawn to her friend. As the final hymn ended and the congregation began to disperse, Elsa made her way to Hanna's side. "Would you like to join me for tea at the café?" she asked gently.

Hanna looked up, relief evident in her tired eyes. "I'd like that very much, thank you."

Lars approached, Sigrid and Anna in tow. "I'll take the girls to the park and run some errands," he offered. "Take your time, ladies."

As they walked to the small café across from the church, Elsa couldn't help but notice how Hanna's steps seemed to drag. They settled into a quiet corner booth, steam rising from their cups of tea.

"Hanna," Elsa began softly, reaching across the table to squeeze her friend's hand. "How are you doing lately?"

The question once again seemed to break something inside Hanna. Tears welled up in her eyes, spilling over onto her cheeks, as they did when Elsa asked the last time. "Oh, Elsa," she whispered brokenly. "Nothing has changed. If anything, it keeps getting worse."

Elsa moved to sit beside her friend, wrapping an arm around her trembling shoulders. "Tell me everything," she urged gently.

Hanna's words tumbled out in a rush, as if a dam had broken. "The farm is falling into more and more disrepair. I'm getting to some of it, but there's not enough time in the day to do it all with only one person. On top of that, there are things that need to be moved and fixed that I'm not physically strong enough to do, the kinds of things Erik always took care of."

She paused, taking a shaky breath. "And Anna... my sweet girl. She's so lonely out there. She tries to help, but she's just a child. She should be playing and learning, not worrying about farm work."

She looked down at her hands, twisting her wedding ring. "I miss Erik so much," she whispered. "Not just for the help with the farm, but for everything. The house is so quiet at night. I lie awake, listening to the wind, and I feel so... empty."

Elsa tightened her arm around Hanna, feeling her friend's pain acutely. "I can't imagine how hard it's been for you," she murmured.

Hanna turned to face her, desperation clear in her eyes. "I'm so lonely, Elsa. I know I should be grateful for what I have, for Anna and the farm. But I can't help longing for more. For a full family again, for someone to share the burden with."

She looked away, shame coloring her cheeks. "Sometimes, I find myself looking at the men in town, wondering what it would be like to have a husband again. Is that terrible of me? To want that so soon after losing Erik?"

Elsa shook her head emphatically. "No, Hanna. It's not terrible at all. It's human. You've been so strong for so long, carrying this all by yourself."

Hanna's shoulders sagged with relief at Elsa's words. "I just don't know what to do anymore. I can't keep running the farm by myself much longer, but I can't bear the thought of selling it. It's all Anna has left of her father, of our life together."

Elsa felt a wave of helplessness wash over her. She wanted desperately to offer a solution, to ease her friend's burden. But what could she do? She had her own farm, her own family to care for.

"I'll pray for you, Hanna," she said finally, the words feeling hollow even as she spoke them. "God won't let you be alone forever."

Hanna managed a weak smile. "Thank you, Elsa. Your friendship means more to me than you know."

As they finished their tea, Elsa's mind raced. She thought of the empty rooms in their big farmhouse, of Sigrid's longing for a playmate. But she pushed the thoughts away. It wasn't her place to offer such a thing, was it?

They made their way back to the church, where Lars was waiting with the girls. Sigrid and Anna were flushed with excitement, chattering about their adventures in the park.

"Mama, can Anna come to our house to play?" Sigrid asked, her eyes shining with hope.

Elsa looked down at the two eager faces before her. Anna, with her mother's dark hair and eyes, looked so hopeful that she felt her heart constrict.

"That sounds like a lovely idea," Elsa said carefully. "We'll have to arrange it soon."

Hanna looked torn between gratitude and embarrassment. As they said their goodbyes, Elsa hugged Hanna tightly.

"Remember, you're not alone," she whispered. "We're here for you, always."

Hanna nodded, blinking back tears. "Thank you," she murmured.

On the ride home, Lars noticed Elsa's unusual quietness. "Everything alright, love?" he asked, concern evident in his voice.

Elsa sighed heavily. "Hanna's really struggling, Lars. The farm is too much for her to manage alone, and she's so lonely. I wish there was more we could do to help."

Lars nodded thoughtfully. "Maybe I could go over and help with some of the bigger repairs?"

"That's kind of you," Elsa said, smiling softly at her husband's generosity. "But I'm not sure it's enough. She needs... more."

Lars raised an eyebrow. "More?"

Elsa shook her head, pushing away the half-formed thoughts swirling in her mind. "Never mind. We'll figure something out."

As they pulled up to their farmhouse, Elsa couldn't shake the feeling that they were missing something important. She watched as Sigrid ran ahead, her laughter echoing across the fields, and thought of Anna, alone on her mother's struggling farm.

That night, after Sigrid was tucked into bed, Elsa found herself standing in one of the empty upstairs bedrooms. Moonlight filtered through the dusty windows, illuminating the bare walls and floor. She ran her hand along the door frame, lost in thought.

Lars appeared in the doorway, concern etched on his face. "Elsa? What are you doing up here?"

She turned to him, tears glistening in her eyes. "I was just thinking... we have all this space, Lars. All these empty rooms. And Hanna and Anna, they're struggling so much."

Lars stepped into the room, wrapping his arms around his wife. "I know you want to help them, love. But we can't take on their problems. We have our own farm to manage, our own family to care for."

Elsa nodded against his chest. "I know. You're right, of course. It's just... when I think of Hanna lying awake at night, so alone... when I think of Anna growing up without a father..."

Lars tightened his embrace. "We'll do what we can for them, Elsa. We'll have them over more, help out where we can. But we can't fix everything."

Elsa sighed, letting her husband's steadiness calm her racing thoughts. "You're right. We'll pray for them, and trust that God has a plan."

As they made their way back to their bedroom, Elsa couldn't quite shake the nagging feeling that there was more they could do. But for now, she pushed it aside, focusing on gratitude for her own blessings and silently praying for Hanna and Anna.

In the quiet of the night, as Lars' steady breathing filled the room, Elsa found herself wide awake. She thought of Hanna, alone in her big empty farmhouse, and of Anna, growing up without the warmth of a full family.

But what could they really do? They had their own responsibilities, their own challenges. And yet... wasn't this what their faith called them to do? To love their neighbor, to bear one another's burdens?

Elsa turned these thoughts over and over in her mind, seeking a solution that seemed just out of reach. As dawn began to break, she finally drifted off to sleep, her dreams filled with images of a joy-filled home, of her daughter dancing and running with a sister in the endless rows of flowers outside, of a family that owed their happiness to the goodness of God even more than it ever had before.

Little did she know that the seeds of an idea had been planted, one that would soon grow into a solution none of them could have foreseen.

Elsa and Hanna had arranged for Anna to visit their farmhouse, as promised to Sigrid. The sound of rickety wheels announced the arrival of Hanna and Anna. Elsa stood on the porch, wiping her hands on her apron as she watched their old horse pull them to a stop. Sigrid burst out of the house, her blonde braids flying behind her as she raced to greet her friend.

"Anna! You're here!" Sigrid cried, throwing her arms around the dark-haired girl as she climbed out of the wagon.

Hanna emerged more slowly, her movements careful and deliberate. Even from a distance, Elsa could see the weariness etched on her friend's face. Yet there was no denying Hanna's beauty—her long, dark red hair caught the morning light, and her hazel eyes, though tired, still sparkled with life.

"Hanna," Elsa called warmly, descending the porch steps. "Welcome. Come in, both of you. I've got coffee brewing and fresh cinnamon rolls in the oven."

As the group made their way inside, Elsa couldn't help but notice Lars' absence. She had seen him slip out to the barn earlier, muttering something about checking on the livestock. It wasn't like him to avoid guests, but Elsa understood. Lars had so many responsibilities.

In the kitchen, the girls chattered excitedly about their plans for the day while Elsa poured coffee for herself and Hanna. The widow sank into a chair at the table, cradling the mug in both hands as if absorbing its warmth.

"Thank you for having us, Elsa," Hanna said softly. "It means more than you know."

Elsa squeezed her friend's shoulder as she sat down beside her. "Of course. We love having you both here."

As they talked, Elsa couldn't help but study Hanna more closely. Despite the clear exhaustion in her eyes, there was a glow about her—the kind that comes from hard work and fresh air. Her skin was tanned from long days in the fields, and her hands, though calloused, were strong and capable.

"How are things on the farm?" Elsa asked gently.

Hanna's smile faltered slightly. "Oh, you know. It's always something. The east fence came down in that storm last week, and I've been struggling to get it back up on my own."

Before Elsa could respond, the back door swung open and Lars entered, his boots leaving muddy prints on the floor. He paused when he saw Hanna, his eyes widening slightly before he quickly looked away.

"Morning, Elsa. Hanna," he said gruffly. "Girls behaving themselves?"

Elsa's cheeks flushed slightly as she nodded. "They're perfect angels, as always."

Lars grunted in acknowledgment, moving to pour himself a cup of coffee. "Lars," she said, an idea forming, "Hanna was just telling me about the fence that came down in the storm. Perhaps you could take a look at it later? Offer some advice?"

Lars's cup paused halfway to his lips. He glanced at Hanna, then quickly back at Elsa. "I, uh... I suppose I could. If Hanna wants."

Hanna's eyes lit up with gratitude. "Oh, would you? That would be so helpful. I've been at my wits' end trying to figure it out on my own."

Lars nodded, his discomfort evident. "Sure. No problem. I'll, uh... I'll go get cleaned up." With that, he hurried out of the kitchen, leaving a trail of muddy footprints behind him.

Elsa bit back a smile as she turned back to Hanna. "Don't mind him."

Hanna laughed softly, a sound that seemed to brighten the whole room. "It's alright. I appreciate the help, truly."

As the morning wore on, the girls disappeared outside to play, their laughter drifting in through the open windows. It struck Elsa how natural it felt, having Hanna in her kitchen, sharing the work and conversation.

Lars, meanwhile, made himself scarce. Elsa caught glimpses of him through the window, always finding some task to occupy himself in the yard or barn. She knew he was trying to be respectful, to avoid any appearance of impropriety. But she couldn't help but feel a twinge of sadness at the distance he was keeping.

After lunch, as Hanna helped clear the table, she paused, her hand resting on the back of a chair. "Elsa," she said hesitantly, "I hope... I hope my being here isn't causing any trouble between you and Lars."

Elsa looked up, surprised. "Trouble? Of course not. Why would you think that?"

Hanna bit her lip, her eyes downcast. "It's just... I've noticed how he avoids being around me. I know I'm a widow, and... well, I wouldn't want to make anyone uncomfortable."

Elsa's heart went out to her friend. She crossed the kitchen and took Hanna's hands in hers. "Oh, Hanna. No, it's nothing like that. Lars is just... he's trying to be respectful. He knows how hard things have been for you, and he doesn't want to do anything that might be misinterpreted."

Hanna's eyes glistened with unshed tears. "You're both so kind. I don't know what I'd do without your friendship."

Elsa pulled her friend into a tight hug. "You never have to find out. We're here for you, always."

As they broke apart, Elsa glanced out the window to see Lars watching them from the barn. Their eyes met, and she saw the conflict in his gaze—the desire to help warring with his sense of propriety. She offered him a small smile, trying to convey her understanding and love.

Later that afternoon, true to his word, Lars accompanied Hanna back to her farm to look at the damaged fence. Elsa watched them go, noting how carefully Lars maintained his distance, how he kept his eyes focused on the task at hand rather than on Hanna's graceful movements.

When they returned, Hanna's eyes were brighter than Elsa had seen in months. "Your husband is a godsend," she declared. "He not only fixed the fence but showed me how to do it myself next time."

Lars, for his part, seemed more at ease. "It was nothing," he said gruffly, but Elsa could see the pride in his eyes at being able to help.

As the day drew to a close and it was time for Hanna and Anna to leave, Elsa found herself reluctant to say goodbye. She watched as Sigrid and Anna hugged tightly, already making plans for their next visit.

"Thank you," Hanna said softly, embracing Elsa. "For everything."

Elsa hugged her back fiercely. "You're family, Hanna. Never forget that."

As the wagon disappeared down the long driveway, Elsa felt Lars' strong arm wrap around her waist. She leaned into him, drawing comfort from his solid presence.

"You're a good man, Lars Holm," she murmured.

Lars kissed the top of her head. "I'm trying to be," he said quietly. "It's not always easy, but... Hanna needs our help. And Anna... she's such a sweet girl. They deserve better than what life's handed them."

Elsa turned in his arms, looking up into his beloved face. She saw there the same conflict she felt—the desire to do more, to somehow ease the burden of their friends' struggles. But she also saw love, deep and unwavering, for her and for their life together.

As they walked back to the house, Sigrid skipping ahead of them, Elsa's mind returned to those empty rooms upstairs.

The seed of an idea that had been planted weeks ago began to take root, growing stronger with each passing day. She didn't know yet what form it would take, but she felt in her heart that God was leading them towards something incredible.

The rooster's crow pierced the early morning stillness, rousing Lars from his slumber. He blinked away the remnants of sleep, turning to gaze at Elsa's peaceful form beside him. A smile tugged at his lips as he quietly slipped out of bed, careful not to wake her.

The floorboards creaked softly under his feet as he made his way downstairs. The familiar scents of their home—wood smoke, fresh hay, and the lingering aroma of last night's stew—filled his nostrils. Lars paused at the kitchen window, taking in the view of their farm bathed in the soft light of dawn.

As he stoked the fire in the stove and set about preparing coffee, Lars found himself humming a hymn from last Sunday's service. His mind wandered to the day ahead—there were fences to mend, livestock to tend, and if time allowed, he hoped to start on that new irrigation system he'd been planning.

The sound of small feet padding down the stairs announced Sigrid's arrival before she burst into the kitchen, her blonde hair a tangled mess and her eyes still heavy with sleep.

"Good morning, sunshine," Lars greeted, scooping her up into a bear hug.

Sigrid giggled, wrapping her arms around his neck. "Morning, Papa. Can I help with breakfast?"

Lars set her down gently. "Of course. How about you gather some eggs while I finish with the coffee?"

As Sigrid skipped out to the henhouse, basket in hand, Elsa appeared in the doorway, wrapping her shawl tightly around her shoulders.

"You two are up early," she remarked, crossing the room to plant a kiss on Lars' cheek.

He pulled her close, breathing in the familiar scent of her hair. "No rest for the wicked," he teased. "Or for farmers, it seems."

Elsa laughed, the sound warming Lars' heart. "Well, this farmer's wife is grateful for the extra sleep. What's on the agenda for today?"

As Lars recounted his plans for the day, Sigrid returned, proudly presenting a basket full of fresh eggs. The family fell into their usual morning routine—Elsa preparing breakfast while Lars and Sigrid set the table and read a passage from the Bible.

Over a hearty breakfast of scrambled eggs, bacon, and fresh bread, they discussed their plans for the day. Sigrid was excited about her reading lesson later - she was making excellent progress with her studies and couldn't wait to start on a new book.

"Can we have a picnic lunch today, Mama?" Sigrid asked, her eyes bright with hope. "By the big oak tree?"

Elsa smiled indulgently. "I don't see why not. It's a beautiful day for it. What do you think, Lars?"

Lars pretended to consider it seriously, stroking his chin. "Well, I suppose I could be persuaded to take a break from my work for such an important occasion."

Sigrid clapped her hands in delight, already planning what treats she wanted to include in the picnic basket.

After breakfast, the family dispersed to their various tasks. Lars headed out to the fields, pausing to ruffle Sigrid's hair as she settled at the kitchen table with her books. Elsa busied herself with household chores, humming softly as she worked.

The morning passed quickly, each member of the family absorbed in their tasks. Lars found a sense of peace in the rhythmic work of mending fences, the sun warm on his back and the breeze carrying the scent of freshly trimmed grass. He offered up silent prayers of gratitude for the blessings in his life—his loving wife, his bright and cheerful daughter, and the bountiful land God had entrusted to their care.

Inside, Elsa moved from task to task with practiced efficiency. As she kneaded dough for the day's bread, she gazed out the window at Sigrid, who had taken her books outside to read under the shade of an apple tree. Pride swelled in her heart at the sight of her daughter, so eager to learn and grow.

When midday approached, Elsa called Sigrid in to help prepare their picnic lunch. Together, they packed a basket with sandwiches, fresh fruit, and some of Sigrid's favorite oatmeal cookies.

"Can we bring extra, Mama?" Sigrid asked as they worked. "In case Papa's extra hungry from all his work?"

Elsa smiled at her daughter's thoughtfulness. "That's a wonderful idea, sweetheart. Your papa will appreciate that."

As the sun reached its zenith, the family reunited under the sprawling branches of the old oak tree. Lars arrived, wiping sweat from his brow, his face lighting up at the sight of his wife and daughter spreading out the picnic blanket.

"Well, this is a sight for sore eyes," he declared, dropping down beside them with a contented sigh.

They ate with gusto, the simple meal made delicious by fresh air and good company. Sigrid regaled them with tales from her morning studies, while Lars and Elsa exchanged fond glances over her head.

After they had eaten their fill, Lars stretched out on the blanket, his head in Elsa's lap. Sigrid curled up beside him, and Elsa began to read aloud from Sigrid's new book. The gentle cadence of her voice, combined with the warm sun and full bellies, soon lulled both Lars and Sigrid into a light doze.

Elsa looked down at her sleeping family, her heart so full of love it felt fit to burst. These quiet moments of togetherness were precious to her, a reminder of all they had to be grateful for.

As the afternoon wore on, they reluctantly packed up their picnic and returned to their tasks. Lars headed back to the fields, while Elsa and Sigrid worked together in the vegetable garden, weeding and harvesting ripe produce.

"Mama," Sigrid said as they worked, her small hands carefully pulling carrots from the rich soil, "do you think we could invite Anna and Aunt Hanna for a picnic sometime?"

Elsa paused, considering her daughter's request. "That's a lovely idea, sweetheart. I'm sure they'd enjoy that very much. We'll have to plan it soon."

Sigrid beamed, already imagining the fun they could have.

As evening approached, the family once again came together, this time in the cozy warmth of their kitchen. Lars washed up at the sink while Elsa and Sigrid prepared dinner, the savory scent of beef stew filling the air.

Over dinner, they shared the highlights of their day. Lars spoke of his progress on the fences and his plans for the irrigation system. Sigrid proudly recounted the chapter she had read in her new book, while Elsa shared news from a letter she'd received from her sister in town.

After the dishes were cleared and Sigrid was tucked into bed with a bedtime story, Lars and Elsa retreated to the porch. They sat in comfortable silence, hands intertwined, watching as the last light faded from the sky and the first stars began to twinkle.

"Days like this," Lars murmured, squeezing Elsa's hand, "they make me realize just how blessed we are."

Elsa leaned her head on his shoulder, breathing in the night air. "We are blessed indeed," she agreed softly. "God has been good to us."

As night fell over the Holm farm, Lars and Elsa sat on their porch, the creaking of their rocking chairs a soothing rhythm in the quiet evening. Sigrid had long since been tucked into bed, her dreams filled with possible future adventures with Anna.

Lars broke the comfortable silence. "Elsa, I can't stop thinking about Hanna and Anna. The state of their farm... it's worse than I thought."

Elsa nodded, her brow furrowed with concern. "I know. Hanna's trying so hard, but it's just too much for one person. Especially with a young child to care for."

"There must be something more we can do," Lars mused, his voice tinged with frustration. "I could go over more often, help with the bigger jobs. Maybe give Anna some tips to make things easier?"

Elsa considered this. "That's kind of you, Lars. I'm sure Hanna would appreciate it. But..."

"But it's not enough," Lars finished for her, sighing heavily.

They sat in contemplative silence for a moment, the weight of their friends' struggles hanging heavy between them.

"What if we sent over some supplies?" Elsa suggested. "Food, seeds for planting, maybe some tools? It wouldn't solve everything, but it might ease their burden a little."

Lars nodded slowly. "That's a good idea. We could spare some from our stores. And maybe... maybe we could hire Hanna for some work here occasionally? Give her a chance to earn a bit extra?"

Elsa reached out, squeezing her husband's hand. "You're a good man, Lars Holm. Hanna's lucky to have us as neighbors."

Lars brought her hand to his lips, pressing a gentle kiss to her knuckles. "We're blessed to be in a position to help. It's what the Lord calls us to do, isn't it? Love our neighbors?"

As they continued to discuss possibilities, neither could shake the feeling that there was more they should be doing, but for now, they could only pray and do what little they could to support their struggling friends.

A few weeks later, Elsa loaded up their wagon with supplies for Hanna. She had spent the morning carefully packing boxes of preserved foods, seeds for spring planting, and some gently used tools that Lars had refurbished. As she rode the familiar road to Hanna's farm, her heart was heavy with concern for her friend.

As she pulled up to Hanna's farmhouse, she couldn't help but notice the state of disrepair. The once-pristine white paint was peeling, and several fence posts leaned at precarious angles. But the sound of children's laughter drew her attention, and she smiled as she saw Sigrid and Anna playing in the yard, their giggles carried on the spring breeze.

Hanna emerged from the barn, wiping her hands on her worn skirt. Her face lit up at the sight of Elsa. "What a wonderful surprise!" she called, hurrying over to greet her friend.

Elsa embraced Hanna warmly. "I brought some things for you and Anna," she explained, gesturing to the back of the wagon. "Just a few supplies we thought might help."

Tears welled up in Hanna's eyes. "Oh, Elsa. You shouldn't have... but thank you. You don't know what this means to us."

As they unloaded the wagon, Elsa took in more details of the farm's condition. The vegetable garden was overgrown with weeds, and the chicken coop looked like it had seen better days. Her heart ached for Hanna, knowing how hard she must be working just to keep things running.

Once the supplies were stored away, Hanna insisted on Elsa staying for tea. They sat at the kitchen table, watching through the window as Sigrid and Anna played an elaborate game of make-believe in the yard.

"They get along so well," Elsa observed, smiling at the girls' antics.

Hanna nodded, her eyes soft with affection. "Anna talks about Sigrid constantly. These play dates mean the world to her... to both of us, really."

As they chatted, Elsa couldn't help but notice the worry behind Hanna's eyes, barely holding up her exhausted shoulders. "How are you, Hanna?" she asked gently.

Hanna's brave facade crumbled slightly. "It's... it's still hard, Elsa. Harder than I ever imagined. We're still behind on so many farm tasks. And Anna..." Her voice broke. "She deserves so much more than I can give her."

Elsa reached across the table, squeezing Hanna's hand. "You're doing an amazing job, Hanna. Anna is happy and loved. That's what matters most."

Hanna managed a weak smile. "Thank you. I don't know what we'd do without you and Lars. Your friendship... it means everything to us."

As they continued to talk, Elsa's eyes wandered around the kitchen. It was clean but sparse, evidence of Hanna's frugal lifestyle. Her gaze fell on an open Bible on the counter, its pages well-worn and marked with notes.

"Would you excuse me for a moment?" Hanna asked, standing up. "I need to check on something in the barn."

Elsa nodded, and as Hanna stepped outside, she found herself drawn to the open Bible. She didn't mean to pry, but something about the passage caught her eye. As she glanced at the text, she realized it was listing the wives of King David.

Her breath caught in her throat as she read the names: Michal, Eglah, Haggith, Ahinoam... The idea that formed in her mind was so unexpected, so unorthodox, that she quickly stepped away from the Bible, her cheeks flushing.

When Hanna returned, Elsa was lost in thought, her tea growing cold in front of her. "Is everything alright?" Hanna asked, unsure if her friend was concerned or simply lost in thought.

Elsa shook herself out of her reverie. "Yes, of course. Just thinking about all the work you have ahead of you. Are you sure there isn't more we can do to help?"

Hanna shook her head, her gratitude evident. "You've done so much already. I couldn't ask for more."

As the afternoon wore on, Elsa found herself watching Sigrid and Anna more closely. The girls were inseparable, their bond evident in every shared laugh and secret whisper. The sight warmed Elsa's heart, even as it made her acutely aware of the loneliness both girls must feel when apart.

When it was time to leave, Elsa hugged Hanna tightly. "Remember, you're not alone in this. We're here for you."

Hanna clung to her, tears threatening to spill over. "Thank you, Elsa. For everything."

On the ride home, Elsa's mind raced with thoughts she could scarcely comprehend. The image of that Bible passage kept returning to her, along with the memory of Sigrid and Anna playing so happily together. An idea was forming, one that both thrilled and terrified her.

But she pushed it aside. It was too unconventional. Surely there had to be another solution, a more traditional way to help Hanna and Anna. And yet... the seed had been planted, and Elsa couldn't quite shake the feeling that God was trying to show her something important.

As she pulled up to their farmhouse, she saw Lars working in the field. He waved to her, his smile brightening as she approached. Elsa's heart swelled with love for her husband, even as a small part of her wondered how he would react if she shared the wild idea forming in her mind.

But no, she decided. This wasn't something to be shared, not yet. She needed time to pray, to seek guidance. For now, she would keep these thoughts to herself, trusting that if this truly was God's plan, He would make it clear in His own time.

That night, as Lars slept peacefully beside her, Elsa lay awake, her mind churning with possibilities. She thought of Hanna's loneliness, of Anna's need for a father figure, of Sigrid's desire for a playmate. And she thought of their own big, empty farmhouse, with rooms that had stood vacant for far too long.

"Lord," she whispered into the darkness, "if this is Your will, please make it clear. And give me the courage to follow where You lead."

As she finally drifted off to sleep, Elsa's dreams were once again filled with visions of a house full of laughter, of children playing in sun-dappled fields, of a family larger and more vibrant than she had ever imagined. And at the center of it all was love—a love big enough to encompass more than she had ever thought possible.

The next morning, Elsa woke with a feeling she couldn't quite explain. As she went about her daily chores, her mind continued to work on the problem of how to help Hanna and Anna. The idea that had taken root the day before still lingered, but she pushed it aside, focusing instead on more practical solutions.

Perhaps they could offer Hanna work on their farm as Lars had suggested, she mused as she gathered eggs from the henhouse. It would provide a steady income and allow Anna to spend more time with Sigrid. Or maybe they could speak to some of the other families at church, see if anyone else could offer assistance or employment.

As she worked in the vegetable garden later that morning, Elsa found herself imagining what it would be like to have Anna there every day, helping alongside Sigrid. The girls worked so well together, their personalities complementing each other perfectly. Sigrid's exuberance brought Anna out of her shell, while Anna's quiet thoughtfulness often calmed Sigrid's more impulsive nature.

As the day wore on, Elsa found herself drawn to the family Bible. While Lars was out in the fields and Sigrid was occupied with her lessons, Elsa sat at the kitchen table, the well-worn book open before her. This time, her fingers traced other familiar Bible stories – Elkanah and Hannah, Moses and the Cushite, David and Abigail.

She had always seen these stories as part of a distant past, not applicable to modern life. But now, with Hanna and Anna's struggles weighing heavily on her mind, she found herself looking at them in a new light. These weren't just historical accounts, she realized, but examples of God's people finding solutions to everyday problems.

Still, the idea that had taken root in her mind seemed too radical, too far outside the bounds of what their community would accept. Elsa closed the Bible with a sigh, sending up a silent prayer for guidance.

That evening, as she prepared dinner, Elsa overheard Lars and Sigrid talking on the porch.

"Papa," Sigrid was saying, "why can't Anna and Aunt Hanna live with us? We have plenty of room, and then Anna and I could play together every day!"

Elsa's breath caught in her throat as she waited for Lars' response.

"Oh, sunshine," Lars said gently, "it's not that simple. Hanna has her own farm to take care of, and... well, families don't usually live together like that unless they're related."

"But we love them," Sigrid insisted. "Isn't that what's most important?"

Elsa had to blink back tears at her daughter's innocent wisdom. Out of the mouths of babes, indeed.

Lars' voice was thoughtful when he replied. "You're right that love is important, Sigrid. But there are... complications in the adult world that you don't understand yet. We'll keep helping Hanna and Anna as much as we can, though. I promise you that."

As Elsa called them in for dinner, she found herself studying Lars more closely. Would he be open to the idea slowly forming in her mind? Could he see past convention to a solution that, while quite unorthodox in the plains of Northern Europe, might be exactly what all of them needed?

But no, she reminded herself firmly. This wasn't something to be rushed into or taken lightly. She needed more time to pray, to seek God's will in this matter. For now, she would keep these thoughts to herself, trusting that if this truly was the path they were meant to take, God would make it clear in His own time.

As they sat down to eat, Elsa looked around the table at her little family. Lars, strong and steady, the rock that seemed to keep them all together. Sigrid, full of life and love, with so much compassion for others. And herself, filled with a growing certainty that God was calling them to something bigger than they had ever imagined.

"Let's pray," Lars said, reaching for their hands. As they bowed their heads, Elsa added her own silent plea to their usual blessing.

"Lord," she prayed silently, "if this is Your will, please open our hearts to receive it. Give us the wisdom to see Your plan, and the courage to follow where You lead. Amen."

As they began to eat, the conversation turned to everyday matters—the progress of the crops, Sigrid's lessons, plans for the coming week. But underneath it all, Elsa felt as if they were on the brink of something momentous. She didn't know yet how everything would unfold, but she trusted that God would guide them. And as she looked at her husband and daughter, she felt a surge of love so strong it almost overwhelmed her.

The following morning dawned bright and clear, the sun casting long shadows across the Holm farm. Lars was up with the roosters, as usual, tending to the animals before breakfast. Elsa stirred shortly after, the aroma of fresh coffee drawing her to the kitchen.

As she prepared a hearty breakfast of porridge and fresh berries, Elsa's mind wandered to Hanna and Anna. She prayed for them, hoping they had enough to eat this morning. The thought of inviting them to live on the Holm farm still lingered, but Elsa pushed it aside, unsure of how to broach such an unconventional idea with Lars.

Sigrid bounded down the stairs, her hair in messy braids and her eyes bright with excitement. "Mama, can I help in the garden today?" she asked, spooning generous amounts of berries onto her porridge.

Elsa smiled, running a hand over her daughter's hair. "Of course, sweetheart. But first, your lessons."

As they ate, Lars discussed his plans for the day. "I need to head into town," he said between bites. "We're running low on feed, and I want to check on that new plow at the blacksmith's."

Elsa nodded. "I should come along. We need a few things for the house, and I promised to drop off some preserves for the church fundraiser."

They decided that Sigrid, at eight years old, was responsible enough to stay home alone for a few hours. She had done so in smaller increments before, and the farm was isolated enough that they felt comfortable leaving her.

After breakfast, Elsa set Sigrid up with her lessons at the kitchen table. "Now remember," she said, cupping her daughter's face, "stay in the house or on the porch. No wandering off, understand?"

Sigrid nodded solemnly. "Yes, Mama. I'll be good, I promise."

With a last hug and kiss, Lars and Elsa set off for town in their wagon. As they traveled down the dusty road, Elsa found herself glancing back at the farmhouse, a strange unease settling in her stomach.

"She'll be fine," Lars assured her, noticing her concern. "Sigrid's a sensible girl."

Elsa nodded, trying to shake off her worry. "You're right. I just can't help thinking... if Hanna and Anna were there, Sigrid wouldn't be alone."

Lars raised an eyebrow. "That's true, I suppose. But they have their own farm to tend to. We can't expect them to be our childminders."

Elsa bit her lip, holding back the words that threatened to spill out. Not yet, she told herself. The time wasn't right to share her idea.

Meanwhile, back at the farm, Sigrid diligently worked through her lessons. But as the morning wore on, she grew restless. Surely it wouldn't hurt to be in the yard for just a little while, she reasoned. She could practice her reading under the big oak tree.

Book in hand, Sigrid made her way to the tree. The sun was high in the sky now, its warmth seeping into her skin. She leaned against the rough bark, losing herself in the story.

So engrossed was she in her book that she didn't notice the low-hanging branch above her head. As she stood up to stretch, her foot caught on a root, and she stumbled backward. Her head connected with the branch with a sickening thud, and pain exploded behind her eyes.

Sigrid crumpled to the ground, tears streaming down her face. Her head throbbed, and when she touched the spot where she'd hit it, her fingers came away sticky with blood.

Panic set in as she realized she was alone. Mama and Papa were in town, and it would be hours before they returned. Sobbing, Sigrid stumbled towards the house, her vision blurry from tears and pain.

In town, Elsa couldn't shake her feeling of unease. As they loaded supplies into the wagon, she found herself rushing Lars. "We should head back," she said, her voice tight with worry. "I have a bad feeling."

Lars, sensing her distress, didn't argue. They made their farewells and set off for home, the horse trotting at a brisk pace.

As they approached the farm, Elsa's heart dropped at the sight of Sigrid huddled on the porch steps, her face tear-stained and a blood-soaked cloth pressed to her head.

"Sigrid!" Elsa cried, leaping from the wagon before it had fully stopped. She gathered her daughter into her arms, examining the wound with trembling hands.

Lars was right behind her, his face pale with concern. "What happened, sunshine?"

Between sobs, Sigrid explained about the tree and the branch. "I was so scared," she hiccuped. "I didn't know what to do."

As Lars cleaned and bandaged the wound, which thankfully looked worse than it was, Elsa held Sigrid close, her mind racing. If someone had been here, her daughter wouldn't have been alone and frightened for hours. If Hanna and Anna lived with them...

The thought struck her with new force. This wasn't just about helping their friends anymore. It was about creating a safer, more supportive environment for all of them.

As the days passed, Elsa found herself increasingly preoccupied with thoughts of Hanna and Anna. The incident with Sigrid had only intensified her conviction that something needed to be done, but she still hesitated to share her idea with Lars.

One afternoon, while Lars was out in the fields and Sigrid was absorbed in her lessons, Elsa retreated to the quiet of their bedroom. She pulled the family Bible from its place of honor on the bedside table and settled onto the bed, her heart racing with a mixture of anticipation and apprehension.

She began her search tentatively, flipping through the familiar stories of the Old Testament. Her fingers traced the lines of text as she read about Abraham and Sarah, about Jacob and his wives, about David and his many marriages. Each account seemed to whisper of a time when such family structures were not only accepted but sometimes even divinely sanctioned.

Yet Elsa couldn't shake the nagging doubt that these ancient stories might not apply to their modern life. She turned to the New Testament, seeking guidance in the teachings of Jesus and the apostles.

As she leafed through the pages, a passage caught her eye. It was in the book of James, chapter 2, verses 15 and 16. Elsa read the words slowly, her breath catching in her throat:

"If a brother or sister is without clothing and in need of daily food, and one of you says to them, 'Go in peace, be warmed and filled,' and yet you do not give them what is necessary for their body, what use is that?"

The words seemed to leap off the page, speaking directly to her heart. Wasn't this exactly what they had been doing? Offering prayers and well-wishes to Hanna and Anna, but not truly meeting their needs when they had the means to do so?

Elsa closed her eyes, her mind whirling with the implications. She had been so focused on finding justification for the unconventional family structure she was considering that she had almost missed the simpler, more profound truth: they were called to help those in need, not just with words, but with actions.

"Lord," she whispered, her voice barely audible in the quiet room, "is this what You've been trying to show me? That it's not about finding a loophole in scripture, but about truly living out Your command to love our neighbors?"

She sat in silence for a long moment, letting the weight of the revelation settle over her. Then, with a deep breath, she stood up, Bible in hand. It was time to talk to Lars.

She found him in the barn, mending a broken harness. The familiar scents of leather and hay filled the air as she approached, her heart pounding in her chest.

"Lars," she called softly, "do you have a moment? There's something I'd like to discuss with you."

He looked up, a warm smile spreading across his face at the sight of her. "Of course, my love. What's on your mind?"

Elsa settled onto a nearby bale of hay, smoothing her skirt nervously. "I've been thinking a lot about Hanna and Anna," she began, her voice steady despite her inner turmoil. "About their situation, and how we might be able to help them more."

Lars nodded, his expression growing serious. "I've been thinking about them too. It's a difficult situation, no doubt about it."

Elsa took a deep breath, then plunged ahead. "What if... what if we invited them to come live with us?"

The words hung in the air between them, heavy with implication. Lars' hands stilled on the harness, his brow furrowing in confusion.

"Live with us?" he repeated, as if trying to make sense of the words. "But Elsa, they have their own farm, their own home."

"A farm that Hanna can barely manage on her own!" Elsa pointed out with a hint of indignation. "A home that's falling into disrepair because she doesn't have the time or resources to maintain it properly..."

Lars set aside the harness, giving Elsa his full attention. "I understand your concern, my dear, but... to invite them to live here? It's a big step. And not one that's typically done outside of family."

Elsa nodded, acknowledging the truth in his words. "I know it's unconventional. But we have the space, Lars. That extra bedroom has stood empty for years. And think of how much easier things would be with another set of hands to help around the farm and the house."

She could see Lars considering her words, weighing the practicalities. But then his expression clouded, a flicker of discomfort passing over his features.

"Elsa," he said, his voice low and hesitant, "I want to help Hanna and Anna, truly I do. But... Hanna is a beautiful woman. To have her here, in our home, day in and day out..." He trailed off, unable to meet Elsa's eyes.

Understanding dawned, and Elsa felt a mixture of love for her husband's honesty and frustration at the obstacle it presented. "You're worried about temptation," she said as she exhaled softly, trying to calm her nerves at the same time.

Lars nodded, his cheeks flushing slightly. "I'm only human, Elsa. The temptation to..." Elsa looked at him with raised eyebrows, appearing surprised that he was going to spell out the nature of the temptation. Unsure how to communicate the obvious to his precious wife, Lars paused for a few seconds as their eyes locked. Everything that needed to be said happened in a few silent moments, then Lars continued, knowing she understood the dilemma, "I don't want to sin in that way, against you, against her, or against God."

Elsa's heart began racing again. This was the moment she had both dreaded and anticipated. Taking a deep breath, she opened the Bible she had brought with her, turning to the passage she had marked.

"Lars," she said, her voice steady despite her inner turmoil, "I want you to read something."

She handed him the Bible, watching as his eyes scanned the highlighted verses. His brow furrowed as he read, confusion evident in his expression.

"James 2:15-16," he murmured, looking up at Elsa. "What does this have to do with Hanna and Anna?"

Elsa leaned forward, her voice intense. "Don't you see, Lars? We've been doing exactly what this passage warns against. We've been offering Hanna our prayers and good wishes, telling her to 'go in peace, be warmed and filled,' but we haven't truly given her what she needs."

Lars nodded slowly, understanding beginning to dawn in his eyes. "You're right. But Elsa, what are you suggesting?"

This was it. The moment of truth. Elsa took another deep breath, silently pleading for guidance and courage.

"What if," she said slowly, each word carefully chosen, "the solution to both Hanna's need and your concern about temptation is the same?" Lars stared at her, innocently oblivious as to where she was going with all of this. He gave a small nod, prompting Elsa to finish her thought. "What if..." She continued, hesitant for a moment. But then, finding the resolve to say what she was meaning to, she confidently finished, "What if you were to take Hanna as a wife?"

The tool Lars was holding fell from his hand onto the hay-covered ground beneath him as the words hung in the air between them, heavy with implication. Lars' eyes widened in shock, his mouth opening and closing wordlessly.

"Take Hanna... as a... wife?" he finally managed to sputter. "Elsa, what are you saying?"

Elsa reached out, taking Lars' hands in hers. "I know it sounds crazy, my love. But hear me out. In the Old Testament, it wasn't uncommon for a man to have multiple wives. And while I know that's not normal in this part of the world, perhaps in this situation, it could be a solution that benefits everyone. It could be just what we all need."

Lars shook his head, still struggling to comprehend. "But... but how? How could this possibly work?"

Elsa squeezed his hands gently, her voice earnest as she laid out her thoughts. "Think about it, Lars. Hanna would have a home, security, and a husband to help provide for her and Anna. Anna would have a stable family environment and a strong father. We would have help on the farm and in the house. Sigrid would have a playmate. And you..." she paused, meeting his eyes steadily, "you would have someone else to love and be loved by, without the guilt of temptation."

Lars listened, his expression a mixture of disbelief and growing consideration. "And you, Elsa? What about you in all this?"

Elsa smiled softly. "I would have a friend, Lars. Someone to share the joys and burdens of running a household with. And even more than that, I would have the peace of knowing that we truly helped our friends in their time of need, not just with words, but with actions."

Lars fell silent, his gaze distant as he processed Elsa's words. She could almost see the thoughts racing through his mind, weighing the pros and cons, grappling with the unconventional nature of the proposal.

"It's... it's a lot to take in," he finally said, his voice hoarse. "I need time to think, to pray about this."

Elsa nodded, relief washing over her. It wasn't a yes, but it wasn't an outright rejection either. "Of course, my love. Take all the time you need. I just ask that you consider it with an open mind—and heart."

Lars nodded, then pulled Elsa into a tight embrace. "You never cease to amaze me," he murmured into her hair. "Your compassion, your willingness to think outside of what's expected... it's one of the reasons I love you so much."

Elsa melted into his embrace, her own emotions a swirling mix of hope, anxiety, and love. "I love you too, Lars. More than you could ever know."

As they parted, Lars picked up the Bible again, his fingers tracing the verses Elsa had shown him. "I'll think about this, Elsa. I promise. And I'll pray for guidance."

Elsa nodded, her heart full. As she left the barn, she offered up a prayer of her own. "Lord," she whispered, "if this is Your will, please open Lars' heart to receive it. And if it's not, please show us another way to truly help our friends."

The days that followed were filled with a strange tension in the Holm household. Lars was quieter than usual, often lost in thought. Elsa caught him several times with the Bible open, poring over passages she knew related to marriage and helping those in need.

Sigrid, perceptive as always, sensed the change in her parents' demeanor. "Is everything alright, Mama?" she asked one evening as Elsa tucked her into bed.

Elsa smoothed her daughter's hair, smiling reassuringly. "Everything's fine, sweetheart. Your papa and I just have some big decisions to think about."

Sigrid's eyes lit up with curiosity. "What kind of decisions?"

Elsa hesitated, unsure how much to share. "Well," she said slowly, "we're trying to figure out the best way to help Aunt Hanna and Anna. You remember how you suggested they could live with us?"

Sigrid nodded eagerly. "Yes! Is that what you're thinking about? Oh, Mama, can we? Please?"

Elsa chuckled at her daughter's enthusiasm. "It's not quite that simple, darling. But we're considering all our options. Now, it's time for sleep. Say your prayers, and we'll talk more in the morning."

As Sigrid obediently closed her eyes and began to whisper her nightly prayers, Elsa's heart swelled with love. Her daughter's innocent desire to help their friends only reinforced her conviction that they were on the right path.

Later that night, as Elsa lay in bed beside Lars, she felt him stir restlessly.

"Can't sleep?" she murmured, rolling over to face him.

Lars sighed, reaching out to pull her close. "My mind won't quiet," he admitted. "I keep thinking about what you proposed. About Hanna."

Elsa's heart quickened. "And?" she prompted gently as she turned to straighten the blanket.

"And... I'm still not sure," Lars said, his voice low in the darkness. "Part of me sees the wisdom in it. The practical benefits, the way it would solve so many problems at once. And I can't deny that the idea of—"

Elsa whipped her head towards him and looked him in the eyes, seemingly holding a smile back as a twinge of playfulness emerged in her heart. "The idea of *what*?" She asked, trying not to laugh before he finished his bashful answer.

Lars nervously cleared his throat as his cognitive function crumbled in the face of Elsa's teasing him. After she let out the first few putters of a laugh that was about to break, she nudged him with her arm and said, "Hannah sure is beautiful, isn't she?"

A nervous smile began to appear on Lars' face. All that the well-intended, but embarrassed, husband could mutter was "I.. uh..." before they both froze for a moment and then suddenly burst out in laughter. The youthful outburst broke any tension, and after they had collected themselves, they both wiped away a few laughter-induced tears as they returned to their conversation.

"Another part of me worries," Lars went on. "About what people would say. About whether it's truly right in God's eyes. About how it might change things between us."

Elsa propped herself up on one elbow, looking down at her husband's troubled face. "Lars," she said softly, "I won't pretend it wouldn't change things. But change isn't always bad. And as for what people might say... since when have we let that dictate our actions?"

Lars chuckled softly, some of the re-surfaced tension easing from his face. "You're right, as usual. But what about God's will in all this? How can we be sure?"

Elsa considered this for a moment. "I believe," she said slowly, "that God's will is for us to love our neighbors, to help those in need. The specifics of how we do that... maybe that's where our own judgment comes in. We pray for guidance, we look to scripture, and then we do what we believe is right."

Lars nodded, pulling Elsa back down to rest against his chest. "You make it sound so simple," he murmured.

"It's not simple," Elsa admitted. "But I believe it's right. I believe this is how we can truly live out the message in James. Not just offering words of comfort, but taking action to meet their needs."

They lay in silence for a long moment, the steady beat of Lars' heart under Elsa's ear a comforting rhythm in the quiet night.

"I need a little more time," Lars finally said. "To pray, to think. But Elsa... I'm not saying no. I just need to be sure."

Elsa felt a surge of hope at his words. "Take all the time you need, my love," she whispered, pressing a soft kiss to his chest. "I'll be here, ready to support whatever decision you make."

As they drifted off to sleep, Elsa's last conscious thought was a prayer of gratitude. They might not have reached a decision yet, but the fact that Lars was truly considering her idea felt like a small miracle in itself.

The next church morning dawned bright and clear, the air crisp with the promise of a beautiful day. As Elsa went about her morning chores, she found herself humming softly, her heart lighter than it had been in weeks.

She was in the kitchen, kneading dough for the day's bread, when Lars came in from the barn. There was a determined set to his shoulders, a clarity in his eyes that made Elsa's breath catch.

"Elsa," he said, his voice steady, "I think it's time we talked to Hanna."

She smiled a huge smile and nodded in agreement, proud of the conviction in her husband's demeanor. With a small but delightful skip in her step, she went upstairs to wake Sigrid so they could get ready for church.

The air nipped at Elsa's cheeks as she stood before the mirror, carefully pinning her blonde hair into a neat bun. Sunlight streamed through the bedroom window, casting a warm glow on her contented face. She smoothed her best Sunday dress, a simple yet elegant navy blue frock that accentuated her slender figure.

"Lars, are you ready?" she called out, her voice lilting with anticipation.

Her husband's deep voice resonated from downstairs. "Just a moment, dear. Polishing my shoes."

Elsa smiled to herself, grateful for the quiet joy that filled their home. As she descended the wooden staircase, the familiar creaks under her feet reminded her of the life they had built together in this modest farmhouse.

Lars stood by the door, his tall frame cut a dashing figure in his pressed suit. His salt-and-pepper hair was neatly combed, and his kind eyes crinkled at the corners as he smiled at his wife.

"You look beautiful, Elsa," he said softly, offering his arm.

She took it, feeling the warmth of his body through the fabric. "And you're as handsome as the day we wed," she replied with a playful wink.

Together, they stepped out into the crisp morning air. The trees lining their property had begun to turn, their leaves a vibrant tapestry of reds, oranges, and golds. The couple's boots crunched on the grassy path as they made their way to their old but well-maintained wagon.

As Lars helped Elsa into the passenger seat, she couldn't help but feel a flutter of excitement. Church had always been a cornerstone of their life together, but lately, it held even more significance. Their routine lunches with Hanna had become a cherished tradition.

The ride to church was filled with a happy silence. Even Sigrid, who usually couldn't restrain herself from relaying her plans for the day, was uncharacteristically quiet as she noticed the hints of anticipation in her parents' smiles. She found herself occupied with guessing what it could be, esteeming the guessing game more fun than begging for information.

The small, white-steepled building stood proudly against the autumn sky, its doors wide open to welcome the congregation. As Lars helped Elsa out of the wagon, they were greeted by the sounds of cheerful conversation and the distant strains of the organ warming up.

Inside, the church was the usual warm haven of polished wood and soft light filtering through stained glass windows. The couple took their usual pew, exchanging nods and smiles with familiar faces. As the service began, Elsa found herself lost in the comforting rhythm of hymns and prayers, her heart full of gratitude.

Throughout the sermon, she couldn't help but glance occasionally at Hanna, who sat a few rows ahead with her young daughter, Anna. The widow's head tilted down under the burden she felt, her once-vibrant red hair dulled by worry and fatigue. Elsa's heart ached for her friend, and she sent up a silent prayer for guidance.

As the congregation filed out after the final hymn, Lars and Elsa made their way to Hanna and Anna. The little girl's face lit up at the sight of them, her freckled cheeks dimpling with a wide smile.

"Mrs. Elsa! Mr. Lars!" Anna exclaimed, bouncing on her toes. "Are we having lunch together today?"

Elsa laughed, reaching out to smooth a stray curl from the child's forehead. "Of course, sweetheart. We wouldn't miss it for the world."

Hanna managed a tired smile, the dark circles under her eyes more pronounced than ever. "You two are too kind," she murmured. "I don't know what we'd do without you."

Lars placed a gentle hand on Hanna's shoulder. "It's our pleasure, truly. Shall we head to the diner?"

The small group made their way down the tree-lined street to the local diner, a cozy establishment that had been a town fixture for years now. The bell above the door jingled merrily as they entered, the aroma of coffee and fresh-baked pie enveloping them.

As they settled into a booth, Elsa couldn't help but notice how Lars' gaze lingered on Hanna for a moment longer than usual. The widow's beauty, though dimmed by hardship, was still evident in her delicate features and graceful movements. Suddenly, Elsa felt a fleeting pang of jealousy, which she quickly recognized as temptation. She immediately pushed it aside, reminding herself of the deep trust and love she shared with her husband.

While Anna chattered excitedly about her Sunday school lesson, the adults perused their menus. Hanna's hands trembled slightly as she held hers, and Elsa noticed her friend blinking back tears.

"Hanna, dear," Elsa said softly, reaching across the table to touch her hand. "What's troubling you?"

Hanna took a shaky breath, setting down her menu. "I... I don't know how much longer I can keep this up," she confessed, her voice barely above a whisper. "The farm... Despite the repairs that we've already made, there's too much left for me to handle alone, and it's not in good enough shape to sell. I'm afraid if things keep going like this, we'll be destitute soon." The needy widow began to cry and raised her head. With the weight of confusion and worry evident in her words, she continued, "How can this be God's plan for me? For my daughter? We've prayed and prayed that God would provide for us, but no answer has come. If things don't turn around by next quarter, we'll be run off our farm with nowhere to go." She looked in Elsa's eyes, and with tears running down her cheeks, she asked, "Where, Elsa? Where is God's provision in all this?"

After catching herself and lamenting her lack of faith, she wiped her tears and quietly apologized for her outburst. At this point, even the children were listening, unsure of how to respond to such seemingly adult problems.

Lars and Elsa exchanged a meaningful glance. This was the moment they had discussed in hushed tones late at night, weighing the possibilities and consequences.

Elsa gave her husband an encouraging nod, squeezing his hand under the table. Lars cleared his throat, causing Hanna to look up. "Hanna," he began, his voice catching slightly, "there's something I... we... wanted to discuss with you."

Hanna's brow furrowed in concern. "Is everything alright?"

Lars nodded quickly. "Yes, yes, everything's fine. It's just..." He trailed off, struggling to find the right words. His palms felt sweaty, and he could feel his heart pounding in his chest. This was much harder than he had anticipated.

Elsa leaned forward, her eyes shining with warmth. "Hanna, we've grown so fond of you and Anna these past years. You know you've become like family to us."

"And family takes care of each other," Lars added, his confidence growing slightly. He took a deep breath, then plunged ahead. "Hanna, we've been thinking a lot about your situation, and we want to help. We... that is, I..."

Lars faltered again, his face flushing. He looked at Elsa desperately, silently pleading for help. Elsa nodded encouragingly, mouthing "Go on" to him.

Hanna leaned closer, her expression a mixture of confusion and concern. "What is it? You can tell me, whatever it is."

Lars nodded, swallowing hard. "Hanna, you and Anna have become so important to us. We care about you deeply, and we want to make sure you're taken care of. I... I know this might seem sudden, or strange, but..." He paused, taking another deep breath. "What I'm trying to say is..."

The tension at the table grew palpable. Anna, sensing the gravity of the moment, remained silent, her fork suspended halfway to her mouth. Sigrid sat wide-eyed, looking between the adults with anticipation.

Lars closed his eyes briefly, steeling himself. When he opened them, he looked directly at Hanna, his gaze filled with sincerity and warmth. "Hanna, we'd like to offer you a place in our home. As... as my..."

Once again, the words stuck in his throat, then Hanna's eyes slowly widened, a flicker of understanding beginning to dawn in them. "As your what, Lars?" she whispered, hardly daring to believe what she thought he might be suggesting.

Elsa, withholding an eager smile that seemed fit to burst, unable to contain herself any longer, blurted out with a joyful shriek, "Oh, Hannah! He's trying to ask you to be his wife!"

A hush fell over the table. Hanna's eyes widened even further, her mouth opening and closing without a sound. Lars, letting out a soft laugh at the way it all happened, offered Elsa a grateful look before turning back to Hanna, his expression a mixture of hope and trepidation.

"Is... is that true?" Hanna breathed, her voice barely audible.

Lars nodded, reaching across the table to take her hand. "Yes, Hanna. I know it's unexpected, and perhaps unconventional, but we've given this a lot of thought. You and Anna need security and support, and we... I... want to provide that for you. I'm offering you marriage, a home with us, and a chance for us to combine our resources and strength to build a better future for both of our children."

He paused, his thumb gently stroking the back of her hand. "I know I'm not the husband you dreamed of, and this isn't a very romantic proposal. But I promise to be a good husband to you, to care for you and Anna, to work alongside you and build a life together. And in time, who knows? Perhaps you might even grow to love me."

Elsa spoke up, her voice gentle. "We both care for you deeply, Hanna. This arrangement would allow us all to support each other, to be a family in every sense of the word. Lars would be your husband, I would be like a sister to you, and together we could raise our children in a loving, stable home."

For a moment, the world seemed to stand still. Hanna sat, stunned, her mind racing to process the enormity of what had just been proposed. She felt as if she were underwater, the sounds around her muffled and distant.

Lars... offering to marry her? To take her and Anna into his home? It seemed too good to be true, an answer to prayers she'd been too afraid to voice. She thought of the struggling farm, of the long, lonely nights, of her fears for Anna's future. And here, sitting before her, was a chance at security, stability, and maybe even happiness.

Slowly, the noise of the diner filtered back in. Hanna blinked, focusing on Lars' anxious face. She became aware of the tears streaming down her cheeks and the trembling of her hands.

"Hanna?" Lars asked softly, squeezing her hand gently. "I know it's a lot to take in. If you need time to think..."

His words snapped Hanna all the way out of her daze. Without hesitation, she gripped his hand tightly, a watery laugh escaping her lips. "I don't need time... Yes, Lars. Yes! With all my heart! Yes!" She had almost shouted her answer, momentarily forgetting all restraint and proper diner etiquette.

The table erupted in cheers. Elsa clapped her hands together, tears of joy in her eyes. Sigrid and Anna jumped out of their seats at the edge of the booth and hugged each other, gasping and giggling with excitement. And Lars... Lars beamed at Hanna, his eyes shining with relief and happiness.

As the initial shock wore off, Hanna found herself swept up in emotions—gratitude, hope, and a budding affection for the couple who had just changed her life so dramatically.

"Oh, Mama!" Anna squealed, excitedly clenching her fists as her and Sigrid climbed back into the booth. "Does this mean we get to live with Sigrid?"

Sigrid was practically bouncing in her seat. "Can we share a room? Please, please, please?"

Elsa nodded at her daughter, and Hanna found herself smiling at the woman who had so graciously offered her to marry her husband. Elsa smiled back at her.

As they finished their dessert, Lars suggested they head to Hanna's farm to start packing. "No sense in waiting," he said with a warm smile. "The sooner you're settled, the better."

The group piled into Lars' wagon, leaving Hannah's behind with a small sign on it that read, "Free for someone in need." The air was buzzing with excitement. The wagon was filled with nervous laughter among the adults and excited giggles among the girls. As they bounced along the dirt road leading to Hanna's farm, a sudden thought struck her.

"Oh!" she exclaimed, turning to Lars. "We'll need a preacher to marry us. How long do you think it'll be before we can get back to town?"

Lars' jaw dropped at the realization that in all the excitement, they had forgotten the part about getting married. He started to rattle off an idea. "That's a good point. I suppose we could—"

"Why wait?" Little Sigrid interrupted, her eyes shining with mischief. "You should get married right here!"

Anna clapped her hands in delight. "Yes! Right now!"

Hanna blushed furiously, stammering, "But, girls, we can't just... I mean, we don't have a preacher or..."

Elsa spoke up, her voice reassuring and her smile from ear to ear. "You know, they have a point. The Israelites didn't always have formal wedding ceremonies. Often, they simply became married at home, in the presence of family."

Lars looked thoughtful for a moment, then a slow smile spread across his face. He pulled the wagon to a stop at the edge of Hanna's property. While everyone was asking why he stopped here, he climbed down, walked around to Hanna's side, and held out his hand to help her down.

Hanna hesitated, her heart pounding. She felt dizzy with the speed at which everything was happening, almost too nervous and excited to speak. But as she looked into Lars' eyes, she saw a new-found confidence there, a strength that made her breath catch. She took his hand and stepped onto the footrest on the side of the wagon to climb down.

Then, with a smile that shone with cheer and masculine resolve, Lars grabbed Hannah's arms and lifted her off the wagon to the ground in front of him. Hanna gasped, suddenly very aware of the strength of his presence. Her once-tired eyes began beaming with a mix of vulnerability and invigoration.

"Hanna," Lars said, his voice low and tender, "will you be my wife? Here and now, with God and our family as witnesses?"

For a moment, Hanna couldn't speak. She was overwhelmed as she felt her feminine frame nearly melt in the face of Lars' confidence. Then, with a clarity that surprised even herself, she knew her answer.

"Yes," she whispered, then louder, "Yes, Lars. I will be your wife!"

"And I, your husband," Lars responded, "to love and to cherish, till death do us part." He then pulled his new wife in towards himself and kissed her lips with a passion that Hannah hadn't felt in over a year, sending what felt like surges of life through her tired bones, a feeling that shot all the way through to her fingers and toes. From the wagon, Sigrid and Anna let out a chorus of "Oooooooh!" followed by giggles and cheers. Elsa wiped away a tear, her heart full of joy for her husband and her friend.

As Lars and Hanna broke apart, both blushing and smiling, Elsa cleared her throat. "Well, I believe that makes it official," she said with a satisfied and playful smile. "Shall we help the bride move into her new home?"

The next few hours found the family working together to pack up Hanna and Anna's belongings. Hanna found herself pausing every now and then, overcome by the enormity of the change in her life. Each time, either Lars or Elsa would be there with a reassuring touch or kind word, grounding her and reminding her that she wasn't alone anymore.

As they packed, Lars busied himself with Anna, helping the little girl choose her favorite toys and books. Elsa couldn't help but smile as she watched him, his gentleness with the child warming her heart. She knew, without a doubt, that they had made the right decision.

By late afternoon, the wagon was loaded with boxes and bags. Lars secured the last trunk in the wagon. "I think that's everything we can fit for now," he said, wiping his brow. "We can come back for the rest later."

Hanna nodded as she stood on the porch, looking back at the weathered farmhouse that had been her home for so long. A lump formed in her throat as she thought of all the memories it held—both happy and sad.

Sensing her emotion, Lars came to stand beside her. "We don't have to sell it, you know," he said softly. "We could keep it, maybe fix it up over time. It could be a place for the children to learn about farming, or a retreat for us when we need a change of scenery."

Hanna looked up at him, surprised and touched by his thoughtfulness. "You'd do that?"

Lars smiled, taking her hand in his. "Of course. It's part of your history, part of who you are. And now, it's part of our family's story too."

Tears welled up in Hanna's eyes, but this time, they were tears of gratitude and hope. She squeezed Lars' hand, unable to find words to express her feelings.

"Ready?" Lars asked softly.

Hanna took a deep breath and nodded. "Ready."

From the wagon, Anna's voice called out, "Mama! Papa! Can we go home now?"

Lars and Hanna exchanged a look, both startled and warmed by Anna's easy acceptance of their new family dynamic. "Yes, sweetheart," Hanna called back. "We're going home."

As they climbed into the wagon, Elsa moved to sit in the back with the girls, giving Lars and Hanna the front seat. The ride back to the Holm farm was filled with chatter and laughter, punctuated by moments of companionable silence.

Hanna found herself stealing glances at Lars, still hardly able to believe the turn her life had taken. She thought of the struggles of the past months—the loneliness, the fear, the constant worry about providing for Anna. And now, in the space of an afternoon, she had a husband to love, a sister in Elsa, and a secure future for her daughter.

Soon, the Holm farmhouse came into view, its white clapboard siding glowing in the late afternoon sun. Flower boxes bursting with late-blooming mums adorned the windows, and a porch swing swayed gently in the breeze.

As Lars brought the wagon to a stop and they approached the farm, Hanna felt a flutter of nervousness. This was to be her home now, her new life. As if reading her thoughts, Lars reached over and took her hand, giving it a reassuring squeeze.

"Welcome home," he said softly as they pulled up to the house.

Anna was the first to hop out, her eyes wide with wonder. "It's so pretty!" she exclaimed, twirling in the yard.

Sigrid was right behind her, jumping out of the wagon and nearly exploding with excitement, "And now you never have to leave! We'll be sisters forever!"

She ran to Anna and the two girls began laughing and squealing and running circles around the house, chasing each other in a burst of happiness that was nothing short of uncontainable. Hannah was positively glowing as she watched her daughter looking so happy with her new sister.

"We can grow flowers together!" Anna yelled.

"And play with the frogs at the creek!" Sigrid yelled back.

The endless possibilities of fun and adventure continued being shouted back and forth between the girls as the adults looked on in grateful amazement.

Glowing as she was, Hanna climbed out more slowly, taking in her surroundings with a mix of awe and trepidation. Elsa came to stand beside her, linking their arms together.

"I hope you like your new home," she said softly yet excitedly.

Hanna turned to her, eyes brimming with grateful tears. "I don't know how I can ever thank you both enough."

Lars joined them, placing a gentle hand on Hanna's shoulder. "No thanks necessary. We're family now."

Together, they made their way into the house. Elsa led Hanna and Anna upstairs, showing them the rooms that would be theirs. Anna squealed with delight at the sight of her new bedroom, complete with a window seat overlooking the orchard.

Hanna's room was next door, a spacious chamber with a quilted bed and a writing desk by the window.

"It's beautiful," she breathed, running her hand over the polished wood of the dresser.

Elsa smiled, squeezing Hanna's hand. "I'm so glad you like it. I want you to feel at home here."

As they began to unpack, the house came alive with activity. Lars carried boxes upstairs, Anna's laughter echoed through the halls, and the aroma of coffee wafted up from the kitchen where Elsa had put on a pot to brew.

By the time dusk fell, most of Hanna and Anna's belongings had found new homes in drawers and on shelves. Exhausted but content, the newly expanded family gathered in the living room, mugs of celebratory hot cocoa in hand.

Anna had fallen asleep on the rug, her head pillowed on her favorite stuffed animal. Hanna sat on the sofa, her eyes heavy with fatigue but shining with happiness. Lars and Elsa occupied the loveseat, their hands intertwined.

"So," Lars said softly, careful not to wake Anna. "How does it feel?"

Hanna looked around the room, taking in the warm glow of the lamps, the family photos on the mantel, and the sleeping child at her feet. A slow smile spread across her face.

"It feels like coming home," she replied, her voice thick with emotion. "Like I can finally breathe again."

Elsa felt her own eyes fill with tears. "We're so glad you're here," she said. "Both of you."

As the evening wore on, they talked quietly about their plans for the future. There was much to figure out—sleeping arrangements, daily routines, how to explain their unconventional family to the town. But for now, in the warm cocoon of the farmhouse, those concerns seemed distant and manageable.

When Hanna yawned for the third time in as many minutes, Elsa stood up. "I think it's time we all got some rest. It's been quite a day."

Lars gently scooped up the sleeping Anna, carrying her upstairs to her new room. Hanna followed, pausing at the top of the stairs to look back at Elsa.

"Goodnight," she said softly. "And thank you... for everything."

Elsa smiled, her heart full. "Goodnight, Hanna. Sleep well."

As Elsa tidied up the living room, reflecting on the day's events, she heard the patter of small feet on the stairs. Looking up, she saw a happy (and sleepy) Sigrid descending, her blonde pigtails lightly bouncing with each step.

"Mama," Sigrid whispered excitedly, her blue eyes wide with wonder, "is Anna really going to be my sister now?"

Elsa's heart melted at her daughter's enthusiasm. Sigrid had been asking for a sibling for years, and the new arrivals seemed like an answer to her prayers as much as anyone else's.

"Yes, sweetheart," Elsa replied, kneeling down to Sigrid's level. "Anna is going to be a sister to you. And Aunt Hanna will be part of our family too."

Sigrid's face lit up with a brilliant smile. "I can't wait to show Anna all my favorite hiding spots in the barn! And maybe I can give her some of my dolls! What do you think, Mama?"

Lars came down the stairs, his expression softening at the sight of his wife and daughter. "What are you doing up, little one?" he asked gently, ruffling Sigrid's hair. "It's past your bedtime."

Sigrid looked up at her father, her eyes pleading. "I was too excited to sleep, Papa. Can I stay up a little longer? Please?"

Lars and Elsa exchanged a glance, both unable to resist their daughter's enthusiasm. "Alright," Lars conceded with a chuckle. "But just for a few more minutes."

The three of them settled on the couch, Sigrid nestled between her parents. "Tell me again how Anna and I are going to be sisters," she requested, her voice full of wonder.

Elsa stroked her daughter's hair, choosing her words carefully. "Well, you know how we've always taught you that family isn't just about who you're born to, but about who you love and who loves you?"

Sigrid nodded solemnly.

"That's what's happening here," Lars continued. "We're choosing to make Hanna and Anna part of our family because we love them and want to take care of them."

"And they'll love us too?" Sigrid asked, her voice small and hopeful.

"Of course they will," Elsa assured her, pulling her daughter close. "They already do."

Sigrid beamed, snuggling into her mother's embrace. "I'm so happy," she murmured. "I've always wanted a sister."

As they sat there, Lars couldn't help but marvel at how easily Sigrid had accepted this change. Her pure, childlike joy at the expansion of their family warmed his heart.

"You know," he said, "I think you're going to be a wonderful big sister to Anna."

Sigrid sat up straight, her chest puffing out with pride. "I'll be the best big sister ever! I'll teach her all about the farm and help her with her reading and protect her from monsters under the bed!"

Elsa and Lars laughed softly at their daughter's determination. "I'm sure you will, sweetheart," Elsa said, kissing the top of Sigrid's head.

As Sigrid's eyelids began to droop, Lars scooped her up in his arms. "I think it's really time for bed now, sunshine," he said gently.

"Okay," Sigrid mumbled sleepily. "But can we have pancakes for breakfast? To celebrate our new family?"

"That sounds like a wonderful idea," Elsa agreed, following Lars up the stairs.

They tucked Sigrid into bed, her room now filled with whispered plans for all the things she wanted to do with her new sister. As they closed her door, leaving it open just a crack the way she liked it, Elsa and Lars paused in the hallway.

The house was quiet now, filled with the soft sounds of a family getting to sleep. Hanna's gentle breathing from one room, Anna's light snores from another, and Sigrid's familiar sighs as she drifted off to dreamland.

Elsa leaned into Lars, feeling the steady beat of his heart. "Our little girl is so happy," she whispered.

Lars wrapped an arm around her waist, pulling her close. "She is. And so am I."

As they made their way to their own bedroom, Elsa felt a profound sense of peace settle over her. Their home was full of love, laughter, and new beginnings. Sigrid's joy at having a sister, Hanna and Anna's relief at finding a safe haven, and their own contentment at being able to help—it all blended together into a beautiful harmony.

As they approached their bedroom door at the end of the hallway, Lars pulled Elsa into a tender embrace. "Are you happy, my love?" he murmured against her hair.

Elsa turned in his embrace, looking up into the face of the man she had loved for so many years. She saw in his eyes the same mix of emotions she felt—joy, nervousness, hope, and above all, love.

"I am," she replied, stretching up to kiss him softly. "Are you?"

Lars smiled, the corners of his eyes crinkling in the way that always made Elsa's heart skip a beat. "More than I ever thought possible."

As they made their way upstairs to their own bedroom, Elsa slipped her hand into Lars', squeezing gently. "Is it your plan to make it official tonight?" She asked as she tilted her head toward Hannah's room, implying the inevitable consummation that would occur.

"As wonderful as that sounds," Lars answered with a soft chuckle under his breath, "I think my new bride's a bit exhausted at the moment. I'm sure she'd appreciate the time to rest and settle in a bit more."

Elsa agreed with a warm smile and nod, deeply appreciating the tenderness and consideration with which Lars was already treating her friend. "I'll go make sure everything's closed up for the night," Lars said as he made his way down the stairs and outside to ensure the farm was in order.

Elsa retreated to their bedroom. A sense of peace settled over her as she opened her Bible where the bookmark was placed, reading with the confidence, maybe now more than ever, that her Heavenly Father was smiling down on them.

If a brother or sister is without clothing or in need of daily food, and one of you says to them, "Go in peace, be warmed and be filled," and yet you do not give them what is necessary for their body, what use is that? Even so faith, if it has no works, is dead, being by itself.

James 2:15-17

Story 2 - Reconciled

Setting – Japan, 2000

The gleaming white hull of the cruise ship towered over Natalie and Jeff Carter as they stepped out of their taxi at the crowded port in Yokohama. Natalie's blue eyes widened with excitement, her blonde hair whipping in the sea breeze. Jeff, tall and broad-shouldered, stretched after the long ride from their Tokyo hotel.

"Can you believe we're finally here, Jeff?" Natalie breathed, clutching her well-worn Bible to her chest. "After all those overtime shifts and penny-pinching?"

Jeff grinned, his warm brown eyes crinkling at the corners. "God is good, sweetheart. He knew how much we needed this break." He hefted their luggage from the trunk, muscles straining slightly under the weight.

Natalie nodded, a serene smile playing on her lips. "Amen to that. I can't wait to see all those little islands. It's like something out of a dream."

As they approached the gangway, Natalie's grip on her Bible tightened. It was a gift from her grandmother, a constant companion on all their travels. The familiar leather cover felt reassuring beneath her fingers, a tangible reminder of God's presence.

A cheerful attendant greeted them at the entrance, checking their tickets and directing them to their cabin. As they made their way through the ship's opulent corridors, Natalie marveled at the intricate artwork adorning the walls—a harmonious blend of traditional Japanese styles and modern cruise ship luxury.

"Oh, Jeff," she whispered, "it's even more beautiful than the brochures."

Jeff chuckled, his free hand finding the small of her back. "And to think, we get a whole week of this. I can't wait to explore those islands with you."

They found their cabin with ease, a snug space featuring a porthole that offered a breathtaking view of the harbor. Natalie immediately set about unpacking, humming a soft melody under her breath as she meticulously arranged their clothes in the compact closet. The gentle sway of the ship added a curious quality to her movements.

Jeff sprawled onto the bed, his long legs dangling off the edge. "You know," he began, a thoughtful expression crossing his face, "I was thinking we could join one of those family groups they mentioned in the cruise itinerary. Could be a great way to meet some interesting people."

"That's a good idea," Natalie responded as she continued unpacking. "It would be nice to connect with some other travellers who've done this before. Might pick up some tips."

As she continued sorting out where everything would go in their room, Natalie's mind drifted to the conversation they'd shared that morning before leaving their hotel. They'd discussed their hopes for the trip, their desire for relaxation, and their eagerness to create lasting memories. It filled her heart with joy to see how quickly their vacation was already shaping up to be everything they'd imagined.

Once they'd settled in, the couple decided to explore the ship before departure. Hand in hand, they strolled along the promenade deck, the sea breeze ruffling their hair. The sun was beginning to set, painting the sky in brilliant hues of orange and pink.

"It's so peaceful out here," Natalie murmured, leaning into Jeff's side. "Reminds me of that verse from Psalms—'He leads me beside still waters, He restores my soul.'"

Jeff nodded, giving her hand a gentle squeeze. "You know, I was just thinking the same thing. I know it's cliché, but it's almost as if God's presence is more tangible out here without all the distractions."

They paused at the railing, watching as the last sliver of sun dipped below the horizon. In the distance, they could see the twinkling lights of the Japanese coastline, a reminder of the exotic world they were about to explore.

"I can't believe we're really doing this," Natalie said, a note of excitement in her voice. "A whole week cruising around these beautiful islands. Jeff, promise me we'll make the most of every moment!"

He turned to face her, his expression soft in the fading light. "I promise, sweetheart. Every single moment." He leaned in, pressing a gentle kiss to her lips.

As they broke apart, the ship's horn sounded, signaling the imminent departure. A thrill of excitement ran through Natalie. This was it—the start of their grand adventure.

They made their way to the upper deck, joining the crowd of passengers gathered to watch as the ship slowly pulled away from the dock. Natalie felt a moment of bitter-sweet nostalgia as she watched Japan's mainland grow smaller in the distance. They'd spent the past week exploring Tokyo and Kyoto, marveling at the blend of ancient traditions and cutting-edge technology.

As the coastline faded into the gathering darkness, Jeff wrapped his arm around Natalie's shoulders. "You know," he said thoughtfully, "I was reading an interesting travel book this morning. There was this quote that stuck with me—'The journey of a thousand miles begins with a single step.'"

Natalie leaned into his embrace, humorously smiling. "Trying to get deep on me, sweetie?" she teased as they shared a quick laugh over it.

"I just keep thinking about how fortunate we are," he continued. "Not just to be on this amazing trip, but to have each other, to have this opportunity to explore and grow together. I really want to appreciate every moment of our travels."

"Absolutely," Natalie agreed. "Hey! Maybe we could start each day by writing in some kind of a travel journal?"

Jeff's face lit up at the suggestion. "That's a great idea. We could use that new notebook with the ugly cat on it your sister gave us for Christmas, since we're obviously not going to use it for anything else..."

"It's the thought that counts," Natalie said as they both shared a small laugh over it.

As they talked, the ship glided smoothly through the dark waters. The deck lights came on, casting a warm glow over the passengers. Around them, conversations in various languages created a gentle hum of excitement.

"Oh, look!" Natalie exclaimed suddenly, pointing towards the horizon. "You can see the first of the islands!"

Sure enough, a dark shape was visible against the star-studded sky. Even in the darkness, they could make out the lush vegetation that seemed to cover every inch of the small landmass.

"Just think," Jeff mused, "tomorrow we'll be exploring places like that up close. Hiking through forests, discovering hidden beaches..."

Natalie's eyes sparkled with anticipation. "I can't wait. Oh, and we have to try some of the local cuisine too! Remember how the travel guide mentioned all those amazing seafood dishes?"

As the night went on, they continued to explore the ship, marvelling at the various amenities—the sparkling pool, the well-equipped gym, the elegant dining rooms. They even peeked into the ship's chapel, a small but beautifully appointed space that immediately grabbed Natalie's attention.

"The pulpit and the artwork in here are beautiful," she mentioned, and Jeff nodded in agreement.

As they were leaving the chapel, Natalie noticed a Japanese couple entering. The woman was petite with sleek black hair, while her husband was tall and distinguished-looking. What caught Natalie's attention, though, was the Bible the woman was carrying—similar to her own.

"Look, Jeff," she whispered, nudging her husband. "I think they might be Christians too."

Jeff glanced over, a warm smile spreading across his face. "I'd assume so. Maybe we'll run into them later."

Natalie nodded, feeling a kinship with the couple even though they hadn't spoken. It was comforting to know that there were other believers on board, as it reminded her of the global nature of their faith.

As they continued their exploration, Natalie and Jeff found themselves in one of the ship's many lounges. A small group had gathered around a piano, where a talented passenger was playing a medley of popular songs. They settled into a cozy corner, content to listen and watch the impromptu entertainment.

"You know," Jeff said, his voice low, "I was thinking about our ministry back home. Do you think Pastor Dave will be okay managing the youth group while we're gone?"

Natalie squeezed his hand reassuringly. "I'm sure he'll be fine. Remember, we prayed about this trip for months. God wouldn't have opened the door if He didn't think the church could manage without us for a week."

Jeff nodded, some of the tension easing from his shoulders. "You're right, of course. I guess I'm just not used to being away from our students."

"That's exactly why we needed this vacation," Natalie pointed out gently. "To rest, recharge, and come back even more energized for our work."

As they continued to chat, Natalie noticed the Japanese couple from earlier entering the lounge. They chose a table not far from where Natalie and Jeff were sitting, and Natalie couldn't help but overhear snippets of their conversation. Though she couldn't understand the words, she recognized the excited tone they used when discussing what seemed to be local landmarks and attractions.

As the evening progressed, Natalie and Jeff decided to head to one of the ship's restaurants for dinner. The dining room was a marvel of elegance, with crystal chandeliers casting a soft glow over white-clothed tables. They were seated at a table for two near a window, offering a stunning view of the moonlit ocean.

Over a delicious meal of miso-glazed salmon and vegetable tempura, they continued to plan their week ahead. "I think tomorrow we're docking at that first island we saw," Jeff said, consulting the itinerary. "There's supposed to be a beautiful hiking trail that leads to a waterfall. Want to check it out?"

Natalie's eyes lit up. "That sounds perfect. We could pack a picnic lunch and make a day of it."

As they ate, they couldn't help but overhear the conversations around them—a mix of Japanese, English, and other languages they couldn't identify. It struck Natalie again how diverse the group of passengers was, all brought together by a love for travel and exploring nature.

After dinner, they decided to take one last stroll around the deck before turning in for the night. The sea air was cool and refreshing, carrying with it the tang of salt that was surprisingly energizing as Natalie breathed it in, tasting the salt in her mouth. Stars twinkled overhead, more numerous and brilliant than Natalie had ever seen in the city.

"It's so beautiful," she murmured, leaning against the railing. "Which reminds me of another Psalm—'When I consider your heavens, the work of your fingers, the moon and the stars, which you have set in place, what is mankind that you are mindful of them, human beings that you care for them?'"

Jeff wrapped his arm around her waist, pulling her close. "It does put things in perspective, doesn't it? We're so small in the grand scheme of things, but being here makes you appreciate the vastness and beauty of the world."

They stood in comfortable silence for a while, simply soaking in the beauty of the moment. Natalie felt a surge of gratitude, thankful for this opportunity and for the man standing beside her.

Eventually, the long day began to catch up with them, and they decided to head back to their cabin. As they walked, Natalie couldn't help but feel the excitement rising through her heart as she thought of all the things they could do here. She made a mental note to review their itinerary and perhaps add a few more fun activities to their plan.

Back in their room, they took turns in the small bathroom, going through their nightly routines. As Natalie brushed her teeth, she could hear Jeff humming his favourite song in the bedroom. The familiar melody brought a smile to her face.

Finally ready for bed, they knelt together beside the narrow bunk. Jeff took Natalie's hands in his, bowing his head.

"Dear Heavenly Father," he began, his voice soft but fervent, "we thank you for this day. For safe travels, for the beauty of Your creation that surrounds us, and for this time we have together. Lord, we ask for Your continued protection as we journey across these waters. Help us to be a light for You, even as we enjoy this time of rest and exploration. We pray for the other passengers and crew on this ship, that they might come to know Your love. In Jesus' name we pray, Amen."

"Amen," Natalie echoed, giving Jeff's hands a squeeze before they rose.

As they settled into bed, the gentle rocking of the ship lulling them towards sleep, Natalie felt herself smile as a feeling of peace settled deep within her. Tomorrow, she and Jeff would see new sights, explore different places, and get new opportunities to share God's love, but right now, wrapped in the warmth of Jeff's embrace and the comfort of God's presence, she was content.

The following morning dawned bright and clear, the sun rising over an endless expanse of shimmering blue ocean. Natalie woke early, the excitement of the day ahead making sleep impossible. She slipped out of bed, careful not to disturb Jeff, who was still snoring softly.

After a quick shower, Natalie decided to head up to the deck for some quiet time with her Bible before breakfast. The ship was docking at their first island stop later that morning, and she wanted to spend a few minutes praying before the day's events began.

The deck was nearly deserted at this early hour, just a few early risers taking their morning jog or sipping coffee as they watched the sunrise. Natalie found a quiet corner and settled into a lounge chair, her Bible open on her lap.

As she read through her daily devotional, Natalie enjoyed a sense of God's presence. The gentle lapping of waves against the ship's hull provided a soothing backdrop to her prayers. She thanked God for this beautiful day, for the safety of their journey so far, and asked for His guidance in the days to come.

Lost in her devotions, Natalie didn't notice a man approaching until he was standing right next to her chair. He was tall and well-built, with a deep tan that suggested he spent a lot of time outdoors. There was something about his stance and the way he was looking at her that made Natalie feel instantly uncomfortable.

"Well, hello there, beautiful," the man said, his voice carrying a slight slur that suggested he might still be feeling the effects of last night's drinking. "What's a pretty thing like you doing up here all alone?"

Natalie closed her Bible and stood up, clutching it to her chest like a shield. "I'm not alone," she said firmly. "My husband is on his way and I'm going to meet him now."

She tried to step around the man, but he moved to block her path. "Aw, come on now," he said, his grin widening. "No need to rush off. Why don't you and I grab a morning drink together? I bet your husband wouldn't mind."

Natalie's heart was pounding now, a mix of fear and anger rising in her chest. "No, thank you," she said, her voice as cold as she could make it. "Please let me pass."

The man's grin faded, replaced by a scowl. He took a step closer, looming over Natalie. "Don't be like that, sweetheart. Can't you see I'm being friendly?"

Just as Natalie was about to call out for help, she heard an accented voice behind her. "Excuse me. Everything... okay?"

She turned to see the Japanese man she had noticed in the chapel the day before. He was standing a few feet away, his wife and two young children clustered behind him. His English was halting but clear, his eyes moving between Natalie and the drunk man with concern.

The drunk man took a step back, his bravado deflating in the face of potential witnesses. "Mind your own business," he muttered.

The Japanese man moved to stand beside Natalie. Despite being shorter than the drunk, he carried himself with quiet confidence. "The lady... she looks not happy," he said slowly, choosing his words carefully. "Maybe you should go."

For a moment, Natalie thought the drunk might argue, but then he shrugged, shooting Natalie one last leer before stumbling away towards the ship's bar.

Natalie let out a breath she hadn't realized she'd been holding. She turned to the Japanese man with a grateful smile. "Thank you so much," she said. "I really appreciate your help."

The man nodded, a small smile on his face. "You are... welcome," he said. "It is good to... help others."

His wife stepped forward then, saying something to her husband in rapid Japanese. The man listened, then turned back to Natalie. "My wife... she asks if you are okay? She is learning English, but not so good yet."

Natalie nodded. "Yes, I'm fine now, thanks to you. I'm Natalie, by the way."

The man's smile widened. "I am Asahi," he said. "This is my wife, Fumiko, and our children, Hiro and Ami." The children, a boy who looked about ten and a girl who seemed closer to seven, bowed politely.

"It's nice to meet you all," Natalie said warmly. She noticed again the Bible that Fumiko was carrying. "I saw you all yesterday. Are you enjoying the cruise so far?"

Asahi's face lit up at the question. "Yes, we are having a wonderful time."

They chatted for a few more minutes, their shared enthusiasm for travel bridging the language barrier. Natalie learned that Asahi and his family were from Osaka, and that this was their first time exploring the smaller islands around Japan.

As they talked, Natalie couldn't help but marvel at how serendipitous it was that this family had been in the right place at the right time to help her. It was a powerful reminder of God's protection and the kindness of strangers.

Eventually, Natalie glanced at her watch and realized Jeff would be wondering where she was. "I should go meet my husband for breakfast," she said. "Thank you again for your help, Asahi. And it was lovely to meet all of you."

Asahi nodded. "Maybe we see you again," he said. "Have good day."

As Natalie made her way back to her cabin, she smiled in gratitude. The unpleasant encounter with the drunk man had been unsettling, but God had provided help just when she needed it.

She found Jeff just finishing getting dressed when she entered their cabin. "There you are, sweetheart," he said, leaning in to give her a quick kiss. "I was starting to worry."

Natalie wrapped her arms around him, holding him close for a moment. "Sorry, I lost track of time," she said. She then proceeded to tell him about her morning adventure.

Jeff's face darkened as she described the drunk man's behavior. "I should have been there," he said, his voice tight with anger. "He better not still be there..."

Natalie put a calming hand on his arm. "It's okay, honey. Nothing happened. And God made sure I wasn't alone." She went on to tell him about Asahi and his family.

As she finished her story, Jeff's anger faded, replaced by a look of wonder. "OK. I'm shaking that guy's hand when I see him." he said. "Isn't God something? Putting that family there just when you needed help."

Natalie nodded, snuggling into Jeff's embrace. "It really is. And you know what? It made me even more grateful for you. I love you so much."

Jeff tilted her chin up, meeting her eyes with a tender gaze. "I love you too, Natalie. More than I can say." He leaned down, capturing her lips in a deep, loving kiss.

When they finally broke apart, both a little breathless, Jeff grinned. "Now, as much as I'd like to continue this, I believe we have an island to explore. Shall we go get some breakfast?"

Natalie laughed, feeling light and happy despite the earlier incident. "Lead the way, my love."

They made their way to the ship's main dining room, where a lavish breakfast buffet was laid out. As they filled their plates with an assortment of Western and Japanese breakfast foods, they continued to plan their day.

"So, we're docking at Miyajima Island in about an hour," Jeff said, consulting the itinerary. "I was thinking we could visit the famous shops first, then maybe do that hike we talked about yesterday?"

Natalie nodded enthusiastically. "That sounds perfect. Oh, and we should try to get some of those maple leaf-shaped cakes the guidebook mentioned. They're supposed to be a local specialty."

As they ate, they couldn't help but overhear the excited chatter of their fellow passengers. Everyone seemed eager to start their island adventures.

After breakfast, they returned to their cabin to prepare for the day. They packed a small backpack with water bottles, snacks, and their guidebook. Natalie made sure to include her Bible—she never knew when she might need it.

As they were getting ready to leave, Jeff pulled Natalie into another embrace. "I'm so glad you're okay," he murmured into her hair. "I don't know what I'd do if anything happened to you."

Natalie leaned back to look up at him, touched by the depth of emotion in his eyes. "I'm fine, Jeff. Really. And I always feel safe with you."

He smiled, pressing a gentle kiss to her forehead. "I'll always do everything I can to protect you, sweetheart. You're my whole world."

Feeling a surge of love, Natalie stood on her tiptoes to plant a big kiss right on his lips.

When they parted, Jeff's eyes were shining. "What was that for?" he asked with a grin.

Natalie shrugged, smiling back at him. "Just because I love you. Now come on, we've got an island to explore!"

Hand in hand, they made their way to the ship's exit, joining the stream of passengers eager to set foot on Miyajima Island. As they waited in line, Natalie spotted Asahi and his family a few people ahead of them. Catching his eye, she gave a friendly wave, which he returned with a smile.

Finally, they stepped off the ship onto the pier. The island rose before them, a lush green jewel set in the sparkling blue sea. In the distance, they could see the bright roofs of the specialty shops glistening in the sunlight.

"Oh, Jeff," Natalie breathed, taking in the beauty around them. "Isn't it amazing?"

Jeff squeezed her hand, his own eyes wide with wonder. "It really is. The beauty that exists in the world never ceases to amaze me."

They set off towards the various attractions, joining the throng of tourists making their way along the island's main street. The road was lined with souvenir shops and food stalls, the air filled with the enticing aroma of grilled seafood and sweet treats.

As they walked, Natalie couldn't help but reflect on the events of the morning. The unpleasant encounter with the drunk man seemed far away now, overshadowed by the kindness of Asahi and his family, and the love and support of her husband.

She took a deep breath, feeling grateful for their safety and for the reminder of the unexpected joys that can come from traveling.

Jeff's voice broke into her thoughts. "Look, Natalie," he said, pointing ahead. "I think those are the maple leaf cakes you wanted to try."

Sure enough, a nearby stall was selling the distinctive leaf-shaped treats. They bought a few to share, the sweet taste of azuki bean paste mingling with the soft cake as they continued their walk.

As they approached the first of the island's architectural wonders, Natalie felt a feeling of awe settle deep within her. The massive vermilion structure seemed to float on the water at high tide, creating a stunning visual effect. They spent the next hour exploring the area, marvelling at the unique architecture and learning about its history from the informational plaques scattered throughout the complex. Despite the crowds of tourists, they had a wonderful time.

As they were leaving, they ran into Asahi and his family again. This time, it was Fumiko who approached them, a shy smile on her face. She said something to her husband, who translated the best he could.

"My wife... she says we are happy to see you again. She hopes you are feeling better after this morning."

Natalie smiled warmly at the couple. "Please tell her I'm feeling much better, thanks to your kindness. We're so grateful for your help."

As Asahi relayed this to his wife, Jeff extended his hand to the other man. "I wanted to thank you personally for helping my wife this morning," he said. "It means a lot to know there are people like you looking out for others."

Asahi shook Jeff's hand, nodding in understanding even if he didn't catch every word. "It is... what God wants," he said simply. "To help others."

They chatted for a few more minutes, the two couples finding common ground in their shared faith despite the language barrier. As they parted ways, Natalie felt a warmth in her heart. It was beautiful to see how faith could bring people together across cultural and linguistic divides.

As they continued their exploration of the island, Natalie and Jeff found themselves continually amazed by the beauty around them. From the peaceful forests to the bustling town center, every part of Miyajima seemed to hold some new wonder.

By late afternoon, they were tired but happy as they made their way back to the ship. As they walked up the gangway, Natalie turned to take one last look at the island, the setting sun casting a golden glow over the scenery.

"What a wonderful day," she said softly.

Jeff pulled her close, pressing a kiss to her temple. "It really was. And you know what the best part is?"

Natalie looked up at him questioningly.

He grinned. "We've got six more days of this to look forward to. What do you say we get cleaned up and then find somewhere nice for dinner?" he suggested.

Natalie nodded, smiling up at him. "That sounds perfect. And maybe afterwards, we could go to the observation deck for a little while? I'd like to take in more of this beautiful scenery."

"Perfect idea," Jeff agreed. "After all, we didn't cruise just to stare at the inside of a ship."

Hand in hand, they made their way back to their cabin, hearts full of love, gratitude, and anticipation for the adventures still to come.

The first few days of the cruise had been nothing short of idyllic. Natalie and Jeff had explored picturesque islands, sampled delicious local cuisine, and spent quiet evenings stargazing on the deck. Their shared faith seemed to deepen with each passing day as they marveled at the beauty of God's creation.

On the fourth night of their voyage, Natalie and Jeff attended a formal dinner in the ship's grand ballroom. Natalie wore a flowing blue dress that matched her eyes, while Jeff looked dashing in a dark suit.

"You look beautiful," Jeff whispered as they entered the ballroom, his eyes full of love and admiration.

Natalie blushed, squeezing his hand. "You're not so bad yourself, handsome."

As they enjoyed their meal, they chatted with the couples at their table, including an elderly pair celebrating their 50th anniversary. Natalie couldn't help but imagine her and Jeff at that age, still as in love as ever.

After dinner, they decided to take a stroll on the deck. The night air was warm, with a gentle breeze that carried the scent of the sea. Stars twinkled overhead, seeming brighter and more numerous than they ever did back home.

"It's so beautiful out here," Natalie murmured, leaning against the railing. "God is truly the greatest Artist of them all."

Jeff wrapped an arm around her waist, pulling her close. "I know what you mean. It's something else, huh?"

As they stood there, enjoying the peaceful night, Natalie noticed something odd. "Jeff," she said, pointing to the horizon, "does that look right to you?"

Jeff squinted, following her gaze. In the distance, they could see the lights of what appeared to be another ship, but it seemed to be moving away from them rather than parallel to their course.

"That's strange," Jeff muttered. "I thought we were supposed to be following the coastline."

Just then, a crew member hurried past them, looking worried. Jeff called out to him, "Excuse me, is everything all right?"

The crew member hesitated, then forced a smile. "Just small correction, sir. Nothing worry. Please enjoy your evening."

But as he walked away, they overheard him muttering into his radio in rapid Japanese. Though they couldn't understand the words, the tone was unmistakably urgent.

Natalie felt a chill that had nothing to do with the night air. "Jeff, I think something's wrong."

They weren't the only ones who had noticed. Other passengers were gathering at the railings, pointing and murmuring in confusion. The ship's movements, which had been barely noticeable before, seemed more pronounced now.

As they made their way back to their cabin, the wind began to pick up, carrying with it the first drops of rain. Natalie said a quick prayer, asking for God's protection over everyone on board.

They were just getting ready for bed when a loud announcement came over the ship's intercom system. The voice crackled with static, making it difficult to understand. "Attention all passengers. Due to unexpected severe weather, we ask that you remain in your cabins until further notice. Please secure any loose items and be prepared for rough seas. We will update you as the situation develops." The announcement was repeated in Japanese.

Natalie and Jeff exchanged worried glances. "I guess that explains the change in course," Jeff said, trying to sound calm. "They must be trying to avoid the worst of the storm. I'm sure it's just a precaution. Why don't we pray together?"

Natalie nodded, grateful for Jeff's steady presence. They knelt beside their bed, hands clasped tightly together.

"Heavenly Father," Jeff began, his voice steady despite the increasing rocking of the ship. "We come to you now, asking for Your protection over this ship and everyone on board. You are the master of the wind and the waves, Lord. We trust in Your power. Please keep us safe through this storm. In Jesus' name, Amen."

"Amen," Natalie echoed, feeling a measure of assurance within her.

As the night wore on, however, the storm only intensified. The ship pitched and rolled, creaking ominously. Items toppled from shelves, and Natalie and Jeff could hear the sounds of panicked voices in the corridor outside. The voices were a cacophony of different languages – English, Japanese, German, and others they couldn't identify.

Through their porthole, when the lightning flashed, they could see that the sea had become a churning mass of white-capped waves. The ship was clearly struggling against the power of the storm, each wave sending shudders through the entire vessel.

"Jeff," Natalie said, her voice tight with fear, "I don't think we're anywhere near where we're supposed to be. The storm couldn't have blown us this far off course so quickly."

Jeff nodded grimly. "I think you're right. Something must have gone wrong with the navigation systems. I get the feeling we're miles off course."

Just then, another announcement crackled over the intercom. "Attention all passengers. We are experiencing technical difficulties with our navigation systems. Our crew is working to resolve the issue. Please remain calm and stay in your cabins. We will provide updates as soon as possible."

Natalie and Jeff looked at each other, the same thought mirrored in their eyes. Technical difficulties didn't begin to cover the situation they were in.

Suddenly, there was a tremendous crash, followed by the screech of tearing metal. The lights flickered and went out, plunging them into darkness. Natalie screamed, clutching Jeff's arm.

"It's okay, Natalie," Jeff said, his voice tight with tension. "We need to get to the lifeboats. Can you find your life jacket?"

They fumbled in the dark, locating their life jackets and putting them on with shaking hands. Just as they were about to open their cabin door, another violent lurch of the ship sent them stumbling. Natalie hit her head on the edge of the desk, crying out in pain.

"Natalie!" Jeff yelled in concern. "Are you all right?"

Before she could answer, the door burst open. A crew member stood there, flashlight in hand, shouting something in rapid Japanese. His eyes were wide with panic, and he gestured frantically for them to follow him.

"What's he saying?" Natalie asked, holding her head.

Jeff shook his head. "I don't know, but I think we need to evacuate. Come on!"

Heart pounding, Natalie grabbed Jeff's hand as they followed the crew member into the chaotic corridor. Passengers were rushing in all directions, some crying, others shouting for loved ones. The ship continued to pitch violently, making it difficult to stay upright.

The narrow hallway was a scene of utter confusion. A group of elderly Japanese tourists huddled together, looking lost and terrified. A German family argued loudly, the parents trying to corral their panicking children. Two crew members were attempting to calm a hysterical woman who was screaming in what sounded like Italian. Jeff, in what was probably an ill-timed attempt to calm Natalie's nerves, joked, "At least everyone's acting like themselves..."

Natalie barely heard it as they clung to each other, trying to follow the crew member's instructions as best they could, but in the darkness and confusion, it was all they could do to keep from being separated by the panicked crowd. They both knew, without having to say it, that their relaxing vacation had turned into a nightmare. Miles off course, battered by a raging storm, and now possibly taking on water, their ship was in dire straits. As they fought their way towards the upper decks, Natalie sent up another silent prayer, hoping against hope that they would somehow make it through this ordeal alive. As they made their way toward the stairs, Natalie and Jeff found themselves caught in a bottleneck of passengers. People pushed and shoved, desperate to move forward. Natalie felt Jeff's hand slip from hers as the crowd surged.

"Jeff!" she cried out, trying to spot him in the sea of faces.

"Natalie! I'm here!" His voice sounded distant, barely audible over the storm and the people shouting.

She pushed against the flow of people, trying to get back to him. A large man bumped into her, knocking her against the wall. She winced in pain but kept moving, calling out for Jeff. Finally, she spotted him, trapped behind a group of passengers who were arguing with a crew member. The crew member was gesturing wildly, trying to direct them up the stairs, but they didn't seem to understand.

Natalie fought her way to Jeff's side, relief washing over her as she grabbed his arm. "I thought I'd lost you," she said, her voice shaking.

"I'm here," he reassured her, pulling her close. "We need to stay together, no matter what."

They joined the throng of passengers slowly making their way up the stairs. The ship's violent movements made the climb treacherous. People stumbled and fell, crying out in pain and fear. The ship was filled with what seemed like all of the world's languages, everyone shouting to be heard over the storm and the groaning of the ship. Halfway up, they encountered a bottleneck. A group of passengers were trying to go back down, shouting something about missing family members. Crew members were attempting to keep order, yelling instructions in multiple languages, but the message was getting lost in the chaos.

"Please, my daughter!" a woman cried out in heavily accented English. "She's still in our cabin!"

A crew member tried to reassure her, but the language barrier made communication nearly impossible. The woman became more agitated, attempting to push past him. Jeff stepped forward, trying to mediate. "Ma'am, I know you're worried, but we need to get to the lifeboats. The crew will make sure everyone is evacuated." The woman looked at him blankly, clearly not understanding. She continued to struggle against the crew member, her cries growing more desperate. Natalie felt helpless, wishing she could do something to ease the woman's fear. She prayed for the child's safety, though it was just one sentence.

The delay caused by this confrontation allowed more passengers to crowd onto the stairs, creating a dangerous crush of bodies. People pushed and shoved, their faces revealing their increasing panic. Natalie felt Jeff's arm around her waist, holding her steady as they were jostled from all sides. Suddenly, a massive wave hit the ship, causing it to lurch violently to one side. People screamed as they lost their footing, tumbling down the stairs. Natalie felt herself falling, but Jeff's strong grip kept her upright.

"Hold on!" he shouted, bracing himself against the wall.

The ship felt like it was beginning to sink, the sound of tearing metal echoing through the stairwell and water seeping in from somewhere below.

"We need to move!" a crew member shouted in English, then repeated it in several other languages. "Quickly, to the upper deck!"

The crowd surged forward again, driven by a new wave of determination. Natalie and Jeff were swept along, struggling to stay together in the chaos. They finally emerged onto the upper deck, only to be met by howling winds and stinging rain.

The deck was a scene of utter pandemonium. Crew members were struggling to launch lifeboats in the turbulent seas, shouting instructions that were lost in the roar of the storm. Passengers huddled in groups, some praying, others weeping. The wind carried snatches of every language—pleas, prayers, and panicked cries blending into a symphony of desperation.

A Japanese crew member approached them, shouting instructions. Jeff tried to ask for clarification in English, but the man just shook his head in frustration, pointing urgently toward the lifeboats.

"Jeff," Natalie cried, her voice barely audible over the storm. "I'm scared!"

He pulled her close, shouting in her ear. "It's going to be okay. We're going to make it through this. Just stay close to me!"

They pushed their way through the crowd towards the nearest lifeboat. The deck was slick with rain and seawater, making every step treacherous. People slipped and fell all around them.

As they neared the lifeboat, they saw a group of passengers arguing with the crew. "There's no more room!" someone shouted in English. "We can't take anymore!"

The crew member was trying to explain something, gesturing towards another lifeboat, but a man pushed forward, trying to force his way onto the already overcrowded boat.

"Stop!" Jeff shouted, moving to intervene. "We need to stay calm!"

But his words were lost in the chaos. The crowd surged forward and Natalie lost her grip on Jeff's hand as people pushed between them.

"Jeff!" she screamed, fighting against the current of bodies that was dragging her away from her husband. "Jeff, where are you?"

She caught a glimpse of him, struggling against the crowd, reaching out for her. Their fingers brushed for a moment, but then another wave hit the ship, sending a wall of water across the deck. Natalie was swept off her feet, tumbling across the slick deck. She slammed against the railing, the impact knocking the breath from her lungs. As she gasped for air, she realized with horror that she was being pulled overboard. She scrabbled desperately for a handhold, but the deck was too slippery.

Just as she was about to be swept into the raging sea, a strong hand grasped her arm. She looked up to see Asahi, the Japanese man who had helped her days earlier. With all of his might, he pulled her back from the brink.

"Hold on!" he shouted, his accent thick but his meaning clear.

Natalie clung to him, her mind reeling. Where was Jeff? She had to find him! But before she could voice her fears, another violent lurch of the ship sent them both sprawling.

Asahi didn't let go of her arm, pulling her to her feet. He pointed towards a lifeboat that had just fallen overboard into the roaring sea below. "We must go!" he yelled over the storm. "Now!"

"But Jeff—" Natalie began, looking around wildly for her husband.

Asahi shook his head, his expression grim. "No time! Ship sinking!"

As if to emphasize his words, there was a deafening groan of metal, and the deck tilted sharply. Natalie stumbled and Asahi half-dragged, half-carried her towards the railing. The lifeboat bobbed violently in the waves below, already drifting away from the ship's hull.

Natalie's eyes widened in horror as she realized what they needed to do. "We have to jump?!" she screamed.

Asahi nodded, his facial expression firm. He gripped her shoulders, forcing her to look at him. "Trust me!" he shouted. "I help you!"

The ship lurched again, and Natalie knew they were out of time. She closed her eyes briefly, sending up a desperate prayer. "God, protect us! Save my husband!"

Asahi climbed over the railing, holding on tightly with one hand while extending the other to Natalie. She took a deep breath and followed, her heart pounding so hard she thought it might burst from her chest.

"On three!" Asahi yelled. "One... Two... Three!"

They leaped together, plunging into the icy, turbulent water. The near-freezing temperature shocked Natalie for a moment. She was disoriented, unsure of which way was up. Before she could gather herself, she felt Asahi's arm around her waist, pulling her to the surface.

They broke through, gasping for air. The waves tossed them about mercilessly, threatening to separate them. Asahi kept a firm grip on Natalie, his eyes fixed on the lifeboat that was now several yards away.

"Swim!" he urged, kicking powerfully against the current.

Natalie tried to match his movements, but her waterlogged clothes and the relentless waves made it difficult. She could feel her strength ebbing with each passing second. "I can't," she gasped. "I can't make it."

"Yes, you can!" Asahi's voice was filled with a mixture of encouragement and desperation. "For Jeff! Swim!"

The mention of Jeff's name sparked something in Natalie. She couldn't give up. She had to find him, had to know he was safe. With renewed determination, she pushed herself harder, fighting against the sea that seemed determined to claim her.

After what felt like an eternity, they finally reached the lifeboat. Asahi guided Natalie to the side, where a rope ladder hung down into the water. "You first," he shouted.

Natalie gripped the ladder, her numb fingers struggling to stay closed. She tried to pull herself up, but her arms felt like lead. She slipped back into the water with a cry of frustration.

"I help!" Asahi positioned himself behind her, boosting her up with his hands. "Climb!"

With Asahi's support, Natalie managed to haul herself over the side of the lifeboat, collapsing onto the floor in exhaustion. A moment later, Asahi pulled himself aboard as well.

As they lay there, panting and shivering, Natalie suddenly realized they had drifted to the edge of the storm and were alone. The small craft, designed to hold a dozen, contained only the two of them. She looked at Asahi, confusion and fear etched on her face.

"Where... where is everyone else?" she asked, her teeth chattering from cold and shock.

Asahi shook his head, his expression grim. "I don't know. This boat... it fall wrong. Maybe others afraid to jump."

The reality of their situation began to sink in. They were alone on this tiny lifeboat, adrift in a raging sea. The cruise ship, now some distance away, was leaning heavily to one side. Even through the darkness and rain, Natalie could see other lifeboats dotting the water, but none were close by.

"Jeff," she whispered, tears mixing with the rain on her face. "Oh God, please let him be okay."

Asahi placed a comforting hand on her shoulder. "We pray," he said simply. "We pray for all."

The storm continued to rage around them, and she had no idea what would become of them, but for now, they were alive, and that small miracle gave her hope. She closed her eyes and prayed fervently, for Jeff, for the other passengers and crew, and for their rescue.

As they pulled away from the sinking ship, Natalie's eyes desperately scanned the calming ocean landscape for any sign of Jeff in the water or another boat, but the residual rain and the darkness made it impossible to see clearly. Tears were continuing to mix with the rain on her face as the horrifying realization set in—she had lost him.

"Jeff!" she screamed into the wind, her voice raw with desperation. "Jeff!" she screamed again, this time her voice cracking and giving out as she fell as if dead on the floor of the boat.

Asahi felt powerless to help her, knowing any comfort would be pushed aside. Her whole world had narrowed to the search for her husband, lost somewhere in this nightmare of wind and waves. The lifeboat pitched wildly in the turbulent sea, threatening to capsize at any moment. Natalie clung to the side, her knuckles white, as she continued to call out for Jeff. But her voice eventually gave out entirely.

As the night wore on, the two occupants of the lifeboat huddled together for warmth, soaked to the bone and shivering. Despite Natalie's determination, her body was giving out and she had lapsed into a kind of numb shock.

Asahi stayed close to her, his presence a silent comfort. He put an emergency blanket over her. "We find him," he said, his broken English barely audible over the storm. "Have hope."

Natalie wanted to believe him, but as the hours passed and there was no sign of Jeff or any other survivors, despair began to set in. She closed her eyes, her lips moving in silent prayer. "Please, God," she whispered. "Please don't take him from me. Please let him be safe."

Just before dawn, the storm in the distance began to subside. As the first weak rays of sunlight pierced the clouds, Natalie could make out the shape of an island in the other direction. Relief washed over both of the occupants of the lifeboat—they had survived the night, and land was in sight.

As they approached the island, the waves grew calmer, making it easier to steer the lifeboat. Asahi and Natalie took turns rowing, their faces grim with exhaustion but determined to reach land. When they finally reached the shore, Natalie stumbled out of the boat on shaky legs. She took a few steps up the beach before collapsing to her knees in the sand. The reality of what had happened—of what she might have lost—again came crashing down on her.

"Jeff," she sobbed, her whole body shaking. "Oh God, please... Jeff..."

Asahi knelt beside her, placing a gentle hand on her back. "We look for him," he said softly. "We not give up hope."

Natalie looked up at him, her eyes red and swollen from crying. She wanted to thank him for saving her life, for staying with her through the night, but the words wouldn't come. Instead, she just nodded, allowing him to help her to her feet.

As Natalie and Asahi stood up, taking in their surroundings, Natalie's eyes scanned the horizon. There was no sign of the ship, no other lifeboats visible, no other survivors. Just the endless expanse of the ocean, now deceptively calm in the morning light.

"We have to search the island," Asahi said after a while. "There can be other lifeboats that have swim here."

Natalie's heart leapt at the possibility. Maybe Jeff had made it after all. Maybe he was on another part of the island, looking for her just as desperately as she was looking for him.

"I'll go," she said, her voice hoarse. "I have to find Jeff."

Asahi nodded, his expression serious. "I come with you," he said. "Not safe alone."

As they prepared to set out, Natalie paused for a moment, looking out over the ocean. The events of the past night seemed like a terrible nightmare, but the ache in her heart and the absence of Jeff's love were all too real.

"Please, God," she prayed silently. "Guide us. Help us find Jeff and the others. Give me strength to face whatever comes."

With one last look at the sea that had torn her world apart, Natalie turned and followed Asahi into the dense vegetation of the island. She knew she had to keep going, had to keep searching. For Jeff, for herself, and for the faith that had always sustained them both. As they disappeared into the island's interior, the sun climbed higher in the sky, its warmth beginning to dry their sodden clothes. But for Natalie, a chill remained in her heart. Where was Jeff? Had he made it to another lifeboat? Was he still out there somewhere, clinging to a piece of wreckage? Or had the sea claimed him?

These questions echoed in her mind as she pushed through the undergrowth, her eyes constantly scanning for any sign of her beloved husband. The search had only just begun, and Natalie was determined to not give up hope. Somewhere on this island, or perhaps still out there on the vast ocean, Jeff might be looking for her too. And until she found him, or learned his fate with certainty, she would not rest.

The sun had climbed high in the sky by the time Natalie and Asahi returned to the beach, their search of the island's perimeter yielding no sign of other survivors. Natalie's heart felt heavier with each step, the hope that had propelled her forward now fading like the morning mist.

As they emerged from the tree line, the stark reality of their situation hit Natalie anew. The beach was littered with debris from the ship—splintered wood, torn life vests, waterlogged suitcases. It was a graveyard of dreams, each piece of wreckage a reminder of the lives disrupted or lost in the night's chaos.

Natalie's legs gave out, and she sank to her knees in the sand. "Jeff," she whispered, her voice breaking. "Jeff..."

Asahi stood silently beside her, his own grief evident in the slump of his shoulders and the tightness around his eyes. After a moment, he knelt down next to her, placing a comforting hand on her shoulder.

"We not give up," he said softly, his broken English carrying a weight of determination. "Maybe others... find island too. We make signal, wait for rescue."

Natalie nodded numbly, grateful for Asahi's steadiness even as her heart ached for Jeff. She knew Asahi must be worried sick about his own family—his wife and children who had been on the ship with them. Yet here he was, trying to comfort her.

"You're right," she managed to say, wiping her tears with the back of her hand. "We need to... to do something. We can't just sit here."

With effort, she pushed herself to her feet. "What should we do first?"

Asahi stood as well, his eyes scanning the beach. "First, we need fire," he said. "For warmth, for signal. Then we look for food, water."

Natalie nodded, clinging to the practicality of these tasks like a lifeline. It gave her something to focus on beyond the gaping hole in her heart where Jeff should be.

They set about gathering driftwood and debris from the wreckage that could burn. As they worked, Natalie's mind kept drifting back to the events of the previous night. The sudden storm, the terrifying moments as the ship began to sink, the last glimpse she'd had of Jeff before the waves tore them apart...

"Jeff was reaching for me," she said suddenly, her voice barely above a whisper. "Just before... before I lost sight of him. He was trying to save me, even then."

Asahi paused in his work, looking at her with sympathy. "Your husband... he good man," he said. "Very brave."

Natalie nodded, fresh tears springing to her eyes. "He is. He's the best man I've ever known. I just can't accept that he's gone."

Asahi was quiet for a moment, then said softly, "My Fumiko... she strong swimmer. Maybe she find way to safety. Maybe she protect our children." His voice caught on the last word, then Natalie saw the sheen of tears in his eyes as well.

Impulsively, she reached out and squeezed his hand. They stood there for a moment, united in their grief and uncertainty, drawing strength from each other's understanding.

As the day wore on, they managed to build a sizeable pile of wood for their signal fire. Asahi, who had some experience with outdoor survival from camping trips, showed Natalie how to use a piece of glass from the wreckage to focus the sun's rays and start the fire. As the flames caught and began to grow, sending a column of smoke into the clear blue sky, Natalie felt a small flicker of hope. Surely someone would see it. Surely help would come.

Their next task was to search the wreckage for anything useful. They found several suitcases that had washed ashore, their contents soaked but potentially salvageable. As they sifted through the sodden clothes and personal items, Natalie couldn't help but think of the people they had belonged to. Had they survived? Were they adrift somewhere, clinging to hope as she and Asahi were?

"Look," Asahi said suddenly, holding up a waterproof bag. "Maybe something dry inside."

They opened it carefully, finding a few items that had been protected from the seawater—a flashlight, some energy bars, and, to Natalie's surprise, a Bible.

She reached for it with trembling hands, running her fingers over the familiar leather cover. It wasn't her Bible. The one her grandmother had given her was lost along with everything else she'd had in their cabin. But holding this one brought a rush of comfort she hadn't expected.

"A Bible," she said softly, looking up at Asahi. "Do you think... could this be a sign? That God is even in all this?"

Asahi's eyes widened in recognition. "You are Christian?" he asked.

Natalie nodded. "Yes, Jeff and I both. We saw you and your family in the ship's chapel that first day. Do you remember?"

A small smile touched Asahi's lips, the first Natalie had seen since the shipwreck. "Yes," he said. "Fumiko and I... we find faith in college. Not many Christians in Japan, but we have small, strong community."

Natalie felt a wave of emotion settle deep within her. Here, in the midst of their desperate situation, God had brought her together with another believer. It couldn't be mere coincidence.

"May I?" Asahi asked, gesturing to the Bible. Natalie handed it to him, and he opened it carefully, leafing through the pages until he found what he was looking for. He began to read aloud:

"'When you pass through the waters, I will be with you; and when you pass through the rivers, they will not sweep over you. When you walk through the fire, you will not be burned; the flames will not set you ablaze.'"

Asahi's voice cracked on the last word. He looked up at Natalie, his eyes suddenly brimming with tears. "Isaiah 43:2," he whispered. "My favorite verse."

Without warning, Asahi's composure crumbled entirely. A heart-wrenching sob escaped his lips, and he dropped the Bible onto the sand. Before Natalie could react, he was on his feet, running towards the water.

"Asahi!" Natalie cried out, scrambling to follow him. "Asahi, wait!"

But he was already in the surf, diving beneath the waves. Natalie watched in horror as he swam out, further and further, his head bobbing up and down as he searched frantically.

"Fumiko!" he screamed between gasps. "Hiro! Ami!"

Natalie waded into the water, her heart pounding. "Asahi, please! Come back!"

For a couple of terrifying minutes, Asahi continued to swim in circles, diving beneath the surface and coming up sputtering. Natalie could see his strength waning, his movements becoming more erratic. Finally, as he came up for air once more, Natalie saw a flash of red in the water around him. Blood.

Without hesitation, she plunged into the deeper water, swimming with all her might towards him. As she reached Asahi, she could see the dazed look in his eyes, the fight draining out of him.

"I've got you," she said, wrapping an arm around his chest. "Let's go back. C'mon Asahi."

Slowly, painfully, they made their way back to shore. As soon as they reached the shallows, Asahi collapsed onto the sand, his body racked with sobs.

Natalie knelt beside him, her own tears mixing with the salt water on her face. She noticed a long gash on Asahi's arm, likely from sharp coral or debris beneath the waves.

"Stay here," she said softly. "I'll be right back."

She hurried to the pile of items they'd salvaged, remembering a small first aid kit they'd found earlier. Grabbing it and the Bible, she returned to Asahi's side.

As she cleaned and bandaged his wound, Natalie spoke softly, her voice trembling but determined. "Asahi, listen to me. I know you're scared. I'm scared too. But we can't give up hope. We have to believe that God is watching over our loved ones, just as He's watching over us."

Asahi's sobs had subsided to quiet weeping, but he nodded slightly, showing he was listening.

Natalie picked up the Bible, finding the passage Asahi had started to read earlier. Her voice grew stronger as she read:

"'When you pass through the waters, I will be with you; and when you pass through the rivers, they will not sweep over you. When you walk through the fire, you will not be burned; the flames will not set you ablaze. For I am the Lord your God, the Holy One of Israel, your Savior.'"

She looked up to find Asahi watching her, his eyes red-rimmed but calmer.

"I'm sorry," he whispered. "I... I lost control. My family..."

"I know," Natalie said, reaching out to touch his arm. "I understand. I'm worried about Jeff too. But we have to trust the Lord. He's all we have right now."

Asahi nodded, taking a deep breath. "You are right. Thank you, Natalie. For saving me... more ways than one."

As the sun began to dip towards the horizon, they sat together on the beach, the Bible open between them. For the next hour, they took turns reading passages to each other, finding comfort and strength in the familiar words. Natalie read Psalm 23, her fears seemingly subsiding with each verse:

"'Even though I walk through the darkest valley, I will fear no evil, for you are with me; your rod and your staff, they comfort me.'"

As darkness fell, Natalie felt a sense of peace settle over her that she wouldn't have thought possible just hours earlier. The grief and fear were still there, a constant ache in her heart, but now there was something else too—a flicker of hope, a reminder that she was not alone.

"We should pray," she said softly, looking at Asahi. "For Jeff and Fumiko and your children. For all the others from the ship. And for ourselves, that we'll have the strength to face whatever comes."

Asahi nodded, bowing his head. Natalie closed her eyes, her hands clasped tightly around the Bible, and began to pray.

"Heavenly Father," she began, her voice trembling but still showing hints of faith. "We come before you now, lost and afraid, but trusting in Your love and mercy. Lord, we pray for our loved ones—for Jeff, for Fumiko, for Hiro and Ami, and for all those who were on the ship with us. Protect them, Father. Guide them to safety if they are lost like we are. And if... if you have called them home to you, Lord, please give us the strength to accept Your will."

She paused, swallowing hard against the lump in her throat. "We ask for Your protection and guidance, God. Help us to remember that You are with us always, even in our darkest moments. Give us the wisdom and strength we need to survive, and please, Lord, send help to rescue us.

We put our trust in You, knowing that You work all things for the good of those who love You. In Jesus' name we pray, Amen."

"Amen," Asahi echoed softly.

As they opened their eyes, Natalie saw that the sun had nearly set, painting the sky in brilliant shades of orange and pink. It was beautiful, a reminder of God's artistry even in this remote and lonely place.

"We should find shelter for the night," Asahi said, rising to his feet and offering Natalie his hand. "Tomorrow, we explore more, look for fresh water."

Natalie nodded, allowing him to help her up. As they gathered palm fronds to create a makeshift shelter near their signal fire, she felt a new resolve growing within her. They were lost, yes, and the road ahead would be difficult. But they were not alone. God was with them, and they had each other.

As night fell, they huddled in their shelter, the Bible tucked safely between them. The sound of the waves lapping at the shore was soothing, almost like a lullaby. Despite her grief and fear, Natalie felt her eyelids growing heavy. She mustered one last prayer, "The Lord gives and the Lord takes away. Whatever comes, I will praise the Lord for He is good."

With that, she drifted off into an exhausted sleep, the Bible clutched to her chest like a talisman against the darkness.

The next morning dawned bright and clear, the horrors of the shipwreck seeming almost like a distant nightmare in the warm tropical sunlight. But as Natalie stirred and opened her eyes, the reality of their situation came rushing back.

She sat up, looking around their makeshift camp. Asahi was already awake, tending to the signal fire to ensure it kept burning.

"Good morning," she said softly, her voice hoarse from sleep and yesterday's tears.

Asahi turned to her, offering a small smile. "Good morning," he replied. "Sleep okay?"

Natalie nodded, though in truth, her dreams had been plagued by images of Jeff lost at sea, calling out for her. She pushed the thoughts aside, focusing on the tasks at hand. "What's the plan for today?"

"We need find fresh water," Asahi said. "And more food. Maybe we explore island more, see if there's better place for camp."

They set about their tasks with grim determination. As they worked, they talked, sharing stories about their lives back home and their loved ones. Natalie learned that Asahi was an engineer, that his daughter Ami loved to draw, and that his son Hiro was learning to play soccer.

In turn, she told him about her life with Jeff, about their large church back home, and about their dreams for the future—dreams that now seemed impossibly distant.

As the day wore on, they managed to find a small freshwater stream inland, and Asahi showed Natalie how to set simple traps for small animals and which fruits were safe to eat. By nightfall, they had improved their shelter and had a small stock of food and water.

As they sat by the fire that evening, Natalie found herself turning to the Bible once again, seeking comfort in its pages.

She read aloud from Romans 8: "'For I am convinced that neither death nor life, neither angels nor demons, neither the present nor the future, nor any powers, neither height nor depth, nor anything else in all creation, will be able to separate us from the love of God that is in Christ Jesus our Lord.'"

Asahi listened intently, then said softly, "Beautiful words. Remind us God's love always with us, even here."

Natalie nodded, feeling a lump form in her throat. "I just... I miss Jeff so much," she whispered. "I keep expecting to turn around and see him there, with that big smile of his. I don't know how to do this without him."

Asahi was quiet for a moment, then said, "I understand. I miss Fumiko, miss children. Heart feels... empty." He struggled to find the right words in English. "But we must have hope. God not abandon us. Maybe... maybe this test of faith."

Natalie considered his words. A test of faith. Was that what this was? It seemed cruel, to be torn away from everything and everyone she loved. But then again, hadn't Job suffered even greater losses? Hadn't he clung to his faith even when all seemed lost?

"You're right," she said finally. "We can't give up hope. Jeff wouldn't want me to give up, and I'm sure Fumiko and your children wouldn't want you to either. We have to believe that God has a purpose in all of this, even if we can't see it right now."

Asahi nodded, his eyes reflecting the flickering firelight. "We pray," he said simply. "We work. We hope. And we trust God."

As they bowed their heads in prayer, Natalie felt herself smile. Yes, they were lost and alone on this island. Yes, the future was uncertain and frightening. But they had their faith, they had each other, and they had the strength that God provided.

The days began to blur together, each one a struggle for survival but also a testament to their resilience and faith. They established a routine—tending the signal fire, gathering food and water, improving their shelter. And each evening, they would read from the Bible, finding new strength and comfort in its words.

A week passed, then two. There was no sign of rescue, no hint that anyone else had survived the shipwreck. But Natalie and Asahi refused to give up hope. They clung to their faith, to each other, and to the belief that God had not forgotten them.

As the sun set on their fourteenth day on the island, Natalie looked out over the endless expanse of ocean. Somewhere out there was home, was Jeff—whether in this world or the next. She prayed for Jeff's protection, as she did every night. With that, she turned back to the camp, where Asahi was waiting with their meager evening meal. Another day was ending, but their journey of faith and survival was far from over.

The days on the island blended into weeks, and weeks into months. Despite their necessary routines and their sometimes difficult task of survival, Natalie and Asahi found moments of peace, even joy, in their shared faith and growing friendship.

As spring gave way to summer, Natalie noticed subtle changes in their relationship. Asahi's English improved rapidly as they spent hours talking, and she found herself picking up Japanese phrases as well. Their conversations, once short and basic, became deeper and more meaningful.

One balmy evening, as they sat by their signal fire watching the sun sink into the ocean, Natalie turned to Asahi. "I'm grateful you're here with me. I don't think I could have survived this alone."

Asahi's eyes softened as he looked at her. "I feel same," he said quietly. "You give me strength, Natalie-san. Remind me to have hope."

There was a moment of charged silence between them, and Natalie felt her heart skip a beat. Quickly, she looked away, focusing on the flames. "We should check the traps before it gets dark," she said, her voice slightly strained.

If Asahi noticed her sudden discomfort, he didn't show it. He simply nodded and stood, offering her a hand up. As their fingers touched, Natalie felt a jolt in her stomach that both thrilled and terrified her. She pulled her hand away quickly, avoiding Asahi's gaze.

That night, as she lay in their shelter listening to Asahi's steady breathing, Natalie found herself consumed by guilt. How could she be feeling this way when Jeff might still be out there somewhere? When Asahi's own family might be searching for him? That night, she prayed for guidance and strength.

As the months wore on, these moments of tension became more frequent. A lingering glance, a brush of hands as they worked together, a shared laugh over some small triumph—each instance left Natalie feeling a confusing mix of warmth and shame.

One day, as they were foraging for fruit in the island's lush interior, Asahi suddenly stopped, his face lighting up with excitement. "Natalie-san, look!" he exclaimed, pointing to a tree laden with ripe mangoes. Without hesitation, he began to climb the tree, his movements graceful despite the months of hardship. Natalie watched as he reached for a particularly juicy-looking fruit near the top.

Suddenly, there was a crack, and the branch Asahi was standing on gave way. Natalie cried out in alarm as he fell, landing hard on the ground with a grunt of pain.

"Asahi!" She was at his side in an instant, her hands fluttering over him anxiously. "Are you all right? Are you hurt?"

He sat up slowly, wincing. "I'm okay," he assured her, though his face was pale with pain. "Just... wind knocked out."

Relief washed over Natalie, so intense it left her feeling weak. Without thinking, she threw her arms around him, hugging him tightly. "Don't scare me like that," she murmured into his shoulder.

For a moment, Asahi stiffened in surprise. Then, slowly, his arms came up to return the embrace. They stayed like that for a long moment, drawing comfort from each other.

When they finally pulled apart, there were tears in Natalie's eyes. "I can't lose you too," she whispered, her voice breaking. "I just can't."

Asahi reached out, gently wiping a tear from her cheek. "You will not lose me," he said softly. "I promise."

The air between them was thick with unspoken emotions. For a heartbeat, Natalie thought Asahi might lean in, might close the distance between them. Part of her longed for it, even as another part recoiled in fear.

But the moment passed. Asahi cleared his throat and looked away. "We should get back," he said, his voice rough. "Storm coming soon."

As they made their way back to their camp, Natalie's mind was in turmoil. She couldn't deny the growing attraction between them, but the thought of moving on, of giving up on Jeff, felt like a betrayal.

That night, as a tropical storm raged outside their shelter, Natalie lay awake, listening to the wind and the rain. She thought of Jeff, of the life they had shared, of the future they had planned together. Tears slipped silently down her cheeks as she wrestled with her conflicting emotions.

"Jeff," she whispered into the darkness, then she prayed. "Father, I miss him so much, but it's been months, and then I've been getting so close to Asahi... Please give me a sign. Help me know what to do."

She drifted off, hoping an answer would come soon.

As summer faded into fall, and fall into winter, Natalie and Asahi's bond continued to deepen. They shared stories of their past lives, their hopes and dreams, their fears and doubts. Natalie learned about Asahi's childhood in Osaka, about his struggle to reconcile his scientific mind with his new-found faith in college. In turn, she told him about growing up in a small town in the Midwest, about meeting Jeff at a church youth group and falling in love over shared volunteer work.

On the anniversary of the shipwreck, they held a small memorial service on the beach. Natalie read from Psalm 23, her voice strong despite the tears that threatened to fall. Asahi added his own prayer in Japanese, the unfamiliar words nonetheless comforting in their sincerity.

As the sun set that evening, painting the sky in shades of orange and pink, Natalie felt a shift in the air between them. They sat side by side on the beach, watching the play of light on the waves.

"One year," Asahi said softly, his English more fluent after months of constant practice. "It feels like a lifetime."

Natalie nodded, her throat tight with emotion. "So much has changed," she murmured. "And yet... part of me still expects to wake up and find this has all been a dream. That Jeff will be there, smiling at me..."

Asahi was quiet for a long moment. Then, hesitantly, he said, "Natalie... I think maybe it's time we talk about future."

She turned to look at him, her heart pounding. "What do you mean?"

He met her gaze steadily, his dark eyes filled with a mix of sadness and determination. "We've been here one year. No sign of rescue. No sign of..." he swallowed hard, "of our families." Seeing her face begin to sadden, he gently grabbed her hand with compassion and continued. "I think it's time..."

Natalie instinctively squeezed his hand and whimpered, "No. I can't," she said as her lips and hand trembled in front of him.

Asahi put his other hand around hers so that her hand was comfortably sandwiched between his. "Natalie.. I know.. Fumiko and my children with Lord. Jeff with Lord too."

Natalie felt tears welling up in her eyes. Part of her wanted to argue, to insist that they couldn't give up hope. But deep down, she knew Asahi was right. They had to face reality.

"I don't know if I can," she whispered. "Accepting that would mean... it would mean giving up on Jeff. On everything we had together."

"Not giving up," he said softly. "Honoring their memory. But also... living. For them, for us."

Natalie looked down at their joined hands, feeling the warmth of his skin against hers. She thought of all they had been through together over the past year, of the bond that had grown between them. And she thought of Jeff, of his love for life, his encouragement for her to always move forward, to embrace new experiences.

Slowly, she nodded. "You're right," she said, her voice barely above a whisper. "I think... I think Jeff would want me to live, not just survive. And I'm sure Fumiko would want the same for you." She paused with a worried look on her face and then continued. "But Asahi, what if the unthinkable happened? What if we did this and then it turned out Jeff was alive? We'll have committed..."

She hesitated to say the word they both knew was next as Asahi bowed his head in acknowledgment, then finished her sentence. "Adultery... We'd commit adultery."

Natalie looked out at the ocean for a minute while each of them silently contemplated their dilemma. Their spouses could certainly be alive, but the likelihood was extremely low, and even if they were, it was becoming less and less likely that they were going to be rescued and reunited with them. Plus, it was somewhat unrealistic to expect that they could live alone on the island another year without connecting in a deeper way.

Breaking the tension, Asahi's grip on her hand tightened slightly. "So... what now?" he asked, his voice hesitant.

Natalie took a deep breath, still looking out towards the sea. "Some time ago, I asked God to give me a sign so that I'd know what to do about Jeff." She wiped a tear away, glanced at Asahi, then looked back at the ocean while Asahi listened intently.

"I had a dream a few nights ago." she continued, with a small smile breaking through her shimmering lips. "It was about Jeff... I was standing at the edge of this beach and I could see him out in the wreckage. He was trying to save other people by putting them on pieces of floating debris." She laughed and looked down for a moment, fondly remembering the picture, then she looked at Asahi. "He was also yelling out to everyone, 'Jesus died for your sins. Repent of your sins. Believe in Him!'"

"Then what," Asahi prompted.

Natalie couldn't help but smile, remembering her husband's courage to do that very thing in real life. "You know," she diverted for a moment, "I heard Christians did the same thing when the Titanic sank. It's incredible. The strength God gives us when we need it most."

Natalie wiped away the rest of her tears and continued telling him the dream with more confidence. "I saw him drown as he was putting one last little girl on a piece of wood. After he was in the water for a few moments, everything went dark, but it was extremely peaceful. I looked down and saw a piece of wood from the crash at my feet. There was something written on it. I picked it up to read it, and written in the prettiest gold I'd ever seen was a fragment of 2 Corinthians 5:8 - 'Absent from the body. At home with the Lord.'"

Asahi immediately recognized the dream as the answer they needed. He smiled warmly as Natalie concluded her thoughts.

She looked at him with more of a peace about Jeff than ever before and said, "I know that the Lord was telling me He'd taken him home. I just didn't want to admit it, but I think I'm ready to now. Now..." Natalie drifted off for a moment, taking one last look at the sea in the direction of the ship's crash. She then looked Asahi straight in the eyes, her blue eyes meeting his dark ones. "Now... we start a new life. Together."

For a moment, they simply looked at each other, years of shared hardship and growing affection reflected in their gaze. Then, slowly,

Asahi leaned in. Natalie's eyes fluttered closed as his lips met hers in a gentle, tentative kiss.

It was sweet and sad and full of promise all at once. When they parted, Natalie felt tears on her cheeks, but she was smiling through them.

"I think," Asahi said softly, reaching up to brush away her tears, "this is what Jeff and Fumiko would want for us. To find happiness, even here."

Natalie nodded, leaning into his touch. "I think you're right," she whispered. "God brought us together for a reason. Maybe... maybe this is part of His plan."

As the last light faded from the sky, they sat together on the beach, hands intertwined, watching the first stars appear. Natalie silently thanked God for His guidance and asked for His blessing on this new part of their lives. The guilt and grief were still there, a dull ache in her heart. She knew she would always love Jeff, always miss the life they had shared. But now, there was something else too—hope for the future, and gratitude for the unexpected gift of love she had found with Asahi.

As they made their way back to their shelter that night, there was a calm and hesitant silence between them, demonstrating the nervousness they both felt in moving forward, but they fell asleep quickly just inches from each other, saying, without words, that tomorrow would begin their new lives.

The next morning dawned bright and clear, a new day full of possibilities. As Natalie stepped out of their shelter, she saw Asahi already up, tending to their signal fire. He turned as she approached, a soft smile lighting up his face.

"Good morning," he said, reaching out to take her hand.

Natalie entwined her fingers with his, returning his smile. "Good morning," she replied. Then, after a moment's hesitation, she added, "I love you, Asahi."

His eyes widened in surprise, then softened with emotion. "I love you too, Natalie," he said, his voice thick with tenderness that she reciprocated.

As they stood there, the warm tropical sun rising over the ocean, Natalie felt herself smile. They had survived the storm, both literal and metaphorical. Now, it was time to live again, to build a life together on this island that had become their home.

The decision to marry wasn't one Natalie and Asahi made lightly. For weeks after acknowledging their feelings for each other, they spent long hours in prayer and discussion, seeking guidance and reassurance that this was the right path.

One evening, as they sat by their signal fire watching the sun sink into the ocean, Asahi turned to Natalie, his expression serious. "I've been thinking," he began, his voice soft but steady. "About us, about our future here."

Natalie nodded, encouraging him to continue.

"In the eyes of God, I believe we are already committed to each other," Asahi said. "We've shared our lives, our faith, our struggles. But I want to make it official, as much as we can in our situation." He took a deep breath, got down on one knee, and looking straight into Natalie's eyes, asked, "Natalie, will you marry me?"

Tears welled up in Natalie's eyes as well as soft laughter in her lips. Despite the unconventional circumstances, despite the lingering grief for Jeff that she knew would never fully fade, she felt a surge of joy at Asahi's words. "Yes," she whispered, and then collecting herself a bit more, repeated, "Yes! I will marry you Asahi!"

Asahi's face broke into a radiant smile. He reached for her hand, bringing it to his lips for a gentle kiss. "I promise to love and honor you, to be faithful to you, and to walk with you in faith for all our days," he said solemnly.

Natalie squeezed his hand, her heart full. "I know you will," she replied, then as a playful laugh started pouring out, she added, "Besides, it's hard not to be faithful to me when we're the only ones here... Unless you're into salamanders or something like that..." They both laughed out loud, as if to make the beginning of their wedded adventure a declaration of the joy they'd share going forward.

They spent the next few days preparing for their simple ceremony. Though they had no officiant and no witnesses beyond the endless sky and sea, they were determined to make their union as meaningful and sacred as possible. Natalie gathered flowers from the island's interior, weaving them into a simple crown. Asahi fashioned rings from polished seashells, carefully carving intricate designs into their surfaces.

On the morning of their chosen day, they rose early, greeting the dawn with prayer. They bathed in a freshwater stream, symbolically cleansing themselves. Natalie put on the cleanest of the dresses they'd salvaged from the shipwreck, a simple white sundress that had faded to a soft ivory after months of island life. She placed the flower crown on her head, the sweet scent of tropical blooms filling the air around her. Asahi wore his best remaining clothes—a white shirt and dark pants that they'd managed to keep in relatively good condition. He had trimmed his beard and combed his hair neatly.

They met on the beach, where the jungle met the sand. The rising sun cast a golden glow over the scene, as if nature itself was blessing their union.

Asahi's breath caught as he saw Natalie approaching. "You look beautiful," he said softly.

Natalie smiled, feeling a blush rise to her cheeks. "You look very handsome yourself," she replied.

They joined hands, facing each other with the vast ocean as their backdrop. Asahi began the ceremony, his voice clear and strong.

"We gather here today, in the presence of God, to join... well... ourselves in marriage," he said, as they snickered once again at their circumstances. "Though we are far from home, though our circumstances are not something we could have ever imagined, we believe that God has brought us together for a purpose."

Natalie nodded, squeezing his hands. "We've faced unimaginable obstacles," she continued. "We've lost so much. But through it all, we've found strength in the Lord, comfort in each other, and love in the midst of hardship."

Asahi smiled, his eyes shining with emotion. "Natalie," he said, "I take you to be my wife. I promise to love you, to honor you, to be faithful to you in good times and in bad, in sickness and in health, for as long as we both shall live."

Natalie felt tears welling up in her eyes as she repeated the vows. "Asahi, I take you to be my husband. I promise to love you, to honor you, to be faithful to you in good times and in bad, in sickness and in health, for as long as we both shall live."

They exchanged the shell rings, each one a unique work of art crafted with love and care. As Asahi slipped the ring onto Natalie's finger, he quoted from the Song of Solomon: "I am my beloved's and my beloved is mine."

Natalie repeated the verse as she placed Asahi's ring on his finger, the familiar words taking on new meaning in this moment.

They had decided to include elements from both their cultural backgrounds in the ceremony. Asahi produced a small cup he had carved from a coconut shell, filling it with fresh water from their stream.

"In Japanese tradition," he explained, "the sharing of sake symbolizes the union of two families. We don't have sake, but we can share this water as a symbol of our new life together."

Before he could lift the cup for them to drink, Natalie, wearing a playful grin, quickly pulled her hand from behind her back and dropped a piece of yuzu in the cup. As Asahi looked down at the fruit in the water, Natalie said, "I know it's not technically sake, but it's closer!"

After sharing a simple laugh, they each took a sip from the cup, the cool water refreshing in the warm morning air. Finally, they turned to face the ocean, hands clasped tightly. Natalie began to pray, her voice carrying clearly over the sound of the waves.

"Heavenly Father, we come before you today with grateful hearts. You have guided us through the darkest of times, and brought us to this moment of joy. We ask for Your blessing on our marriage. Help us to love each other as You have loved us. Give us strength and wisdom to navigate our life together, and always keep our hearts turned towards You."

Asahi continued the prayer in Japanese, trying to use phrases that Natalie would be familiar with. As he finished, they both said "Amen."

Then, with smiles of pure joy, they sealed their vows with a kiss. It was sweet and tender, full of promise for their future together.

As they broke apart, Natalie couldn't help but laugh, overcome with happiness. "We did it," she said. "We're married!"

Asahi grinned, pulling her close. "Yes, we are," he replied. "Husband and wife!"

They spent the rest of the day in celebration. They had prepared a special meal from the best of their island provisions—fresh fish grilled over an open fire, tropical fruits, and even a sweet treat made from coconut and wild berries.

As the sun began to set, casting a warm glow over the beach, Natalie and Asahi sat side by side, watching the play of light on the waves. Despite the joy of the day, there was a touch of bittersweetness in the air.

"I wish our families could have been here," Natalie said softly. "I wish Jeff could have known that I found happiness again."

Asahi nodded, understanding in his eyes. "I feel the same about Fumiko and our children," he replied. "But I believe they know, somehow. I believe they would be happy for us."

Natalie leaned her head on his shoulder. "I think you're right," she said. "Jeff always said that love was the greatest gift we could give each other. I think he would be glad that I've found love again, especially given these wild circumstances."

They sat in companionable silence for a while, lost in thoughts of the past and dreams of the future. As the last light faded from the sky and the first stars began to appear, Asahi stood, offering his hand to Natalie.

"Shall we retire for the night, Mrs. Tanaka?" he asked with a soft smile.

Natalie took his hand, allowing him to pull her to her feet. "Lead the way, Mr. Tanaka," she replied, her heart fluttering with a mix of excitement and nerves.

They made their way to the shelter they had built together over the past year, now adorned with fresh flowers and leaves in honor of their wedding day. Inside, they had laid out the softest blankets they possessed, creating a cozy nest. As they stood facing each other in the dim light of a small fire outside, Natalie felt a moment of shyness. Despite the months they had spent together on the island, this felt like a new beginning, a crossing of a threshold they hadn't yet passed.

Asahi seemed to sense her hesitation. He reached out, gently cupping her face in his hands. "We don't have to do anything you're not ready for," he said softly. "This is a big step for both of us."

Natalie leaned into his touch, grateful for his understanding. "I want to," she whispered. "I'm just... it's been so long, and everything is so different now."

Asahi nodded, stroking her cheek with his thumb. "We'll take it slow," he assured her. "We have all the time in the world."

Slowly, reverently, they began to undress each other and consummate their marriage. There was no rush and no desperate passion, just a tender rediscovery of intimacy long forgotten in their struggle for survival. Afterwards, they lay in each other's arms, listening to the sound of the waves and the night time chorus of the island's wildlife.

"I love you," Natalie murmured, tracing patterns on Asahi's chest.

He pressed a kiss to her forehead. "I love you too," he replied. "More than I ever thought possible."

As they drifted off to sleep, Natalie finally felt blissfully content. Yes, their situation was still precarious. Yes, there was still grief and longing for the lives and loved ones they had lost. But in this moment, wrapped in the arms of her new husband, she felt truly at home for the first time since the shipwreck.

The next morning, Natalie woke to the sound of gentle rain pattering on the roof of their shelter. For a moment, she was disoriented, the events of the previous day seeming almost like a dream. Then she felt Asahi stir beside her, and a warm smile spread across her face as she remembered—they were married now.

"Good morning, husband," she said softly, turning to face him.

Asahi's eyes crinkled at the corners as he smiled back at her. "Good morning, wife," he replied, leaning in for a gentle kiss.

As they lay there, listening to the rain, Natalie felt herself smile. This was the first day of their new life together, the beginning of a journey they would walk side by side.

"What should we do today?" she asked, propping herself up on one elbow.

Asahi considered for a moment. "Well," he said with a playful glint in his eye, "we could stay here and continue celebrating our marriage..."

Natalie laughed, swatting his arm lightly. "As tempting as that is," she replied, "I think we should use this rainy day to plan for our future. We're not just survivors anymore—we're building a life together."

Asahi nodded, his expression growing more serious. "You're right," he agreed. "We should think about improving our shelter, maybe even expanding the garden. And of course, we need to keep maintaining the signal fire and watching for any signs of rescue."

As the rain tapered off and the sun began to peek through the clouds, Natalie and Asahi emerged from their shelter hand in hand. Upon lifting the covering, Natalie looked down and noticed two hermit crabs right in front of the entrance, engaging in a little "celebration" of their own. She snickered and gestured with her eyes for Asahi to look down. He let out a little laugh as well.

"Oh my," Natalie teased. "Looks like we're not the only ones on our honeymoon..."

The two of them laughed and stepped out onto the beach as husband and wife; no longer just two lost souls clinging to survival—they were partners, bound by love and faith.

Nine months had passed. The tropical sun had barely crested the horizon when Natalie awoke, her hand instinctively moving to her swollen belly.

She felt the baby shift beneath her touch and smiled, marveling at the miracle growing within her. Beside her, Asahi slept peacefully, his face relaxed in the soft morning light.

As Natalie carefully eased herself up, trying not to wake her husband, she reflected on the whirlwind of the past nine months. After their island wedding, she and Asahi had thrown themselves into improving their little corner of paradise. They had expanded their shelter into a cozy hut, complete with a thatched roof that kept out even the heaviest tropical rains. Asahi had proven to be quite the engineer, designing an ingenious system to collect and filter rainwater.

Their garden, once just a dream, now flourished with an array of fruits and vegetables. Papaya trees, banana plants, and even a few stubborn tomato vines that had somehow adapted to the tropical climate provided a variety of fresh food to supplement their diet of fish and coconuts.

But the most surprising and joyous development had been Natalie's pregnancy. They had discovered it about two months after their wedding, and the news had filled them both with equal parts excitement and trepidation. Bringing a child into the world was daunting enough in normal circumstances—on their remote island, it seemed almost impossible.

Yet, with faith as their foundation and love as their strength, they had faced every hurdle as it came. Asahi had fashioned crude prenatal vitamins from the most nutrient-rich plants they could find, meticulously researching each one to ensure its safety. Natalie had woven soft blankets from the fibers of certain trees, preparing as best she could for the baby's arrival.

Natalie waddled out of their hut into the warm morning air, sending up a silent prayer of gratitude. Despite the hardships, despite the lingering grief for the lives they had lost, she felt truly blessed.

"Good morning," Asahi's voice came from behind her, still husky with sleep. He wrapped his arms around her, his hands coming to rest on her belly. "And how are my two favourite people today?"

Natalie leaned back into his embrace, smiling. "We're good. Someone's been doing somersaults all night, though."

Asahi chuckled, pressing a kiss to her temple. "Already an acrobat. Must take after you."

As they went about their morning routine—tending the signal fire, checking their water collection system, gathering fresh fruit for breakfast—Natalie couldn't shake the feeling that something was different today. There was an energy in the air, a feeling of anticipation that made her skin tingle. By midday, as the tropical heat reached its peak, Natalie knew what that feeling had been heralding. The first contraction hit her as she was washing some mangoes in their freshwater stream.

"Asahi!" she called out, her voice tight with a mixture of excitement and fear.

He was at her side in an instant, his face etched with concern. "Is it time?"

Natalie nodded, gripping his hand as another contraction washed over her. "I think so. Oh, Asahi, we're really doing this, aren't we?"

His eyes were wide, but his voice was steady as he helped her back to their hut. "We are. Remember everything we've planned, everything we've prepared for. You can do this, Natalie. We can do this."

The next few hours passed in a blur of pain, sweat, and determination. Asahi was a rock, his calm presence anchoring Natalie through each contraction. He wiped her brow, fed her sips of water, and murmured encouragement in a mixture of English and Japanese.

As the sun began to set, painting the sky in now-familiar hues of orange and pink, Natalie gave one final, mighty push. The sound of a baby's cry split the air, more beautiful than any music she had ever heard.

"It's a boy," Asahi said, his voice choked with emotion as he cradled their newborn son. "Natalie, you did it. He's perfect."

Tears streamed down Natalie's face as Asahi placed the baby on her chest. She looked down at their son, taking in his shock of dark hair, his tiny nose, his perfect little fingers. "Hello, little one," she whispered. "We've been waiting for you."

As night fell, the new family huddled together in their hut, marveling at the miracle they had created. The baby nursed contentedly, his little fist wrapped around one of Asahi's fingers.

"He needs a name," Natalie said softly, stroking the baby's cheek.

Asahi nodded, his eyes never leaving their son's face. "I've been thinking about that," he said. "What about Noah? It seems fitting, given our circumstances..."

Natalie gave him a cute and snarky look, clearly getting the joke but unwilling to name their baby for a gag. "Or maybe," she said with a playful tone, "we could name him something *actually* meaningful."

After a short laugh, they spent about 10 minutes offering name suggestions back and forth. Natalie offered English names while Asahi offered Japanese names. But no matter how many they considered, none seemed to be the right fit.

"Perhaps, we should put his name on hold until it comes to us," Asahi suggested.

Natalie agreed. "You're right. It'll come when the time is right. Who knows? Maybe God will give us the perfect name."

Their son, blissfully unaware of the deliberations surrounding his identity, continued to thrive. He had his mother's blue eyes and his father's olive skin, a perfect blend of their heritages. He was a calm baby, rarely fussing except when hungry or wet.

One morning, about a week after the birth, Natalie was sitting outside their hut, the baby cradled in her arms as she watched the sunrise. Asahi joined her, wrapping an arm around her shoulders.

"You know," Natalie said thoughtfully, "we can't just keep calling him 'the baby'. We really need to decide on a name."

Asahi nodded, a wry smile on his face. "I never thought naming our child would be more difficult than surviving on a deserted island."

Natalie laughed, then winced as the movement jostled her still-tender body. "Maybe we're overthinking it. We should just pick something simple, something meaningful to both of us."

They sat in companionable silence for a while, watching as the golden light of dawn spread across the beach. Suddenly, Asahi straightened, his eyes lighting up.

"I have an idea," he said mischievously. "Why don't we call him Akachan for now? In English, it means, "the baby."

Natalie looked at him, rolling her eyes but grinning. "Until when?"

Asahi's smile widened. "Well, until we can agree on a name."

Asahi leaned in and kissed his son on the forehead. "Welcome to the world, Akachan."

Natalie giggled. Their days revolved around the baby's needs—feeding, changing, bathing—while still maintaining their survival tasks. They took turns watching the baby while the other tended the garden, checked the traps, or maintained the signal fire.

One evening, as they sat on the beach watching the sunset, the baby sleeping peacefully in Natalie's arms, Asahi turned to his wife with a serious expression.

"Natalie," he said softly, "I've been thinking. About rescue."

Natalie felt her heart skip a beat. It was a topic they hadn't discussed much since the baby's birth, both of them focused on the immediate needs of their growing family.

"What about it?" she asked, her voice equally quiet.

Asahi sighed, running a hand through his hair. "I think we need to come to terms with this island being our home for the rest of our lives."

Natalie nodded slowly. It was a thought that had crossed her mind as well, especially since the baby's birth. "I know," she said. "I've been thinking about it too. Part of me still hopes, still watches the horizon every day for a ship or a plane. But another part..."

"Another part has started to think of this place as home," Asahi finished for her.

"Yup. Home." Natalie agreed. She looked down at the baby, sleeping peacefully, unaware of the weight of the conversation happening above him. "You know, when I first realized I was pregnant, I was terrified. How could we possibly raise a child here, I thought. But now..."

"Now it seems like the most natural thing in the world," Asahi said, smiling as he stroked the baby's cheek gently.

Natalie leaned into her husband's side, drawing comfort from his steadiness. "So what do we do? Do we just... accept this as our life now?"

Asahi was quiet for a moment, his gaze fixed on the horizon where the sun was sinking into the sea. "I think," he said slowly, "that we need to find a balance. We keep hoping, keep watching for rescue. We maintain the signal fire and keep our eyes on the sky. But at the same time, we build our life here. We make plans for the future—our future, and the baby's future."

Natalie nodded. "You're right," she said. "We can't put our lives on hold waiting for rescue that may never come. We owe it to the baby to give him the best life we can, right here and now."

As they did most nights, they sat in silence for a while, each lost in their own thoughts as they watched the last light fade from the sky. As the first stars began to twinkle overhead, Natalie felt a surge of love for her little family. Against all odds, they had not just survived, but thrived. They had created a life filled with love, faith, and hope.

"You know," she said softly, "when I think about it, we're incredibly blessed. We have each other, we have the baby, we have this beautiful island. It's not the life we planned, but it's a good life."

Asahi pressed a kiss to her temple. "It is," he agreed. "And who knows? Maybe one day, the baby will have a little brother or sister to share it with."

Natalie laughed, the sound carrying across the quiet beach. "Let's get through the toddler years first, shall we?"

As if on cue, the baby stirred in her arms, his little face scrunching up as he prepared to wail for his next meal. Natalie and Asahi shared a look of amused resignation before heading back to their hut.

That night, as Natalie nursed the baby by the light of their small fire, she found herself humming an old hymn her grandmother used to sing. "Great is Thy faithfulness, O God my Father, there is no shadow of turning with Thee…"

Asahi, who was mending one of their fishing nets, looked up with a smile. "That's beautiful," he said. "What is it?"

"It's called 'Great Is Thy Faithfulness'," Natalie explained. "My grandmother used to sing it to me when I was little. I'd almost forgotten it, but for some reason, it just came back to me."

Asahi set aside his work and moved to sit beside her. "Will you teach it to me?" he asked. "I'd like to learn it. For the baby."

Natalie's heart swelled with love for this man who had become her partner in every sense of the word. "Of course," she said. "Then we can teach him together."

As they sat there, softly singing the old hymn to their son, Natalie felt a profound feeling of gratitude settle deep within her. Their situation was far from perfect, their future still uncertain. But in this moment, surrounded by the love of her family and the beauty of their island home, she knew that they would be okay.

Three months later, the sun had barely crested the horizon when Natalie stirred from her sleep. She glanced over at Asahi, still peacefully slumbering, and then at the makeshift crib where their three-month-old son lay. A smile touched her lips as she watched the baby's chest rise and fall with each tiny breath.

"Good morning, little one," she whispered, gently stroking his cheek. The baby's eyes fluttered open, bright and curious. "Still no name for you, huh? Your daddy and I really need to figure that out."

As if on cue, Asahi began to stir. He sat up, rubbing his eyes, and smiled at his wife and child. "Good morning, my loves," he said softly.

Natalie was about to respond when a faint sound suddenly caught her attention. She froze, straining her ears. "Asahi," she whispered urgently, "do you hear that?"

Asahi tilted his head, listening intently. His eyes widened as he recognized the distant hum of an engine. Without a word, he sprang to his feet and rushed outside their shelter.

Natalie quickly wrapped the baby in a blanket and followed, her heart pounding. As she stepped onto the beach, she saw Asahi standing at the water's edge, shading his eyes against the morning sun as he peered out to sea.

And there, cutting through the waves, was a small boat heading directly for their island.

"Is it real?" Natalie breathed, hardly daring to believe her eyes. "Asahi, tell me I'm not dreaming."

Asahi turned to her, his face a mixture of joy and disbelief. "It's real," he confirmed, his voice thick with emotion. "Natalie! We're being rescued!"

As the reality of the situation sank in, a heavy mix of emotions swept through Natalie. Joy, relief, excitement... and a twinge of something else. Uncertainty? Fear? She pushed the feeling aside, focusing instead on the approaching boat. As it drew closer, they could make out two figures aboard. The couple waved frantically, shouting to attract attention, though it was clear the boat had already spotted them.

When the small craft finally reached the shallows, two men in official-looking uniforms jumped out and waded to shore. They spoke rapidly in Japanese, and Asahi responded, his words tumbling out in a rush of relief and gratitude.

One of the men turned to Natalie and spoke in broken English. "We are... police. Search... many months. Very happy... find you."

Tears streamed down Natalie's face as she nodded, unable to form words. The baby in her arms began to fuss, drawing the attention of the officers. Their eyes widened in surprise, and they exchanged meaningful glances.

As Asahi continued to converse with the officers, explaining their situation, Natalie noticed another boat approaching in the distance. Her brow furrowed in confusion—had they sent two rescue boats?

"Did you find any other survivors?" Asahi asked the officers.

"Only one other" they replied. "Everyone else drown."

The second boat drew closer, and Natalie could make out a solitary figure aboard besides the operator. As it neared the shore, she felt Asahi stiffen beside her. He muttered something in Japanese that sounded like a prayer... or perhaps a plea."

The boat reached the shallows, and a woman jumped out, her eyes scanning the beach frantically. When her gaze landed on Asahi, she froze, her hand flying to her mouth in shock. For a long moment, she stood there, unmoving, as if she couldn't believe what she was seeing.

"Asahi?" she whispered, her voice barely audible over the lapping waves. "Asahi, is it really you?"

Asahi's face had drained of all color. He took a shaky step forward, his eyes never leaving the woman. "Fumiko?" he breathed, his voice filled with disbelief and a hint of fear. "How... how is this possible?"

Fumiko's paralysis broke, and she began to run towards them, her feet kicking up sand as she sprinted across the beach. "Asahi!" she cried out, her voice breaking with emotion. "Asahi!"

Natalie watched in stunned silence as Fumiko threw herself into Asahi's arms. It took her a moment to understand what was happening, but when she did, it felt like the ground had dropped out from beneath her feet. This was Asahi's wife. His first wife. The one they had believed dead for two years.

Fumiko was sobbing uncontrollably, her words coming out in a jumbled mix of Japanese and the English she had learned since the crash. "I thought... I thought you were dead," she managed between gasps. "They told me... the ship... no survivors..."

Asahi held her tightly, his own eyes brimming with tears. "We thought the same," he said softly, his voice filled with wonder and confusion. "Fumiko, I... I can't believe you're here. How did you survive? Where have you been all this time?"

As the reunited couple clung to each other, Natalie stood frozen, the baby clutched tightly to her chest. She felt like an intruder in a moment she shouldn't be witnessing, yet she couldn't look away. The joy on their faces was palpable, a testament to a love that had endured even when all hope seemed lost.

But then, slowly, inevitably, Fumiko's eyes drifted from Asahi's face to take in their surroundings. Her gaze landed on Natalie, confusion flickering across her features. And then, almost in slow motion, her eyes dropped to the baby in Natalie's arms. The joy on Fumiko's face morphed into confusion, then disbelief, and finally, a storm of emotions too complex to name. She pulled away from Asahi abruptly, her eyes darting between him, Natalie, and the baby.

"Asahi," she said, her voice trembling, "what... what is this? Is she the woman... and that baby... That baby not two years old..."

Asahi's face was a mask of anguish as he realized the full implications of the situation. "Fumiko," he began, his voice pleading, "please, let me explain. We thought you were dead. We all did. I... I never imagined..."

But Fumiko wasn't listening. Her eyes, filled with pain and betrayal, were fixed on the baby. "Is it yours?" she whispered, her voice barely audible. When Asahi didn't immediately respond, she repeated the question, louder this time. "Is it yours, Asahi?"

Asahi closed his eyes, a look of deep pain crossing his face. "Yes, and Natalie is my wife," he said softly. Then, in an attempt to get everything out that needed to be said quickly, he continued. "Fumiko, please understand. We thought you were gone. We mourned for you. I never meant to—"

"How could you!?" Fumiko cried out with a screech, cutting him off. The pain in her voice was raw, visceral. "I was out there, alive, hoping every day that I would see you again. And you... you just replaced me? Replaced our family?"

Tears were streaming down Fumiko's face now, her body shaking with sobs. The anger was there, simmering beneath the surface, but it was overshadowed by a profound sadness that seemed to emanate from her very soul.

"Did our love mean so little to you?" she asked, her voice breaking. Asahi attempted to comfort her with an embrace, but she screamed, "Was I so easy to forget!?" pushing Asahi away and beating his chest several times in an explosion of grief.

As she stepped back, Asahi reached out to her again, his own face wet with tears. "No, Fumiko, never. I loved you... I still love you. But I thought you were gone. We all did. I was lost without you. I—"

Fumiko shook her head, backing away from his outstretched hand. "And so you found someone else," she said, her voice hollow. "You built a new life, a new family. While I was fighting every day just to survive, clinging to the hope of seeing you again."

Her eyes turned to Natalie, who stood rooted to the spot, unable to speak. "And you," Fumiko said, her voice a mixture of anger and despair. "You knew it! You knew I was his wife when you married him! When you had his child!"

Natalie opened her mouth to respond, but no words came out. What could she possibly say in this situation?

Fumiko didn't wait for an answer. She turned back to Asahi, her eyes filled with a pain so deep it was almost tangible. "I don't know you anymore," she whispered. "The Asahi I loved... he would have waited. He would have known, somehow, that I was still alive."

"Fumiko, please," Asahi begged, his voice cracking with emotion. "Let me explain. We couldn't have known—"

But Fumiko was already backing away, once again shaking her head violently. "No," she said. "No explain. No more lies."

Without warning, after one last glance at Natalie and the baby, she turned and ran back to the boat she had arrived on. Asahi called after her, his voice filled with desperation, but she didn't look back. The boat's engine roared to life, and within moments, it was speeding away from the island, leaving behind a scene of joy turned to heartbreak.

Asahi stood at the water's edge, watching the boat disappear into the distance, his shoulders slumped in defeat. Natalie remained where she was, the baby now crying softly in her arms, as the full gravity of what had just happened settled over them like a heavy shroud. The rescue they had longed for had come, but with it came a complication none of them could have foreseen. A heavy silence fell over the beach. The police officers shifted uncomfortably, unsure of how to proceed. Natalie felt numb. The baby in her arms began to cry, perhaps sensing the tension in the air, and she automatically began to soothe him. This small, familiar action anchored her, giving her something to focus on besides the chaos of emotions threatening to overwhelm her.

One of the officers cleared his throat, breaking the tense silence. He spoke to Asahi, who nodded mechanically in response. Then, turning to Natalie, the officer said, "We go now. Other boat... come soon. Take you home."

Home. The word echoed in Natalie's mind. What did that even mean now? Where was home?

As if in a daze, Natalie and Asahi gathered their meager possessions—the few tools they had fashioned, some clothing, and the precious Bible they had found in the wreckage. The baby's cries had subsided to whimpers, and Natalie held him close, drawing comfort from his warmth. A larger boat arrived within the hour. As they prepared to board, Natalie took one last look at the island that had been their home for the past two years. The shelter they had built together, the garden they had tended, the beach where their son had been born—it all seemed like a dream now, fading away in the harsh light of reality.

The journey back to civilization was a blur. Natalie and Asahi sat side by side on the boat, the baby nestled between them, but an invisible chasm seemed to have opened up. They spoke little, both lost in their own thoughts, grappling with the enormity of what just happened. As the familiar skyline of a Japanese city came into view, Natalie felt a surge of panic. What would happen now? What did this mean for their future—for their family? She looked down at the baby, still unnamed, innocent and unaware of the turmoil surrounding him. Then she glanced at Asahi, who met her gaze with eyes full of sorrow, confusion, and something else—determination.

The boat docked, and they were ushered through a whirlwind of medical examinations, police interviews, and curious stares. It was late evening by the time they were finally cleared to leave.

"Asahi... where are we going?" Natalie asked hesitantly as they climbed into a taxi.

Asahi gave an address to the driver, then turned to Natalie. "Home," he said softly. "My home. Our home now, I suppose."

The drive was silent, the unfamiliar cityscape blurring past the windows. Natalie felt like she was in a dream—or perhaps a nightmare. Everything was happening so fast, and yet time seemed to have slowed to a crawl.

When they finally arrived at a modest townhouse, Natalie felt a fresh wave of anxiety settle deep within her. This was Asahi's home—the home he had shared with Fumiko. What would they find inside?

Asahi fumbled with his keys, which had miraculously survived their ordeal in a waterproof pouch. As the door swung open, Natalie held her breath, unsure of what to expect. The apartment was... empty. Not completely—the furniture was still there, the walls still decorated with photos and art. But it was clear that someone had been here recently, clearing out personal belongings.

"Fumiko," Asahi murmured, his voice barely audible. "She must have come here after..."

He trailed off, unable to finish the sentence. Natalie felt a pang of guilt, mixed with a confusing blend of other emotions she couldn't quite name. They moved through the apartment like ghosts, taking in the half-empty shelves, the bare spots on walls where photos had once hung. In the bedroom, the closet door stood open, revealing empty hangers where Fumiko's clothes had once been.

"I'm sorry," Natalie whispered, not knowing what else to say.

Asahi shook his head, his expression unreadable. "We should get settled. The baby needs to sleep."

They went through the motions of unpacking their few belongings, setting up a makeshift bed for the baby in what had once been a guest room. Natalie fed and changed him, grateful for the familiar routine in the midst of so much uncertainty.

It was late when they finally collapsed onto the couch in the living room, physically and emotionally exhausted. The baby was asleep in the other room, his soft breathing audible over the baby monitor they had found in a drawer. For a long moment, neither of them spoke. The silence stretched between them, heavy with unspoken thoughts and fears. Before they drifted off to sleep, they muttered a weary "I love you" to each other, both of them seeing the confusion, exhaustion, but also love in each other's eyes.

When morning came, the couple woke up before the baby, who had miraculously slept through the night, probably as a result of the previous day's adventure. They silently made some tea and prepared a simple breakfast, exchanging a few soft touches as they navigated the traditional Japanese kitchen.

When they sat down, Natalie finally broke the silence. "Asahi," she said softly, "what... what happens now?"

Asahi sighed, running a hand through his hair, as was his usual gesture when deep in thought. "I don't know," he admitted. "I never thought... I never imagined we'd be in a situation like this."

"Me neither," Natalie agreed. She hesitated, then asked the question that had been weighing on her mind. "What about Fumiko? Do you think she'll come back?"

Asahi's expression darkened. "I don't know," he said again. "She was so angry, so hurt. I've never seen her like that before."

Natalie felt tears prickling at her eyes. "I'm so sorry, Asahi. This is all my fault. If I hadn't gotten pregnant—"

"No," Asahi interrupted firmly, taking her hand in his. "Don't say that. Our son is not a mistake, Natalie. He's a blessing. No matter what happens, I will never regret him. Or you."

Natalie squeezed his hand, drawing comfort from his touch. "But Fumiko... she's your wife. Your *real* wife."

Asahi shook his head. "You're my wife too, Natalie. Maybe not legally, not here. But in my heart, in the eyes of God... you are my wife. And I love you."

The words hung in the air between them, a beacon of hope in the midst of their tumultuous situation.

"I love you too," Natalie whispered. "But I can't help feeling terrible for Fumiko. What she must be going through..."

Asahi nodded, his eyes filled with sorrow. "I know. I keep thinking about her, wondering where she is, if she's okay."

They fell silent again, each lost in their own thoughts. After a while, Natalie spoke up. "Well, I think we should pray for her."

Asahi looked at her, surprise and gratitude mingling in his expression. "You'd do that? Pray for Fumiko?"

Natalie nodded. "Of course. She's hurting. And... she's still your wife. If we believe that God is truly working in all this—and I believe He is—we should pray for her."

Asahi's eyes shimmered with unshed tears. "Thank you," he said softly.

They bowed their heads to pray, but found themselves at a loss for words. What exactly should they pray for in this impossible situation? For every solution they could think to ask for, something seemed terribly lacking in the arrangement. They were both—but Natalie especially—a bit confused as to what to say the Lord.

After a few moments of silence, Asahi spoke up. "Natalie, there's something I need to tell you. This... Well, it might sound strange to Western ears, but... in much of Asia, including Japan—"

Natalie interrupted him there. "Polygamy, right?"

Asahi froze and just stared at her, totally surprised that the thought had crossed her mind.

Natalie provided a hesitant smile. "That's the official term for having more than one wife, right? I think it's Greek, or something like that..." she continued as she took a deep breath to relieve her own tension.

Asahi found himself still unable to formulate a response and continued staring, giving a slight nod to positively answer Natalie's question about the word's etymology.

After taking another deep breath, calming the rest of her nerves, she proceeded to tell her husband how she knew about it.

"The topic came up at a Bible study back in the States," she began. "Jeff and I had only been married a few months. We were discussing David and Bathsheba. While someone was reading God's response to David through Nathan, my friend Sarah interrupted and pointed out that God took credit for giving David his multiple wives. We all kind of froze until she asked the leader a pretty intense question. She said, 'How can polygamy be a sin if God is the One who gave David his wives? And apparently, according to this, He would have given him more!' We all froze, including the leader. That's when Jeff spoke up. He pointed out that the Bible never technically condemns having multiple wives and that God even prescribed it in some of His laws, so it would be wrong to say that it's a sin."

Asahi, listening intently, raised his eyebrows, seemingly impressed by Jeff's insight.

Natalie continued. "But there was a girl in the group who was not happy with that at all. She kind of let him have it in front of the whole Bible study. She told him that there was no way God would be okay with something so selfish and abusive. They got in an argument. Which, by argument, I mean she yelled at him while he gently tried to get her to consider what the Bible had to say about it. But she wasn't having it. With her Bible closed and her mind made up, she stormed out of the Bible study, leaving Jeff—and everyone else—stunned at how mad she'd gotten."

Natalie paused, looking down and off to the side.

"Who was she?" Asahi asked. "A friend?"

Natalie looked back up at him with a humble smile. "Me." she answered. "The girl who yelled at him and questioned his character in front of half the church was me... his wife."

"Oh." Asahi said, unsure of what else to say.

"Later on," she continued, "I was beyond embarrassed for the way I acted. Before Jeff got home, I got my Bible out and started skimming through the Old Testament, looking for any other mentions of polygamy. I sure learned my lesson when I found out Jeff was right. There was nothing in there to suggest that polygamy was a sin, or even abnormal for that matter. In fact, I found myself counting more polygamists than monogamists among God's best men throughout the Bible. Clearly, this was not the issue I'd felt it was. I was just going off of what I'd been told my whole life."

Natalie took a breath and a sip of her tea. "Anyway," she continued. "When he got home, we talked about it and I apologized. I was still pretty uncomfortable with the idea. I certainly couldn't think of any modern-day application for an arrangement like that, but Jeff had at least put my mind at ease that he wasn't a crazy pervert."

Natalie laughed a little, taking a couple of seconds to remember that night. "Turns out I was due for a little more humility than I thought, because here I am, in the 21st Century, innocently married to a man who's already married." She then let out an audible sigh, as if to come to terms with what God was doing in her heart. "I guess it's for some people after all."

She took another sip of her tea, marking the conclusion of her story.

Asahi smiled with a little trepidation, unsure of how freely he should speak about the topic. "It's not legally practiced in Japan anymore," he said, "but there are still other places in the world where it's common." He paused for moment and then continued. "I'm not really sure what else to say. What do you think about all this?"

Natalie, with a little bit of confidence rising in her voice, answered. "Well, if it was good enough for stand-up guys like Moses and Josiah, I guess it should be good enough for me. And in a situation like ours... I don't see another way. Do you? Certainly God doesn't want you to divorce either one of us, and technically, it's already the situation that we're in. I don't see any Biblical reason to change it."

Asahi's eyes widened slightly at her words. "You... You really think so? You'd do that? For Fumiko? For me?"

Natalie reached for the Bible they had found earlier. "If I'm remembering correctly, 1 Corinthians 7 says a lot about specific marriage circumstances, right? Maybe we'll find the answer we need there."

Asahi scooted his chair over to skim the chapter with her. Suddenly, her finger stopped on a verse. "Asahi, look at this. Verses 10-11: 'But to the married I give instructions, not I, but the Lord, that the wife should not leave her husband (but if she does leave, she must remain unmarried, or else be reconciled to her husband).'"

They looked at each other, the implications of the verse sinking in.

"The Bible... it's saying Fumiko only has two options," Asahi said slowly. "Remain alone, or... reconcile with me."

Natalie nodded, her heart beginning to race. "And I don't see an exception for if her husband has remarried." She flipped the Bible on its front cover, then the back cover, then flipped through the maps at the end, humorously implying that she was looking for an exception. "Nope. Nothing."

They smiled at the joke, then Natalie continued with a resolute tone. "According to this, God's will would be for Fumiko to return as your wife. It's as simple as that."

They sat in stunned silence for a moment, the weight of this revelation settling over them.

"So, what does this mean for *us*?" Natalie whispered, as the theoretical discussion quickly transitioned into reality for her.

Asahi took a deep breath. "I think... I think it means we need to pray for reconciliation. For all of us. It won't be easy, but if this is what God's word is telling us..."

Natalie nodded slowly. "You're right. It's not what I expected, but... if this is God's will, we need to trust in His plan."

They bowed their heads once more. This time, their prayer was clear: for Fumiko's return, for her pain to be eased, for her heart to be softened, for understanding and forgiveness to find its way into her soul. They looked at each other, a mix of fear and hope in their eyes, which was promptly interrupted by the baby's cry echoing through the monitor. Natalie and Asahi shared a small smile.

"I'll get him," Asahi said, standing up. "And then we pray. For Fumiko, for us, for our future. Whatever it may hold."

Natalie nodded, watching as Asahi went to tend to their son. As she sat there, surrounded by the remnants of Asahi's old life and the beginnings of their new one, she felt a glimmer of hope. It wouldn't be easy, but with faith, love, and determination, they would find a way through this. Together, they would build a future—unconventional as it might be—filled with love, forgiveness, and the grace of God.

The days following their return to civilization passed in a blur of adjustment and uncertainty. Asahi and Natalie settled into a routine in the apartment. Every night, they prayed together for Fumiko's return, their hearts hopeful, but also heavy with the weight of their circumstances. Asahi tried calling Fumiko a few times but she didn't return his calls. On one occasion, Natalie spotted her at the market while grocery shopping. She tried to approach her, but with a scowl, Fumiko avoided her and got in her car and drove off. They continued to pray, but as the weeks turned into months, there was no sign of her.

"Do you think she'll ever come back?" Natalie asked one evening, as they sat on their balcony watching the sunset. The baby, now six months old and still unnamed, gurgled happily in her arms.

Asahi sighed, habitually running a hand through his hair. "I don't know," he admitted. "But we have to keep hoping, keep praying. It's all we can do."

Natalie nodded, leaning her head on his shoulder. Despite the uncertainty that clouded their future, moments like these reminded her of the love that had brought them together on that distant island. The baby squealed, reaching out for Asahi. With a soft chuckle, he took the infant from Natalie's arms, lifting him high in the air. The baby's laughter echoed across the balcony, a joyful sound that never failed to lift their spirits.

"You know," Natalie said, watching them with a smile, "we really should give him a name. We can't keep calling him 'the baby' forever."

Asahi grinned, bringing the baby back down to his chest. "I thought we agreed to wait until we could decide on something we both liked?"

"I know..." Natalie trailed off, her expression growing thoughtful. "Maybe I'm just overthinking it again."

As if in mocking agreement, the baby let out another happy squeal, his tiny hands patting Asahi's face. They both laughed, the sound mingling with their son's giggles in the warm evening air.

Later that night, as they lay in bed, Natalie curled into Asahi's side. "I love you," she murmured, tightly wrapping her arm around his chest. "I know this isn't how we imagined things would be, but I'm grateful for every day we have together."

Asahi pressed a kiss to her forehead. "I love you too," he replied. "More than I ever thought possible. You and our son... you're my world now."

They fell asleep in each other's arms, the baby's soft breathing a comforting soundtrack to their dreams.

The next morning, the baby was teething, his cries of discomfort piercing the early morning quiet. Natalie paced the living room, bouncing him gently and murmuring soothing words. Asahi emerged from the bedroom, his hair tousled from sleep. Without a word, he took the baby from Natalie's arms, pressing a cool teething ring to the infant's sore gums. Gradually, the cries subsided to whimpers, then to contented coos.

"You're amazing with him," Natalie said, watching them with a tender smile.

Asahi shrugged, but his eyes shone with pride. "He makes it easy. He's such a good baby."

As the day progressed, they fell into their usual routine. Asahi worked from home, his computer set up in a corner of the living room. Natalie tended to the baby and kept the household running, occasionally assisting Asahi with translations or research.

In the afternoon, they took a walk in the nearby park, the baby strapped to Asahi's chest in a carrier. As they strolled along the path, Natalie's hand found Asahi's, their fingers intertwining naturally.

"Do you ever regret it?" she asked suddenly, her voice soft. "Coming back here, I mean. Sometimes I wonder if we should have just stayed on the island."

Asahi was quiet for a moment, considering her words. "No," he said finally. "I don't regret it. Our life there was... it was beautiful in its own way, but I think if we stayed, we would've been running from reality. This.." he gestured around them at the bustling park and the city beyond, "this is real. It's imperfect and complicated, but it's where we belong."

Natalie nodded, squeezing his hand. "You're right. And who knows? Maybe this is all part of a bigger plan. Maybe Fumiko..."

She trailed off, not wanting to voice the hope that still lingered in both their hearts. Asahi brought their joined hands to his lips, pressing a kiss to her knuckles.

"Maybe," he agreed softly. "We just have to keep faith."

That evening, as they prepared dinner together, the baby watching from his high chair, Natalie found herself humming the old hymn she had taught Asahi, 'Great Is Thy Faithfulness'. Asahi paused in his chopping of vegetables, listening with a smile.

He set aside his knife and moved to stand behind her, wrapping his arms around her waist and singing it in unison with her.

"Great is Thy faithfulness, O God my Father
There is no shadow of turning with Thee
Thou changest not, Thy compassions, they fail not
As Thou hast been, Thou forever will be
Great is Thy faithfulness
Great is Thy faithfulness
Morning by morning new mercies I see
All I have needed Thy hand hath provided
Great is Thy faithfulness, Lord, unto me
Summer and winter, springtime and harvest
Sun, moon and stars in their courses above
Join with all nature in manifold witness
To Thy great faithfulness, mercy and love..."

The weeks continued to pass. The baby grew stronger, his personality blossoming. His blue eyes, just like his mother's, were as luminescent as ever and his olive skin glowed, just like his father's. His dark hair made him a perfect blend of both his parents.

One lazy Sunday afternoon, Natalie and the still-unnamed baby sat together on the balcony while Asahi was getting things done in the kitchen. Natalie was busy making the baby laugh when a knock at the door startled them both. She exchanged a puzzled glance with Asahi—they weren't expecting anyone.

"I'll get it," Asahi said, putting down the dish and the rag he was holding.

Natalie nodded, scooping the baby into her arms and following a few steps behind, curiosity piqued. As Asahi opened the door, she heard his sharp intake of breath before she saw who was standing there.

"Fumiko," Asahi breathed, his voice a mixture of disbelief and hope.

Natalie's heart skipped a beat as she peered around Asahi's shoulder. There, on their doorstep, stood Fumiko. She was wearing a modest Sunday dress, clutching a Bible to her chest. Her eyes were red-rimmed and puffy, evidence of recent tears, but there was a resolute set to her jaw. She was clearly about to burst, but she was trying to maintain a sense of propriety.

"Asahi," Fumiko said softly, her gaze flicking between her husband and Natalie. "I... I hope I'm not intruding."

For a moment, no one moved. The air seemed thick with tension and unspoken words. Then, as if snapping out of a trance, Asahi stepped back.

"No, of course not," he said quickly. "Please, come in."

Natalie found her voice then, offering a tentative smile. "Yes, please come in, Fumiko."

Fumiko hesitated for a moment before stepping over the threshold. Her eyes landed on the baby in Natalie's arms, and a flash of emotion—too quick to identify—crossed her face.

They moved to the living room, an awkward dance as they tried to figure out where to sit. Finally, Fumiko perched on the edge of the sofa, while Natalie and Asahi sat across from her, the baby nestled between them.

"I owe you both an apology," Fumiko began, her voice a little shaky. "My behaviour when we first... when I first saw you on the island... it was unforgivable."

"Fumiko, no," Asahi started, but she held up a hand to stop him.

"Please, let me finish," she said. "I was hurt, and angry, and I lashed out. But I've had time to think, to pray... and most importantly, to listen."

She opened her Bible, flipping to a marked page as tears began to escape her eyes. "This morning, at church, my pastor preached on this passage. I think... I think God was speaking to me through it."

She began to read aloud, her voice gaining strength with each word: "But to the married I give instructions, not I, but the Lord, that the wife should not leave her husband (but if she does leave, she must remain unmarried, or else be reconciled to her husband.)"

Natalie and Asahi exchanged a look of amazement. It was the very same passage that God had used to guide them months ago.

Fumiko looked up, realizing what their facial expressions implied. "You... you read this too?"

Asahi nodded. "We did. We were struggling with our feelings, with the situation we found ourselves in. This passage... it gave us hope that there might be a way."

"For us," Natalie added quickly, "We were hoping for your return."

Fumiko's eyes fully welled with tears. "I had no idea. I thought... I thought you had simply moved on."

"Never," Asahi said firmly. "Fumiko, you were always in our hearts. We mourned you, yes, but we never forgot you."

Fumiko nodded slowly, taking a deep breath. "When I heard these words today, it was like a veil lifted from my eyes. I left my husband... And God gives me two choices. I can remain alone forever or I can come back to you, even if... even if it means not being your only wife."

She paused, gathering her thoughts. "I realized that my anger, my hurt... it was pushing me away from God's plan, and from the man I love. But more than that, even though I had a choice to make, only one choice would truly bring reconciliation; not just with my husband, but in my heart."

"And you chose to come here," Natalie said softly. "That must have taken a lot of faith."

"It did. I was... I am... terrified. But I knew I had to try." Fumiko's gaze met Asahi's, her eyes brimming with more tears. "God has softened my heart today, Asahi. And I choose reconciliation. If... if you'll have me." Her crying was saturated with the doubt that her husband and his new wife would not agree to such a unique family structure.

"Of course I'll have you, Fumiko," Asahi said. He leaned forward, his eyes intense. "We never wanted to hurt you. When we thought you were gone... it was like the world had ended. Natalie and I, we found each other in our grief, in our struggle to survive."

Natalie nodded in agreement. "We never expected to be rescued. We thought we would die on that island. And in that despair, we found each other."

"I understand that now," Fumiko said. "It's taken time, and a lot of prayer, but I can see how impossible your situation was. Please, will you both forgive me?"

Asahi's own eyes glistened as he reached across the coffee table, taking Fumiko's hand in his. "There's nothing to forgive," he said softly.

"We prayed for you," Natalie added gently. "Every day..."

Fumiko's gaze shifted to Natalie, surprise evident in her expression. "You... you prayed for me? Even after how I treated you?"

Natalie nodded, offering a small smile. "Of course. You're Asahi's wife. And... and I hoped that maybe, someday, we could be family too."

Fumiko's eyes widened at this, and for a moment, she seemed at a loss for words. Then, slowly, she spoke again. "I... I don't know what to say. Your kindness, in the face of everything... it's humbling."

She turned back to Asahi, squeezing his hand. "When I ran away that day on the island, I was so consumed by my own pain that I couldn't see anything else, but as the weeks passed, and I reflected on what happened, I began to understand. You both thought I was dead. You waited a year. I wouldn't expect you to do anything else."

Fumiko's gaze drifted to the baby, who was now cooing softly. "And you created a new life together. A beautiful life."

She took a deep breath, her voice wavering slightly. "It would be so easy to let my hurt and jealousy rule me, but that's not what God wants. He wants reconciliation. He wants forgiveness. And He wants love."

Asahi nodded. "That's all we want too, Fumiko. We never wanted to replace you or push you out."

A sob escaped Fumiko, and before anyone could react, she moved around the coffee table and enveloped both Natalie and Asahi in a tight embrace. The baby, caught in the middle, let out a surprised coo that turned into a delighted giggle.

As they pulled apart, all three adults wiping at their eyes, Fumiko's gaze fell on the baby. "He's beautiful," she whispered. "What's his name?"

Natalie and Asahi exchanged a slightly sheepish look. "Well," Natalie said, "we actually haven't named him yet. We've been... waiting."

"Waiting?" Fumiko asked, confused. "Waiting for what?

Asahi and Natalie exchanged a mutual nod, silently affirming to each other what they both knew was the right move.

"For you." Natalie said with a warm smile and a few tears. "I believe we've been waiting for you."

Fumiko gasped, her hand flying to her mouth.

"Will you name him?" Natalie asked, Asahi smiling and nodding in agreement.

Fumiko, fully aware of the honor being bestowed upon her, and subsequently unable to hold back more tears, asked, "You want... you want me to name your son?"

Natalie nodded, smiling warmly. "*Our* son, Fumiko. If you want him to be."

For a long moment, Fumiko just stared at them, overwhelmed. Then, slowly, she reached out, gently stroking the baby's cheek. The infant gurgled happily, reaching out to grasp her finger. The range of emotions that flooded Fumiko's soul was an indescribable experience. The love of her husband, the new-found family in her co-wife, the excitement of getting to help raise a new child; it was enough to make her insides feel as though they would burst.

After staring at the baby and touching his cheek for almost two minutes, she finally collected herself and took a deep breath, as if she knew she had thought of the right name. "Yuuto," she said softly. "His name is Yuuto."

"Yuuto," Asahi inquisitively repeated, tasting the name. "It sounds great."

"What does it mean?" Natalie asked.

Fumiko smiled, her eyes never leaving the baby's face. "Yuuto means 'to help give peace.'"

The whole family gathered closely around the baby, basking in the depth of meaning that this name implied. It went unspoken in this moment, but clearly, God was orchestrating it all.

"Our little Yuuto." Natalie lovingly said through tears of joy.

"Who helped give us peace." Asahi concluded, wrapping his arms around both of his wives, their child being held in the center of them.

As if recognizing his new name, the baby—Yuuto—let out a joyful squeal, kicking his legs excitedly. All three adults laughed, the sound mingling with Yuuto's giggles in a symphony of Christ-exalting happiness.

Now all these things are from God, who reconciled us to Himself through Christ and gave us the ministry of reconciliation.

2 Corinthians 5:18

Story 3 -
She Shall Become His Wife

Setting – Philippines, Modern Day

Henry Green jolted awake, his heart pounding. The sheets were damp with sweat, clinging to his skin like a second layer. He blinked, trying to orient himself in the darkness of the bedroom. The digital clock on the nightstand glowed an eerie red: 3:17 AM - Chicago, IL - 57°

The dream lingered, vivid and haunting. He could still see his sister Emily's face, frozen in that final moment of terror. The gunshot echoed in his ears, a sound that had become all too familiar in his nightmares over the years.

Beside him, his wife Lily stirred. "Henry?" she murmured, her voice thick with sleep. "Are you okay?"

He took a deep breath, willing his racing heart to slow. "Yeah," he managed. "Just a dream."

Lily's hand found his in the darkness, her touch warm and comforting. "The same one?"

Henry nodded, forgetting for a moment that she couldn't see him. "Yeah," he said again, his voice barely above a whisper.

Lily sat up, the rustle of sheets loud in the quiet room. She reached over and switched on the bedside lamp, casting a soft glow over their faces. Henry squinted against the sudden light, taking in his wife's concerned expression.

"Do you want to talk about it?" she asked gently.

Henry shook his head. "Not really. It's always the same anyway."

Lily nodded, understanding in her eyes. She knew the story well—the day Henry's sister had been killed, shot by a criminal during a botched robbery. The day that had set Henry on his path to becoming a police officer, driven by a need for justice that sometimes bordered on obsession.

"I'm here if you need me," Lily said, squeezing his hand.

Henry managed a small smile. "I know. Thanks."

As Lily settled back down, Henry's gaze drifted to the cross hanging on the wall opposite their bed. It was a wedding gift from Lily's parents, a symbol of the faith that had become such an important part of her life over the past year.

He remembered the day she'd told him about her conversion. They'd been married for only a few months, and at first, he'd been worried it would drive a wedge between them. But Lily had never pushed her beliefs on him, content to live out her faith quietly and pray for him in private.

Henry's eyes lingered on the cross, a familiar mix of emotions swirling in his chest. Part of him envied Lily's peace, the certainty she seemed to have found in her faith. But another part of him recoiled from it, knowing that to embrace that same faith would mean having to forgive the man who had taken Emily from him. And that was something Henry Green wasn't sure he could ever do.

As the first rays of dawn began to creep through the curtains, Henry finally drifted back to sleep, his dreams mercifully empty this time.

Later that morning, Henry stood in front of the bathroom mirror, adjusting his tie. The face that stared back at him looked older than his 35 years, etched with lines of grief and anger. He heard Lily in the kitchen, humming a hymn as she prepared breakfast.

"I made your favorite," Lily said as he entered the kitchen. "Blueberry pancakes."

Henry managed a small smile. "Thanks, hon."

As they sat down to eat, Henry found himself studying his wife. Her faith had changed her in subtle ways over the past year. There was a calmness about her now, a quiet strength that he admired even if he didn't fully understand it.

"I've got that community outreach thing at the church today," Lily said between bites of toast. "You're still okay with me borrowing the car, right?"

Henry nodded. "Of course. I'm working a double shift anyway."

A flicker of concern crossed Lily's face. "Another one? Henry, you've been pulling so many extra hours lately. Are you sure you're not pushing yourself too hard?"

Henry felt a twinge of guilt. He knew his work habits worried Lily, but he couldn't bring himself to slow down. The job was the only thing that made him feel like he was making a difference, like he was honoring Emily's memory.

"I'm fine," he assured her, reaching across the table to squeeze her hand. "Really. It's just been busy at the station lately."

Lily didn't look entirely convinced, but she didn't push the issue. Instead, she gave him a small smile and said, "Well, I'll be praying for you to stay safe out there."

Henry nodded, feeling gratitude and discomfort at her words. He appreciated her concern, but the mention of prayer always left him feeling slightly awkward.

As they finished breakfast and prepared to go their separate ways for the day, Henry found himself lingering in the doorway, watching Lily gather her things. She looked up, catching his gaze.

"What is it?" she asked, a hint of amusement in her voice.

Henry shrugged. "Thanks for... you know, last night."

"Always," Lily replied, her eyes soft with affection.

As he held her, Henry closed his eyes, savoring the moment of peace. Whatever their differences, he knew that this—their love for each other—was real and solid.

As Henry entered the precinct, it buzzed with its usual morning energy. He nodded to fellow officers, his demeanor shifting into the confident, no-nonsense detective his colleagues knew.

"Green!" called out his partner, Jake. "We got a lead on that convenience store robbery."

As they pored over security footage, Henry's mind kept drifting back to his nightmare. The grainy images on the screen morphed into that fateful night, the robber's face blurring into the man who had taken his sister from him.

"Earth to Henry," Jake's voice cut through his thoughts. "You with me, partner?"

Henry blinked, refocusing. "Yeah, sorry. What've we got?"

They spent the morning following up on leads, interviewing witnesses. As they left the last interview, Jake suggested grabbing lunch at their usual diner.

Over burgers and fries, Jake studied his partner. "You seem off today, man. Everything okay?"

Henry shrugged, pushing a fry around his plate. "Just... thinking about Emily."

Jake's expression softened. "Your sister? It's been what, seven years now?"

"Eight," Henry corrected, his jaw tightening. "Eight years, and that lowlife is still out there somewhere."

Jake leaned back, choosing his words carefully. "Look, I know it's not my place, but have you ever considered... I don't know, talking to someone about it? It's eating you up, man."

Henry's eyes flashed. "What's there to talk about? He killed her, Jake. End of story."

Before Jake could respond, their radios crackled to life. A robbery in progress, not far from their location. As they raced to the scene, adrenaline coursed through Henry's veins, momentarily pushing aside his troubling thoughts.

The suspect was cornered in an alley when they arrived. As Henry approached, gun drawn, the world seemed to slow down. The terrified face of the young man before him seemed to transform into the phantom that haunted his dreams.

"Drop the weapon!" Henry shouted, his voice raw with emotion.

The suspect hesitated, his hand trembling. For a moment, Henry saw himself reflected in the young man's eyes—the same fear, the same desperation.

Jake's voice cut through the tension. "Come on, kid. Don't make this worse than it has to be."

Slowly, the suspect lowered his gun. As Jake cuffed him, Henry leaned against the alley wall, his heart racing. The line between past and present had blurred dangerously, and he knew he was losing his grip.

That evening, Henry found himself at O'Malley's, the local cop bar. The burn in his throat from his whiskey was a welcome distraction from the turmoil in his mind.

"Thought I'd find you here," came a familiar voice. Henry looked up to see David, an old friend from the academy and now a chaplain for the department.

Henry grunted in response as David slid onto the bar stool next to him.

"Rough day?" David asked, ordering a club soda.

"You could say that," Henry muttered.

They sat in companionable silence for a while, the din of the bar washing over them. Finally, David spoke. "You know, Lily's been coming to prayer meeting every week. She's worried about you and we've been praying for you."

Henry tensed. "Dave, don't start. Not tonight."

David held up his hands. "I'm not here to preach, Henry. I'm here as your friend. But I gotta ask—how long are you going to let this eat you up?"

Henry swirled the amber liquid in his glass, watching the light refract through it. "Until I find him," he said quietly. "Until I make him pay for what he did."

David sighed. "And then what? Will that bring her back? Will it actually make you feel better?"

Henry slammed his glass down, anger flaring. "What do you want me to do, Dave? Forgive him? Pretend it never happened?"

"No," David said gently. "I want you to live, Henry. Really live, not just survive. What happened to Emily was tragic, but you're coming unglued. You lost a sister to a bullet, but Lily's losing a husband to vengeance. No sense in the guy killing both of you."

Henry's anger deflated, leaving behind a bone-deep weariness. "I don't know how to let it go," he whispered.

David placed a hand on his friend's shoulder. "It starts with a choice, Henry. A choice to forgive, even when it feels impossible. Now, I won't tell you Who can help you. You already know that. But I will tell you that you're drinking poison and waiting for your enemy to die. It'll get you nowhere, my friend."

As Henry drove home that night, David's words echoed in his mind. The streets of the city blurred past, each corner holding memories of his life before—before the shooting, before the grief, before the anger had taken root in his soul.

He pulled into the driveway, noting the soft glow of lamplight from the living room window. Lily was waiting up for him, as she always did. A wave of guilt washed over him as he realized how much his inner turmoil affected her too.

Inside, Lily looked up from her bible, her face wearing concern and love. "Hey," she said softly. "I was getting worried."

Henry hung up his jacket, avoiding her gaze. "Sorry, I lost track of time. I was with Dave at O'Malley's."

Lily's eyebrows raised slightly. "Oh? How is David doing?"

Henry sank into his armchair, suddenly feeling every one of his years. "He's good. We talked about... stuff."

Lily set her bible aside, giving him her full attention. "Do you want to talk about it?"

For a moment, Henry was tempted to brush it off, to retreat behind the walls he'd built. But something in Lily's eyes—the unwavering love and acceptance—broke through his defenses.

"I don't know how to forget about it, Lily," he said, his voice cracking. "I've tried, for you, for us. But every time I close my eyes, I see Emily. I hear that gunshot. How am I supposed to let that go?"

Lily moved to kneel beside his chair, taking his hands in hers, her eyes shining with unshed tears. "Healing isn't about forgetting, Henry. It's about choosing to release the hold that person has on you. It's about forgiveness."

"Forgiveness," Henry repeated. Something inside him suddenly hardened at Lily's words. He pulled away from her touch, standing up abruptly. "No," he said, his voice low and tight. "You don't understand, Lily. You've never had someone stolen from you."

Lily stood as well, a hint of frustration at hearing these words for the hundredth time flickering across her face. As a tear escaped one eye, she answered him. "Maybe not by someone else, but I'm certainly losing someone!"

They both froze, Henry, unsure how to respond to his wife's outburst, and Lily, unsure how she felt about doing it. She took a breath and closed her eyes for a moment, clearly trying to exercise patience and self-control. "But Henry," she continued, "G—"

"But what?" Henry interrupted, his tone sharp. "But I should just let it go? Pretend it never happened? Is that what God wants?"

Lily flinched at his words. "That's not what I'm saying. Forgiveness doesn't mean—"

Henry scoffed, pacing the room now. "There's no forgiveness for what he did, Lily. He shot my sister. He destroyed our family. And you want me to just... what? Pray about it?"

Lily took another deep breath, trying to keep her voice calm. "I know you're hurting, Henry. I can see how much pain you're in. But this anger is affecting our marriage, your work—"

"Don't," Henry warned, his eyes flashing. "Don't you dare bring our marriage into this. This has nothing to do with us."

"It has everything to do with us," Lily replied, her own frustration beginning to show its face again. "Every day, I watch you struggle. Every day, I watch this eat away at you. Every day, I wonder when I'm going to get my husband back!" Lily's momentary frustration suddenly turned into sadness as she started crying. "And it breaks my heart because I know there's a way out for you, if you'd just—"

"Just what? Find Jesus!?" Henry's laugh was bitter. "That's the answer to everything for you!"

Lily recoiled as if she'd been slapped. "That's not fair, Henry. My faith isn't some magic fix-it-all. It's about finally having peace. Peace with God, peace with other—"

"Well, I don't want peace!" Henry shouted, causing Lily to step back. Seeing her reaction, he lowered his voice, but the intensity remained. "I don't want to find peace with this, Lily. I want justice. I want that scumbag to pay for what he did. And if that means I have to carry this anger for the rest of my life, then so be it."

Lily wrapped her arms around herself, as if trying to hold herself together. "So that's it? You won't even try? You won't talk to someone, or—"

"There's nothing to talk about," Henry cut her off. "I can't forgive him, Lily. I won't. And I don't want to talk about it anymore."

With that, he turned and walked out of the room, leaving Lily standing alone, tears streaming down her face. The sound of the front door slamming echoed through the house with a finality to it that sent a chill through Lily's heart.

As she sank onto the couch, Lily buried her face in her hands. She prayed silently, desperately, for a miracle—for something to break through the walls Henry had built around his heart.

The cool night air hit Henry's face as he stormed out of the house. He had no destination in mind; he just needed to walk, to put some distance between himself and the pain he'd seen in Lily's eyes. As he strode down the quiet suburban streets, the adrenaline from their argument began to fade, leaving behind a hollow ache in his chest. The weight of his words settled on him, each step a reminder of the hurt he'd inflicted on the one person who had stood by him through everything.

A stray cat darted across his path, disappearing into the shadows of a nearby alley. Henry paused, watching as two more felines emerged from behind a dumpster, cautiously approaching a discarded takeout container. Their wary movements reminded him of himself—always on guard, never truly at peace.

He found himself at a small park, empty at this late hour. Sinking onto a bench, Henry buried his face in his hands, the events of the evening replaying in his mind. Lily's gentle touch, her words of love and support—and how he'd thrown it all back in her face.

"What have I done?" he muttered to himself, the irony of his involuntary prayer not lost on him.

As he sat there, he thought back to the day he'd met Lily, a chance encounter that had changed his life forever.

| It had been a routine call—a reported break-in at a small bookstore. Henry had arrived on the scene to find Lily, the owner, shaken but unharmed. As he'd taken her statement, he'd been struck by

her kindness and the way she'd focused on the well-being of her elderly neighbor who'd called 911 rather than on her own ordeal.

In the weeks that followed, Henry had found himself thinking of her often. He'd stop by the bookstore to "follow up" on the case, and soon their conversations had extended far beyond the details of the break-in. Lily's warmth had drawn him in, offering a glimmer of light in the darkness that had consumed him since Emily's death.

Their romance had culminated in a small, intimate wedding just six months after they'd met. Henry remembered the joy on Lily's face as they'd exchanged vows, the hope he'd felt for their future together.

About a year into their marriage, Lily became a Christian, but Henry was always hesitant to attend church, and although he was somewhat wary of her new faith, he always respected it. From the very start, he found the Christian message of catch-free forgiveness insulting and somewhat childish in light of what he had gone through.

Drawing on God's strength, Lily had remained steadfast. Her love for him never wavered, even in the face of his worst moments. She met his anger with patience, his bitterness with kindness. Time and again, she'd extended grace to him when he least deserved it. |

A soft meow drew Henry's attention. The stray cat from earlier had followed him, its green eyes regarding him with what seemed like curiosity. As Henry watched, the cat cautiously approached, eventually settling next to him on the bench.

"At least someone's not afraid of me," Henry murmured, gently stroking the cat's matted fur. The simple act of comfort, even to this stray animal, sparked something in him—a reminder of the man Lily saw in him.

Their second anniversary was approaching in just a month. Henry had been so consumed by his inner turmoil that he'd barely given it any thought. Now, sitting in the quiet park with an unlikely companion, he found himself reflecting on the vows he'd made to Lily. He'd promised to love and cherish her, in good times and in bad.

The cat purred softly, leaning into his touch. Henry smiled despite himself, feeling a small crack in the armor he'd built around his heart.

He thought of Lily, probably still awake and worrying about him. The guilt intensified, but with it came a determination to make things right.

Standing up, Henry gave the cat one last scratch behind the ears before heading home. The walk back seemed both longer and shorter than his aimless wandering earlier. With each step, he rehearsed what he would say to Lily, knowing that a simple "I'm sorry" wouldn't be enough to heal the hurt he'd caused.

As he approached their house, Henry saw that the living room light was still on. Taking a deep breath, he opened the front door.

Lily was curled up on the couch, her bible open on her lap, though her red-rimmed eyes suggested she hadn't been reading for some time. She looked up as he entered, her expression a mix of relief and apprehension.

"Lily, I—" Henry began, but the words caught in his throat. Instead, he crossed the room in three long strides and knelt before her, taking her hands in his. "I'm so sorry," he whispered, his voice thick with emotion. "What I said, how I acted—it was inexcusable. You deserve so much better than this."

Lily's eyes welled with fresh tears as she squeezed his hands gently. "Oh, Henry," she said softly.

They talked long into the night, Henry opening up about his fears and struggles in a way he had never allowed himself to do before. While they didn't resolve everything, it felt like a first step towards healing—for both of them.

Henry woke up early the next morning, his mind already formulating a plan. He called the precinct and requested a day off, something he'd never done before. Then, as Lily slept, he set about preparing a surprise.

When Lily finally stirred, she found a handwritten note on Henry's pillow: "Meet me downstairs when you're ready. Dress for a day out. Love, Henry."

Confused but intrigued, Lily got ready, her heart lightening at the thought that Henry had taken a day off work.

Downstairs, she found Henry waiting with a bouquet of her favorite flowers—daisies, simple and cheerful, just like her. "Good morning, beautiful," he said, a shy smile on his face. "I thought we could use a day just for us."

Lily's face lit up with a radiant smile, the kind that never failed to make Henry's heart skip a beat. "Henry, this is wonderful! But what about work?"

"Work can survive without me for a day," Henry replied, taking her hand. "You're more important."

He led her to the car, refusing to divulge their destination despite her playful attempts to guess. As they drove, Henry found himself relaxing, enjoying the simple pleasure of Lily's company.

They soon arrived at one of the most luxurious hotels in the city. Lily gasped in surprise as Henry handed the keys to the valet. "Henry, this is too much!"

"Nothing's too much for you," he said softly, guiding her inside.

They spent the day indulging in all the hotel had to offer—a tour through their art gallery, a leisurely lunch by the rooftop pool, and a stroll through the hotel's beautifully manicured gardens. Henry had even booked them a relaxing couple's massage at the spa.

When they approached the spa desk, a pleasant young man checked them in. As Henry was finishing paying, the clerk motioned towards the entry door where two massage therapists had just walked through, smiling and waiting for the couple to finish at the counter. "There are your massage therapists now," the clerk politely informed them, continuing.. "I've got Erica for Mr. Green and Trevor for Mrs. Green."

The couple looked over and awkwardly froze for a moment, as a reasonably pretty young woman stood next to a young man so handsome, Henry thought he was staring at the next lead actor for Baywatch. He nervously swallowed as Lily cleared her throat and looked down, wearing a small smirk on her face. Henry turned around to the clerk and leaned in close. "I'm not sure I like Trevor," he said in a low voice. Lily comically played with her ring, smiling at the therapists waiting for them at the door.

Henry continued. "Can we get someone else for my wife? Like, someone named Susan, or Jenny, or something? You get where I'm coming from, brother?" The clerk grinned, and even had to hold back a laugh when he saw the humorous expression on Lily's face.

"Of course, sir." The clerk replied as Henry looked back at Lily, lightheartedly asking what she found so funny.

"Ah!" The clerk said, looking at his computer screen. It looks like Florence is available. She'll be right out.

Henry lightly whacked the counter. "Florence sounds great." He replied.

At a prompt from the clerk, Trevor smiled and waved at the couple—knowing full well what had happened—and retreated back into the spa area. A few seconds later, a woman who seemed to be in her 50s took his place outside the door, wearing the name tag, "Florence."

Henry sighed in relief as he turned back to the clerk to shake his hand. "That's much better. I think my wife will love Florence." Henry said as he gave a small laugh.

But as he was chuckling, Lily cleared her throat loudly. Henry turned around to see her staring at him with wide eyes. She moved her eyeballs to the two female therapists then back to Henry.

"What?" Henry whispered.

Lily cleared her throat again, but this time slowly and with a very defined break between the syllables "Ah" and "hem."

Henry looked at the young, pretty therapist and the 50 year old woman at the door and suddenly got the message. He leaned into the clerk and whispered, "On second thought, *I'll* take Florence."

"You got it, sir." The clerk replied as he adjusted the form and sent the couple off to their massage.

Lily cheerfully wrapped her arm around Henry's as they walked toward the door and greeted their massage therapists, humorously adding, "I bet a massage is just what we need. Are you excited for yours?" They laughed at the whole situation as they entered the spa area.

As evening approached, Henry suggested they get ready for dinner at the hotel's renowned restaurant.

Lily emerged from the bathroom in a stunning blue dress that brought out the color of her eyes. Henry, who had changed into a suit, felt his breath catch at the sight of her. "You are the most beautiful woman I've ever seen," he said, drawing her close.

At dinner, over candlelight and soft music, they talked—really talked—for what felt like the first time in months. They discussed their upcoming anniversary, reminiscing about their courtship and wedding day.

"I can't believe it's been almost two years," Lily mused, her eyes sparkling. "So much has changed."

Henry nodded, a hint of sadness crossing his face. "I know I haven't made it easy, Lily. But I want you to know how much I appreciate your patience, your love. I don't deserve you, but I'm so grateful for you."

Lily reached across the table, taking his hand. "Henry, love isn't about deserving. It's about choosing each other, every day. And I choose you, always."

As they finished their meal, the sound of a live band drifted in from the hotel's ballroom. Henry stood, offering his hand to Lily. "May I have this dance, Mrs. Green?"

Lily beamed, taking his hand. "I thought you'd never ask, Mr. Green."

They swayed together on the dance floor, lost in their own world. As they danced, they continued to talk about their hopes and dreams for the future.

"I've been thinking," Henry said hesitantly, "maybe we could start trying for a family soon. If you want to, that is."

Lily's eyes widened in surprise and joy. "Really? Oh, Henry, I'd love that. But are you sure you're ready?"

Henry took a deep breath. "I can't promise I'll be perfect, Lily. I still have a lot to work through. But being here with you, today—it's reminded me of the life we wanted to build together. And I want that. I want a future with you, children, a home filled with love."

Tears glistened in Lily's eyes. "That's all I've ever wanted, Henry. For us to face life together, the good and the bad."

As the music swelled around them, Henry pulled Lily closer. "I love you," he whispered. "And I promise, I'm going to do better. For you, for us, for our future family."

Lily leaned her head on his shoulder, her voice soft but full of conviction. "We'll do it together, my love. One day at a time."

Henry woke early the next morning, his mind clearer. As he watched Lily sleep peacefully beside him, he reflected on their conversation from the night before. He had promised to do better, to work towards the future they both wanted, but the desire for justice still burned within him. He couldn't let that go, but he could try to keep it from poisoning the love he and Lily shared.

Then, just days before their anniversary, Henry received a call that changed everything.

"Detective Green," came the gruff voice of his captain. "We've got a lead on the Emily Green case. Credible intel suggests the suspect has been hiding out in the Philippines."

Henry's heart raced, his hand tightening on the phone. "How solid is this information, sir?"

"Solid enough to warrant further investigation. But Henry," the captain's voice softened slightly, "I know what this case means to you. If you want to pursue this, you need to keep a level head. We can't risk an international incident."

"I understand, sir," Henry replied, his mind already racing with possibilities. "I'll handle it professionally."

After hanging up, Henry sat at his desk, conflicting emotions warring within him. He had promised Lily a family. But this... this was what he'd been waiting for, for eight long years.

That evening, as Lily prepared dinner, Henry approached her with what he hoped was a convincing smile. "Honey, I've been thinking about our anniversary."

Lily looked up, her eyes bright with curiosity. "Oh? What about it?"

"Well," Henry said, taking her hands in his, "how would you feel about a trip? I was thinking... the Philippines."

Lily's eyes widened in surprise and delight. "The Philippines? Henry, that sounds wonderful! But can we afford it? And what about your work?"

Henry squeezed her hands gently. "I've been saving up, and I've got some vacation time due. I thought it would be nice to really get away, just the two of us. What do you say?"

Lily threw her arms around him, her joy palpable. "Yes! Oh, Henry, this is going to be amazing!"

As he held her, Henry felt a twinge of guilt. He hated lying to her, even by omission, but it was necessary. Still, he needed to find a way to balance his search for Emily's killer with giving Lily the anniversary trip she deserved.

In the next few days, Henry coordinated with local law enforcement in Manila, arranging meetings under the guise of professional development. He also booked a beautiful hotel in a tourist-friendly area, determined to give Lily the vacation she was so excited about.

As they boarded the plane, Lily's hand clasped tightly in his, Henry felt the familiar surge of anticipation that came with a new case, but this time, it was tempered by a sense of unease. He was walking a dangerous line, and he knew it.

As their plane touched down in Manila, the humid air enveloped them and they stepped off the aircraft. Lily's hand tightened in his.

"It's so warm!" she exclaimed, her eyes bright with wonder. "I can't believe we're really here."

Henry squeezed her hand, pushing aside his guilt to focus on her joy. "Believe it, sweetheart. Happy anniversary."

As they made their way through the airport, Henry found himself unconsciously scanning faces, a habit born from years on the force. He forced himself to relax, reminding himself that for now, he was just a tourist with his wife.

Their hotel was luxurious and situated in the heart of the city. As they entered their suite, Lily gasped at the view of the Manila skyline.

"Oh, Henry," she breathed, moving to the floor-to-ceiling windows. "It's beautiful."

Henry wrapped his arms around her from behind, resting his chin on her shoulder. For a moment, he allowed himself to simply be present, to feel the warmth of her body against his and share in her excitement.

"Not as beautiful as you," he murmured, pressing a kiss to her neck.

Lily turned in his arms, her eyes shining with love and happiness. "Thank you for this," she said softly. "Being here with you, it feels like heaven."

Henry pushed aside the guilt he felt at her words.

On their first full day in Manila, they explored the historic Intramuros district, marveling at the centuries-old Spanish colonial architecture. Lily was particularly taken with San Agustin Church, its baroque facade a testament to the country's rich history.

As they walked hand in hand through the cobblestone streets, Henry found himself genuinely enjoying the experience. Lily's enthusiasm was infectious, and he found himself seeing the city through her eyes—not as a detective looking for clues, but as a man rediscovering the simple joy of exploration.

They stopped for lunch at a small restaurant recommended by their hotel concierge. The smell of garlic and spices filled the air as they were seated at a tiny table in the corner.

"What should we try?" Lily asked, her eyes wide as she perused the menu filled with unfamiliar dishes.

Henry grinned, feeling a sense of adventure. "How about we ask the waiter for his recommendations? When in Rome, right?"

Their meal turned out to be a delightful adventure for their taste buds. They sampled adobo, a savory meat dish simmered in vinegar and soy sauce, and sinigang, a sour tamarind-based soup that made Lily's eyes water but left her wanting more.

As they shared a plate of sweet, golden mangoes for dessert, Henry found himself studying Lily's face. The joy radiating from her was heart-touching, and he was left feeling regret for the secret he was keeping.

"What are you thinking?" Lily asked, catching his gaze.

Henry reached across the table, taking her hand. "Just how lucky I am to be here with you," he said, and in that moment, it was the complete truth.

As evening fell, they made their way to Rizal Park, joining the locals in their nightly ritual of strolling through the expansive green space. The park was alive with activity—families picnicking on the grass, elderly couples doing tai chi, and young people gathered around buskers playing traditional music.

They found a bench near a fountain, sitting close together as they watched the world go by. Lily leaned her head on Henry's shoulder, letting out a contented sigh.

"I wish we could stay like this forever," she murmured.

Henry wrapped an arm around her, pulling her close. "Me too," he said.

Lily smiled. "Any chance we can move here? The Philippines need cops too, right?"

Henry laughed. "Something pretty crazy would have to happen for us to move here, sweetheart."

"You never know what God is up to." Lily said, as she buried herself further into Henry's side.

As they made their way back to the hotel, reality began to creep back in. Henry knew that in a few short hours, while Lily slept, he would be meeting with his local police contact to discuss the latest leads on Emily's killer.

The guilt of lying to her gnawed at him as he watched Lily prepare for bed, her movements slow and languid with contentment and fatigue from their day of exploration.

"Today was perfect," she said, snuggling up to him as they lay in bed.

Henry held her close, breathing in the familiar scent of her shampoo. "Get some rest. We've got another big day ahead."

He waited until her breathing evened out, indicating she had fallen into a deep sleep. Then, with practiced stealth, he slipped out of bed and dressed quietly in the darkness.

The night air was still warm and humid as Henry made his way through the dimly lit streets. He found himself in a less touristy area of the city, where the buildings were more run-down and the streets narrower.

His contact, a local detective named Ramon, was waiting for him in a small, dimly lit bar. The place was nearly empty, save for a few locals nursing their drinks in the corners.

"Detective Green," Ramon greeted him in heavily accented English. "I hope your stay in our city has been pleasant so far."

Henry nodded, taking a seat across from Ramon. "It has, thank you. But let's get down to business. What have you found?"

Ramon slid a manila folder across the table. "We've narrowed down the suspect's possible locations to three areas in the city. My team has been conducting surveillance, but we need to move carefully. We don't want to spook him."

Henry opened the folder, his heart racing as he looked at the grainy surveillance photos. One, in particular, caught his eye—a man exiting a rundown apartment building, his face partially obscured but achingly familiar.

"This is him," Henry said, his voice tight with suppressed emotion. "I'd recognize him anywhere."

Ramon nodded solemnly. "We believe he's been living under an assumed name, working odd jobs to stay under the radar. But he's gotten sloppy recently. That's how we were able to track him."

As they discussed strategy and potential next steps, Henry felt the familiar surge of adrenaline that came with closing in on a suspect. The meeting went on for hours, and by the time Henry made it back to the hotel, the sky was beginning to lighten with the first hints of dawn. He slipped back into bed, careful not to wake Lily.

That morning, Henry barely got any sleep. Lily was still asleep when he got a text from Ramon telling him the location of a diner the suspect frequently went to for lunch, alongside several pictures of him in the diner.

Henry woke Lily with a gentle kiss when it was time to rise. "Hey, beautiful. I was thinking maybe you'd like to spend the day at the hotel spa? My treat."

Lily stretched and yawned, smiling up at him. "Even if another Trevor awaits?" She teased with a laugh.

"Maybe skip the massage…" Henry replied, half joking, half serious.

"A day at the spa sounds heavenly." Lily continued. "But what about you? Don't you want to do something together?"

Henry forced a casual shrug. "I thought I might check out some of the local Henryets, maybe pick up some souvenirs. I know shopping isn't really your thing."

Lily studied him for a moment, but then she smiled. "Alright, if you're sure. But promise we'll have dinner together tonight?"

"Of course," Henry agreed, relieved she hadn't pressed further. "I'll make reservations at that rooftop restaurant you liked."

As soon as Lily left for her spa day, Henry changed into nondescript clothing and headed out. He took a series of taxis to throw off any potential tail, his police instincts kicking in despite the voice in his head telling him he was being paranoid.

The diner wasn't exactly what Henry had imagined. He had pictured a rundown, hole-in-the-wall haven for drug dealers and prostitutes, but it turned out to be a very nice, lively place. Families were present, the staff was friendly, and one of the outdoor tables was hosting what seemed to be some sort of bible study. Henry settled into a corner booth, sipping a beer as he scanned the room. Hours passed with no sign of his target. Just as he was about to give up, his phone buzzed with a text from Lily that alerted him to how late it had gotten.

"Where are you? I'm at the restaurant. Everything okay?"

Henry cursed under his breath as he read Lily's message. He'd lost track of time and forgotten about their dinner plans. He made it to the restaurant in record time, his mind racing as he tried to come up with a plausible excuse. Lily was waiting at their table, worry etched across her face.

"Henry! What happened? I was getting worried."

He leaned down to kiss her cheek, hoping she wouldn't notice the smell of alcohol in his breath. "I'm so sorry, honey. I got turned around in the Henryets and my phone died. I feel terrible."

Lily's worry melted into relief, though a hint of doubt lingered in her eyes. "It's okay. I'm just glad you're here now. Did you find any good souvenirs?"

Henry's stomach twisted with guilt as he realized he hadn't bought a single thing. "Uh, not really. Nothing seemed quite right. But tell me about your day at the spa. Was it as relaxing as you'd hoped?"

As Lily launched into a description of her treatments, Henry tried to focus, to be present in the moment, but his mind kept drifting back to the diner, to the man that he'd been waiting for. He was so close to finally getting justice for Emily.

Throughout dinner, Henry found himself only half-listening to Lily, his responses curt as he mentally reviewed what he'd learned and planned his next move. It wasn't until Lily fell silent that he realized she asked him a question and was waiting for an answer.

"I'm sorry, what was that?" he asked, forcing himself to meet her gaze.

Lily's eyes were filled with hurt and concern. "Henry, what's going on? You've been distracted all evening. Actually, you've been off since this morning. Is something wrong?"

For a moment, Henry was tempted to tell her everything, to unburden himself of the secret he'd been carrying. But the words stuck in his throat. How could he explain what he'd done, the lies he'd told? How could he make her understand why this was so important to him?

"It's nothing," he said finally, reaching across the table to take her hand. "I guess I'm just... overwhelmed. Being here, away from everything. It's stirred up a lot of memories."

Lily's expression softened. "Do you want to talk about it, my love?"

Henry shook his head, forcing a smile. "No, it's okay. I'm sorry for being so distant. This is supposed to be our anniversary trip. Let's focus on us."

Back in their hotel room, as Lily prepared for bed, Henry stood by the window, looking out over the twinkling lights of the city.

"Henry?" Lily's voice was soft, tentative. He turned to find her watching him, concern evident in her eyes. "Are you sure you're okay?"

Henry felt a lump form in his throat. He took Lily's hand, running his thumb over her wedding ring.

"Lily," he began, his voice thick with emotion. "There's something I need to tell you."

Henry hesitated, the words catching in his throat as he looked into Lily's trusting eyes. No. He couldn't bring himself to shatter the peace of the moment, so he swallowed hard and forced a smile.

"I just wanted to say... I love you more than anything and words can't describe how grateful I am that you've stayed with me and loved me for two whole years. You sure are incredible."

Lily's face softened. She leaned in, pressing a gentle kiss to his lips. "I love you too, Henry. Always."

The next few days fell into a pattern. During the day, Henry made sure to be fully present with Lily, exploring the vibrant city and its surroundings, but in the evenings, while Lily slept, he would slip out of their hotel room. He'd cite insomnia or a desire for a late-night snack, but in reality, he was meeting with local police contacts, poring over reports, and following leads on the whereabouts of Emily's killer.

One evening, about a week into their trip, Henry found himself in another dimly lit bar in a less touristy part of Manila. He was waiting for his contact, Ramon, who had promised new information. He didn't have to wait long. The local detective slid into the seat across from him five minutes later, his face grim.

"We have a problem, Detective Green," Ramon said in a low voice. "Our suspect seems to have gotten wind of our investigation. He's gone underground."

Henry felt his heart sink. "How? I thought we were being careful."

Ramon shook his head. "We were. But this guy.... We think he might be planning to flee the country."

The news hit Henry like a physical blow. After all these years, to be so close only to have his quarry slip away... it was almost more than he could bear.

"We need to move fast," Henry said, the anxiety evident in his voice. "What's our next step?"

They spent the next few hours strategizing, mapping out possible hideouts and escape routes. By the time they finished, it was well past midnight. Henry emerged from the bar into the humid night air, his mind racing with plans and contingencies.

Lost in thought, he barely registered the young woman walking in his direction until he nearly collided with her on the narrow sidewalk. He stumbled, reaching out to steady her instinctively.

"I'm so sorry," he began, then paused as he got a good look at her.

She was young, probably about twenty, with delicate features and large, expressive eyes. She was clearly a Filipina native. Despite the late hour and the less-than-reputable neighborhood, she was dressed simply but elegantly in a sundress that accentuated her slender figure.

"It's okay," she said softly, her English accented but clear. "No harm done."

Henry found himself staring, transfixed by her beauty and the hint of vulnerability in her eyes. He knew he should move on, get back to the hotel before Lily woke and noticed his absence. But something kept him rooted to the spot.

"Are you... are you alright?" he asked, noticing a slight tremor in her hands. "It's late to be out alone."

She smiled in a way that tugged at something in Henry's chest. "I could say the same to you," she replied. "But yes, I'm fine. Just... thinking. I've been going through a lot lately and I thought a walk would help."

Henry nodded, understanding all too well the need for solitary reflection. "Can I... would you like me to walk you home? I imagine it's not very safe out here at night."

She hesitated for a moment, then nodded. "That would be kind, thank you."

As they walked, Henry found himself opening up to this stranger in a way he hadn't with anyone in years. Perhaps it was the anonymity of the night, or the fact that he'd never see her again, but he found himself talking about Emily, about his quest for justice, about the guilt that ate at him for lying to Lily.

The young woman, who introduced herself as Lola, listened without judgment, offering quiet words of understanding and empathy. By the time they reached her modest home, which clearly housed other sleeping family members, Henry felt lighter than he had in years.

She walked him to an exterior staircase that led to her second-story room. "Would you like to come up for a cup of tea?" Lola asked, her eyes holding invitation and uncertainty.

Henry knew he should say no. He thought of Lily, waiting for him in their hotel room. He thought of his wedding vows, of the trust he'd already betrayed by keeping his investigation a secret.

But in that moment, feeling a momentary lifting of his burden and the intoxicating presence of this beautiful, understanding stranger, Henry's resolve crumbled.

"Yes," he heard himself say. "I'd like that."

Henry lost himself in the moment, pushing aside thoughts of Lily, of Emily, of everything but the present...

...It wasn't until later, as he lay in Lola's small bed watching the first hints of dawn creep through the window, that the full weight of what he'd done crashed down upon him. He slipped out of bed, dressing quickly and quietly.

Lola stirred, her eyes fluttering open. "Henry?" she murmured sleepily. "When will I see you again?"

The question caught him off guard. He turned to look at her, taking in her tousled hair and hopeful expression. It struck him as odd that she asked him that question. Didn't she know this was a one-time mistake? Didn't she remember that he was married?

"I... I don't think you will, Lola," he said softly. "This was... it shouldn't have happened. I'm married, and I love my wife. I'm so sorry."

He saw a flicker of both hurt and confusion in her eyes, quickly masked by a forced smile. As Henry made his way back to the hotel, the city coming to life around him, he felt hollow.

The guilt was overwhelming, threatening to consume him. He had betrayed Lily in the worst possible way, all while lying to her about the real reason for their trip.

He slipped back into their room just as the sun was fully rising. Lily was still asleep, her face peaceful and trusting. Henry felt a surge of self-loathing so strong it nearly brought him to his knees.

As he showered, trying to wash away the evidence of his infidelity, Henry made a decision. He couldn't continue like this. The lies, the betrayal... it was destroying him, and worse, it was threatening to destroy the one good thing in his life.

***

Lola stood at the living room window of her family's modest home, her eyes fixed on the street outside but her mind far away. The events of the previous night played on a loop in her head.

She hadn't meant to tell her family, but she knew that she had sinned and simply couldn't keep it inside. The words had spilled out during their morning devotions, her guilt too heavy to bear alone. Now, she wished she could take them back and stuff them back inside where they couldn't hurt anyone but her.

Behind her, she could hear her mother's quiet sobs and her father's angry pacing. The floorboards creaked with each of his heavy steps, a physical manifestation of the tension that filled the room.

"Lola," her father's voice was low, controlled, but she could hear the fury simmering beneath the surface. "You will tell me who this man is. Now."

Lola turned slowly, her heart pounding. Her father stood in the center of the room, his usually kind face twisted with anger and disappointment. Her mother sat on the deep red sofa, dabbing at her eyes with a handkerchief.

"Papa, please," Lola pleaded, her voice barely above a whisper. "It was my fault. He... he didn't force me. I invited him in."

Her father's eyes flashed. "It doesn't matter! He took advantage of you, of your innocence. He must make this right."

Lola felt a surge of panic. "Make it right? Papa, what do you mean? He's an American. You can't possibly mean—"

Her father's jaw set in a determined line. "The bible is clear, daughter. If a man takes advantage of a virgin, he must pay the brideprice and marry her. God's Law doesn't change just because this man is a foreigner. Who else is supposed to restore your honor? Who else will marry you now that you've been defiled? Have you thought about *that*?"

The words hit Lola like a physical blow. She stumbled back, gripping the windowsill for support. "No," she whispered. "Papa, you can't. He's... he's married. He has a wife. He's a tourist, and where he's from, they can only have one wife anyway. In his country—"

"Your honor comes before his country!" Her father's expression hardened further. "If he's married, he has sinned doubly by deceiving his wife, but the bible is clear."

"But papa," Lola pleaded. "The Law doesn't have to apply to us. I know it—"

"Ah!" Her father interrupted. "So, that's why you thought you could get away with it." He looked at her as if he had just figured something out.

Lola took a nervous step back, a tear falling from one eye. "Papa, I..."

Her father looked at her mother and then back at her. "You thought that you'd get out of this because this man can't take another wife. Is that it?"

Holding back more tears from her confused and anxious eyes, Lola replied. "I thought... I wasn't thinking. It just happened and I didn't think at all." Her face began to give way to her tears.

At the sight of her evident struggle, her father softened, though just a little, toward his daughter, then he continued. "The letter of the Law, no. But the spirit of the Law, yes. If God deemed it a good idea for His people then, it's a good idea for His people now. There was no exception for married men then and there is no exception for married men now. We are going to find this man and he is going to redeem you. I will not accept my daughter being treated like a harlot and then the perpetrator running back home without consequence."

Lola's mind raced. She thought of Henry, of the pain and guilt in his eyes as he'd left her room. She thought of his wife, waiting for him in their hotel room, blissfully unaware of her husband's deception.

"Papa, please listen to me," Lola said, forcing her voice to remain steady. "This man... he won't understand. He's probably not even Christian. He doesn't understand the bible. And he's hurting, Papa. He told me about his sister, about the pain he's carrying. He made a mistake, but he doesn't deserve to have his life destroyed because of it."

Her father shook his head, unmoved. "His pain does not excuse his actions, Lola. And what of *your* life? Your honor? Who will marry you now, knowing you've been defiled?"

The word 'defiled' kept cutting through Lola like a knife. She felt tears welling up in her eyes again but blinked them back fiercely. "I don't care about that, Papa. I care about doing what's right, and I don't think you should expect this of him."

Her father's expression softened slightly, but his resolve remained firm. "Lola, this is exactly why we have the word of God. We don't abandon its wisdom because our situation is unique. If anything, we cling to it all the more, knowing that what it says transcends our own wisdom, no matter what the case may be."

Lola watched in horror as her father grabbed his jacket and headed for the door. "Papa, stop! Where are you going?"

"To find this man," he replied, his hand on the doorknob. "You said he's staying at a hotel. It can't be that difficult to find an American tourist."

Panic surged through Lola. She darted forward, placing herself between her father and the door. "Papa, please. You can't do this. It will only cause more pain, more suffering. Is that what our faith teaches us?"

Her father didn't listen. As he picked up his keys, she sank onto the sofa next to her mother, who wrapped an arm around her shoulders.

Lola's heart raced as she watched her father's face harden, his jaw reset in a determined line.

"Papa, please," she pleaded, her voice trembling. "You can't do this. It was my mistake too."

"Enough, Lola," he growled, checking his jacket pockets to ensure his wallet was in one. "This man must face the consequences of his actions."

Lola's mother sat silently on the faded sofa, continuing to dab at her eyes with a handkerchief. The weight of her silent disappointment pressed down on Lola with palpable force.

As her father reached for the doorknob, Lola stood and said, "If you must go, let me come with you!"

For a brief moment, Lola thought she saw a flicker of hesitation in her father's eyes, but it vanished as quickly as it had appeared.

"Very well," he said, his voice low and dangerous. "Come with me."

As they shut the door behind them, Lola's mother remained on the couch, weeping for her daughter. She knew that if she interrupted her husband, it would make things worse. She had never seen him so angry. She also knew that arguing with him would teach Lola a terrible lesson, one of defying both the wisdom in the bible and one's father. After a couple of minutes of crying, she grabbed the bible sitting on the small table next to the couch. She opened it up to the passage her husband was referring to, and read—

Deuteronomy 22:28-29 – "If a man finds a girl who is a virgin, who is not engaged, and seizes her and lies with her and they are discovered, then the man who lay with her shall give to the girl's father fifty shekels of silver, and she shall become his wife because he has violated her; he cannot divorce her all his days."

With one hand resting on this passage in her bible, she prayed, "Oh Lord God. You have watched over our family for so long and protected our children for so long. This is the wisdom Your word has to offer us, so

I pray that what the devil meant for evil, you will take and use for good. I pray you give my husband your wisdom, forgive my daughter her sin, and save this man's soul. In the most precious name of Jesus, I pray. Amen."

Henry sat across from Lily at a quaint beachfront cafe, the gentle lapping of waves providing a soothing backdrop to their conversation. Despite the beautiful setting, he couldn't shake the gnawing guilt that had plagued him since his indiscretion with Lola. He watched Lily's face, animated as she described the colorful local market she'd visited that morning, and felt a sharp pang in his chest.

"Henry? Are you listening?" Lily's voice cut through his thoughts.

He blinked, forcing a smile. "Sorry, I was just... thinking about how beautiful you look in this light."

Lily beamed, reaching across the table to squeeze his hand. Henry felt the weight of his wedding ring, a constant reminder of his betrayal.

As he opened his mouth to respond, a commotion near the cafe entrance caught his attention. His blood ran cold as he recognized Lola, standing beside an older man who bore a striking resemblance to her. Their eyes met for a brief moment before Lola pointed directly at him.

Time seemed to slow as the man—undoubtedly Lola's father—strode towards their table, his face a mask of barely contained fury. Henry stood, instinctively placing himself between the approaching man and Lily.

"You!" Lola's father spat, his accent thick with emotion. "You're the one who violated my daughter! How dare you treat my daughter like a harlot? Have you no shame!?"

Henry felt the blood drain from his face as Lily's confused voice piped up behind him. "Henry? What's he talking about?"

Before he could formulate a response, Lola's father continued his tirade, laying bare Henry's transgression in excruciating detail. Henry watched helplessly as understanding dawned on Lily's face, quickly followed by hurt, betrayal, then disgust.

"Lily, I—" Henry started, but she was already pushing back her chair, tears welling up in her eyes.

By this point, all of the cafe's customers had stopped eating and turned to watch what was happening. All eyes were on the American couple, which was too much for Lily to handle.

"I need... I can't..." Lily choked out before turning and fleeing the cafe.

Henry moved to follow her, but found his path blocked by Lola's father. "You're not going anywhere until we deal with this," the man growled.

Frustration and panic welled up in Henry. "Look, I'm sorry for what happened, but I need to talk to my wife."

He tried to push past, but suddenly found himself surrounded by about a dozen local men who had risen from their tables, their faces set in grim determination.

"You heard the man," one of them said. "Sit down and face what you've done." The others nodded and gestured in agreement.

Realizing he was outnumbered and in a precarious situation, Henry sank back into his chair, his mind racing. He looked at Lola, who stood off to the side, her expression a mix of guilt and apprehension.

"I'm truly sorry," Henry said, addressing Lola's father. "What I did was wrong. I made a terrible mistake, and I'm prepared to face the consequences." Although this was less of a confession than a strategic move to remain unharmed by the crowd, his quick admission of guilt seemed to reduce the tension, be it ever so little.

To Henry's surprise, the older man's demeanor somewhat shifted. The fury in his eyes dimmed a little, leaving only fortitude in its place. He pulled up a chair and sat down across the small table from Henry. The other men followed suit, some pulling up a chair of their own and others standing in a more relaxed posture.

"Well now, young man," Lola's father said, his voice becoming more calm as he composed himself. "You're in quite the predicament, and I'm sure you want out, but you're not leaving this cafe until we settle things. You can be sorry for your sin all you want, and so you should be, but there are consequences to our actions, and we're about to find out what yours should be."

Henry blinked, caught off guard by the crowd's suddenly more relaxed demeanor. "Consequences?" Henry asked, looking around at the large group of men that could easily get the best of him.

The older man nodded, a challenging gleam in his eye as he glanced around the room at his support. "I saw your wife was holding a bible, so you must know what God demanded of a man in your shoes, correct? There's only one way to make this right—"

"I'll pay whatever fine is necessary," Henry said quickly. "I'll make a donation to your church, anything you want. I don't know what the bible says and I don't care. Just let me go talk to my wife."

Lola's father's face re-hardened, and he shook his head. "Oh no. Money can't restore my daughter's honor. Only marriage can do that."

Confused, Henry blurted out, "So let her get married. What's that got to do with me?"

Her father looked at another man in the cafe and rolled his eyes. The man humorously shrugged and shook his head with a smirk in response. The two were clearly communicating their disdain for the American's ignorance.

Turning to Henry, he clarified. "Oh, my confused friend. Only marriage to *you* can do that. You're going to marry my daughter, just like the bible says."

Henry's jaw dropped as he scanned the room to find any indication that he was joking, but he could see on the faces of the locals that he wasn't. "Marry? But I'm already married. And no offense, but I barely know your daughter."

One of the onlookers, a middle-aged man with a thick mustache, laughed heartily. "Ah, the men of the West! With all their fairy tales and princess weddings. If their view of marriage was any narrower, it'd pass right through the eye of a needle." Others joined him in laughing.

"Indeed," another man chimed in, while leaning in closer to Henry with a devious smile. "So tell me this, Mr Rich American. Why is it that you men can want more than one house, more than one car, and more than one computer, but not more than one wife?"

"Maybe they like toys more than women," another answered, as the whole cafe erupted in more laughter at Henry's expense.

"I think I saw one kissing his car goodnight one time!" a man from the bar shouted over, causing the laughter to continue. Even Lola's father couldn't help but let out a chuckle at the local's mockery.

Henry's head was spinning. He looked to Lola for help, but she merely shrugged, looking as bewildered as he felt.

"Look," Henry tried again, hoping to squirm out of this situation. "I appreciate the, uh, offer, but I'm not even a Christian. Surely you wouldn't want a non-believer marrying your daughter? Besides, I'm only here for a week."

To his dismay, Lola's father's grin only widened as he let out a curious groan while looking at the others, as if he did indeed see the problem. Looking back at Henry, he said, "Well, you're certainly right about that. Can't have my beautiful baby girl marrying a heathen, now can I?"

"Exactly," Henry replied.

Lola's father raised his hands and then slapped them down on his knees, looking around at the whole cafe. "He's right," he said in somewhat comical admission. "I guess there's only one thing to do."

Henry stood to his feet. "I'm glad you see that sir. I'm sorry again for what happened," Henry said as he took a step away from the table.

Lola's father looked at him with humorous confusion. "Where are you going?" He then turned to a man sitting behind him and asked, "Where is he going?" while gesturing toward Henry with his arms.

The man behind him shrugged and chuckled as the man at the bar, who made the joke about the car, shouted over, "He has no time to marry your daughter. He has a hot date with a Toyota."

The whole cafe, including Lola's father, was again reduced to laughter as Henry grew more uncomfortable. As the laughter subsided, the group gestured for him to sit back down, which he nervously did.

"Henry," Lola's father began. "We have ourselves quite the situation here. On one hand, the bible says you should marry my daughter. On the other, the bible also says that she must not marry outside the faith. Now, the way I see it, there's only one way out of this mess."

He smiled and looked at Henry in the eyes as Henry expressed bewilderment as to what he was getting at.

Then, Lola's father put a hand on Henry's shoulder. "We're going to make a Christian out of you, my friend. That'll solve it."

The solution was met with hearty nods and vocal expressions of approval by the onlookers.

Removing his hand from Henry's shoulder, he continued. "I understand you're not from around here, but I'll make a deal with you. If I can make you a genuine disciple of Jesus Christ within thirty days, you will marry Lola. If I fail, I'll let you go and never speak of it again."

"A month?" Henry sputtered. "We're here on a week's vacation. I have work to do here and back in the States—"

A new voice entered the conversation—a local police officer who had been observing the scene. "I'm afraid it won't be possible for you to just leave, sir. By engaging in fornication, you've committed a crime. There's a substantial fine to avoid jail time." The officer looked at Lola's father and winked, signaling to him that he was trying to help.

Henry felt panic rising in his chest. "Jail? Surely we can work something out. I don't have much money but—"

"Now, now," Lola's father interrupted. "Let's not start bribing officers of the law. I'm sure we can come to an arrangement that benefits everyone."

The officer nodded, a mischievous glint in his eye. "Perhaps a period of... cultural exchange?"

"Exactly!" Lola's father exclaimed. "Cultural exchange!" He then turned to Henry. "You will come to our daily bible study every morning for the next month. If you're a Christian by the end of it, you take my daughter as your wife. If not, we won't press charges and you're free to go."

Henry just sat there, continuing to look baffled by the situation.

The officer added, "It's either that or jail, Mr Henry."

Henry's mind raced, searching for a way out. "But what about my wife? My job? I can't just... disappear for the month!"

An elderly woman at a nearby table spoke up, her voice filled with wisdom. "Young man, sometimes the path to redemption requires sacrifice. Perhaps this is the very thing God is using to save your life."

"But—" Henry started, only to be cut off by another onlooker.

"Think of it as an adventure!" the man said enthusiastically. "How many people get the chance to immerse themselves in a new culture like this?"

Henry looked around desperately, feeling like he had stepped into some bizarre alternate reality. The cafe had grown quiet, all eyes on him as they awaited his decision.

"I... I need time to think," he stammered.

Lola's father leaned back and faced the officer. "How much time do we give him?"

The officer, looking at Henry, said, "You've got the night. If you're not at bible study in the morning, you'll be in cuffs by lunch."

The crowd gestured in agreement, as if they were bearing witness to the terms.

As the group waited for his response, Henry felt a surreal detachment from the situation. Part of him wanted to laugh at the absurdity of it all, while another part wanted to break down and weep. In the end, faced with the prospect of jail time in a foreign country and the realization that his marriage to Lily was likely over regardless, Henry reluctantly agreed to their terms. As the group dispersed, satisfied with the arrangement, Henry remained seated, staring out at the ocean.

The sun was setting. It should have been beautiful, but to Henry, it felt like the final curtain falling on the life he had known. He thought of Lily, wondering where she had gone, if she would even speak to him again.

He thought of his job back home, of the investigation he had come here to pursue. It all seemed so distant now, like a half-remembered dream.

Lola approached him cautiously, her eyes filled with guilt and something else—hope, perhaps? "I'm sorry," she said softly. "I never meant for this to happen."

Henry looked at her, really looked at her, for the first time since that fateful night. She was beautiful, yes, but so young, so full of life and potential. He felt ancient in comparison, weighed down by his mistakes and regrets.

"Neither did I," he replied, his voice hoarse. "But here we are."

As Lola walked away, Henry turned his gaze back to the ocean. The waves continued their endless dance, indifferent to the turmoil of human lives. He had a month ahead of him—a month to face his mistakes, to grapple with questions of faith and morality he had long ignored, to try and make sense of the mess he had made of his life.

For a moment, he allowed himself to imagine what it would be like to stay here, to start anew in this vibrant, complicated country. To embrace a faith he had always viewed with skepticism, to build a life with Lola. It was a seductive thought, an escape from the guilt and pain that awaited him back home.

But as quickly as the thought came, he dismissed it. He knew he couldn't run from his responsibilities, from the hurt he had caused Lily. Whatever happened in the coming month, he owed it to her—and to himself—to face the consequences of his actions.

With a heavy sigh, Henry stood up. The cafe had emptied, leaving him alone with his thoughts. He walked slowly towards the beach, letting the warm sand sink between his toes. As the gentle waves lapped at his feet, he closed his eyes and took a deep breath.

As the last light faded from the sky, Henry opened his eyes. The first stars were becoming visible, pinpricks of light in the deepening darkness. He thought of all the times he and Lily had stargazed together, planning their future, dreaming of the life they would build.

"I'm sorry, Lily," he whispered to the night. "I'm so sorry."

With one last look at the vast, indifferent ocean, Henry turned and walked back towards the town. His thoughts were solely focused on finding Lily.

He quickened his pace as he approached their hotel, hoping against hope that she had returned there. But as he entered their room, he was met with an oppressive silence. Lily's suitcase remained untouched, her purse still on the nightstand where she had left it that morning.

Anxiously running his hand over his face, Henry tried to think where she might have gone. Then it hit him—the beach. Lily had always found solace near the water.

He made his way to the shoreline where the two of them had previously walked, and scanned the beach, his heart leaping when he spotted a familiar figure sitting alone in the sand.

Henry approached slowly, uncertain of his welcome. Lily sat with her knees drawn up to her chest, her gaze fixed on the rolling waves. As he drew closer, he could see the tear tracks on her cheeks.

"Lily?" he said softly, his voice barely audible above the sound of the surf.

She turned to look at him, and Henry braced himself for the anger and hurt he expected to see. But to his surprise, Lily's eyes held only a deep sadness and... something else. Understanding?

"Henry," she replied, her voice hoarse. "I've been praying."

He sank down into the sand beside her, careful to maintain a respectful distance. "Lily, I... I don't even know where to begin. What I did was unforgivable."

To his astonishment, Lily didn't raise her voice or lash out in anger in any way. She looked at him, her face red from crying. "No, Henry. Nothing is unforgivable. It hurts—" She began to weep. "It hurts so much."

She then took a minute to cry into her arms as Henry just watched the results of his actions unfold in front of him. After composing herself a little, Lily turned her head and looked at him. "I forgive you, Henry."

Henry felt something break inside him at her words. Tears welled up in his eyes as the full weight of her grace washed over him. "How?" he choked out. "How can you forgive me so easily?"

Lily's eyes shimmered with more tears. "It's not easy, Henry. But it's what we're called to do. 'Forgive us our trespasses, as we forgive those who trespass against us.' If God can forgive me for my sins, how can I not forgive you for yours?"

Her words struck Henry like a knife in his side. If Lily could forgive him for this betrayal, shouldn't he be able to forgive the criminal he'd been hunting all these years? The thought was both terrifying and liberating.

"There's... there's more," Henry said hesitantly. He proceeded to explain the bizarre situation with Lola's father and the locals, watching as Lily's expression shifted from confusion to shock.

"They want you to what?" Lily exclaimed, her voice rising. "But that's... that's ridiculous! It's certainly not Christian! Multiple wives are for cult leaders, not Christians! What in the world...?"

Henry nodded, feeling a surge of relief at her reaction. "I know, I agree. But they're saying it's either this deal or prison. They tried to explain that having more than one wife is normal for them. They even talked like it's in the bible, but..."

Lily shook her head, her brow furrowed. "This is... I don't even know what to think. God knows it'd be an answer to prayer for you to be around Christian men, especially the kind that are strong enough to confront you for your actions. But what kind of Christians would recommend something like this? What they're suggesting is not just wrong. It's disgusting and evil."

She stood up suddenly, brushing sand from her clothes. "I need time to pray about this, Henry. I just need to be alone with my bible for a while."

As Henry watched her walk away, he felt hope and trepidation. He had expected anger, recrimination, perhaps even the end of their marriage. Instead, he had been met with forgiveness and a willingness to seek God's will. It humbled him in a way he had never experienced before.

Back at the hotel, Henry paced the room, his mind racing. He thought about Emily, about the anger and grief that had driven him for so long. For the first time, he allowed himself to consider the possibility of letting go, of forgiving. The very idea terrified him, but he couldn't deny the seed of hope it planted in his heart.

Meanwhile, on the beach, Lily sat with her bible open on her lap. She flipped through the pages of Exodus, Leviticus, and Deuteronomy, searching for the passages the men had mentioned. To her surprise, she found several references that seemed to regulate and even encourage having multiple wives—something she had never noticed before.

Her fingers trembled slightly as she turned to Deuteronomy and found the passage they had spoken of. There it was, in black and white: a man who seduced a virgin was required to marry her, with no exception for married men.

Lily closed her eyes, her heart conflicted. Everything she had been taught, everything she believed about marriage, seemed to be at odds with what she was reading. She took a deep breath and began to pray, surrendering her will and asking for guidance.

As the stars came out above her, Lily felt a sense of peace settle over her. She couldn't say she understood or agreed with everything she had read, but she felt a certainty that this was the path they needed to follow—for Henry's sake, for her own, and for the sake of their marriage.

With a mix of trepidation and resolve, Lily made her way back to the hotel. She found Henry sitting on the edge of the bed, his head in his hands. He looked up as she entered, his eyes red-rimmed and anxious.

"Lily," he said, standing up. "I... what did you decide?"

She took a deep breath, meeting his gaze steadily. "I think you should meet with those men for their daily bible studies, Henry."

His eyes widened in surprise. "Are you sure? Lily, we don't have to do this. We could find another way—"

She held up a hand to stop him. "I've prayed about it. I've read the scriptures they mentioned. I can't say I understand it. But Henry, you need Jesus, so I believe this is what we're being called to do. You need to go to that bible study, and I'll be praying my heart out that you find Jesus while you're there."

Henry stared at her in awe, overwhelmed by her strength and faith. "Lily, I don't deserve you..."

She smiled softly, but still avoided getting too close to him. "It's not about deserving, Henry. It's about grace. And maybe... maybe this is the grace we both need right now."

The morning sun filtered through the curtains of Henry and Lily's hotel room, shining brightly on their faces. Henry stirred first, his eyes fluttering open to meet the reality of the day ahead. He turned to look at Lily, still peacefully asleep beside him, and felt a pang of guilt twist in his chest.

Gently, he rose from the bed, careful not to wake her. As he dressed, his mind raced with thoughts of the impending bible study. What would it be like? How would they receive him? The uncertainty gnawed at him, but beneath it all, there was a glimmer of... curiosity? Hope? He couldn't quite place the feeling.

Henry paused at the door, looking back at Lily's sleeping form. He wanted to wake her, to ask her to come with him, but something held him back. This was his burden to bear, his journey to start. With a soft sigh, he slipped out of the room and into the Manila morning.

The walk to the bible study location was both too long and too short. Henry's feet seemed to move of their own accord, carrying him through streets alive with the sounds and smells of a city waking up. Vendors called out their wares, the aroma of freshly baked pan de sal wafting through the air. It all felt surreal, like a vivid dream he couldn't quite shake.

Before he knew it, Henry found himself standing before a modest building situated on a busy area of the beach, its walls a faded yellow in the morning light. He hesitated for a moment, his hand on the door handle. Taking a deep breath, he pushed it open and stepped inside.

The room was larger than he'd expected, filled with the low murmur of conversation. Henry blinked, his eyes adjusting to the dimmer light inside. He counted at least thirty men, more than he'd anticipated. His gaze fell on familiar faces—the local officer, some men from the café, and at the center of it all, Lola's father, who was clearly the leader of the group.

A hush fell over the room as they noticed his presence. Henry felt the weight of their stares, curiosity, judgment, and something else he couldn't quite define. He swallowed hard, fighting the urge to turn and flee.

Lola's father stepped forward, his face a mask of stern authority softened by a hint of... was that compassion? "Welcome, Henry," he said, his voice carrying easily through the quiet room. "We're glad you've joined us."

The officer stood up and shook Henry's hand to welcome him and the other men murmured their greetings, some nodding, others offering small smiles. Henry felt some of the tension leave his shoulders. "Thank you," he replied, his voice steadier than he felt. "I... I'm here to learn."

As Henry took a seat, one of the men asked, "Where is your wife?"

Henry shifted uncomfortably. "I... I wasn't sure if she should come," he admitted. "This is all very new to me."

Lola's father nodded, understanding. "Of course. Please, invite her to join us tomorrow. The women fellowship together and watch the children while we study." He pointed towards the outdoor area through the rear living room doors. Henry saw a couple dozen women and their children talking and playing on the patio and the connected beach area. "She would be most welcome." Lola's father assured him.

As the bible study began, Henry found himself drawn in, despite his initial reservations. Lola's father led the group in prayer, followed by prayers from a few others. He then looked up, and with a smile, addressed the group. "Brothers. Today, we are going to skip our normal study. So you can leave your bookmarks in Matthew 17 for tomorrow, but today we are going to hear a couple of testimonies and then I'm going to share the gospel, because, in case some of you haven't noticed, we have a particularly mischievous sort with us today." He looked at Henry and smiled as the group laughed a little, a couple of men giving Henry a slap on the shoulder to reassure him they were just kidding around. Henry lightened up and found himself able to laugh along with them.

Two of the men shared their stories of how they came to Christ years ago. Henry listened closely as the men shared their stories. One used to be a gang member and a drug addict. He came to Christ after his best friend was killed by the drugs he was selling, when a girl from his school invited him to her youth group. The other man was a Catholic his whole life (the dominant religion in the Philippines) but came to Christ when a street preacher stopped to talk to him. He told of how the preacher walked him through the Ten Commandments, asking him if he'd lied, stolen, used God's name in vain, or lusted after women. His conscience was bothered for days, and after reading the bible for himself, he put his faith in Christ and left the Catholic church, even though his family and friends treated him harshly for doing so.

These testimonies weren't anything like what Henry was going through, but he still marveled at the instant change these men experienced. It made him wonder if he, too, could experience a deep inner change with God's help.

After their stories, Lola's father took about ten minutes to present the gospel. He spoke of how holy and perfect God is and how unholy and sinful people are. He posed the question, "If God is good, we must ask ourselves, what does He do with people like us?"

This question brought the first true feelings of conviction that Henry had ever experienced. He suddenly found himself on the edge of his seat, eagerly awaiting the answer to this problem.

Lola's father went on to explain how a just God must punish sinners, or else he wouldn't be just. The more he made the case, the more Henry felt a war waging within his soul. Surely, he couldn't be that bad? He frantically scrambled to compile evidence in his own mind of his good deeds outweighing his bad behavior, but as he filled the scales, he heard

Lola's father's voice pierce through his thought process with startling conviction. "The problem, my dear friends, is not that you have sinned. The problem is—you've never done anything *but* sin."

Henry absorbed these words like a knife going through his chest. Even his good deeds began to reveal themselves as having been done with selfish motives. His drinking, unforgiveness, and occasional harsh treatment of Lola whirled around in his head as the message continued.

"But there is hope!" the zealous speaker continued. "Two thousand years ago, God sent His Son, Jesus of Nazareth, to pay the price for our sin. We broke God's Law, and He must see that justice is done, but He is rich in mercy and willing that none perish, so He provided a Savior. On that cross, all of the anger and punishment that we deserve for our sin, God poured out on His willing Son in our place. That way, God can legally dismiss our case because our debt was paid by another. We are all going to face God on judgment day. It is a date that none of us can postpone or avoid. So now, God tells all of us to repent of our sins and trust alone in Jesus, to believe in what He did for us on that cross. And He promises that everyone who comes to Jesus will be forgiven of their sins, made a brand new creation on the inside, and given the free gift of everlasting life."

After scanning the room, Lola's father, with tears shimmering in his eyes, invited everyone to bow their heads as he prayed. "Father in Heaven, I pray that if anyone in this room does not know You, that You would convict them by Your Holy Spirit and draw them to Yourself before it's too late. In Jesus' powerful Name, amen."

With that, everyone lifted their heads and echoed, "Amen."

Henry had listened intently, feeling something stir within him—a sense of reality he had never felt before. This message was not like the clips of TV preachers he had seen or the ones he had heard the few times he went to church with his grandmother as a teenager. This message didn't promise him happiness and ease or a perfect marriage and a good job. It went straight for his sin and left him without any excuse before God for his actions. He knew it was true and left the study with a heavy conscience, but he tried his best to set it to the side as he returned to Lily.

Back at the hotel, Henry found Lily waiting for him, her eyes full of questions. As he recounted the morning's events, he watched her expression shift from concern to curiosity to optimism. The gospel message he relayed to her was so strong, it even helped Lily grow in her own understanding of her faith. She kept it to herself, but she was overjoyed to hear that Henry was fellowshipping with genuine, strong, Christian men.

"I'm glad it went well," Lily said softly, reaching out to take his hand.

"So am I," Henry said, smiling as he squeezed her hand. "They were asking you to come tomorrow."

"Oh? And do you think I should come?"

Henry nodded, giving her hand another squeeze. "I think it would be good for both of us. The women have their own fellowship while the men study. And Lily..." he paused, meeting her gaze. "I think this might be what we need. What *I* need..."

Lily's eyes shimmered with unshed tears. She nodded, a small smile tugging at her lips. "Then we'll go together."

The next morning dawned bright and clear, a perfect Manila day. As Henry and Lily made their way to the bible study, there was a nervous energy between them.

Upon arrival, they were greeted warmly by the group. Lily found herself ushered towards a group of women, their faces open and welcoming. As Henry joined the men, he cast one last glance at his wife, offering a reassuring smile before turning his attention to the study.

Lily followed the women out back to the patio and ocean-side area, which was filled with the cheerful sounds of playing children. She watched in amazement as the women effortlessly managed the group, their patience and love evident in every interaction. The children, ranging from toddlers to pre-teens, played together.

As she observed, Lily couldn't help but compare this scene to what she was used to back home. These families clearly had less in terms of material possessions, yet there was a richness here that touched her deeply. The contentment and joy were palpable, challenging her preconceptions.

Three of the wives, including Lola's mother, approached Lily with warm smiles. "Would you like to talk?" Lola's mother asked gently. "We know this must be a difficult time for you."

Lily nodded, grateful for the opportunity to open up. They sat down at a small table on the patio, and as the other children played, Lily poured out her heart. She spoke of her pain, her confusion, and her struggle to reconcile her faith with her current situation.

The women listened with compassion, offering comfort through gentle touches and understanding nods. When Lily finished, Lola's mother spoke softly. "We understand your pain, Lily. What your husband did was wrong, but we believe God is in the business of redemption."

"And reconciliation," one of the other wives, named Carmelita, added with a smile. She looked to be in her 20s. "I know the idea of multiple wives seems strange to you. It's not overly common here, but it is normal. In fact, I'm one of four women here who has a co-wife."

Lily's eyes widened in surprise. "Really? But everyone seems so…" Lily glanced at the three women's faces as one raised her eyebrows, waiting for her to finish the sentence. "…normal." Lily concluded. "I thought polygamy was the stuff of Mormon horror stories. How… How do you even make it work?"

The women exchanged a knowing glance, smiling. "It's not always easy," Lola's mother admitted. "Just like being the only wife isn't always easy either. Some struggles come from being alone. Others come from being together. Nothing is perfect this side of eternity. But we believe in working together, in supporting each other. And when you add biblical wisdom to the mix, sometimes that teamwork is best carried out by having more wives at home."

"But can't you just help each other as friends?" Lily asked. "Why turn it into such a—" Lily chose her words carefully, not wanting to offend her kind hosts. "different… way of living?"

The third woman chimed in, who looked to be in her late 30s. "Well, if help around the house was all we were after, perhaps that would fit the bill, but there are more important issues at stake—like finding husbands for our daughters. The West seems to want girls to do everything but start a family, but here, while women do all sorts of wonderful jobs, we count it as our highest calling to raise a godly family."

Lily gave her a look that communicated she understood the problem, but was still confused as to how polygamy was the solution.

Carmelita clarified further. "The problem is, there's not always enough good men to go around. Tragically, many Christians in our country settle for letting their daughters marry Catholics because there simply aren't enough Christian men available. A few years ago, when I was ready for marriage, three men approached my father about me. One was a married Christian. Two were single Catholics. What would so many fathers have done? They would have given their precious daughter, who they're supposed to be protecting from falsehood, to an unbeliever, leaving her to walk the Christian road alone in her marriage. What kind of solution is that? The bible never says a woman can't marry a married man, but it most certainly says that we can't marry unbelievers. The Christian was a good man, and if anything, he proved that he was worth marrying because he already had demonstrated how well he could take care of a family. I will always be grateful that my father gave me to my husband. And not only that, but my co-wife is now my best friend. Who could ask for more?"

Processing what she was hearing, Lily looked around them, not seeing the strange, foreign culture she had expected, but a community bound by love, faith, and mutual support.

As the women settled deeper into their conversation, Lily felt a mix of nervousness and relief. The warmth in their eyes and the gentle touch of Lola's mother's hand on her arm provided a comfort she hadn't realized she desperately needed.

"I... I don't even know how to begin accepting all this," Lily admitted, her voice barely above a whisper. "Everything's happened so fast, and I feel like I'm drowning in confusion and hurt."

Lola's mother, who had introduced herself as Maria, nodded sympathetically. "Take your time, dear. We're here to listen."

The wife in her thirties, named Sarah, added, "Sometimes, just speaking our fears out loud can help us make sense of them."

Lily took a deep breath, steadying herself. "I love Henry. I've loved him for years, through all the pain he's carried since his sister's death. But this... I never imagined he could betray me like this. And now, to be told that the solution is for him to marry another woman? It goes against everything I've ever believed about marriage."

Lily paused for a moment, glancing away before continuing her thought. "Everything you're saying makes sense, but I don't know how to make it normal to me. I just feel so lost right now."

As she spoke, Lily felt tears welling up in her eyes. She blinked them back, determined to maintain her composure.

Maria's voice was gentle when she responded. "Your pain is understandable, Lily. What your husband did was wrong, and it's natural to feel hurt and betrayed. But tell me, what does the bible say about forgiveness?"

Lily paused, considering what she knew about forgiveness and how she certainly tried to forgive Henry the other night on the beach. "The bible teaches us to forgive as we have been forgiven. But this feels so much bigger than any forgiveness I've had to offer before."

Sarah leaned in, her eyes bright with understanding. "Forgiveness doesn't mean forgetting or excusing the wrong. It's about releasing the anger and bitterness that can poison our own hearts. Sometimes it's a process."

"But how?" Lily asked, her voice cracking. "How do I even begin to forgive something like this?"

Maria smiled softly. "One day at a time, dear one. And remember, forgiveness is as much for you as it is for Henry. It frees you from the burden of resentment."

As they talked, Lily found herself opening up more, sharing her fears and asking more questions about the whole situation.

"How do you manage the jealousy, the competition?" Lily asked.

Carmelita's laugh was warm and genuine. "Oh, sweetie. You've got Disney-princess theology in your head. Jealousy? Why would I be jealous of the woman who frees up my husband to have more time for me? The bible never once tells of a woman being jealous for her husband, only men for their wives. And that is a godly thing. What reason would I have to be jealous? It's not as if he loves me less just because he loves her too. And as for competition? We have our struggles like any family. But we're sisters in Christ, not rivals. We support each other and share the burdens of running a household and raising children. In many ways, our family is stronger for it."

'Disney-princess theology?' Lily thought to herself. She felt rebuked, seeing that these words came from a woman around ten years younger than her. It made her feel a little childish for only thinking in terms of jealousy and romantic dreams.

Maria, though the only wife in her family, added her wisdom. "The key is communication, respect, and a shared commitment to putting the family first. It's not about one wife being better than another, but about each bringing their unique strengths to the family unit."

"Right," Sarah added. "Like we all know who brings the cooking strength to *Carmelita's* family unit..." she teased, as the three women laughed.

"Hey!" Carmelita replied, faking indignation. "I'm working on it!"

As they continued to talk, Lily found herself fascinated by their stories. They shared tales of everyday life in their families—the challenges, the joys, the unexpected moments of humor. She learned about how they navigated things like household duties, time with their husband, and raising children together.

"But what about intimacy?" Lily asked, blushing slightly. "Doesn't it feel... strange?"

Maria's response was matter-of-fact. "Intimacy is just one part of a marriage, Lily. An important part, yes, but not the only part. We focus on building strong emotional connections, on supporting each other in all aspects of life."

"Spoken like a true grandmother," Carmelita joked, as Maria rolled her eyes, clearly expecting a more 'youthful' response to follow.

"It's only strange if you make it strange," Carmelita continued. You just let the moments of passion inspire you and take them as they come, just like if you were alone. Besides, with a friend to split the load, you don't get hounded for sex all the time..."

Maria gasped at the word 'sex' and comically slapped Carmelita with her napkin, causing the others to laugh.

Lily jokingly added, "I guess it wouldn't be so bad to walk through my own house without getting pounced on 24/7..."

The three women continued to laugh and Lily found herself slowly relaxing. The womens' openness and willingness to answer her questions, no matter how personal, helped ease some of her fears. She began to see that while their way of life was different from what she knew, it wasn't the loveless, oppressive arrangement she had imagined.

"The kids also seem so happy." Lily said, as she watched them playing near the water.

Then, as if on cue, a squabble broke out between two of the younger children. The women resumed their laughter as Sarah went to manage it, seeing that one of the squabblers was hers. "See?" Maria said with a grin. "It's not always perfect, but it is family."

Lily found herself laughing along, feeling a weight lift from her shoulders. As Sarah returned, smoothing her skirt, she added, "And honestly, having multiple wives can be a blessing when it comes to managing a household and raising children. There's always someone to lend a hand or offer support. I've even bugged my husband about getting on board so I can have it as easy as Carmelita." The two younger wives laughed and slapped each other over the joke.

"Anyway..." Maria concluded with another roll of her eyes. "I'm sure you'll find that it's more of a blessing than an obstacle. And Lola is a wonderful girl. I—"

The other two women smiled and said in unison, "I don't raise any other kind," clearly mocking the fact that Maria says this about her own mothering often.

Maria waited for them to stop chuckling, and then a devious smirk appeared on her face. Grabbing Lily's wrist and leaning in to her, she whispered, "She's certainly a better cook than Carmelita..."

Suddenly feeling like a young girl with best friends again, Lily and Sarah "oooooh'd" in unison while looking at Carmelita, followed by shared laughter between the four of them.

As their conversation continued, touching on topics from faith to child-rearing to managing household duties, Lily felt a growing sense of connection with these women. Their lives were so different from hers, yet she found herself admiring their strength, their faith, and their commitment to their families.

"Thank you," Lily said softly, looking at all three women. "For your honesty, your kindness. I still have a lot to process, but you've given me so much to think about."

Maria smiled warmly. "That's all we can ask, dear. Take your time, pray about it. And know that whatever happens, you have support here."

When Henry came outside to get her, Lily's eyes were bright with a new understanding. As they walked back to their hotel, hand in hand, she felt a sense of peace she hadn't experienced in days.

"How was it?" Henry asked tentatively.

Lily squeezed his hand, a small smile playing on her lips. "It was... enlightening," she replied. "I think I'm beginning to understand. And Henry?" She stopped, turning to face him. "I think we're where we need to be right now."

That day, as the evening sun dipped below the horizon, Henry and Lily sat across from each other at a beach-side restaurant. The gentle lapping of waves provided a soothing backdrop, but there was still enough tension to keep both of them mostly quiet.

Henry pushed his barely-touched seafood paella around his plate, stealing glances at Lily. Her eyes were fixed on the ocean, a faraway look on her face. The last two days had been a whirlwind of bible studies, cultural immersion, and soul-searching, leaving them both raw and uncertain.

"The fish is good," Henry offered weakly, desperate to break the silence.

Lily nodded, her lips curving into a small smile. "Yes, it is."

The conversation died as quickly as it had begun, leaving them once again in uncomfortable silence. Henry felt a weight pressing on his chest, the words he needed to say caught in his throat like shards of glass.

As the waiter cleared their plates, Henry stood abruptly. "Would you like to take a walk on the beach?"

Lily looked up, surprise flickering across her face. "Sure," she said softly, rising to join him.

They made their way down to the shore, their shoes sinking into the cool sand. The beach was nearly deserted, most tourists having retreated to their hotels or nightlife spots. Henry and Lily walked side by side, close but not touching, each lost in their own thoughts.

After a few minutes, Lily broke the silence. "How are the bible studies going?" she asked, her voice barely audible above the sound of the waves.

Henry took a deep breath, his hands clenching and unclenching at his sides. "They're... intense," he admitted. "The message, the idea of sin and redemption—I understand it intellectually, but..."

He trailed off, his jaw tightening. Lily waited patiently, sensing he had more to say.

"But I just can't bring myself to forgive him, Lily," Henry finally continued, his voice cracking. "The man who killed Emily. I know I'm supposed to, but every time I think about it, I feel this rage burning inside me and—"

Lily reached out, gently taking his hand. "It's okay, Henry. Sometimes, forgiveness is a process," she said, remembering the same words being spoken to her earlier. "You'll get there."

Henry shook his head, tears welling up in his eyes. "But what if I don't get there? Before, I only had to worry about losing some sleep. Now I have to worry about going to Hell."

He stopped walking, turning to face the ocean. The moonlight reflected off the water, creating a shimmering path that seemed to stretch to infinity. Henry felt something break inside of him, a dam of emotion he'd been holding back for years.

"I have to tell you something, Lily," he said, his voice thick with emotion. "The real reason we came here… it wasn't just for our anniversary."

Lily's hand tightened in his, but she remained silent and just stared at the water, giving him space to continue.

"I got a tip," Henry confessed, the words tumbling out now, "about Emily's killer. That he was here, in the Philippines. I thought… I thought I could find him—bring him to justice. Or maybe…" He trailed off, unable to voice the darker thoughts that had driven him.

Lily's deep intake and exhale of breath was audible even over the sound of the waves. She wasn't sure what to say, but she was glad he had come clean.

The weight of his deception, of everything that had happened since they arrived, came crashing down on Henry. His legs gave out, and he sank to his knees in the sand, tears streaming down his face.

"I'm so sorry, Lily," he sobbed, his whole body shaking. "For lying to you, for everything. For not being the husband you deserve. For letting my anger control me for so long."

Lily knelt beside him, wrapping her arms around his trembling form. She held him as he wept, her own tears falling silently.

"I forgive you, Henry," she said softly, her voice filled with pain and compassion. "I really do forgive you and I really do love you."

They sat there on the beach, the waves lapping at their feet, as Henry poured out years of pent-up grief, anger, and regret. Lily listened, offering comfort and understanding, her own heart breaking for the pain her husband had carried for so long.

As Henry's sobs subsided, he took a shuddering breath. "I don't know how to move forward from here, Lily. How do I let go of this? How do we… how do we deal with everything that's happened since we came here?"

Lily was quiet for a moment, her fingers absently tracing patterns in the sand. "I think," she said slowly, "that we take it one day at a time. We keep going to bible study, we keep learning, and we keep growing. And we face whatever's next together."

Henry nodded, feeling a glimmer of hope in his chest. "Together," he repeated, the word feeling like a lifeline.

They sat in silence for a while, watching the moon's reflection dance on the waves. The night air was warm and heavy with the scent of salt and tropical flowers. In the distance, they could hear the faint sounds of music and laughter from a beach-side bar.

"Henry," Lily said suddenly, her voice hesitant. "What about Lola? And her family's expectations?"

Henry got tense again, having almost completely forgotten about that. "I don't know," he admitted. "I've been so focused on my own issues, I haven't really let myself think about that part of it."

Lily nodded, her expression thoughtful. "I was talking with the women in the bible study," she said. "Learning about their culture, their way of life. It's so different from what we know, but there's a beauty to it, a sense of community and support that's... well, it's helping me see things differently."

Henry looked at her, surprise evident on his face. "What are you saying, that you want—?"

She shook her head quickly. "No, not exactly. I'm just saying... I think we need to approach this with open minds and open hearts. We need to pray about it, seek guidance. And we need to consider Lola's feelings in all of this too."

Henry nodded slowly, feeling a mix of emotions he couldn't quite name. "You're right," he said. "We can't just run away from this. We need to face it head-on, whatever the outcome."

Lily leaned her head on his shoulder, and Henry wrapped an arm around her, pulling her close. They sat like that for a long time, the rhythm of the waves soothing their troubled hearts.

As it got late, Henry stood, reaching down to help Lily to her feet. "We should head back," he said softly. "Get some rest before the bible study."

Lily smiled and nodded in agreement and they returned to their hotel room for what they'd hoped would be a good night's sleep.

On their third day, Henry and Lily made their way to the bible study, their hands intertwined, drawing strength from each other. As they approached the familiar yellow building, Henry felt a flutter of nervousness in his stomach. He squeezed Lily's hand, receiving a reassuring smile in return.

"I'll see you after," Lily said, giving him a quick kiss before joining the other women.

Henry watched her go, marveling at her strength and grace. Taking a deep breath, he stepped into the men's study room.

The atmosphere inside was warm and welcoming, as always. A different man stood at the front, his face lighting up when he saw Henry enter.

"Welcome, brother," he said, reaching out his hand to shake Henry's. "I'm Alon. I pastor the church that most of these guys attend. I usually give a message here on Fridays. I'm glad you're here."

Henry nodded, managing a small smile as he took his seat. As the other men filed in, he couldn't help but notice their curious glances. Had word of his emotional breakdown on the beach spread? He pushed the thought aside, focusing instead on Pastor Alon as he began to speak.

"Forgiveness." Pastor Alon began, his voice filled with passion, "My message this morning is on forgiveness."

Henry felt a lump forming in his throat as he thought of Emily, of the years he'd spent consumed by anger and the desire for vengeance. He also thought of Lily, of her unwavering love and forgiveness despite his mistakes. Something inside of him began to squirm at that word, "forgiveness."

Pastor Alon began preaching from Matthew 18. He told the story of the master who had forgiven his slave a great debt, but when that slave refused to forgive others, the master handed him over to the torturers for punishment. Then the pastor read verse 35 - "My heavenly Father will also do the same to you, if each of you does not forgive his brother from your heart."

Upon hearing these words, Henry's life began flashing before his eyes. The whirlwind of guilt and conviction that was raging in his soul became uncontainable. Suddenly, he stood up, his chair scraping loudly against the floor.

"I... I need help," he said, his voice shaking. "I need Jesus right now."

Pastor Alon nodded encouragingly, gesturing for Henry to come to the front, but while it looked like Henry was trying to step forward, he seemed frozen in place. His fists clenched and his jaw tightened.

"I want to let it go but I'm so angry!" Henry said as his arms and torso began to vibrate. He felt himself unable to say anything else. His heart beat fast and the room became a blur. In a desperate attempt to save his own life, though unable to speak, Henry silently called to Jesus for help, begging Him for salvation. Suddenly, he heard Pastor Alon's authoritative voice cut through his darkness and fear. "Devil! Let him go!"

Henry immediately felt an infusion of divine power, as all of the rage he had felt for years seemed to have leapt out of his body in an instant. In a matter of seconds, his heart steadied and his senses returned to him, followed by a deep sigh that brought the most liberating feeling he had ever experienced. In that moment, Jesus had become real to him, not just as a message, but as his personal deliverer. He looked around the room at the praying men for a moment or two, and then fell to his knees and wept, crying out to God in praise, thanking Him for saving his life.

The men gathered around Henry, laying hands on him as Pastor Alon led them in prayer. After a few minutes, Henry began to compose himself and rose to his feet, receiving hugs and welcomes to the family of God from the men around him.

Lola's father broke through the group to embrace Henry with tears in his eyes. "Well, my friend. I'd ask if you'd like to accept Jesus, but something tells me we're past all that!"

"There's no doubt about it," Henry said, with the most joyful smile he had ever smiled. "I couldn't tell you what happened, but I know that Jesus saved me!"

Upon this confession, Pastor Alon shouted, "Let the angels rejoice! Hallelujah!!!"

The other 30 or so men began echoing his praise, cheering and applauding what God had done in their midst.

The commotion reached to the outdoor area where the women were fellowshipping. They all looked over to try and ascertain what was happening, some rising from their chairs as they mumbled to each other what could be going on. Right then, one of the young men ran outside, waving his hands. "The American!" he shouted, and then he looked at Lily, "Your husband! He's been delivered! He's given his life to Christ! Come and see!"

Lily gasped, her hand flying to her mouth as the other women followed with gasps of their own, excitedly murmuring to each other about the news. Lily ran inside to find Henry, surrounded by praying and celebrating men, his face tear-stained but radiating a peace and a joy she'd never seen before. As tears broke through her own eyes, she pushed through the circle of men to throw her arms around Henry.

"Oh, Henry," she sobbed, her tears soaking into his shirt. "Oh, thank God. Thank you Jesus!"

Henry held her tightly, his own tears flowing freely. "I'm sorry," he murmured into her hair. "I'm sorry it took me so long to get here. But I promise you, Lily, from now on, I'm going to do things right. I'm going to be the man you deserve."

They stood there, locked in their embrace, as the men around them offered more words of congratulation and welcome. Henry felt as if he was seeing the world through new eyes, everything sharper, brighter, more vivid than before.

As the excitement began to die down, Henry became aware of a figure approaching from the side. He turned, still holding Lily, to see Lola standing there, an excited yet hesitant smile on her face.

"I hope I'm not interrupting," she said softly. "I just... I wanted to officially introduce myself to your wife."

Henry felt Lily stiffen slightly in his arms, but to his surprise, she pulled away from him with a warm smile.

"Lola," Lily said, her voice kind and broken amidst catching her breath after crying. "It's nice to officially meet you."

Lola's smile widened, relief evident in her eyes. "I'm so happy for you both," she said sincerely. "What happened today... it's beautiful."

Henry watched in amazement as Lily reached out to take Lola's hand, squeezing it gently. The joy of the moment seemed to have temporarily eclipsed the complicated emotions surrounding their situation.

After exchanging a few more words with Lily, Lola's eyes twinkled with charm as she turned to Henry. "Well," she said, her tone lighthearted, "looks like I'll only be single for 26 more days..."

With that, she turned and walked away, leaving Henry and Lily standing there, slightly stunned. As the reality of Lola's words sank in, Henry felt a familiar knot of uncertainty forming in his stomach. He looked at Lily, searching her face for any sign of distress, but to his surprise, Lily was still smiling, though her eyes held a hint of that very same uncertainty.

Later that night, back at their hotel, Henry and Lily reviewed the joy of the day over and over, thanking God together for everything He had done for them, and while they were still uncertain on how to move forward with regard to their family, they decided that they at least needed to spend time with Lola over the next few weeks.

So, the next 25 days were filled with daily bible study, attending Pastor Alon's church on Sundays, and daily outings with Lola, some just between her and Henry, some just between her and Lily, and some comprising all three of them. Both Henry and Lily were growing in their faith by leaps and bounds, more than they ever had back in the States. The people around them offered encouragement and support like no one else they had ever known. Not once did the locals bug Henry about the "deal," giving him all the room he needed to grow in Christ.

He was quickly becoming the man that Lily had been praying he would be. Lily and Lola continued to build a friendship, one that was littered with awkward moments of silence at first, but was steadily developing into a genuine, heart-warming friendship, despite the ten year difference between them. A constant matter of amusement to them was what to do about the fact that their names sounded so similar. It opened the door to a sense of comradery and even sisterhood.

On their 28th night in Manila, Henry and Lily found themselves in their hotel room, needing to make a decision. They had two days left to decide between Lola and jail. And while the past month had been one of extraordinary growth, they still hadn't settled this matter, but it was time to do it now.

Henry was getting dressed for the night and Lily was sitting on the bed.

"Lily," Henry began, his voice barely above a whisper. "I don't know what to do."

Lily patted the space beside her on the bed, inviting him to sit. As he did, she reached out and put his hand in hers, her touch warm and reassuring.

"Henry," she said softly, "these past few weeks have been... transformative. For both of us. I've seen you change, seen you open your heart to God in a way I never thought possible."

Henry nodded, feeling a lump forming in his throat, nervous as to what conflict might arise over the delicate issue of marrying Lola.

"But this decision," Lily continued, her voice steady despite the gravity of the situation, "it's not just about us anymore. It's about Lola—her honor, about the people here, about the promise you made."

Henry closed his eyes, memories of the past month flashing through his mind. The bible studies, the long talks with Pastor Alon and Lola's father, the growing sense of belonging he felt among these people. And

Lola... the guilt of his transgression still stung, but it was tempered now by a genuine care for her well-being.

"I've been praying about this," Lily said, drawing his attention back to her. "Henry. I think you need to honor your commitment."

Henry's eyes widened in surprise. "You mean...?"

Lily nodded, a small smile playing at the corners of her mouth. "Yes. I think you should marry Lola. And not only that, I think we should stay... here. In the Philippines. With this church. I don't think we could ever find a better home."

The words hung in the air between them, heavy with implication. Henry felt a mix of emotions swirling within him—relief, fear, gratitude, and something else he couldn't quite name.

"Are you sure?" he asked, searching Lily's face for any sign of doubt. "This is... it's a huge change. For both of us."

Lily's smile widened, her eyes shining with hope for the future and gratitude for her husband's salvation. "I'm sure, Henry. In fact, I don't think I've ever been more sure of anything in my life. I believe this is where God wants us to be. This is where we've been growing, so why would we want to leave? It seems like all the most important things in life are right here."

Henry pulled Lily into a tight embrace, burying his face in her hair. He felt overwhelmed by her strength, her faith, her unwavering love. As they held each other, the city sounds faded away, leaving only the sound of their synchronized heartbeats.

When they finally pulled apart, Henry felt a sense of clarity he hadn't experienced in years. "Okay," he said, his voice firm. "Let's do this. Let's make Manila our home."

The morning was beautiful, as if the weather itself was celebrating their decision. Henry and Lily made their way to the bible study, hand in hand, their steps light despite the magnitude of what they were about to share.

As they entered the familiar yellow building, they were greeted by warm smiles and enthusiastic welcomes. Pastor Alon approached them, his face lighting up at their presence.

"Henry, Lily," he said warmly, "it's good to see you both. You look... different today. Like everything's right with the world."

Henry exchanged a glance with Lily before turning back to Pastor Alon. "We have some news," he said, his voice steady. "Is everyone here?"

Pastor Alon nodded, his expression curious. "Yes, we were just about to start our morning prayers. Would you like to share with the group?"

Henry took a deep breath, feeling Lily's reassuring squeeze on his hand. "Yes," he replied. "Yes, we would."

As the group gathered, both the men and the women, Henry felt a mix of nervousness and excitement bubbling up inside him. He looked out at the sea of faces—faces that had become familiar and dear to him over the past month. His eyes landed on Lola, sitting with her parents, her expression one of hope and apprehension.

"Brothers and sisters," Henry began, his voice carrying across the hushed room. "As you all know, I began coming here under less-than-ideal circumstances, but as you also know, the last few weeks have been truly life-changing for us. And now, Lily and I have made a decision. A decision to follow what we believe is God's will for our lives."

He paused, looking at Lily, who nodded encouragingly. As Lola's father put his hand on his wife's, his eyes widening with hope, Henry continued. "We've decided to honor my commitment. I will take Lola as my wife."

Lola's father breathed a huge sigh of relief and gestured to Henry in appreciation for his integrity as the rest of the room nodded and said "Amen" in agreement with Henry's decision.

"But more than that," Henry continued further, "we've decided to make this our home." After pausing for a moment and seeing the slight confusion on some people's faces, Lily blurted out in excitement, "We're moving to Manila!"

The news brought a rush of joy among their new family. Everyone cheered and got up to embrace them and welcome them to the Philippines for good.

When everyone got back in their seats, Lily stepped in front to share something with the group. "We've found something here that we never knew we were missing. A sense of family, of true faith. We don't want to lose that. We want to be part of it, to contribute to it, and to grow with all of you."

Pastor Alon and Lola's father moved to the front, their eyes beaming with joy. "Henry, Lily," Pastor Alon said, his voice thick with emotion. "This... this is a blessing beyond words. We welcome you with open arms and with all our hearts."

What followed was another round of hugs, tears, and heartfelt congratulations. Henry found himself enveloped in the warmth of the community, feeling a sense of belonging he'd never experienced before.

As the excitement began to die down, Lola approached, her steps hesitant. "Henry, Lily," she said softly. "I... I don't know what to say. Are you sure about this?"

Lily reached out, taking Lola's hands in hers. "We are," she said, her voice gentle but firm. "We're choosing this, Lola. We're choosing to build a life here, with this community. With you."

Lola's eyes filled with tears as she looked between Henry and Lily. "I promise," she said, her voice cracking, "I promise to be a good wife, a good sister. I'll do everything I can to make this work."

Henry suddenly felt a surge of affection for this young woman, who had finally become so much more than just a reminder of his mistake. "We know you will," he said softly. "And we can't wait."

As the news spread, the church erupted into activity. Plans for a celebration dinner were quickly put into motion, with everyone eager to contribute. Henry watched in amazement as the community came together, each person offering what they could—food, decorations, music.

As evening fell, the outdoor area behind the church was transformed. Tables groaned under the weight of a feast, the air filled with the tantalizing aroma of Filipino dishes. Fairy lights twinkled overhead, casting a warm glow over the gathering.

Henry stood to the side, taking in the scene before him. Lily was deep in conversation with some of the women, her face animated as they discussed plans for the upcoming wedding. Lola moved among the guests, her shy smile growing more confident with each interaction.

Pastor Alon approached, clapping a hand on Henry's shoulder. "How are you feeling, my friend?" he asked, his voice warm with anticipation.

Henry took a moment to consider the question. "Overwhelmed," he admitted. "But in the best possible way. It's like... like I'm finally waking up after a long sleep."

Pastor Alon nodded, his eyes twinkling. "That's the Holy Spirit at work, Henry. Embrace it. Let Him guide you."

As the evening wore on, Henry found himself marveling at the easy camaraderie and the genuine joy that filled the outdoor space. This was so different from the life he'd known back home, where relationships were often superficial, where true community was hard to come by.

Finally, as the meal was winding down, Lily stood, tapping her glass with a spoon. The group fell silent, all eyes turning to her.

"I'd like to propose a toast," she said proudly. She looked around the patio, her gaze lingering on Henry and Lola before sweeping across the gathered faces.

"To new beginnings," Lily continued, raising her glass. "To faith that moves mountains and love that knows no bounds. To this beautiful family that has welcomed us with open arms. And to the journey ahead—may it be filled with love, laughter, and enduring blessings."

A chorus of agreement filled the night air as glasses clinked together. Henry's eyes swept across the scene, taking in the twinkling fairy lights strung between trees and the faces of people who had, in such a short time, become like family. He watched as Lily chatted animatedly with a group of women, her face alight with happiness. Lola moved gracefully between tables, offering food and ensuring everyone was comfortable. The sight of them, so at ease in this new world they were embracing, filled Henry with a warmth he couldn't quite describe. As he took a sip of his punch, he found his mind wandering to the journey that had brought him here. The anger that had fueled him for so long seemed like a distant memory now, replaced by a peace he'd never thought possible. He closed his eyes for a moment, savoring the feeling.

When he opened them again, something caught his attention. A man, clearly not from the local community, had entered the beachfront area where they were celebrating. He was Caucasian, perhaps in his late forties, with graying hair and a nervous demeanor. Henry watched as the man's eyes darted around the gathering, seemingly searching for someone.

Suddenly, the stranger's voice cut through the chatter. "Excuse me," he called out, his American accent obvious. "I'm looking for the American officer. Is he here?"

The onlookers fell silent, all eyes turning to the newcomer. Henry felt a chill run down his spine, a long-forgotten tension seeping into his muscles as he faced the man who had spoken.

Their eyes met, and in that instant, Henry felt the world tilt on its axis. Recognition slammed into him like a physical blow. This was the man. The killer. The one who had taken Emily from him.

Henry's hand tightened around his glass, his knuckles turning white. He was vaguely aware of Lily moving to his side, her hand coming to rest on his arm. But he couldn't tear his gaze away from the man who had haunted his dreams for so long.

"It's you," Henry said, his voice low and intimidating.

The stranger nodded, his face a mask of regret and fear. "Yes," he replied, his voice shaking. "My name is Michael. And I... I'm the one who killed your sister."

A collective gasp went through the crowd. Henry felt rooted to the spot, a maelstrom of emotions churning within him. The anger he thought he'd left behind threatened to resurface, battling with the freedom he'd embraced.

Michael took a hesitant step forward, his hands raised in a placating gesture. "Please," he said, his voice thick with emotion. "I know I have no right to ask this, but... I need to explain."

Henry felt Lily's grip on his arm tighten. He glanced at her, seeing the concern in her eyes. Taking a deep breath, he nodded. "Go on," he said, surprised by his own restraint.

Michael swallowed hard, his eyes never leaving Henry's face. "After... after what happened with your sister, I was consumed by guilt. I couldn't eat, I couldn't sleep. And then, in my darkest moment, I found Jesus. Or, perhaps, He found me."

Henry's eyes widened, his heart pounding in his chest. He was aware of the entire gathering holding its breath, waiting to see how this unexpected confrontation would unfold.

"I wanted to turn myself in," Michael continued, his voice gaining strength. "To face the consequences of what I'd done. But I was a coward. I was afraid... afraid you'd kill me if you found me. So I ran. I came here, thinking I could escape my past."

Michael's eyes filled with tears as he spoke. "But I couldn't escape the guilt. It followed me everywhere. And then, a few days ago, I heard about an American officer who was after me, and how he got saved here. I knew it had to be you."

Henry felt his tension ease. The anger he'd expected to feel was there, but it was muted, overshadowed by something else. Something he couldn't quite name.

"I'm not asking for forgiveness," Michael continued, his voice breaking. "I know I don't deserve it. But I needed you to know how sorry I am. How much I regret what I did. And I needed to face you, to accept whatever judgment you see fit."

The beachfront was silent, the tension palpable. Henry could feel all eyes on him, waiting to see how he would respond. He closed his eyes, taking a deep breath. In that moment, he felt the weight of his journey pressing down on him—the years of anger, the recent weeks of transformation, the love and support of his new church family. When he opened his eyes, Henry was surprised to feel tears streaming down his face. He took a step forward, closing the distance between himself and Michael.

"For years," Henry began, his voice low but clear, "I dreamed of this moment. Of finding you, of making you pay for what you did." He paused, aware of the collective intake of breath from those around him. "But now... now I realize that the person I wanted to punish doesn't exist anymore. Just like the man I was doesn't exist anymore either."

Michael's eyes widened, a glimmer of hope breaking through his fear. Henry continued, each word feeling like it was being pulled from the depths of his soul.

"What you did... it can't be undone. Emily is gone, and that pain will always be a part of me." Henry's voice cracked, but he pressed on. "But holding onto that anger, that need for vengeance... it was destroying me. And I can't... I won't let it control me anymore."

Henry took another deep breath, suddenly feeling the presence of God in a way he'd never felt before. "Michael," he said, his voice steady now. "Jesus forgave me. So I forgive you."

Upon hearing those words, Michael's legs seemed to give out, and he sank to his knees, sobbing. Without hesitation, Henry knelt in front of him, embracing him on the ground.

Around them, the gathered community began to murmur prayers, their voices rising in a soft chorus of support and praise. Lily and Lola moved to Henry's side, their presence a silent affirmation of his decision.

As Michael's sobs subsided, he looked up at Henry, his eyes filled with gratitude and disbelief. "I... I don't know what to say," he whispered. "Thank you doesn't seem like it's enough."

Henry helped Michael to his feet, feeling a lightness in his heart that only Jesus could make possible. "It's enough," he said softly. "We're brothers in Christ now. That's what matters."

Michael nodded, wiping his eyes. "I'm leaving the Philippines," he said, his voice steadier now. "Going back to face whatever consequences await me in the States. But before I go, I want to do something to help you start your new life here."

He reached into his pocket, pulling out a set of keys and some papers. "My house here and my car... they're yours now. I've already arranged for the transfer. And when I get back to the States, I'll pack up your old house and ship your belongings here. It's the least I can do."

Henry felt overwhelmed by the gesture, but before he could respond, Pastor Alon stepped forward. "Michael," he said, his voice warm and welcoming. "Why don't you join us for dinner? Share in our celebration before you go?"

Michael looked around, seemingly surprised by the invitation. But as he met the kind gazes of those gathered, he nodded, a small smile forming on his lips. "I'd be honored," he said softly.

As the group moved back to the tables, the atmosphere on the beach shifted. What had begun as a celebration of new beginnings had transformed into something even more profound—a testament to the power of forgiveness.

Henry found himself seated between Lily and Michael, with Lola across from them. As plates were filled and conversations resumed, he felt a sense of completion he'd never known before. The journey that had brought him here, with all its twists and turns, suddenly made sense. Henry observed the interactions around him with a new perspective. He watched as Michael was welcomed into the community, albeit tentatively at first. He saw the way Lily and Lola worked together, their initial awkwardness giving way to a meaningful friendship. And he felt, deep in his soul, that this was exactly where he was meant to be.

Later, as the stars began to twinkle overhead and the party wound down, Henry found a quiet moment alone. He looked up at the night sky, thinking of Emily. For the first time in years, the memory of her brought a smile to his face rather than a stab of pain.

"I hope you can see this, sis," he whispered to the stars. "I hope you know that I'm okay now. That Jesus really healed me."

A warm breeze rustled through the beachfront, carrying with it the scent of jasmine. Henry closed his eyes, and when he opened them, he caught sight of Lily and Lola, their heads bent together in conversation. The sight filled him with a mix of emotions—love, gratitude, and a touch of apprehension about the path they were taking, but as they looked up and smiled at him, Henry felt any doubts melt away.

This was his family now. Unorthodox, unexpected, but bound together by something stronger than blood—faith, hope, and love.

The next morning, Lily and Henry waited for Lola to arrive at the beachfront café as Lily's fingers tapped nervously on the worn wooden table, her eyes scanning the growing crowd of tourists and locals. Even in the midst of their growing friendship with Lola, something about this pre-wedding breakfast tempted old nervousness to resurface.

"Relax," Henry said softly, reaching across to still Lily's hand. "Everything's going to be fine."

Lily took a deep breath, inhaling the salty air mixed with the smell of freshly brewed coffee. "I know. It's just... this is all so surreal. A month ago, I never would have imagined..."

Her words trailed off as she spotted Lola approaching. The young woman moved gracefully through the throng of people, her long dark hair swaying gently in the ocean breeze. Lily felt a flutter in her stomach—a mix of nervousness and an unexpected warmth.

"Good morning," Lola said softly as she reached their table, her shy smile revealing a dimple in her left cheek.

Henry stood up, pulling out a chair for her. "Good morning, Lola. We're glad you could join us."

As Lola settled into her seat, Lily found herself studying the younger woman's face. There was an innocence there, but also a quiet strength that Lily admired. She realized with a start how much she genuinely liked Lola—not just out of obligation or acceptance of their unusual situation, but as a person.

A waiter appeared, handing them menus and pouring water into their glasses. "What would you recommend?" Lola asked, her eyes wide as she scanned the menu. "I've never been here before."

"The mango pancakes are delicious," Lily offered. "Light and fluffy, with just the right amount of sweetness."

Lola's face lit up. "That sounds perfect. I love mangoes."

As they placed their orders, the initial awkwardness began to dissolve. Henry regaled them with stories of his early days on the police force, his animated gestures drawing laughs from both women. Lily found herself relaxing, swept up in the easy friendship that was continuing to develop.

As they continued to talk, sharing stories and laughter over their meal, Lily felt a warmth spreading through her chest. She watched as Henry and Lola engaged in a playful debate about the best way to eat a mango, and she marveled at how natural it all felt.

Lola spoke of her desire to become a teacher, her eyes shining as she described her volunteer work at the local school. Henry shared his newly discovered passion for community outreach, inspired by the church group that had brought them all together. Lily spoke of her love for children and her hope that the three of them would raise their children together.

As their plates were cleared away, Lily found herself reluctant for the meal to end. She realized that she had genuinely enjoyed every moment of it.

"Lola," she said, reaching out to touch her hand, "would you like to come shopping with me today? We still need to find you a dress for tomorrow."

Lola's face lit up with joy and surprise. "Really? You'd do that for me?"

"Of course!" Lily said exuberantly, squeezing her hand. "Every bride deserves to feel special on her wedding day."

As they stood to leave, Lily caught Henry watching her with a mix of love and gratitude in his eyes. She leaned in, kissing him softly on the cheek.

"I'll see you later," she murmured. "Take care of any last-minute details for tomorrow, okay?"

Henry nodded, his hand lingering on the small of her back. "I love you," he said softly. "Both of you," he added, including Lola in his gaze.

As Lily and Lola walked away from the café, arm in arm, Lily felt a sense of peace settle over her. This wasn't the life she had imagined for herself, but somehow, in this moment, it felt absolutely right.

In the marketplace, Lily and Lola weaved their way through the crowds, the younger woman's eyes wide with excitement.

"I've never been to this part of the market before," Lola admitted, her gaze darting from one stall to the next. "It's usually for tourists."

Lily smiled, gently steering them towards a row of clothing shops. "Well, today we're on a mission and I don't know where else to shop, so let's find you the perfect dress!"

As they entered the first shop, a cool blast of air conditioning welcomed them. Racks of dresses in every color imaginable lined the walls, and Lily watched as Lola ran her fingers reverently over the soft fabrics.

"See anything you like?" Lily asked, noting the way Lola's eyes lingered on a rack of white sundresses.

Lola bit her lip, hesitating. "They're all so beautiful."

"Oh, this one's lovely," Lily said, pulling out a flowing white dress with delicate lace sleeves. "Why don't you try it on?"

Lola disappeared into the changing room, and Lily found herself pacing nervously. When Lola emerged, Lily's breath caught in her throat. The dress fit perfectly, accentuating Lola's slender frame and giving her an ethereal glow.

"You look beautiful," Lily said softly, blinking back unexpected tears.

Lola twirled in front of the mirror, a radiant smile lighting up her face. "I feel like a princess," she admitted with a laugh.

"Then it sounds like it's time for shoes!" Lily said while she put up her hand for a high-five.

"Oh," Lola responded as she whacked Lily's hand with spunky attitude. "It is *definitely* time for shoes."

When they concluded their shopping with lunch at a local restaurant, Lola broke a moment of silence with a very sincere thought. "I never had a sister," she said softly. "But I think... I think this must be what it feels like."

Lily felt her heart swell with emotion. "Neither have I, but I do now."

Lola let out a couple of tears, overwhelmed at the kindness Lily was showing her.

The next day, the beach was bathed in the warm glow of the setting sun as guests began to gather for the ceremony. Lily stood in front of the mirror in the small beach-side cabana, making last-minute adjustments to her hair. She wore a simple, coral sundress, with a flower tucked behind her ear.

A soft knock at the door drew her attention. "Come in," she called, expecting to see Henry or perhaps one of the other guests.

Instead, Lola stepped into the room, resplendent in her white dress.

"Oh, Lola," Lily breathed, crossing the room to take her hands. "You look absolutely stunning."

With an excited hug, they encouraged each other for the big event.

As they stepped out onto the beach, Lily was struck by the beauty of the scene before her. Tiki torches lined a makeshift aisle in the sand, their flames flickering in the gentle breeze. At the end of the aisle stood Henry, looking handsome in a light linen suit, his face a picture of love and anticipation.

The small gathering of friends and church family turned to watch as Lily and Lola made their way down the aisle. Lily could feel Lola trembling slightly beside her, and she gave her arm a reassuring squeeze.

As they reached Henry, Lily sat down as Lola's father took his place to give away the bride. She caught Henry's eye and gave him a smile that melted away any fears he had left.

The ceremony was simple yet profound. When it came time for the kiss, Lily held her breath for a moment. But as Henry leaned in to gently kiss his new bride, Lily found herself cheering along with everyone else. As the small crowd erupted in applause and congratulations, Lily made her way to the newly married couple. She embraced them both, congratulating them and welcoming Lola to the family.

"I'm so proud of you," she said to Henry lovingly, cupping his face in her hands. "I'm so proud of the man you've become."

Henry pulled both women into a group hug, his voice thick with emotion as he spoke. "I never thought I could be this happy, this blessed. Thank you both for giving me this chance."

As the celebration continued around them, with music playing and people dancing on the beach, the three of them stood together, watching the sun dip below the horizon, each of them basking in the glow of the possibilities to come with their new life together.

And hope does not disappoint, because the love of God has been poured out within our hearts through the Holy Spirit who was given to us.

Romans 5:5

Story 4 - Called By Your Name

Setting – India, 2050

This story is written in a somewhat "Bollywood" form—some over-dramatization, occasional forced comedy, and a seemingly less realistic premise. Like most Bollywood tales, if you try to take it too seriously, you'll be disappointed. Just let yourself have a good time. The dialogue was crafted with Indian accents and their manners of English speech in mind, and is meant to be read accordingly.

Aneeth refilled his glass with whiskey as he rested his back in his chair, swirling it around. He was present in a rooftop bar filled with people drinking, smoking, and dancing around him. However, his attention was only fixed on the woman sitting across from him. She looked stunning. Her dark hair, being slightly burgundy, fell over her shoulders, and her deep brown eyes were completely focused on his.

The girl took a sip of her drink while she kept her eyes on him. "So, what are your thoughts about the war?" she asked, leaning onto the table a little bit. "Things seem to be getting worse, with the fighting making its way through Pakistan. I heard on the news that some border towns are already feeling the impact. It's intense, right?"

Aneeth gave her a smirk, not really interested in serious topics. He kept his glass on the table and said, "Oh, come on... that's all happening far away," waving it off casually. "We don't have to be worried about something so far away from us."

The girl raised an eyebrow in response. "Really? It's not *that* far anymore. I have family in Lahore who are worried it might spread over the border. There's been talk of refugees crossing into Pakistan now. We might feel the effects sooner than you think."

Hmm... she's pretty, but talking about the war? Aneeth thought to himself. *Why does she want to ruin the mood?*

He closed his eyes for a brief moment before opening them again. He tilted his head, flashing his usual smile. "You know, I'd rather focus on the real important things... like how amazing you look tonight."

Her smile widened, but she wasn't letting go of the topic yet. "Aren't you scared that things might get worse? I mean, the news is full of it."

Aneeth took another sip of his drink, his eyes never leaving hers. "Look, I'm not scared of some war going on in another country. We're in Delhi, living it up... Why let it bring us down?"

She should be more worried about me losing interest than anything else. She's too pretty to be talking about this stuff.

He gave her another playful grin, tilting his head slightly. "The only thing I'm scared of is letting this night end without getting to know you better."

She laughed softly, finally warming up to his charm. "You really don't care, do you?"

Aneeth raised his eyebrows and shrugged, leaning back in his chair. "Life is too short to be worried about something you can't control. And me? I'd rather focus on something that's right in front of me. Like you."

He let his eyes wander, slowly taking in the woman in front of him. Her dress hugged her body just right, showing off curves that made him forget about anything serious she might have been saying.

Aneeth had never been one to settle down. He was constantly surrounded by beautiful women, always dating someone new, but never for long. His relationships were fleeting, casual affairs—just enough to keep things interesting without getting too serious. He preferred it that way, free from the complications of commitment. Love, in his eyes, was just another distraction.

He once again checked her out before closing his eyes and biting his lips. *Man... she's gorgeous,* he thought with a smile.

She gave him a sharp look and crossed her legs. He couldn't help but look down for a second. *Perfect.* His mind was already drifting to how the night could end. But first, he had to keep her engaged.

He gave her a slight grin and leaned forward. His voice got deep, just enough to sound more intimate. "You know. I was thinking that you're way too gorgeous to get stressed about the world falling apart. Why don't we just leave everything and enjoy the night? And who knows what it could turn into..."

She giggled as she glanced away for a moment while shaking her head. "You're really not interested, are you?" She teased him and playfully raised her eyes, a hint of curiosity in her voice.

Aneeth grinned. *Got her.* He raised his head and shook it while lowering his voice again. He looked like he was about to share a secret. "I'm only interested in one thing..." he paused, letting the suspense build before giving her a smile. "Finding a reason to spend more time with you."

She laughed, clearly enjoying the attention, but her expression softened after a moment. "But seriously, Aneeth. With everything happening in the world... don't you ever think about it? I mean, things could change overnight, right?"

He looked at her for a second, surprised she was still stuck on the topic. *Come on... I'm trying to make this fun.*

He gave a small sigh but softened it with a smile. He hummed and said, "You're right. Things are a mess right now." He huffed and leaned back, his hands resting on the back of his chair. "People are fighting, the economy's crashing, and sometimes... yeah, it feels like everything's falling apart." His eyes flicked over her once more. *But not tonight, not here.*

He stood up from his seat and went to sit beside her. "I think the closer we sit, the less we get distracted." Then, he reached out, gently removing a strand of hair from her face and tucking it at the back of her ear. "But you know what?" His voice dropped to almost a whisper as he moved his face closer to her ear. "None of that matters right now. Because you're here, and that's the only thing worth focusing on." He said and moved back to see her reaction.

Her eyes widened slightly at his touch, then she smiled, clearly taken by the moment. But there was still concern in her eyes. "It's just... things are getting worse everywhere. My brother's stuck abroad because of the war. I'm scared it's going to reach us, and we'll be dragged into it too."

Aneeth paused for a second, watching the real worry cross her face. *Okay, maybe I've gotta take this seriously...* He gave her a warm smile and moved in a little closer, gently putting his hand on hers, his tone softening.

"Hey... I understand how difficult things are right now. But don't worry about that," he said, looking straight into her eyes. "Things might be tough, but I promise... we're safe. You're safe with me..." Aneeth gave her a smile and squeezed her hand to reassure her. "And besides, if things ever did get messy... I'd have a plan."

She looked at him, a little relieved but still unsure. "You think so?"

Aneeth smiled, that charming grin sliding back onto his face. "Absolutely."

Then he looked at her with a playful look in his eyes. "You know what... What if I take you somewhere to get your mind off of it?" He winked. "You wanna see my mansion?"

She laughed, her earlier worry melting away as she shook her head. "Hmm. That's your solution to everything?"

He leaned back in his chair, shrugging with a grin. "Hey, it's not just a mansion... it's an experience." He gave her a playful look. "And trust me when I say this. You'll forget all about wars and politics once you see the view from my bedroom."

She chuckled and rolled her eyes at his statement, but her smile said she was very much interested in knowing. "You're impossible," she said, laughing. "But, let's go. I will explore this mansion of yours."

Aneeth guided her toward the valet, keeping things light and playful as they made their way through the busy street. When they reached the stand, he gave the valet a quick nod. She was standing beside him, looking around, waiting for his car.

"So, which one is yours?" She asked while raising her eyebrows.

Aneeth smirked, feeling a rush of excitement. "You'll find out soon enough."

A loud roar of an engine suddenly broke through their conversation. The valet pulled up in Aneeth's sleek, black Lamborghini. The car was shining under the streetlights. Its low, sharp lines looked like something out of a dream. Her eyes widened the second she saw it.

"Whoa," she whispered, clearly impressed. "That's yours?"

Aneeth bowed to her with a grin and opened the passenger door for her. "Yeah, I told you, right? You will have a wild ride."

She chuckled at his choice of words and sat down in the car. Eagerly, Aneeth went to the driver's seat, slipped inside, and started the ride to his mansion.

When he pulled away from the club, he glanced over at her, watching as she ran her hand along the dashboard, taking it all in. "Not bad, right?" he asked. His voice was casual, but he already knew what the answer would be.

"Not bad?" she repeated while still trying to register what was happening. "This is crazy! I have never stepped into a car like this."

Aneeth's smile grew wider as he sped off to join the rest of the traffic. He playfully glanced at his date, pressing the gas a little harder as they zipped through the city streets, the lights of Delhi flashing by in a blur.

She hummed and leaned back in her seat, clearly enjoying the speed and the smoothness of the ride. "Where are we headed?" she asked, glancing over at him with a curious smile.

"My place is on the other side of town," he said simply. "Don't worry. You'll love it."

They went through the city, eventually leaving the crowded streets behind. Soon, they were driving through a quieter, upscale neighborhood. Large houses with gated driveways appeared on either side of the road, but none of them compared to what was waiting for her.

When they finally pulled up to Aneeth's mansion, she gasped. The massive house stood tall, glowing by soft lights along the driveway, highlighting the modern design. The entrance was grand, with wide steps leading up to double doors framed by tall windows.

She stepped out of the car and let out a little "Wow" while taking in what she was seeing. "This is amazing!"

Aneeth smiled, walking up beside her. "Told you. Ready to see inside?"

She gave him a sweet smile and nodded, following him up the steps as he opened the door to his luxurious home, revealing the stunning interior.

They stepped inside his mansion, and the moment she entered, her eyes went wide. The interior was just as impressive as the outside—marble floors, high ceilings, and glass walls that gave a perfect view of the city skyline. The soft glow of designer lights lit up the place in a warm, welcoming way. Not to mention, it was spotless.

"Whoa," she whispered as she went further in. "This is something else... You really live here?"

Aneeth smiled as he shut the door and turned towards her. "Yup. Every day. Do you like it?"

"Like it? I'm in love with it," she said, her eyes still looking around the mansion, capturing all it had. She was impressed to see the thick leather furniture, the art pieces mounted on the walls, and a large TV hanging above a fireplace. "What do you do for a living? I mean... how do you afford it all?"

Aneeth chuckled, watching her take it all in. "I work in tech. You know, apps, software... that kind of stuff."

"Must be some serious apps," she said, shaking her head, still amazed.

Before Aneeth could reply, his phone buzzed in his pocket. He pulled it out and saw the name flashing on the screen. *John*. His friend and co-worker. He quickly took a look at her and turned back to his phone. He didn't want to be rude to her but he knew that if John was calling him, it must be something important.

"Uh, sorry, I've gotta take this real quick," Aneeth said, stepping to the side but still in view. He answered the call, lowering his voice. "Hey, man, what's up?"

On the other end, John's voice came through way too loud. "Bro, let's meet. It's been too long since we had free time."

"Yeah, sure. I was thinking the same. Let's meet soon." Aneeth replied while looking at his date.

"Wait! Why don't we meet at the church near your house?" John said, then waited for his reaction.

"The church? No way, man. You know that I don't go to those places." Aneeth said while frowning. "Why don't we meet at the restaurant near our office?"

"No, no. Let's meet at the church this Sunday." John said while trying to make him agree.

"Let it be. I don't wanna meet you there. If you want, we can meet somewhere else. But a church? No chance." Aneeth replied while shaking his head.

He was about to hang up when John spoke again. "Bro, you HAVE to come to church this Sunday. There's a new wave of single women. And man, they are *gorgeous!*"

Aneeth's eyes darted to the woman, who was still looking around, thankfully not paying attention to his phone call. He quickly turned his back to her, lowering his voice even more. "Uh... yeah, uh... let's talk in code, man. You know, in case... uh, you know."

John laughed on the other end, clearly not getting it at first. "Code? What, are you a spy now? Anyway, I'm telling you, man, the scenery is looking *real* good this Sunday."

John was a Christian and was constantly trying to get Aneeth to go to church, but was never successful. This was his latest in a long line of creative attempts to get his co-worker to step foot in a place of worship.

Aneeth pinched the bridge of his nose. "Bro, stop talking like that. Uh... the 'flowers' in the 'garden'—how do they look? Yeah, that's what I'm asking. How's the *garden?*"

There was a long pause before John caught on, and then he snorted, trying to hold back his laugh. "Ohhhh, the *garden*. Yeah, bro, the garden is in full bloom! Bright colors, soft petals, and all that. You're gonna love it."

Aneeth stole another glance at the woman, who was admiring one of his paintings. He again turned his back and replied, "Right, right... I'll have to check it out then. But why Sunday? Why not any other day?"

John, still holding back his laughter, replied, "Sunday's when the best 'flowers' are around, bro. Trust me, you don't wanna miss it. Plus, we've got some... uh, *garden keepers* talking about *planting new seeds*. You know, future stuff."

Aneeth tried not to laugh out loud. "Planting seeds, huh? Yeah, sounds... interesting. I'll let you know."

Just then, the woman turned around, looking at him curiously. Aneeth quickly put on his best innocent face, pretending like the conversation was nothing. "Alright, man, I gotta go. Talk later."

John shook his head and chuckled. "Don't forget. Sunday at the garden."

Aneeth hung up and slipped his phone back into his pocket. He turned to her, giving her a sheepish grin. "Sorry about that. Just a friend checking in."

She raised an eyebrow, clearly not buying it. "You and your friend... garden?"

Aneeth laughed nervously. "Yeah, you know... just guy stuff. Gardening. Really into plants these days."

She looked at him with squinted eyes and gave him a smile while teasing him. "Uh-huh. Sure."

Aneeth grinned, walking over to her, trying to steer the conversation back to where it was. "So, I am sure you liked it. Want to come with me and see the balcony? The view from there is killer."

She laughed, shaking her head but clearly charmed by his demeanor. "Lead the way, Mr. Gardener."

As they headed toward the balcony, Aneeth couldn't help but chuckle to himself. *That was close. But at least Sunday should be interesting...*

As they stepped onto the balcony, the girl let out a little gasp, looking up in front of her. The view was definitely mesmerizing. The lights from tall buildings and other mansions shimmered. As it was almost midnight, the streets below were empty and silent. In the distance, the river reflected the glow of streetlights. The dark sky was clear, hundreds of stars visible. A cool breeze brushed Aneeth and the girl making them sigh, feeling calm.

"I must say. This view is amazing." She said while giving him a soft smile. "I'd love to spend more time up here next visit."

After showing her around the mansion, Aneeth and the woman ended up back in the living room. She seemed a little tired, and after a few more minutes of small talk, she stretched her arms and smiled.

"I should probably get going," she said softly, picking up her bag from the couch. "Thanks for tonight, though. Your place is really something."

Aneeth nodded, giving her a polite smile, but his mind was already drifting elsewhere. "Yeah, anytime. Glad you enjoyed it."

She headed towards the door, and as Aneeth opened it for her, she gave him one last glance. "Maybe next time, I'll see it in the morning, too?"

"Definitely," Aneeth replied, his heart beating faster at the thought of her staying the night.

He watched from a living room window as his interested date climbed into her taxi, paying her one last wave.

Once the door clicked shut behind her, Aneeth let out a small sigh and tossed his phone onto the couch. He walked to the balcony, looking out over the city lights. But Aneeth's mind wasn't on the view. It was on what John had said during the call.

Aneeth leaned against the railing, his thoughts making him lost. For a brief moment, the empty mansion reminded him of home, his father's house. He hadn't thought about it in years, but tonight, something about the stillness brought those memories rushing back...

***

A young Aneeth stood in the doorway of his father's study, watching as his father sat at the desk, head down, going through piles of paperwork. The room was dim, lit only by the desk lamp, casting a soft glow over the old wooden desk. His father, a tall, stern-looking man in his early 50s, barely looked up as Aneeth entered.

"Dad," Aneeth said quietly, clutching a cricket bat in one hand. "Can we play for a bit? You said we could go out today."

His father glanced at him briefly, a tired smile on his face. "Not today, beta. I've got too much work to do. Maybe this weekend."

"You always say that!" Aneeth blurted out, his frustration boiling over. "You never have time! You're always working."

His father sighed heavily, pushing the papers aside for a moment. He looked up at Aneeth, his expression softening. "I know, and I'm sorry. But I have to do this... for us. To provide for you, for your future."

Aneeth rolled his eyes, unable to hide the anger in his young voice. "I don't care about the money or the work! I just want you to be around. You're never home!" He stormed out of the room, leaving his father sitting there, looking even more exhausted.

***

Standing on his luxurious balcony, Aneeth felt the same tightness in his chest as he did back then. He hadn't realized how much those words hurt his father at the time or how much he would regret them now.

His father had tried to balance work and family, but Aneeth never saw it that way. He only saw the absence, not the effort. And now, years later, with his father far away, there was no way to make amends. No way to apologize for the coldness that grew between them.

Aneeth reached for the whiskey glass on the table behind him, taking a slow sip. The bitterness of the drink matched the heaviness in his heart. He was the one who pushed his father away. Maybe that's why he never stuck around with anyone for long. Relationships were too complicated, and commitment? That was something his father had tried to give him, but Aneeth had rejected it.

Slowly, his mind wandered from his father back to meeting John in the morning.

"Church...," he muttered to himself, almost laughing. "Me, at a church?"

He had never been the kind of guy to bother with that stuff. The church seemed boring, full of rules, prayers, and old people. But then he remembered what John had said about the "garden" and all the "flowers" waiting for him on Sunday.

"More women, huh?" he said, pacing inside. *John has the best taste.. If he says the women are gorgeous, they must be something.*

Aneeth leaned against his kitchen counter, taking another sip of his whiskey, thinking it over. *The church isn't really my place,* he thought. *But if it's packed with pretty girls... maybe it's worth checking out.* He smiled to himself, the idea slowly taking shape in his head.

"More women," he again said out loud, almost as if testing the thought. And as the words left his mouth, he couldn't help but chuckle. "Ahh... Sunday might not be so bad after all."

He walked over to the couch, plopped down, and stretched out his legs. The idea of sitting through some boring service didn't exactly excite him, but the idea of meeting a whole bunch of women? That was enough to get him thinking.

"Going there is a good idea," Aneeth said with a smirk, already imagining how Sunday would turn out. Maybe John was onto something after all.

Aneeth's car stopped in front of the church. He slid his window down and took a look at the building. He carefully checked it out and looked at the people going inside it. There were a few people purchasing candles and flowers to bring in with them.

He boringly looked at it and thought, *I hope it's worth coming here.* Sighing, he parked his car. Stepping out, he noticed a few people looking at him, obviously because of his Lamborghini. He sighed again and made his way inside the church while fixing the collar of his expensive designer shirt and adjusting his watch.

While walking towards the church, many heads again turned towards him, likely because of his expensive clothing. He went past the people, being charmingly confident about himself. He entered the church, expecting a lively crowd inside. But his expectations were turned upside down when he noticed the gloomy atmosphere in the sanctuary.

The environment was full of sadness, and the usual hum of light chatter was replaced with soft murmurs and serious expressions. Aneeth frowned at the energy in the church. He expected it to be more lively, with several girls surrounding him, but it was the total opposite.

Nevertheless, Aneeth looked around, trying to catch sight of John. He saw him sitting near the front row, looking up at the pastor, and made his way over to him.

John looked up at Aneeth, and they greeted each other with a quick, friendly nod. Aneeth sat down next to him, whispering, "Hey, man." John nodded his head in acknowledgment.

"What's with the mood? I expected the atmosphere to be cheerful. But, man, it's so dull." Aneeth said while looking around the church.

John rolled his eyes and gave him a tight smile. He moved closer to him and whispered, "Yeah, today's a little different. The pastor is talking about the ongoing war. Just listen to it."

Not again! Aneeth thought and sighed while leaning back in the pew. The service then began after a few minutes. The choir started to sing a slow, soothing hymn and Aneeth found himself growing impatient.

He wanted to see the girls John told him about. He looked at the people sitting around him but noticed everyone paying attention to the pastor.

Finally, the typically light-hearted and comical pastor stepped up to the pulpit, his face and tone weighed down in serious consideration. He was a shorter man, stocky, with a thick mustache and wiry glasses. He started to speak softly at first, but his voice carried through the room.

"Brothers and sisters, we have gathered here today with heavy hearts," the pastor began, his tone gloomy. "In the past six months, there have been twenty precious women in our congregation who have been widowed. There have been twenty families that were torn apart by the devastation of war. These people are our friends, families, sisters, our neighbors."

While listening to the pastor's speech, Aneeth shifted uncomfortably in his seat. He wasn't expecting this before coming here. The pastor stopped for a moment, and Aneeth noticed a few women in the congregation dabbing their eyes with tissues.

"We sit here, safe in this church," the pastor continued, "but out there, lives are being shattered. Fathers, sons, husbands... lost in the senseless violence. And it is not just across the world, it is touching us here, in our community. We must pray for them, for their strength, and for peace."

Aneeth, for the first time, thought about the ongoing war. He had never really cared much about it. It always seemed so distant, so irrelevant to his life. But now, sitting among people who had been directly affected, he could feel the weight of their grief.

The pastor sighed, looked in front and continued in a soft voice. "Now, we'll maintain silence for a few moments in remembrance of those who are no longer with us. Let us also mention their families in our prayers, especially the women who are left behind, carrying burdens no one should have to bear."

Aneeth glanced at John, who was sitting with his head bowed. For the first time, Aneeth felt out of place. He had come here expecting something entirely different. He had expected lighthearted conversations, maybe even him flirting around. Instead, he was surrounded by this solemn environment, with people mourning their loss.

After a few moments of silence, the pastor spoke up again, his voice steady but filled with emotion. "There's often a question that goes around in our head. 'What can we do about situations like these?' We may feel powerless, but remember, even in times of despair, we are called to love, to support one another, and to find hope in God's grace."

The pastor stopped, letting the people feel the importance of his words. After a moment, he again continued, his voice firm.

"Brothers and sisters, we are called to do more than just pray. We are called to take action and to care for those who are struggling. These women, who are just like our sisters, have lost their husbands, their providers, and their partners. It is our responsibility, as a community of faith, to make sure they have what they need. Food, shelter, companionship. They should never feel abandoned."

He carefully looked at the women seated in front, the widows who had been forced to bear the unbearable.

"If we take a look at the Scripture, we are reminded of our responsibility. 1 Timothy 5:14 says, 'So I would have younger widows marry, bear children, manage their households, and give the adversary no occasion for slander.'" The pastor finished and looked at the people.

"The Bible encourages the younger widows to remarry, build a new life, and find hope and joy again. But during these hard times, with the uncertainty around us, it is difficult. Because of this, many lives have been lost. And now, looking for someone who can take on the responsibility of a wife, of another household, is becoming harder."

The pastor's voice grew softer but still remained purposeful. "Many men are afraid. Afraid of the weight that comes with taking care of another person in times like these. But fear is not from God. We are called to love and serve, even when it is difficult, even when it costs us something."

Aneeth noticed a few nods in the congregation, some men shifting uncomfortably, likely considering the pastor's words. The widows stared ahead, some with blank expressions, others with eyes that seemed to hold pain and hopelessness.

The pastor raised his hand slightly and placed it on his chest. "Let us keep in mind that these women are not just burdens to be carried. They are blessings, a part of our community who deserve love and respect from us. We must stand by their side as a church family and support them in every way we can."

Aneeth's eyes drifted to the group of women sitting a few rows ahead. He scanned the row, appraising each one from one side to the other. Seven of those women stood out, not just for their elegance, but because they were noticeably young for widows, yet their faces were bathed in sorrow. Despite their heads being bowed in grief, there was no denying their beauty.

Aneeth's lips began to curve. His imagination, as usual, took a wild turn. In his mind, the somber church scene melted away, replaced by the fantasy forming in his head. He leaned back, letting his thoughts take over to the tune of his favorite dance song.

The seven pretty widows were no longer grieving. Instead, they were surrounding him, all in colorful, stunning dresses, dancing across the marble floors of his luxurious home. Smiling at him, their sorrow was long forgotten as they showered him with affection, their movements synchronized to the tune in his head, while Aneeth stood in the center, enjoying their attention like a king.

He imagined them cooking for him and taking care of him and his house, gasping and clutching their breath at his signature charming smile. One of them brought him a glass of champagne while another wrapped a silk scarf playfully around his neck. Dust wands were waved and dishes were seasoned in perfect rhythm with the music.

Slowly but surely, his grin in the dream transitioned to a grin in real life...

John turned to Aneeth and noticed him staring at those women with a goofy smile. He shook Aneeth's hand and whisper-yelled at him. "Bro, what are you doing?" His voice jolted him out of his daydream.

Aneeth blinked, realizing he was still in the church, surrounded by the quiet grief of people mourning real losses. The vision of dancing widows in his mansion vanished in an instant, replaced by the dull feeling inside the church. He shifted nervously, feeling a bit guilty for letting his mind wander so absurdly at a time like this.

John frowned slightly, leaning in. "This is serious, man. You can't just zone out like that. These women... they've lost everything."

Aneeth nodded while John turned to the front again, listening quietly to the pastor. Whereas Aneeth's mind was stuck on one thing—seven attractive widows in the front row. He was unable to take the pastor's words out of his mind, especially the part about younger widows remarrying. The verse had stuck with him like a challenge, a chance to turn his day around.

As he sat through the rest of the service, his thoughts spun wildly. This service wasn't just a coincidence, he thought; it was an opportunity for him.

By the time the service ended and people began filing out, Aneeth had a plan forming in his mind. To him, those widows were ripe for the picking, since their pastor just told them they were supposed to get married. Surely, he could score a date with at least one of them.

Or, what about seven of them? He thought and chuckled. It would be tricky, but he was confident in his charm. After all, he had dated a lot of girls. How hard could it be to impress these widows? And the cherry on top was that the pastor had practically given him the green light. He just needed to make them believe he was a serious Christian.

As the church emptied, Aneeth stood up alongside John, who was still looking at him suspiciously.

"Let's go, man. You looked like you were about to doze off," John said, giving him a nudge.

Aneeth grinned, shaking off John's concern. "Nah, I'm good. Actually, I was thinking... maybe I should start coming to church more often. You know, get into the groove of things."

John raised an eyebrow, clearly not buying it. "You? *Wanting* to come to church? You've got to be kidding me."

But Aneeth wasn't kidding, at least not in the way John thought. He was serious about this new "mission" of his. As they walked out of the church, Aneeth looked at each of the seven women one last time. They were still sitting together, talking amongst themselves.

Perfect, he thought. *Just perfect.*

Before they could leave, the pastor stood at the church entrance, greeting the congregants as they left. Aneeth, seizing the moment, tapped John's arm. "Wait up, I want to meet the pastor."

John gave him a curious look but shrugged. "Alright, go ahead."

Aneeth approached the pastor with a charming smile, extending his hand. "Hello, Pastor. I'm Aneeth. I was really moved by your speech today, especially what you said about younger widows remarrying. It really got me thinking."

The pastor smiled warmly, shaking his hand. "I'm glad to hear that, Aneeth. I'm Pastor Manoj. It's always good when the Word touches someone's heart, especially when it has the power to divert one's attention from a row full of pretty widows..."

John snickered behind Aneeth, fully aware of his pastor's jovial and witty nature. Pastor Manoj, staring at Aneeth, widened his eyes with a smirk.

Aneeth fumbled for words, not realizing the pastor had caught him staring during the service. "I... I just care so much." Aneeth lied with a nervous smile. He then composed himself and more skillfully faked genuine compassion. "Those who have lost people in the war are so dear to my heart. I just want what's best for them."

"Of course you do!" Pastor Manoj exuberantly agreed, his playful sarcasm evident. He then interrupted more stammering words from

Aneeth by putting a hand on his shoulder. "I hope to see you around more often, Aneeth." The pastor said with sincerity.

With a final handshake, Aneeth left the pastor, already imagining his next steps.

Later that evening, back at his mansion, Aneeth stood in front of the bathroom mirror, washing his face as he replayed the scene from the church in his head. He needed a plan. He couldn't just walk into the church next week and ask these women out. That would be too forward and too abrupt. No, he needed to blend in first to be seen as one of them. The Bible verse the pastor had quoted gave him the perfect idea. He decided that he would pretend he was a devoted Christian, a man of faith who cared deeply about their loss, and slowly, he'd work his way into each of their hearts.

Aneeth walked out of the bathroom and sat down at his desk. He opened his laptop and began looking for information related to Christianity. He specifically searched for verses in the Bible that related to widows, love, care, and kindness. He thought he should memorize a few important verses, which he could talk about during the conversations with his targets. That would definitely impress them. *This is going to be easy.* He chuckled to himself.

He laid down on his roomy king bed and sighed. "Ahh! It was a good decision to go to church today." He fell asleep while thinking about his plan.

The next morning, Aneeth woke up feeling even more determined, rushing through his morning stretches to get started with his mission.

Coming out of the shower, he hurriedly grabbed the Bible from his cupboard which he once bought as a decoration. He sat down at his dining table with a cup of coffee in one hand and the Bible in the other, determined to grasp Christianity for his own benefit. He flipped through the pages aimlessly at first. He huffed and muttered, "Alright! Let's see what pearls of wisdom I can find in here."

He consciously flipped through various passages, not really reading the verses. He was just looking for words that stood out. His eyes landed on a verse in Matthew: **"Blessed are the poor in spirit, for theirs is the Kingdom of Heaven."**

Aneeth smirked. "Poor in spirit? Guess that means it's good to be sad all the time. Easy enough." He jotted it down in his notepad.

Step one: Be sadder.

He flipped another page and landed on something about the Ten Commandments. **"Thou shalt not covet thy neighbor's wife,"** he read out aloud. Aneeth scratched his head, his brow furrowing in confusion. "Does that mean I shouldn't… want to date these women? But the pastor practically said they need new husbands!" He shrugged it off. "Nah, that must be about some other kind of neighbor. These widows are fair game."

He continued flipping through the pages until he stopped at a passage in Psalms. **"The Lord is my shepherd; I shall not want."** He paused. "I shall not want?" He repeated and frowned. "What shall I not want? That doesn't make any sense. Why would God not want people to want stuff? How are you supposed to get anything if you don't want it?"

He scribbled down a note, deciding that it probably had something to do with being modest and not showing off his wealth. "Fine," he sighed. "I'll wear less expensive clothes, but the watch stays. I need at least one thing to flex."

Step two: Look poor.

As he flipped through more pages, he found a verse about turning the other cheek. "Ah, yes," he said aloud, nodding in agreement. "This is probably telling me that when one widow rejects me, I should try another. You know, don't take it personally. Just keep going." He marked that passage for the future, feeling quite proud of himself for figuring it out.

Step three: Don't take 'no' for an answer.

Next, he stumbled upon the story of Jonah being swallowed by a whale. He read it with wide eyes. "Man, this guy Jonah had it rough. But hey, at least he got out of the whale eventually. Maybe that's a metaphor? If I get in trouble, I can just charm my way out, like Jonah escaping the whale. No big deal!" He chuckled, writing another step down.

Step four: Use charm to get out of whale-sized problems.

He then reached a passage in 1 Corinthians; **"Love is patient, love is kind."** "Now this," he muttered, "this is gold. The widows would definitely love this stuff. I'll memorize it word for word. It actually sounds kind of romantic... I'll throw it in a conversation when things get serious. They'll be impressed for sure." He practiced saying it out loud in front of the mirror a few times, trying to make his voice sound deeper and more soulful, imagining himself talking to the widows.

After rehearsing for a few minutes, he recalled several 'Christian' words he'd heard that he could use to prove his sincerity. "What are some of them?" He mused. "Oh, right! It goes like 'God bless,' and, uh, 'Amen,' and… something about 'fellowship'?" He wrote down a few keywords, deciding that if he just used them in sentences randomly, it would sound real.

Aneeth spent another hour flipping through the Bible, finding random verses that seemed helpful to make his plan succeed but often completely misinterpreting their meaning. **"Judge not, lest ye be judged,"** caught his eye. "Okay, so this verse basically says that no one can call me out on my plan, or they're the bad guy. Perfect!" He closed the Bible proudly, fully convinced of his ability to make the widows believe he was a devout Christian.

Standing in front of the mirror, he adjusted his more modest shirt, practiced his "devout" facial expression, and held the Bible in his hand for dramatic effect, wanting to portray his habit of carrying it around. "You've got this," he whispered to himself. "Just a few verses, some sad looks, and a little fake modesty. They'll fall for you in no time." Satisfied, Aneeth made his way out the door, heading to the church with confidence.

He headed to the office door on the side of the church, Bible in hand, trying to look as sincere as possible. His plan was simple. He would pretend that he was there to help the widows. However, all he was truly after was their addresses.

He entered the office, being greeted by the smell of old paper and the soft noise of a ceiling fan. Behind the desk sat a middle-aged woman with a kind face. She smiled at him warmly.

"Good morning! How can I help you today?" she asked.

Aneeth smiled charmingly, being careful to keep his voice soft and humble. "Good morning." He began. "Lately, the pastor's words have affected me deeply. I was wondering if I could be of any help. I was hoping to assist the widows in our congregation. You know, bring them food, check on them, and help them buy the necessities."

Her face lit up. "That's wonderful! We always need more volunteers. The widows would appreciate your help. Let me see if I can find a list of addresses for you."

Aneeth's heart raced as she turned to a filing cabinet and started flipping through some papers. Till now, the plan was going smoothly. Soon, he would have exactly what he needed.

"Here you go," she said, handing him a small list with the names and addresses of the widows. "These are the twenty widows that we have in our congregation right now. God bless you, beta."

Aneeth nodded, taking the paper. "Thank you, Madam. It's the least I can do." He gave her one last smile before walking out of the office. He smirked at the list, then tucked it in his pocket. He couldn't help but snicker to himself. This was too easy.

Sitting in his car, he started the engine with a roar. He pulled out the paper for another look and sighed while looking at the names. *Twenty widows. Looking for seven.* He had to figure out which widows were the pretty ones he saw on Sunday. "I'll just cross them off one at a time," he said with a confident smile. "I'll be done by tomorrow."

The first house he visited was a modest one. He parked across the street, watching from behind his sunglasses. The woman who stepped out of the house was older, probably in her fifties. Aneeth scrunched his nose and shook his head.

"Nope, too old," he muttered under his breath, crossing her off the list.

He visited the next house, but it wasn't much better. Another older widow, hair tied back in a messy bun, was pushing a grocery cart up the driveway. Aneeth sighed and struck her name off the list without a second thought.

But then, on the third visit, he saw a younger woman, maybe in her early thirties, stepping out of her front door. Her long, dark hair fell down her back as her skin shone under the sun. She adjusted her purse on her shoulder while walking away from the house. Aneeth's eyes lit up.

"Now we're talking," he whispered, squinting his eyes, trying to get a good look, but the limited visibility his sports car provided made it hard to see from where he was.

He stepped out of the car, carefully placing himself behind bushes so as not to be seen. But while staring at the woman much longer than was necessary to recognize her, he felt something move around his right pocket. He slowly looked down to see a small, furry hand sliding his phone right out of his pocket. He jumped and turned around, only to see a monkey making off with his phone up the tree behind him. The monkey had stopped at a branch too high for Aneeth to reach, joining another as the two animals curiously examined the piece of technology.

Aneeth attempted to talk the monkeys into returning his property, speaking in a high, welcoming tone, but the monkeys, after holding up his phone—as if acknowledging they knew what he wanted—instead threw a stick at him, knocking his designer sunglasses off of his face and onto the ground. The two amused primates laughed as Aneeth picked up his broken glasses.

He looked over the bushes, ensuring he wouldn't be seen by the woman he was scouting, then turned around and began climbing the tree in a huff of frustration. The monkeys moved higher and higher, occasionally stopping to look back and laugh at their pursuer, clearly amused at his efforts to retrieve his phone.

"Give me that," he grunted, swiping up to intimidate the thieves. But the angrier he got, the more the monkeys laughed at his expense.

Finally, halfway up the tree, his hair disheveled and clothes torn from the climb, he remembered he had a treat in his pocket. He reached into his left pocket, drawing the monkeys' curious attention. He pulled out a treat, unwrapped it, and offered it to the monkeys in exchange for his phone. After examining it, the monkey whose hands were free grabbed it and began to eat.

"Can I have my phone now?" Aneeth pleaded in exasperation. Without even looking at him, the monkey holding his phone—rather than handing it to him—threw it to the ground to complete their trade.

When Aneeth descended the tree, he picked up his phone to see the screen cracked. He looked up at the monkeys, who were thoroughly enjoying their treat, and showed them his phone. "Thanks for the trade!" He said sarcastically, shaking his phone at them. But the monkeys just laughed at his continued calamity.

A defeated mess, Aneeth returned to his car to continue spying on the woman across the street. When he spotted her, he realized she was heading in his direction, to the car that was parked right behind his. He pretended to fiddle with his phone as she walked to her car and drove away. He added a checkmark next to her name, making a mental note. *Definitely keep her on the list, but park on the other side of the street next time...*

The next twenty-four hours was more of the same. He parked outside each house, waiting to catch a glimpse of the women inside. Some didn't pass his test as they were too old or too plain, but then there were the others. The ones who made him sit up straighter in his car, the ones who made his heart beat faster. By the end of his little spying mission, Aneeth had recognized and marked down the seven attractive widows he'd seen in church. Each one was stunning in her own way, and he believed that each could be part of his plan.

"Seven's a good number..." he muttered, leaning back in his seat with a satisfied smirk.

As he drove away from the last house, the sun beginning to set behind him, Aneeth couldn't help but chuckle to himself.

"Time to begin the fun..."

He then lifted his phone to examine the screen... "And time to get a new phone as well," he sighed while sourly recalling his encounter with the mischievous monkeys.

The next day, Aneeth arrived at the first widow's house, Anjali, parking his car down the street so as not to cause suspicion. As he approached the tiny house, he saw her baking in the kitchen through the thin curtains of her window. The scent of freshly made bread flowed through the air, getting mixed with the sweet smell of cake or cookies. Her movements were graceful as she was lost in her work, kneading the dough and occasionally checking the oven.

Aneeth saw that she clearly had a love for baking, and this could be his way in. If there was one thing he knew how to do, it was use someone's interests to his advantage. He looked around for an opportunity, his eyes halting when he saw a bakery's delivery truck down the street. A plan suddenly formed in his mind. *Perfect!* He thought. He stared at the truck to assess the scene.

A young man wearing a white cap hopped out to make his delivery, leaving the back of the truck slightly open. Aneeth's pulse quickened. Now was his chance...

He casually walked over to the van, pretending to be deep in his thoughts. He looked around, making sure no one was watching him. When he was confident no one was looking, he hopped inside the truck. Inside was a basket filled with freshly baked bread, still warm and smelling delicious. Without hesitation, he grabbed it, tucking it under his arm as if he owned it. He could almost feel the warmth of the bread through the basket's cloth cover.

His heart raced as he made his way towards Anjali's house with the stolen goods in tow. When he reached the small concrete slab in front of her house, he took a deep breath, adjusted his shirt, and knocked on the door.

The door opened, and there she was. Anjali. Dressed in a simple yet elegant floral dress, her hair loosely tied back, and a faint dusting of flour on her hands. She seemed surprised to see him standing there with a basket of bread, but she greeted him politely.

"Hello," she said, being curious. "Can I help you?"

Aneeth gave her a warm smile, holding up the basket. "Good afternoon! I have a delivery for this address. Some fresh bread, I believe."

Anjali frowned slightly, glancing from the basket to him. "A delivery? I didn't order any bread."

Faking his confusion, Aneeth looked at the basket and then back at her. "Oh? That's strange. I think this was the address I was told. Maybe there has been a mix-up."

He hesitated for a moment, then acted as if he suddenly got an idea. He looked at her with a smile and said, "Well, since I'm here, and this bread is fresh out of the oven, I wouldn't want it to go to waste. Do you enjoy eating bread? I baked these myself."

Her eyes widened in surprise. "You... made these?"

Aneeth nodded confidently, smiling widely. "Yes, I love baking. It's my passion. I've been trying out different recipes lately, and I thought I'd try to sell it... and, uh... give the money to the poor."

Anjali's frown softened into a smile, though she still looked a bit confused. "That's impressive. I didn't think you would have baked it."

"Well, I wouldn't say I'm a professional," he replied, slightly shrugging his shoulders. "But I do enjoy it. There's something calming about the process, don't you think? You must enjoy baking, yourself. I could smell it from outside, and it smelled incredible. What were you making?"

Anjali's eyes lit up at the mention of her own baking, clearly pleased that he had noticed. "Oh, that was just some bread and a few treats for my sister's kids. They love my cookies, and I love making them treats."

"Cookies? Now that sounds delicious," Aneeth said, being genuinely enthusiastic. "Maybe you could give me some tips. I've always wanted to perfect my cookie recipe."

Anjali chuckled softly, and the tension between them seemed to dissolve. She looked at the basket in his hands again and stepped aside, gesturing for him to come in. "Well, since you brought this lovely basket, why don't you join me for a bit? I've just finished making some tea, and I'd love to hear about your baking experiences."

Aneeth smirked slightly. This was going exactly the way he planned. He stepped inside, carefully placing the basket on her kitchen counter, which was still slightly messy from her earlier baking session. The scent of spices and freshly baked bread filled the room. Aneeth inhaled deeply, letting the warmth of the kitchen wrap around him.

"It smells amazing," he said, looking at the trays and mixing bowls scattered across the counter. "It's clear you're passionate about this."

Anjali smiled as she poured two cups of tea. "I've always loved baking. It's something my mother taught me when I was young. I find it relaxing, especially when I'm stressed. What about you? How did you get into it?"

Aneeth leaned back in his chair, giving her a thoughtful expression. "It started as a hobby. I love baking different things with different flavors and seeing what I can create. There's something satisfying about watching a loaf of bread rise or pulling cookies out of the oven just when they're perfectly golden."

She nodded, clearly impressed. "I can relate to that. Baking is like a form of therapy for me. Plus, it makes people happy, which is the best part about it."

They chatted easily for the next hour, Anjali sharing baking tips and Aneeth sharing made-up baking stories, with Anjali becoming more and more comfortable as the conversation went on. By the time Aneeth was preparing to leave, he knew he had successfully impressed her.

At the door, he turned back, giving her a warm smile. "This was really nice. Maybe next time, I could bring something else I've baked, and we can share some recipes?"

Anjali smiled warmly, her guard completely down now. "I'd like that. It's been nice talking to someone who has the same interest as me."

Aneeth nodded, feeling a sense of achievement as he stepped outside. "I'll see you soon, then." As he walked back to his car, he couldn't help but grin.

"First one down..." he whispered to himself as he drove off. "Six more to go."

***

Aneeth's success with Anjali had him feeling confident, and the next morning, he was ready to move on to the next target, Ruhi. She lived in a quiet neighborhood, her house neat and well-kept. From his earlier observations, he knew she was attractive and slim, with short hair that complimented her face delicately. However, Ruhi seemed more reserved, and Aneeth knew he would have to be careful to not overwhelm her.

As he approached her house, Aneeth noticed through the glass door that Ruhi was sitting on the couch, watching a movie on her TV. He leaned in slightly to see the title and recognized the film immediately. Singham Returns. He watched for a moment, observing her laughing at some of the action scenes, clearly enjoying herself. The DVDs stacked neatly on her shelf indicated that she was a fan of movies, especially Bollywood films.

Aneeth grinned to himself. He saw an opportunity to use her love for movies as a way to connect with her. He quickly retreated, heading back to his car. Now, all he had to do was wait for the right moment.

About twenty minutes later, Ruhi stepped outside, still in casual clothes, looking as if she had just taken a break from watching the movie. This was Aneeth's cue. He opened his music app and found the Singham theme. He cranked up the volume, letting the iconic tune blast from his speakers as he pretended to search for something inside his car's trunk.

Ruhi stopped in her tracks, looking up in surprise. The music had caught her attention, and she smiled, clearly recognizing the theme. She made her way towards Aneeth.

"Hey!" Ruhi called out. "That's some good music you're playing there!"

Aneeth smiled as if it was nothing special. "Yeah, I'm a big fan of the movie. It's one of my favorites."

Ruhi's face lit up. "No way! I was just watching it. What a coincidence!"

Aneeth raised an eyebrow, faking surprise. "Really? I love that movie! I watch it all the time. It's one of those films that never gets old."

Ruhi chuckled, clearly delighted by the coincidence. "I know, right? The action. The humor. It's perfect! Do you watch a lot of Bollywood movies?"

Aneeth, though he had little interest in Bollywood, nodded smoothly. "Oh, definitely. I've seen them all. Singham, Dabangg, Dhoom... I love the energy and the music in those films."

Turning off his stereo and walking over to Ruhi, Aneeth smiled. "You know, *I* can dance and sing pretty well, too."

Ruhi laughed and raised an eyebrow, clearly unconvinced. "Oh, really? And why should I believe you?"

Aneeth grinned, sensing a challenge. Without hesitation, he slid to her side and started singing "Jhoome Jo Pathaan," cycling through his best dance moves as he circled around her.

Ruhi burst out laughing, trying to cover her mouth but failing. "What are you doing?!"

Aneeth spun dramatically, pretending to take his performance very seriously. "Why are you laughing? Don't you like my dancing?"

Ruhi sarcastically replied, "Yes, of course. A true Pathaan in the making..."

Aneeth concluded his dance in front of her and leaned in closely, asking with a deeper voice, "Ah, Ruhi... Who do you think taught Pathaan all those moves in the first place?"

She laughed again, playfully pushing him away. "Okay, okay. You're not so bad, I guess."

"Not so bad?" Aneeth asked with overdone shock on his face. He leaned back in, delivering his next line in a smooth tone like the movie actors. "Aneeth and Ruhi would be a more explosive duo than Tiger and Zoya..."

Rolling her eyes, Ruhi smiled and pushed him away again. She reached out and squeezed his moderately-toned bicep. "Not exactly Tiger, I'm afraid." She joked as she pulled her arm away.

Aneeth backed away, holding a hand to his heart. "Ouch." He said with a comical look of offense, causing Ruhi to chuckle.

Aneeth turned towards his car, closed his trunk, and leaned against it, keeping his tone light. "I was thinking of catching a movie in theaters this weekend. Would you like to join me?"

Ruhi blinked in surprise at the invitation but then smiled warmly. "That sounds like fun! I haven't been to the movies in ages."

"Great," Aneeth replied, his grin widening. "We can pick a good one and make a day out of it. I'll text you the details later?"

Ruhi nodded as he wrote down her phone number. "That sounds perfect. I'm looking forward to it."

As Ruhi started walking back to her house, Aneeth climbed into his car and lowered his window. Ruhi turned around and called out with a smile, "You won't stand me up, will you?"

Aneeth flashed her his signature grin from his Lamborghini seat. "Pathaan's promise." He said with a wink, causing Ruhi to chuckle as she went inside.

As Aneeth drove away, leaving the Singham theme on to his own amusement, he felt satisfied. Another connection was made. His plan was unfolding perfectly. "That's two... five more to go," he muttered, increasing the speed of his car.

***

After his success with Anjali and Ruhi, Aneeth knew that Ishika, the third widow, would be more of a challenge. She was commanding, energetic, and turned many heads, though her typical spirited nature was somewhat restrained since her husband died. One Friday evening, he decided to check in on her. He pulled up near her apartment and noticed Ishika stepping out, dressed to impress for a night out. In one way, she seemed full of life. In another, it seemed she couldn't quite shake a certain sadness. Aneeth's curiosity increased as she called a taxi and quickly slipped inside. He instinctively followed her, keeping a safe distance.

The taxi drove to a local jazz club, where Ishika stepped out, her heels clicking on the pavement. Aneeth's heart raced with excitement. "Alright," he muttered to himself, "time to change plans."

He hurried home, quickly changed into a well-fitted suit that made him feel confident and returned to the jazz club. Inside, the warm atmosphere and soft lighting created a friendly setting. He scanned the room until he spotted Ishika at a table near the stage, sipping a cocktail and enjoying the music.

Aneeth took a deep breath and approached her table, exuding confidence. "Hello, how are you?"

Ishika looked up at him with a curious expression. "Hello. Never saw you before. Are you new here?"

"Yeah. Just changed cities. Heard that this place was good, so I decided to give it a visit," he replied smoothly, glancing at the jazz band playing softly in the background.

She raised an eyebrow, clearly not convinced but entertained by his charm. "Really? That's nice. How much time has it been since you moved?"

Aneeth chuckled, leaning closer. "It's been a month, and quite a boring month at that. But maybe tonight will be good, now that I've met you."

Ishika chuckled and crossed her arms, a playful smile on her face. "You think you can just stroll in here and charm me? You might be in for a surprise."

"Challenge accepted," he said with a wink, taking the seat next to her. "So, tell me, what's your favorite part about coming here?"

"The atmosphere, definitely. And the music. It's so relaxing," she replied, her demeanor warming slightly. But then, her smile faltered for a brief moment. "Although," she added, her voice a bit softer, "it's been hard to truly enjoy myself since my husband passed away. Nights like these have become so rare."

Aneeth noticed the shift in her tone and softened his approach. "I'm really sorry to hear that," he said, his voice filled with genuine sympathy. "Losing someone you love... I can't even imagine how hard that must be."

Ishika gave a small nod, her gaze momentarily distant. "It's been almost six months now, but sometimes it feels like yesterday. I try to go out, be with people, but..." She trailed off, her expression unreadable.

Aneeth leaned in slightly, lowering his voice. "I understand. Grief doesn't follow a schedule. But you're strong, Ishika, even for just stepping out tonight. You deserve to have someone who can take care of you, even if it's just for one evening."

Ishika gave him a small, appreciative smile, the sadness in her eyes easing a little. "Well, I try to keep things fun, but it can be exhausting always being the one to plan everything."

"I can imagine," he said, leaning back casually. "How about a night off? Let me take you out for dinner, and maybe even dancing. No planning on your part, just fun."

She looked at him, her expression indicating growing interest. "Dinner and dancing? You think you can keep up with me?"

Aneeth smiled, a spark of excitement in his eyes. "I believe so. Life is too short to be serious all the time."

Ishika hesitated, her brow furrowing as she considered his offer. "And why should I trust you, Mr. Aneeth? I'm a Christian woman. Don't let this nice dress fool you. I don't go dining and dancing with just anyone."

Aneeth froze for a moment, remembering that proving his faith would be key with all of the widows, sooner or later. Recalling the passage about love he'd memorized, he attempted to make the connection. "Ah, yes. I am a Christian too." He said with a smile. "I know all about Christian love."

"Oh really?" Ishika replied, somewhat unconvinced.

Aneeth drew back, comically gasping. "You mean... you don't... believe me?"

Ishika took a sip of her drink with a smirk. "Not really, no."

"Well," Aneeth said with humorous indignation. "I happen to know that love is ancient, love is blind, love is—"

Ishika cut him off. "Really? Ancient and blind? I think you mean patient and kind."

Aneeth quickly realized he had tragically misquoted the passage, but played it off as if he was joking the whole time. "Yes." He recovered with a playful smile. "Love is patient and kind, which I'm sure you will be with me, given that you're a Christian woman and all."

She stared at him for a moment, then her expression softened, and she smiled. "Alright, I'm interested. But you better make it worth my time."

Aneeth's grin widened. "I promise you won't be disappointed. How about going for dinner after spending a little time here?"

"Sounds good," she replied, her eyes showing the first signs of excitement. "Let's see what you've got planned."

Aneeth led her to his car, her reaction typical of his dates who first saw his symbol of wealth. He took her to his favorite restaurant, playing the part of a gentlemen perfectly. As the night wore on, he noticed how her guard was slowly coming down. They shared personal stories, and Ishika revealed her passion for music and travel.

"I've always wanted to go to Paris," she admitted, her eyes gleaming with excitement. "The art, the culture, the food, it all sounds magical."

"It is magical," Aneeth replied, a hint of sincerity in his tone. "I've been, and it's a place that changes you. Maybe I could take you one day."

Ishika looked at him, her expression a mix of surprise and intrigue. "You travel a lot, then?"

"Whenever I get the chance," he said with a shrug. "Life's too short to stay in one place."

As they finished their meals, the lights dimmed, and the band began playing a casual, upbeat song. Aneeth stood up and extended his hand. "Shall we dance?"

With a playful smile, Ishika took his hand. "You really do know how to keep a girl entertained."

As they danced, Aneeth felt the chemistry building between them. Their movements remained friendly, as Aneeth sought to respect Ishika's conservative sentiments.

As the night came to an end, Aneeth walked Ishika to her taxi, their laughter mingling with the cool evening air. "I had a great time tonight," she said, her eyes sparkling. "You're not like the others."

"Neither are you," he replied, feeling a sense of accomplishment. "I hope this is just the beginning for us."

"Let's see where it goes," Ishika said, stepping into the taxi. "But you better keep it interesting if you want to keep me around."

"Trust me," he said with a smile, "I've got plenty of ways to impress."

As the taxi drove away, Aneeth watched her go, feeling delighted. Ishika was a fun challenge, and he was determined to keep her interested. This game was just beginning, and he was ready for whatever came next.

"Three down..." he whispered to himself, starting the car. "Four more to go... and it keeps getting better."

***

Aneeth's next target was Ankita. She lived with an elderly couple from church in a quiet neighborhood, out of the way of the city's hustle and bustle. Aneeth had observed her from a distance; she was tall and graceful, with striking features that caught his attention immediately. Though a bit older than the others—probably in her 40s—her elegance set her apart.

This time, Aneeth decided to take a different approach. Instead of bringing gifts or attempting to impress her with his usual antics, he wanted to meet her directly. He parked his car a few blocks away from her house and walked to her door. As he knocked, a neighbor passing by noticed him and called out, "Are you looking for Ankita? She's at the library this afternoon!"

"Can you tell me where the library is?" Aneeth asked, hoping it was nearby.

"You'll find it in the street before this one." The neighbor replied.

"Thank you!" Aneeth said, being grateful for the information.

Aneeth peeked inside the house through the window and saw books lining the shelves in the living room. He decided to head to the library to find her.

Upon entering the library, he noticed the warm and inviting atmosphere. He spotted Ankita seated in a cozy armchair, engrossed in a book. Aneeth approached quietly, taking a seat in the chair next to hers. A small table separated them, and he noticed a few interesting titles at her side.

"Mind if I join you?" he asked with a friendly smile.

Ankita looked up, surprised but pleased. "Oh! I didn't see you there. Of course, you can join me."

Aneeth leaned forward, glancing at the book in her hand. "What are you reading?"

"It's a novel by an author I really enjoy. What about you?" she replied, her eyes sparkling with interest.

He picked up a book from the nearby shelf, holding it up for her to see. "I just started this one. I've heard great things about it, and I thought it might be impressive."

Ankita raised an eyebrow. "Ah, I've read that one! It's fantastic. What do you think of it so far?"

Aneeth placed the book on the table between them, allowing her to see the title clearly. "I'm still in the early chapters, but I can already tell it has a lot of depth. I'd love to hear your thoughts on it."

She smiled, her interest piqued. "Well, if you enjoy character development, you're in for a treat. The protagonist goes through quite the transformation."

As their conversation flowed, Aneeth continued to pick books from the shelves, placing them on the table so Ankita could see what he was reading. "What about this one?" he asked, holding up a classic novel.

"Oh, that's a great choice!" Ankita exclaimed. "It's a timeless story. You have good taste."

"Thank you!" he said, feeling the connection growing. "I believe that books can offer so much insight and companionship, especially during tough times."

Ankita's expression softened, his comment about tough times reminding her of her husband's death just a few months ago. "You're right." She said somewhat solemnly. "They have a way of taking us away from our problems."

As they exchanged thoughts on literature, Aneeth could see that she was warming up to him. "If you ever want to discuss books or just need someone to talk to, I'm here," he offered, his tone gentle.

"That's very kind of you, Aneeth. It's not often you find someone who genuinely cares," she replied, her voice filled with gratitude.

"I think it's important to support one another," he said sincerely. "Especially during difficult times. It's what I'm called to do as a Christian, no? After all, love believes all things and hopes all things," he concluded with a charming grin.

"So you're a Christian?" Ankita sought to confirm.

"Of course I am." Aneeth replied. "And so are you. I can tell by the kindness you've shown to me."

Upon learning Aneeth was a Christian, Ankita began to feel drawn to him. Their conversation continued with ease.

After a while, Ankita glanced at the clock. "I didn't realize how much time has passed. It's refreshing to have such an engaging conversation."

"I agree. I really enjoy talking to you," Aneeth replied, smiling. "How about we visit the bookstore nearby sometime? I'd love to continue this conversation and maybe discover some new titles together."

Ankita's face brightened. "I'd like that very much. It's been a while since I've been to that bookstore."

"Perfect! I'll text you, and we can arrange a day," he suggested, feeling happy that she agreed.

As he stood to leave, her phone number in hand, he flashed her his signature smile. "I'm really glad I met you today, Ankita. I look forward to our bookstore adventure."

"Me too, Aneeth. Thank you for making my afternoon special," she said, her eyes shining with appreciation.

As he walked back to his car, Aneeth felt that familiar rush of satisfaction. *Huff! Four down, only three left,* he thought, grinning to himself as he replayed the meet-up in his mind.

***

Aneeth was ready to meet Sonali. As he arrived at her complex, he spotted her walking out of her apartment. Shorter than the rest, she boasted an adorable smile and large, glowing eyes. Aneeth couldn't help but enjoy the simplicity about her, thoroughly admiring her look in a simple pink t-shirt and jeans. Quickly parking his car, he got out and followed her on foot to a local coffee shop nearby.

Once inside, he noticed an employee smock hanging on a coat rack. Seizing the opportunity, he put it on and waited behind the counter, preparing for their encounter.

When Sonali entered the coffee shop, she approached the counter, looking at him with curiosity. "Excuse me, are you new here?"

Aneeth flashed a friendly smile. "Yes! I just started today. I'm still getting the hang of things. What can I get for you?"

She raised an eyebrow, intrigued. "Hmm, I'll have a cappuccino, please."

"Coming right up!" he replied, pretending to expertly make her drink. As he handed her the cappuccino, he added, "You know, I've heard the pastries here are really good. Have you tried them?"

Sonali shook her head, being interested. "Not yet. I usually come in for the coffee."

"Would you like me to recommend a pastry? You won't regret it," he asked, trying to engage her further.

"Sure! What do you recommend?" she replied, looking at him with genuine curiosity.

"I suggest the almond croissant. It's my personal favorite," Aneeth said confidently. "Let me grab one for you."

He quickly fetched the pastry and placed it on the counter. "Here you go! A cappuccino and an almond croissant on the house. Consider it a welcome gift from the new guy."

Sonali smiled, pleasantly surprised to see "Love is Kind" written on her drink in whipped cream. "That's very kind of you. I appreciate it. So, how are you finding the job so far?"

"It's been great! The people are friendly, and I enjoy talking to customers. Speaking of which, what brings you here today?" Aneeth asked, taking the opportunity to learn more about her.

"I'm just taking a break from my routine. I love trying out different coffee shops," she replied, taking a sip of her amateur cappuccino. "This place has a nice atmosphere." Tasting the sub-par drink, she made a sour face as she pulled the cup from her lips, wondering why it tasted so bad.

"I agree! There's something comforting about the aroma of fresh coffee," Aneeth said, glancing around the shop. "What's your usual go-to drink?" His question redirected her from the confusion over her drink.

"I usually stick to lattes, but I'm always open to trying something new," Sonali replied cheerfully. "I love experimenting with different flavors."

Aneeth leaned forward, intrigued. "Do you have a favorite flavor?"

"I'm a sucker for vanilla," she admitted with a laugh. "You can't go wrong with a classic!"

"True! I'm more of a caramel person myself," he shared, grinning. "Maybe we should have a caramel versus vanilla taste test one day."

"I like the sound of that! Challenge accepted," Sonali replied, her laughter brightening the atmosphere.

As the conversation flowed, Aneeth seized the moment to engage her more. "So, do you have any hobbies besides exploring coffee shops?"

Sonali's expression remained bright. "I enjoy painting in my free time. It's a nice way to express myself."

"Really? That's awesome! I've always admired artists. What do you like to paint?" he asked, genuinely interested.

"Mostly landscapes and abstract pieces," she said, her passion shining through. "It helps me relax and clear my mind."

"I can see how that would be therapeutic," Aneeth agreed. "I'd love to see some of your work someday."

"Maybe I can show you sometime. I have a few pieces displayed at home," Sonali suggested, her tone inviting.

"I'd really like that," Aneeth said, feeling the connection deepen. "You know, I've heard there's an art exhibit opening next week. How about we check it out together?"

Sonali seemed taken back by the offer, but after a moment, she smiled. "That sounds like fun. I'd love to go."

"Great! Let's exchange numbers so we can coordinate," he said, reaching for his phone.

As they exchanged contact information, Aneeth felt a familiar rush of excitement. He had made a good impression on Sonali, and he couldn't wait to see where this connection might lead.

"Looking forward to our coffee adventure," he said as they finished up.

"Me too! It was nice to meet you, uh..." she trailed off, looking for his name.

"Aneeth," he said, redirecting her from spotting his incorrect name tag. "And you're Sonali, right?" he added, glad they had finally introduced themselves properly.

"Exactly! Nice to meet you, Aneeth," she replied, smiling as she waved goodbye.

As Aneeth left the shop, he satisfyingly said to himself, "Five down... two more to go."

However, his victorious musings were abruptly interrupted by the sound of a man yelling behind him. "You! Where are you going with my smock?! You don't even work here!"

Aneeth froze, looking down to see that he had forgotten to take off the smock he'd borrowed. Turning around, he saw what could only have been the store's owner chasing him, his face red with anger. Aneeth began running from him down the sidewalk, desperately trying to untie the back of the smock as he ran. When he finally got it off, he threw it behind him, hoping the owner would cease his pursuit now that he'd gotten his smock back.

Aneeth ran under a tree before stopping to turn around. The owner was holding the smock up angrily, telling him off from a distance, using Hindi phrases that even Aneeth wouldn't repeat in public.

"You have your smock, old man!" Aneeth yelled from the shade of the tree. He then held his phone up above his head. "If you keep pursuing me, I'll call the police!" The shop owner dismissively waved his hands, then turned around to go back to his coffee shop.

Relieved that the chase was over, Aneeth brought his hand down to put his phone back in his pocket, but when he looked in his hand, his phone was gone. Confused, he looked up to see a pair of familiar monkeys holding his phone in the tree, wildly amused by their repeated shenanigans.

"No, no, no!" Aneeth lamented, getting louder with each 'No.' He stepped back and took a good look at the tree and his surroundings, realization dawning on him that this is where his phone was stolen the last time.

"I know this tree," he said under his breath. Then, looking up at the amused monkeys, he pointed at them as his face contorted with frustration. "You!" He exclaimed. "Give me my phone back!"

The monkeys looked at each other for a moment, almost as if they were deliberating. Then the one holding the phone extended it towards Aneeth.

"Good monkey," Aneeth patronized. "Just a little further," he prompted while reaching for the phone.

When his hand was only inches away from retrieving his device, the monkey suddenly threw it in the other direction, the screen shattering as soon as it hit the pavement. Aneeth anxiously hurried over to assess the damage while the monkeys wildly threw their arms up and down, mocking their victim's exasperation.

Admitting defeat, Aneeth walked back to his car to head home for the night, the sound of the monkey's laughter fading behind him.

***

Next on his list was Payal, and she was unlike anyone he'd dealt with so far. Aneeth had spotted her jogging around the park near her house. She was athletic, fit, and full of energy, her long hair bouncing in a ponytail as she ran. She had a spark about her that immediately caught his attention. But he knew she wouldn't fall for soft words or thoughtful gifts. He needed a different trick. One that played into her active lifestyle.

The next morning, Aneeth showed up at the park, dressed in gym clothes, ready to bump into Payal. He had timed it perfectly, arriving just as she finished her run. As she slowed down near a bench to catch her breath, Aneeth made his move.

"Hey, I've seen you around here before," he said, flashing her a grin as he wiped pretend sweat from his forehead. "You're fast. I'm trying to get back into running myself."

Payal looked him up and down with a sassy expression. "Yeah? You look like you could use a few more laps."

Aneeth laughed, loving her fiery attitude. "You're right about that. How about a running buddy sometime? I could use someone to push me."

She raised an eyebrow, intrigued but cautious. "You sure you can keep up?"

"Like the bible says," Aneeth replied, "I'll run in such a way as to win."

Payal's eyebrows raised at his mention of scripture, suddenly giving serious thought as to whether or not he was worth her time.

Aneeth saw that his bible trick had earned him a chance. "Besides," he continued, "it's more fun with company, don't you think?"

Payal paused, then shrugged. "Alright. Tomorrow morning, same time. Let's see what you've got."

Perfect.

The next morning, they ran together, and Aneeth managed to keep up... barely. Payal was competitive, constantly challenging him to run faster or go further. But by the end, they were laughing together, and Aneeth could tell she enjoyed his company.

As they finished their run, Aneeth casually asked, "How about grabbing a smoothie afterward? My treat."

Payal smirked, still catching her breath. As she unwrapped her phone holder from her arm, she delivered a serious comment. "I'm a widow, Aneeth."

Before he could offer consolation, she continued matter-of-factly. "I don't have time for boys or games. I'll spend my time with a man of God, and nothing less." She lifted her head just a tad, along with her eyebrows, silently prompting him to confirm if he was such a man.

Aneeth put his hand to his chest, demonstrating his sincerity. "I promise, I will not waste your time."

"Alright," Payal responded, her tone reverting to its previous spunk. "But if you slow me down again tomorrow, you're paying for breakfast."

"Deal," Aneeth said with a wink, knowing he had her hooked.

Six down... last one to go.

***

Later that day, Aneeth approached the seventh widow's house, Bhumika, and noticed her taking care of her garden in the backyard. His curiosity increased as he leaned over the fence and called out to her.

"Hello there! Your garden looks amazing!" he exclaimed, admiring the colorful flowers and neatly arranged plants.

Bhumika turned, slightly surprised. "Thank you," she replied, then turned back to continue her work.

"Could I be of any help?" Aneeth asked, hoping she would agree.

"I appreciate your offer, but I really don't need any help," she replied politely without looking at him.

Aneeth turned away from the fence in disappointment. Clearly, Bhumika was the cautious type who couldn't be bothered with strangers. When he dropped his head to think of a plan, he noticed a large Bandicoot rat moving along the sidewalk, and an idea came to his mind. With a mischievous glint in his eye, he quietly pushed the rat through a hole at the bottom of the fence, hoping it would head for her precious vegetables.

Moments later, Bhumika shrieked, dropping her gardening tools as the rat darted towards her plants. "What on earth is that?!" she cried out, stepping back in fright.

Aneeth quickly opened the gate and rushed through. "Ma'am! Are you alright?" he asked, pretending to be concerned. "I saw that rat! Do you need help?"

Bhumika's eyes were wide with shock as she nodded. "Yes, please! It's in the garden!"

He carefully approached the rat, gently shooing it away from her garden and back on the street. "There, it's gone now. You're safe," he said, trying to reassure her.

As she took a deep breath, Bhumika managed a small laugh. "Thank you for saving me, or, I should say, my plants. That was the biggest rat I've ever seen!"

Aneeth smiled warmly. "I'm glad I could help. It seems like you could use some company after all. Would you like to chat for a bit? I'd love to hear more about your garden."

Bhumika hesitated, then nodded, her expression softening. "Sure, that sounds nice. I could use a break after the surprise."

They both settled down on her patio, a little more at ease. "So, what do you enjoy growing in your garden?" Aneeth asked, genuinely curious.

As they began to talk, the initial tension faded away, and Bhumika started to share her gardening tips and experiences. Aneeth felt a sense of accomplishment; his plan to connect with her worked like a charm.

All seven in the bag, he thought to himself as he left Bhumika's house. She had agreed to have him over again, making his entire mission a glorious success.

***

Aneeth drove home, feeling unstoppable. He had won over every single one of the widows, and all that was left was to figure out how to date them without getting caught. But the challenge excited him.

He smiled to himself as he walked through his front door, thinking about how smoothly everything had gone. A part of him wondered how long he could keep this up before things went out of control. Seven women, all at once... it was bound to get messy eventually.

But not yet, he thought, his grin widening. *Not yet.*

Over the next two weeks, Aneeth secured the interest of the widows, playing to each of their interests and personalities, proving to each he was the kind of man worth having around. He saw each of them once or twice a week, balancing work and his scheduled dates while managing keeping them from discovering each other.

It started off smoothly. Baking with Anjali, movie nights with Ruhi, nights on the town with Ishika, book clubs with Ankita, art gallery tours with Sonali, morning runs with Payal, and gardening with Bhumika.

Within two months, he established a great bond with all seven. Between his increasing propensity for injecting bible verses at appropriate points of conversation and his irresistible charisma and charm, Aneeth found himself winning the hearts of each widow with little difficulty. He even became a master at consoling them when thoughts of their husbands resulted in fluctuating emotions. The comfort he learned to provide drew the hearts of the women to him in a very deep way. He was evolving from a charming womanizer to a master manipulator, flawlessly juggling his relationship with all seven women. In his mind, he was as successful as any man could ever hope to be. Seven beautiful widows. And they were all his.

Aneeth pulled into his driveway just as the evening ended. The day for him was exhausting. He had gone to the gym with Payal in the morning, had lunch with Ishika in the afternoon, and finished the day by having dinner with Bhumika, using fresh vegetables picked from the garden they'd been growing. He managed it all perfectly. The date circle became routine. It was like a game of chess with multiple opponents, and so far, he hadn't been caught.

But tonight, he felt weirdly different.

As he reached the door of his mansion, something began to feel off. His mother's car was in the driveway, the door was slightly ajar, and the golden light of the chandelier in the foyer was visible. Aneeth's mother was always careful. She never left the door open like this when she visited.

A feeling of unease crept up in his heart. He stepped inside, calling out for his mother. "Maa?" he called out softly as he went further inside. His voice echoed in the silence. The house was quiet... too quiet.

He placed his keys on the table near the door and glanced around. His heart started to race. The light in the living room was on, and the low noise coming from the TV filled the background, which was flashing images of chaos and war. Headlines related to the conflicts in neighboring countries and violence erupting between the factions were displayed. Although he had seen little glimpses of those headlines before, he always felt distant. It was something that never mattered to him. But that was about to change.

He heard soft, muffled sobs as he followed the sound and went inside the living room.

Aneeth's stomach twisted as he moved towards the side where the sound was coming from. As he rounded the corner, the sight before him made his breath catch. His mother sat on the floor while clutching a crumpled piece of paper in her hands. Her shoulders were trembling, and her face was stained with unstoppable tears. He had never witnessed his mother so broken and fragile before.

"Maa?" He let out a whisper, moving towards his mother, but she didn't reply. Behind him, the news still broadcasted the situation of war, showing the violence and destruction in some far-off place. But her focus wasn't on the news; it was on the paper she was holding.

She looked up at him, and the vulnerability in her eyes hit him like a punch to the gut. "Aneeth…" Her voice cracked, barely audible as she faced difficulty in catching her breath. She shook her head and let out a loud sob, unable to continue.

Panic rushed through him, "What is it, Maa? What's wrong?" He bent down towards her and grabbed her shoulder. His mind raced with a thousand possibilities, but nothing could prepare him for what she said next. He held her up and had her sit on the couch. He knelt down in front of her and looked at her, waiting for her to speak.

"Your father…," she choked out, her voice trembling with the weight of the words. "He's gone, Aneeth. He's gone," she revealed, then broke down again.

For a moment, Aneeth was unable to register her words. "Gone?" he repeated, confused. His father had been traveling for work, like always. He was a successful businessman, always flying from one country to another, working on different deals and partnerships that Aneeth never fully understood. They hadn't been that close as his father was always away and always busy. But gone? No. It didn't make any sense to him.

"He… he was killed," she continued, her voice breaking as tears streamed down her face. "He was in Pakistan… for work. There was crossfire when he was on his way home. He… he didn't make it through."

Aneeth blinked, unable to take in his mother's words. He stared at her, his brain unable to process the information. Killed? Dead? His father? His father, who looked like he was untouchable, firm, and always in control of things, was now… dead?

"No… no, that can't be true," he stammered, shaking his head as if denying it would make it untrue. His chest tightened, and he faced difficulty in breathing. The room spun around him, and he felt his body trembling.

"They called me today," his mother said, her voice barely above a whisper. "The embassy. They said… it was quick. That he didn't suffer, that he didn't feel any pain."

Aneeth stood up while breathing heavily, pushing his hair back. He sank down onto the nearest chair, his legs unable to support him anymore. His father. The man who had always been a distant figure in his life was now suddenly gone. Forever. And he didn't even get the chance to meet him and say goodbye for the last time. He didn't get the chance to fix the relationship between them, to ask him questions he'd always kept in his heart.

His mother's sobs filled the silence, but Aneeth could barely hear them. His head started to hurt. The war, which he never cared for. The war, the one he had seen in passing on the news, had seemed so far away. It wasn't supposed to touch them, to invade their lives like this. His father was simply traveling for business, just like he always had. And now, because of a war that had nothing to do with him, he was gone.

"I... I didn't know how to tell you this," his mother whispered, her voice shaking. "I... I thought he would come back. Like always."

He looked at his mother, her face showing grief, and felt a pang of guilt hitting him. For years, he had resented his father's absence and built walls between them. But now that his father was gone, all those unresolved feelings had no place to go.

"What are we going to do?" his voice cracked as he finally managed to speak.

His mother shook her head, wiping her tears. "I don't know. The embassy will help with arrangements... to bring him home."

Bring him home. The words echoed in Aneeth's mind.

His world, which had revolved around the excitement of his plans and distractions, felt little now. Meaningless. The seven women he had been dating, the lies he had told them so effortlessly, suddenly seemed like childish games. None of it mattered in the face of this crushing reality.

Later that night, as it stormed outside, Aneeth felt the weight of everything pressing down on him. His father's sudden demise had shaken him to his core. He sat alone in his room with the rain pounding against the windows. Lightning flashed outside, illuminating his room. Aneeth felt small, powerless. His mind turned to the women he had been deceiving. The seven widows, each one trusting him and falling for his lies. Just hours ago, he had been caught up in the thrill of his tricks, feeling unstoppable. But now, it all seemed meaningless.

His eyes drifted towards the Bible on the shelf. It had been there for years, left untouched and covered in dust. Only in the wake of his phony Christianity had he ever even bothered to open it. But now, in his life's most tumultuous moment, he wondered, perhaps, if it had any answers. Why was he alive? What was even the meaning of life? Where would he go when he died? These questions and so many more drew him to the once-neglected holy book.

Aneeth stood up and went towards the shelf. He reached out for the Bible and grabbed it with trembling hands. He flipped through its pages, unsure of where to start. But he knew he had to find something, anything, that could help him make sense of his life. His eyes scanned the verses, skipping over lines that felt distant to him. Then, he stumbled upon a passage that stopped him in his tracks.

"For what does it profit a man to gain the whole world and forfeit his soul?"

The words struck him deep, hitting him hard. Aneeth had spent so much of his life chasing after pleasure, power, and control. He had built his life around betrayal, lying to people, playing games, and manipulating everyone around him. And now, standing on the edge of loss and grief, he felt empty. The excitement that once filled him up now felt like he had captured himself in a cage he had built for himself.

He stared at the verse, reading it over and over again. **"What does it profit a man...?"** The words roamed around in his mind, growing louder with each repetition. For the first time in a long time, Aneeth felt like his games were exposed.

His father was dead. The seven women he had been lying to had no idea who he really was. And worst of all, *he* didn't know who he was anymore.

Aneeth's grip tightened around the Bible as he sat back, his heart pounding in his chest. He had spent years ignoring these questions of life, pushing away anything that made him feel too serious. But now, with the storm roaring outside and the grief of his father's death pressing down on him, he couldn't escape reality anymore. He had been living for himself, and for what?

He placed the Bible in his lap and closed his eyes. For the first time in his life, Aneeth prayed. Not because he was supposed to, not because someone had told him to, but because he didn't know what else to do in that moment. His praying wasn't eloquent, but it came from a place of deep need.

"God," he began, his voice low and shaky, "I don't know what to do. I've made so many mistakes. I've lied, cheated, and betrayed people. And now… my father's gone. I don't know how to fix any of this. I… I don't even know why I'm alive. Please, show me what to do. Help me make this right. If you are real, I beg You, show me the way to go."

As he prayed, the storm outside grew louder, the wind making the windows bump together. But inside, Aneeth felt a small hint of peace within himself. It wasn't a solution, not yet, but it was something. A small ray of hope that maybe, just maybe, he could change.

The guilt of his actions with regard to the women began to weigh heavier on his heart. He had used them, taken advantage of their trust, all for his own selfish games. Now, with his father's death forcing him to confront the brittleness of life, Aneeth couldn't ignore the truth anymore. He couldn't keep living this way—lying, manipulating, and living for no one's gain but his own.

"What do I do about them?" he whispered, thinking of Anjali, Ankita, Payal, Ishika, Bhumika, Sonali, and Ruhi. Each of them had fallen for a man he pretended to be. None of them knew the real Aneeth, the one who'd been playing a dangerous game with their hearts. "I don't know how to fix this" was the last thing he muttered before he fell asleep from the day's exhaustion.

The next morning, Aneeth woke up feeling drained. He lay in bed, staring at the ceiling, the words from the Bible still echoing in his mind:

"For what does it profit a man to gain the whole world and forfeit his soul?"

Everything felt different now. The thrill of going out with seven women, which had once made him excited, suddenly seemed ridiculous. He felt lost and unsure of how to move forward. He didn't know how to fix his life, but he knew he couldn't continue down the same path.

That day, as Aneeth sat in the living room with his phone, he made a decision. He would cancel his plans for the week. No more dates, no more lies, no more pretending. He needed space to think. One by one, he sent messages to Anjali, Ankita, Payal, Ishika, Bhumika, Sonali, and Ruhi, giving excuses about work and family emergencies. The replies came quickly, being concerned, understanding, and filled with questions. But Aneeth didn't care about the responses. For the first time in months, he felt relieved to be free from the exhausting web of lies he had spun.

Meanwhile, while Aneeth was at home, wrestling with life's most difficult questions, the widows—all twenty of them—met at the church with Pastor Manoj. He scheduled this meeting with all of them to see how they were doing and inquire as to how the church could help meet their needs. Though some still lived in reasonable houses and apartments, their money was quickly running out.

Most of the widows, being part of a bigger (though not necessarily wealthy) church, didn't know each other well, but a few were close with each other. They met with the Pastor in one of the larger meeting rooms. Foldable metal chairs with cushions on the bottom were scattered around in front of a desk where the pastor sat. The room was dimly lit, with flowers in vases lining the two window sills.

The women greeted each other and sat down, preparing to share with the pastor—and each other—the things they were going through, both financially and emotionally. Some reported their steady progress, while others testified of crippling sorrow and overwhelming debt. All of their husbands had died as a result of the war, leaving each one to fend for themselves amidst the nation's struggling economy. That, along with most everything else, they had in common. But there was one topic only the seven youngest among them could report on. Romance.

"You know," Anjali began, "I wasn't sure I'd ever find love again after my husband passed. But there's this wonderful man I've been seeing. His name is Aneeth. He's charming, thoughtful... and even with all that's going on, I think I might be falling for him. It's been quite the unexpected blessing."

Several other women smiled and nodded, their faces lighting up at the mention of love.

"That's funny," Ishika said, her smile slightly fading. "I've been seeing someone too. His name is Aneeth as well. He's lively, adventurous... rich..." The group laughed at the last-mentioned trait. Ishika continued, "He's been such a bright spot in my life these past few months. We've gone to the best restaurants in town, the most romantic locations; it's almost felt too good to be true."

Payal cleared her throat, drawing everyone's attention to her. "I am also dating a handsome man named Aneeth." She said with a neutral expression.

The room suddenly grew quiet, unsettling suspicion beginning to materialize in everyone's minds.

"Is your Aneeth rich?" Pastor Manoj asked Payal with a smirk, still unwilling to believe what most had already begun theorizing.

Payal sighed with a sense of relief. "No. The Aneeth I've been seeing is no traveler or fine diner. He's a bit of a homebody who's just gotten back into working out. Most of the time we spend together is at the gym or on runs."

Murmurs and chuckles of relief spread throughout the room, most being content to accept that the three women were simply dating men with a common name. That is, until Bhumika spoke up...

"I have a boyfriend now, as well." She conceded, her expression unreadable.

When everyone turned to look at her, she clarified. "His name is Aneeth."

The entire room froze for a moment, though none were willing to accept their unspoken suspicions just yet.

"When do you go on dates with this Aneeth?" she asked her three increasingly uncomfortable peers.

Payal answered first. "Our dates are always in the morning. That's when we run and hit the gym."

"Ours are always in the evening, usually around dinner," Bhumika responded.

"See, you worry for nothing," Ishika replied. "Ours are in the evening as well."

"What days of the week?"

Everyone looked at Ruhi, who had suddenly broken her own silence. She repeated, "What days of the week do you see him in the evening?"

Bhumika smiled. "Only on Mondays and Thursdays. He works the other nights."

Ishika's eyes got wide. "Our evening dates are only on Fridays and Saturdays. He... works the other nights."

More eyes in the room went wide, shifting their gaze back to Ruhi.

"Ruhi?" Pastor Manoj pressed. "Why do you ask?"

Ruhi put a tentative hand on her chest, as if trying not to come to terms with the worst. "I, too, am dating a man named Aneeth. Our movie nights are on Tuesdays and Wednesdays," she said in a low, nervous tone. Then, after looking around the room, she looked straight at Bhumika and Ishika. "He works the other nights."

"Sunday."

Everyone looked at Anjali in horrific anticipation.

"Our baking night is every Sunday." Anjali expounded. "He... he works the rest of the week."

A long, uncomfortable pause settled among the widows. And unbeknownst to the rest of the group, Ankita and Sonali, the oldest and youngest of Aneeth's victims, had been looking at each other in fearful revelation, realizing that they too had been part of the scheme.

Pastor Manoj noticed their silent exchange. "Ankita? Sonali? Is there something you'd like to share?"

Ankita spoke first. "My Aneeth meets me for lunch on most weekdays."

Sonali followed. "My Aneeth meets me for lunch on most weekends."

There was another pause.

"*My* Aneeth meets me for breakfast every other Tuesday," Pastor Manoj teased. The room looked at him. He was barely able to contain his snickering. "What?" He said between breaths. "He's dating seven of you. What's one more?" He hit his desk as he tried to refrain from bursting out laughing.

The women, who usually loved his sense of humor, had mixed internal reactions to his probably ill-timed joke. The Pastor, seeing that this wasn't the time, calmed himself and asked the group. "How tall is Aneeth? All of you answer at once."

"About six feet." The seven widows said in perfect harmony.

The room went deafeningly quiet. Then, the truth officially hit them all.

They were dating the same man.

Shock turned to disbelief. Disbelief, to outrage. The room suddenly erupted in anger, confusion, and felt betrayal as the seven widows realized that Aneeth was lying to all of them.

"He's been deceiving us all!" Anjali said, her voice firm. "What are we going to do? I was making plans to marry him!"

"So was I!" Bhumika echoed, followed by similar declarations from the other deceived widows.

As a chorus of intended vengeance and hurt rose among the women, two of the older widows turned to look at Pastor Manoj, as if expecting him to handle the situation.

The Pastor looked back at them and shrugged. "What? *I* wasn't planning to marry him..."

The three of them snickered as the betrayed widows angrily exchanged more facts about their shared boyfriend.

Eventually, Payal stood up, causing the others to quiet down out of curiosity.

"Payal. What are you doing?" Pastor Manoj asked.

Payal ripped her shirt sleeve off and began wrapping it around her wrist and knuckles. "I'm going to kill him. Who wants to join me?"

One by one, in order of the most to the least rambunctious, the other six stood to their feet, vocalizing their agreement with the drastic plan.

"Hold on. Hold on." Pastor Manoj pressed, as he raised his hands and gestured for them to relax. "Why don't you all sleep on it and see if you still want to kill him in the morning?"

Payal finished wrapping her hand in unquenchable determination. Then, looking at the Pastor, she replied, "What do you care? You only dated him every other Tuesday..."

With a playful smirk, Payal made her way out of the office, the other widows following behind her, dead set on teaching their boyfriend a lesson he'd never forget.

As they walked through the hallway, Anjali asked, "How will we get there? Half of us took cabs to this meeting."

"The church van," Ankita suggested. "That will fit all of us."

The women nodded and voiced their agreement as they exited the church and walked towards the van.

"Who's driving?" Bhumika asked curiously.

"I am," Ruhi said with glaring confidence, the rest of the group taken back by her sudden vitality.

"What?" Ruhi said, looking at the shocked women. "Watching movies isn't my only hobby. My father lets me drive his race car on Saturdays."

The women nodded with grins on their faces, then piled into the 15-passenger vehicle.

Their ride in the van was a spectacle to behold as the seven women tried to make sense of it all. What began as shock and anger slowly transitioned to comical disbelief; all that could be expected of seven angry Indian women sharing a ride under such circumstances...

"I still can't believe it!" Bhumika exclaimed, her voice rising. "We really fell for it, all of us! What is he, a magician?"

"Magician or not," Ishika shouted from the back, taking off her heels. "I'm going to stab him in the eye with my shoe!"

The women laughed and voiced their approval of her proposed solution.

"That will only work if he hasn't died from the poisonous mushroom I feed him from my garden!" Bhumika added.

More lively laughter, accompanied by high-fives, followed her threat.

"I was just planning on beating him to death the old-fashioned way," Payal said with her wrapped fist held in the air, prompting more laughter.

"I was planning on replicating this torture scene I saw in a movie last week, where they cut this terrorist to death an inch at a time," Ruhi said with a chillingly neutral tone.

The van went quiet as all eyes turned to Ruhi, who was forcefully staring at the road in front of her.

"Are you sure you should be watching those movies," Sonali asked gently.

Ruhi looked at everyone's nervous expressions in the rearview mirror. "What?" She asked. "Did I take it too far?" A moment of silence was followed by another outburst of laughter.

As the laughter died down, Ankita chimed in. "We should've known something was wrong. I mean, I know we're sad about our husbands, but are we really so desperate that we fell for this scheme?"

Ishika leaned forward from the back, still holding her heels in one hand. "I should've known something was off when he started quoting Bollywood dialogues like he was Shah Rukh Khan."

"Speaking of SRK," Ruhi interjected. "Did anyone else get a goofy dance number?"

"Yup," said one, followed by positive answers from the others.

Ruhi indignantly gasped. "What song did he sing all of you!?"

The widows looked at each other for a moment, grinning as if they all knew their answers were the same. Then, in perfect unison, they all began singing and dancing; "Jhoome jo Pathaan, meri jaan, Mehfil hi lut jaaye." With half the chorus finished, they all fell into each others' laps in fits of laughter.

As they emerged from the hilarity, Anjali shouted to everyone, "And what did he say after he promised to never leave you?"

The other six answered in a symphony of sassy unison. "Pathaan's promise..."

They once again succumbed to laughter as they uncovered more and more of Aneeth's common tricks, finding so much entertainment in it by this point that they had almost forgotten to be angry.

Bhumika gasped for breath between laughs. "Forget confronting him! We should make a movie about this!" The others continued laughing in agreement.

They were so distracted by their mockery that they completely missed the black Lamborghini passing them on the other side of the road...

While the widows were plotting their revenge and bonding over their shared embarrassment, Aneeth had reached the lowest he'd ever been. Desperate for answers, he was on his way to the church to speak with the pastor. He, too, was too distracted to notice the van full of girlfriends that passed by.

When the seven women finally pulled up in front of Aneeth's mansion, they marched out of the van and rang the doorbell repeatedly, but no one answered.

"Just open the door," Ishika said, barefoot with heels in hand. The door was unlocked, so they entered. The grandness of the mansion did nothing to soothe their anger.

"I'll bet he's hiding from us," Anjali muttered as they searched the house.

On the other side of town, Aneeth walked into the church, his footsteps heavy on the wooden floor. The atmosphere inside was calm and quiet, the air filled with the scent of candles and fresh flowers from the window sills. The widows from the previous meeting had already left the building, leaving no one there but Pastor Manoj. Aneeth's heart pounded in his chest as he made his way to the pastor's office. The weight of his actions, his lies, and his double life pressed down on him, making it hard to breathe.

When he knocked on the door, Pastor Manoj looked up from his desk, surprised to see him. "Can I help you?" the pastor said, a curious look on his face. He didn't recognize Aneeth from the one time he'd met him at church a few months ago.

Deeply troubled, Aneeth sat down, burying his face in his hands. "Pastor, I have to confess... I've done terrible things. I don't even know where to start."

Pastor Manoj closed the Bible on his desk and leaned forward, his expression shifting from confusion to concern. "Take your time, beta. Whatever it is, God is here to listen."

Aneeth swallowed hard, his throat dry. "I've been living a lie. I pretended to be someone I'm not. I pretended to be a Christian. But the truth is... I've been using the church for my own selfish reasons."

"Using the church?" Pastor Manoj questioned. "What do you mean?"

Aneeth continued, though barely able to get the words out. "I've been dating seven widows from the church at the same time. I've deceived them, lied to them. I've never believed in God before, but I'm scared for my life now. Pastor, what do I do?"

Pastor Manoj's eyes widened in shock as he realized who was sitting before him. Unable to keep a serious attitude in light of the coincidence at hand, he smirked, folded his arms, and leaned back in his chair.

"Seven widows, you say.." The Pastor inquired while stroking his chin. "I'm no prophet, nor the son of a prophet, but I'd bet my church your name is Aneeth."

A humungous smile emerged on the pastor's face as Aneeth looked up.

"Yes... My name is Aneeth. You remember from when we met three months ago?"

"No." Pastor Manoj chuckled. "But I remember you from when the widows figured it out not twenty minutes ago..."

Aneeth's eyes went wide, his face red. He was paralyzed in light of this information.

Pastor Manoj clapped his hands together and laughed, unable to restrain himself any longer.

After a few moments, tears beginning to well in his eyes, Aneeth said to the Pastor, "With all due respect, pastor… I'm trying to confess and you're laughing at me."

Pastor Manoj deeply sighed as he pulled himself together. "Oh, beta. I'm not laughing at you. I'm laughing about the seven women who are probably at your house this very moment, looking to kill you."

Aneeth swallowed hard, at least understanding the comical nature of the situation, but still unable to move on from his crippling guilt.

Recognizing the need to deal with Aneeth's soul, Pastor Manoj's tone shifted. He leaned forward, slowly crossing his arms over his desk.

"Aneeth," he said with kindness in his eyes, "I know you feel bad about deceiving these women, but why are you really here?"

Aneeth fidgeted in his seat for a few moments, then tears began to fall from his eyes. "My father was killed in Pakistan because of the war. I found out last night."

Pastor Manoj took a deep breath, then encouraged him to continue.

"My whole life," Aneeth began to expound, "I haven't given God a second thought. And now, I don't even know where my father is, or where I'm going when I die. What can I be sure of, pastor? It's like every wrong thing I've ever done is screaming at me that I'm a criminal. What can I do to get right with God? How can I even know who God is?"

Pastor Manoj looked at Aneeth with a heart full of compassion. He recognized the convicting work of the Holy Spirit in this young man's life, and knew he was being called out of darkness and into light.

"Aneeth." Pastor Manoj got his attention. "Tell me. What is the biggest religion in India?"

Aneeth wiped tears away from his eyes. "Hinduism, of course."

The pastor nodded. "And in Pakistan?"

"Islam… of course," Aneeth answered with a curious look, wondering where this was going.

"And what about China? What's the big religion there?"

"Buddhism," Aneeth replied. "But pastor, what does this have to do with anything? What does it prove other than the fact that people believe different things? How am I supposed to know which one is right?"

Pastor Manoj ignored Aneeth's questions and continued his train of thought. "Now, tell me, what do all those religions have in common?"

Aneeth shrugged, but then took a moment to think. He put his head down in a contemplative manner, then after thinking it through, raised his head to look at the pastor.

"They are all trying to get to God?" Aneeth guessed. "What else is religion for?"

Pastor Manoj smiled, sitting up straight in his seat. "That's exactly right. They're all trying to get to God. Would you like to know the difference between all those belief systems and Christianity, Aneeth?"

Aneeth nodded, desperation for answers still evident in his eyes.

Pastor Manoj leaned forward over his desk. "The difference, beta, is all of those religions are trying to get to God, but in Christianity, God is trying to get to us."

Aneeth looked at him, puzzled, not sure he understood.

"All of the false religions in the world," Pastor Manoj continued, "they teach a man how to work his way to God. Good works, annual pilgrimages, daily prayers, etc. Whereas the Bible tells the story of how God came down to us when we did absolutely nothing to deserve it."

Aneeth felt he was catching on. "But why would God do that if we didn't deserve it?"

Pastor Manoj answered, "That's the question that the gospel answers, my friend. How can God be just, and yet show mercy to people who don't deserve it?"

The pastor paused, momentarily studying Aneeth's face. Aneeth was well aware of his faults. He couldn't be brought any lower, and so the pastor began to give him the good news that could cure his condition.

"Aneeth. I would tell you that you're evil, but you are clearly already aware of that. The bible tells us that no thief, no liar, and no fornicator will inherit the kingdom of heaven. These are all things you have been your whole life. But it is while you were still a sinner, not someone who deserved it, that God demonstrated His love for you in Christ Jesus."

Love. This word struck Aneeth like no religious word ever had before. Certainly, he thought, the other religions he'd heard about didn't speak of love. They spoke of worship, duty, vengeance, but never love, especially not that of God. He then thought of his father, whose love—if it was ever there—was never shown. *How could God demonstrate love for me?* He pondered.

Pastor Manoj broke through Aneeth's thoughts. "You see, Aneeth. God is rich in mercy, and He is willing that none perish. If you were to continue on the path you're on, you would rightly suffer in a Lake of Fire, but God did something that can rescue you from the fires of judgment."

God did something for me? Aneeth considered. *Why... How... How could that be possible?*

"Aneeth, two thousand years ago, God sent His Son to this world. His name is Jesus. Jesus did what you and I couldn't. He lived a perfect life, never doing anything that displeased His Father in heaven. He performed many miracles—healed the sick, cast out demons, and raised the dead. After being with us for thirty-three years, He was crucified on a cross at the request of His own people. They couldn't see that He had come to save them, but He came to save them nonetheless. On that cross, Jesus suffered the punishment from God that we deserve, as well as the vicious cruelty of men, and then... He died." He paused for a moment, ensuring he had Aneeth's attention. "For you, Aneeth... He died for you."

The Pastor paused again, as Aneeth's eyes began to be filled with tears and unfamiliar emotions. "But..." Aneeth muttered. "But why? Why would He die for people who hated him?"

Pastor Manoj warmly smiled. "So that *you* wouldn't have to, my friend. God loved the world in this way, that He gave His only Son, that whoever would believe in Him will not perish, but have everlasting life."

There was that word again. *Love.* More tears began to fill Aneeth's eyes as he leaned forward to hear the rest.

The Pastor continued. "Aneeth. Jesus died for you. You deserve to be punished for your sins, but Jesus was punished *for* you. As He hung on that cross, He knew that Aneeth would lie and steal and cheat, yet He died for you anyway. Then, a couple of days later, this Jesus who died was raised back to life by the power of God and appeared to hundreds of witnesses alive!"

This was the moment Aneeth believed. When the Pastor told of Christ's resurrection, something instantly came alive in Aneeth's soul. He perked up on the chair, tears streaming down his face and wide-eyed in amazement.

"That's right, Aneeth!" The pastor joyfully shouted with a smile, seeing that God was working right then. "He died and was raised again for you! Now come to him, beta! Repent of your sins and believe that God sent Jesus for you, and you will be saved! And you will know Him, and He will know you! And the love of God will be poured out in your heart, never-ending for all eternity! Jesus died... Now you can live!"

Aneeth broke. He fell off the chair and onto his knees, sobbing uncontrollably and calling on the name of the Lord. As he came to Jesus on that old, worn-out floor, Pastor Manoj spread out his arms and looked toward heaven. "Thank You, Father." He rejoiced quietly, tears of his own beginning to flow. "Thank You for saving Aneeth this day."

Meanwhile... Back at Aneeth's house, the widows, after searching for a while and finding no one, decided to return to the church, realizing they had missed him.

"If he knows what's good for him, he left town," Ishika said, putting her heels back on in front of his house.

Bhumika was the last to exit the house, accidentally leaving the front door ajar. "And he won't come back, either." She added, descending the steps of his porch.

"C'mon ladies. Let's head back to the church," Anjali said, gesturing for everyone to get back in the van. "Pastor Manoj is probably praying that we don't commit murder..."

With a chuckle, the women filed into the van and pulled out of Aneeth's luxurious driveway to return to the church and inform their pastor that Aneeth wasn't home.

Back at the church, Aneeth had regained his composure and was embracing Pastor Manoj as they rejoiced in new-found salvation.

As they came apart, Pastor Manoj let out a satisfied sigh and returned to his desk chair. Aneeth sat back down in the chair in front of the desk.

"Well, Aneeth." The joyful pastor said. "You are right with God. How does it feel?"

"Like nothing I've ever felt before, pastor," Aneeth replied, still wiping away the last of his tears. "I know now that God is not going to punish me, and it is the greatest feeling ever. What other problems have I to fear?"

Pastor Manoj smiled. "Well, my friend, you may be saved from the wrath of God,"—he leaned over his desk, his eyes comically widening—"but how will you escape the wrath of the widows?"

Aneeth froze. In the rush of all that transpired in the office, he had completely forgotten about the women.

Pastor Manoj fell back into typical form and burst out laughing at Aneeth's panicked expression.

Aneeth buried his face in his hands. Then, as the pastor regained his composure, Aneeth lifted his head up. "Pastor... What do I do?"

Pastor Manoj chuckled, slowly shaking his head back and forth with a smile. "Well, if you want to live, I wouldn't advise going home. I don't think they were planning on bringing you back alive." The pastor tried—and failed—to contain his snickering.

Aneeth stood up from his chair and began anxiously pacing the office. The pastor looked at him, and after observing for a few moments, invited him to sit back down.

"Aneeth," the pastor said, his laughter having run its course (for now), but his expression still light, "in all seriousness, you do need to take responsibility for what you've done to them."

Aneeth sighed. "I know, but what do I do?"

Pastor Manoj looked him in the eyes. "Go home, confess to them what you've done, and take whatever they dish out. What else can you do?" He finished with a shrug.

Aneeth felt a sense of determination rise up within him. He stood from his chair, ready to accept responsibility, whatever that looked like.

"Thank you, pastor," Aneeth said with a nod. "I'll go home and take care of this."

"I'll be praying for you, brother," the pastor said as Aneeth turned to leave his office. "Lord knows you'll need it..." he said to himself with a chuckle as Aneeth closed the door behind him.

After more amused laughter, he lightheartedly lifted his eyes upward and sighed. "Oh, Father... I love it when someone gets saved right before they die..." He once again burst into laughter, unable to keep his mind from wandering to the possible scenes that could unfold at Aneeth's mansion.

Ruhi navigated the church van onto the highway, the six other women continuing to vent their frustration and ruthlessly mock their manipulative boyfriend. In fact, they were so distracted by their mockery that they completely missed the black Lamborghini passing them on the other side of the road...

As the ladies were heading back to church to inform the pastor they had missed Aneeth, Aneeth was speeding home to confess to the women.

When Aneeth arrived at his house, he exited his car, curiously looking for a church van that wasn't there. As he approached the front door, thoughts of what awaited him caused his heart to beat faster as he found the front door ajar. *Are they waiting inside to kill me? Is there an ambush set?* He slowly pushed the front door open, unsure of his fate once he entered the house. Slowly, carefully, he made his way through the rooms of his mansion, expecting the women to jump him at any moment...

Meanwhile, back at the church, the seven women parked the van and stormed back into the pastor's office.

"We didn't find him!" Ruhi lamented.

"He wasn't home." Payal clarified, unwrapping the cloth from her knuckles.

"Of course he wasn't." Pastor Manoj said with restrained amusement. "He was here."

The seven women, who were still murmuring about their misfortune, suddenly became quiet, all turning to look at the pastor.

"He was... here?" Ankita asked.

"Indeed." Pastor Manoj said with a wide grin. "He showed up right after you left."

The seven women surrounded his desk, bursting into a flurry of rapid Hindi interrogation, asking things like, "Why didn't you call us?" and "How could you let him go?"

Sonali's voice finally rose above them all, a tear running down her cheek. "Why didn't you let us punish him, pastor?"

The other seven people in the room took note of her emotional question, quieting down to give her room.

Pastor Manoj gestured for the women to gather in front of his desk, and looked each one of them in the eyes, starting with Sonali. His expression was serious and meaningful. "Because Jesus was punished in his place." He looked at all the women again, who just stared back in thoughtful silence. He again locked eyes with Sonali. "That's why, beta."

"But pastor," Anjali sincerely inquired, "he's not a Christian."

Pastor Manoj respectfully chuckled. "He is now."

The women's eyes went wide in shock, darting back and forth between each other and their pastor.

"Pastor, what are you saying?" Payal asked, genuinely wanting an answer.

"That is why Aneeth came here." The pastor explained. "He came to talk to me about his soul. He confessed what he'd done to all of you, along with everything else he could think of. I then shared the gospel with him and he received Christ. Right there, on the floor where all of you are standing."

Some of the women took a few hesitant steps back. Ishika sat in the chair. They looked down and around at each other, their shoulders dropping in consideration of what they'd just learned. It was clear their desire to get even and their desire to act like Christians was at war within them.

"Whether you all can stomach it or not," Pastor Manoj continued in a calming tone, "Aneeth is your brother in Christ now. Jesus has forgiven him for this sin." He looked around the room, locking eyes with some of the widows. "Can you?"

The women seemed frozen, clearly conflicted as to how to respond.

Pastor Manoj continued in a passivizing tone. "I know that he hurt all of you, but we must not get our own revenge, no matter how much we want to. What does the scripture say? 'Vengeance is mine. I will repay, saith the Lord.'"

Ishika nodded. "And I am his willing servant. May He avenge through me," she said as she removed her heels and rose from her chair with attitude.

The other six women held her, all trying to calm her down, eventually convincing her to get back in her seat and put her shoes back on.

As Pastor Manoj was chuckling at the commotion, his phone beeped, alerting him to a text message. He picked it up and saw that it was from Aneeth. Reading the message, he couldn't keep himself from grinning.

"Ladies," he said, trying to quiet any leftover commotion. "Why don't we all sleep on it tonight? I will call Aneeth here tomorrow evening and each of you can confront him properly. What do you say?"

"So that's it?" Bhumika pressed. "All he gets is a good night's sleep?"

Pastor Manoj snickered, turning his phone to face the women. "Oh, I don't think he'll be getting much sleep tonight..."

The women all leaned in to read the text from Aneeth.

"Pastor. I can't find the women anywhere. I think they're hiding. Do you think they will kill me in my sleep?"

The eight of them burst into laughter in response to Aneeth's obvious distress. The women agreed to let the matter rest for the night and confront Aneeth tomorrow evening with the pastor.

They exited his office and made their way down the hallway and into the parking lot, where each of them said their goodbyes before heading home.

In the office, Pastor Manoj was replying to Aneeth's text, clearly amused by what he was writing...

"See you tomorrow evening, my friend. IF you survive the night..."

The pastor put his phone down and leaned back in his chair, snickering at Aneeth's predicament, as well as rejoicing in his salvation.

269 | POLYGAMY

The next evening, Aneeth nervously walked toward the church, his heart pounding in his chest and his palms sweating. He knew this moment was unavoidable. The time had come to face the seven women he had deceived. He'd spent the entire day praying, asking for strength to handle what was to come. Now, as the church doors were opened before him, all he could do was take a deep breath and step inside. He walked down the long hallway and turned into Pastor Manoj's office.

Then he saw them.

The seven widows were seated in folding chairs in front of the pastor's desk, their eyes fixed on Aneeth, showing their anger and hurt. The tension in the room was thick, and Aneeth felt a wave of guilt crash over him. They had every right to be upset.

Before he could say a word, Anjali stood up, her voice sharp. "How could you do this to us, Aneeth? How could you lie to all of us like this?"

Payal followed, her tone more heated. "You played us, made us all believe we were special. How could you be so heartless?"

They all stood up and got in his face, the questions coming at him all at once, a rapid-fire mix of English and Hindi. At one point, Ishika began angrily removing a heel, which prompted Pastor Manoj to get up and hold her back.

Aneeth tried to speak, but his words were drowned out by their rising voices.

"I trusted you!" Ankita shouted, her hands shaking with frustration. "I let you into my life, and you turned it into a joke!"

"How can I return to my garden!?" Bhumika shouted. "Now every time I eat a pepper we planted, I'll be reminded of your lies!"

Ruhi pointed in his face. "I'll bet you don't even *like* Bollywood movies, do you!? At least Singham has muscles! What are you?"—She squeezed his bicep, letting out an indignant chuckle—"A twig!?"

Suddenly, in the midst of the chaos, Sonali stepped forward. Without warning, she slapped Aneeth across the face. The sound echoed through the hall, leaving everyone silent and stunned. Aneeth's head snapped to the side, his cheek stinging from the impact. He blinked, momentarily shocked by the slap.

Sonali gasped and covered her mouth with her hands, her eyes widening in disbelief of what she'd done. "I'm... I'm sorry," she whispered, her voice barely audible as she took a step backwards, tears brimming in her eyes.

Aneeth, still reeling from the slap, slowly raised his hand to touch his reddened cheek. But instead of anger, all he felt was the weight of his own guilt. He had caused all of this. He had hurt these women deeply, and now, he had to own up to it.

Taking a deep breath, he stepped forward, his voice low but steady. "I deserve that," he said, looking at Sonali, then at the rest of them. "I deserve all of it. What I did was wrong, and I have no excuse."

The widows watched him blankly, remaining silent as he continued.

"I lied to all of you. I made each of you think you were the only one, and that was cruel. I was selfish, thinking only of my own desires, without any thought of how it would affect you. I don't deserve your forgiveness, but I am truly sorry."

He paused, his voice thick with emotion. "I don't expect you to forgive me right away, or maybe even ever. But I need to tell you that I'm sorry. I've spent the last few days reflecting, praying, and trying to understand how I could have been so blind to the hurt I was causing."

Aneeth looked at each of them, his eyes pleading for understanding, though he didn't expect any. "I've spoken to the pastor, and I'm trying to change. I want to make things right as much as I can, though I know it won't undo the damage I've caused."

The women exchanged glances, their anger beginning to abate. There was something different now. His words had softened the sharp edges of their pain, though they weren't ready to let go just yet.

Anjali was the first to speak, her voice quieter but still firm. "We've heard apologies before, Aneeth. What makes this one any different?"

Aneeth nodded, understanding their hesitance. "You have every right to doubt me. I can't ask you to believe me, but I can promise that I'm done lying. I came here to be honest, and I will be, no matter how hard it is."

For a long moment, no one spoke. The room was heavy with the weight of unspoken emotions. Then, slowly, Ishika sighed and shook her head as she sat down to strap her heel back onto her foot.

"I don't know if I can trust you again," she said, slipping her shoe on, "but I appreciate that you came here to apologize."

One by one, the others began to nod, their expressions softening just a little. It was clear that the wounds he had caused wouldn't heal overnight, but the fact that he had shown up, stood before them, and admitted his faults had made a small difference.

Aneeth knew there was still a long road ahead, but for the first time, he felt a small sign of hope. He had taken the first step, and now it was up to him to continue down the path of honesty and repentance.

Pastor Manoj sat in his chair, confident that Ishika was no longer a physical threat to Aneeth... "Why don't we all sit down?" He suggested, motioning for everyone to sit in a chair.

They arranged the chairs in a circle in front of the pastor's desk. When they were all seated, Pastor Manoj sighed and looked at Aneeth.

"Aneeth," he prompted. "Is there anything else you'd like to share with the group?"

Aneeth hesitated for a moment, then looked around to meet the eyes of the onlooking widows. "Yes," he conceded. "Two days ago, I learned that my father was killed because of the war."

The women responded sympathetically, though some more than others. Responses ranged from widened eyes to soft gasps from covered mouths.

"It made me think about my life," Aneeth continued. "I read in the Bible, **'What does it profit a man to gain the whole world and forfeit his own soul?'** It was then that I realized I was only living for myself. I had made my whole life a game, one that was all about me, and it was soon going to cost me my soul. I drove to see pastor yesterday, to find out what I was missing. Then, right here in this office, Pastor Manoj told me about Jesus, how He died for me so that I can be forgiven of my sins. As I listened, something happened to me." Tears began welling up in Aneeth's eyes. "It was as if God Himself reached down and touched me. I suddenly began to know that my sins were gone, and I was becoming someone new." He wiped some tears away from his eyes with his hands. "And I know that I can't fix everything I've done overnight, but I truly am sorry for what I did to all of you."

Pastor Manoj handed a tissue to Anjali, who passed it on to Aneeth. Aneeth blew his nose, holding back more tears. He then looked around the room, taking in the sight of these precious women before him, whom he had hurt so deeply.

"The truth is," Aneeth continued, "the whole thing started as a game. I simply wanted to see if I could date all of you at the same time for fun. But then, as days turned into weeks, I found myself enjoying my time with all of you so much, that I didn't want any of it to end."

He turned toward Anjali. "Anjali. It's true that I had never baked before, but every Sunday, I so looked forward to baking with you at your house. Watching you work your magic brought so much joy to my heart," Aneeth said while lifting his hand over his heart, the sincerity of his words evident to all.

Anjali smiled and nodded. "I had fun, too, Aneeth."

He then turned his head to face Ruhi. "I'm sorry to say, I really don't like Bollywood movies. I actually much prefer American films."

"I knew it," Ruhi said in a soft huff.

"But I loved watching you laugh at them when we'd watch together," Aneeth continued. "Your smile made me wish the movies were longer."

Ruhi softened a bit, though she still refrained from smiling. "I will admit, it was kind of nice to have company for a change."

He then turned to face Ishika, whose face suggested her heel could come back off with one wrong word.

"Ishika..." Aneeth said with a nervous smile. "Beautiful, gorgeous, wonderful Ishika... I didn't know that one could have so much fun around town without doing the things that I... that I *used* to do. You showed me how much fun it was to just be with someone you care about."

To everyone's surprise, Ishika's comical scowl slowly turned into a warm smile. "It's true, you know," she said to both Aneeth and the group. "We did have fun."

Aneeth took a deep breath, clearly relieved that he would no longer be attacked by pointy footwear. He then faced Ankita.

Before he could speak, Ankita asked, in a matter-of-fact tone, "You've never read a book, have you?"

Aneeth cleared his throat. "I... well... no... I have actually never read a book."

Ankita sighed while staring at him, silently communicating disbelief in his stupidity.

"But," Aneeth recovered, "I learned something with you that I never knew about myself."

"And what is that?" Ankita asked.

"That I love to read," Aneeth said with a genuine smile. "It simply took someone as special as you to show me that. And for that, I am grateful." He put his hands together in a praying fashion and bowed his head to Ankita as a display of gratitude.

Ankita's expression was somewhat unreadable, but she was clearly considering what he had to say about her.

Aneeth turned and looked at Sonali, putting his hand up to his recently assaulted cheek. "Sonali. Thank you for slapping me."

The group laughed at his statement, a sign that more and more tension was releasing from the room—and their hearts.

Aneeth continued while looking at Sonali. "I so enjoyed our coffee dates and museum tours together. Your company always made my day brighter. Even now, looking in your eyes warms my heart."

Sonali blushed. "Thank you, Aneeth. I enjoyed our dates too." She shrunk back a little and looked around the room. "What?" She shrugged. "Apart from the constant deception, the dates were quite good."

The women—and Pastor Manoj—once again succumbed to a small round of laughter.

Aneeth then turned to Payal, who looked back at him with a face full of forced seriousness.

"Thank you, Payal," Aneeth said sincerely.

"For what?" She responded coldly.

"Well," Aneeth smiled, "I've never been in better shape in my whole life."

Warm, hearty laughter filled the room, then Aneeth leaned closer in towards Payal. "Honestly," he said just loud enough for everyone to hear, "can we still work out together? Ruhi says I'm a twig..."

That joke did it. The women erupted with laughter, the kind that they'd shared in the van together. The barriers between Aneeth and his former victims were starting to crumble, as he finally turned his gaze toward Bhumika.

"Save it, Aneeth," Bhumika said before he could speak. "The peppers we planted will remind me of your stupidity, yes..." Everyone chuckled, while Bhumika warmly smiled. "But they'll also remind me of your transformation and courage."

Everyone, including Pastor Manoj, nodded as if to agree with Bhumika's sentiment. Then, after a few moments of nervous silence, everyone unsure of where to go next, a faint voice broke through the quiet.

"Aneeth."

Everyone turned to see Sonali looking up at Aneeth, her eyes looking straight at his, hesitant tears beginning to form in them.

"I forgive you," Sonali said softly, exhaling a breath she hadn't realized she'd been holding.

Pastor Manoj smiled, encouraged by her Christ-honoring display. Then, to both his and Aneeth's surprise, "I forgive you" began escaping through each of the widow's lips, one after the other, until all had offered Aneeth their forgiveness.

Tears began falling from Aneeth's eyes as the flood of forgiveness completely overwhelmed him. "I don't deserve this," he said between breaths.

"No, you don't," Payal said as she got up and walked over to him, putting a hand on his shoulder. "But you're our brother now."

Aneeth looked up at her, his eyes swelling with emotion.

"*We* forgive you." She continued. "We forgive you, brother."

Aneeth burst into tears, kissing the hand that was on his shoulder, completely overwhelmed by the grace he'd been shown. The other six widows got up and joined Payal in embracing Aneeth, assuring him that they indeed forgave him. Pastor Manoj looked on from his desk, silently giving thanks for the glorious sight he was beholding in his office.

The moment passed and the widows returned to their seats, each nervously adjusting as they silently pondered the question that had yet to be asked. Pastor Manoj, slowly realizing what was causing the awkward silence, fell into his all-too-familiar comedic form and blurted out, "So? You all were wanting to marry this man. Which one of you gets him?"

An ear-to-ear smile emerged on his face as he watched the widows shuffle around, each unsure how to respond to the question. They all looked back and forth at each other, saying—without saying—what each of them was thinking. They were all interested in marrying Aneeth, especially in light of his genuine conversion, but none were willing to stake such a claim, knowing that staking it would put them at odds with the other six women.

As the widows and Aneeth sat in uncomfortable silence, Pastor Manoj noticed a silent notification appear on his phone. He picked it up and read a text message, his countenance falling as his eyes traversed the screen. Ankita, noticing the pastor's unease, spoke up softly. "Pastor Manoj? Are you okay?"

All eyes moved to the typically jovial pastor. He raised his head from the phone and looked at the group with a severely concerned expression. Sweat began beading on his forehead as he slowly reached for a remote on his desk and turned to power on the small T.V. behind him.

A breaking news report flashed across the screen. The headlines were terrifying. Everyone leaned forward to watch the report as Pastor Manoj increased the volume.

"The war is now at our doorstep." An Indian woman reported from central Delhi. "We've just received news that Muslim extremists have attacked Indian citizens near the edge of the city. They have entered defenseless homes and demanded money in exchange for safety. They have raped women and kidnapped children who cannot pay, and are threatening to attack the city tomorrow. The Indian army is—"

Pastor Manoj turned the T.V. off and turned towards the group as a tear fell from his eye.

"Pastor?" Anjali said, her voice quivering. "What do we do?"

"We all live alone or with elderly people in the city," Bhumika added. "How will we be safe?"

Murmuring about the dangerous situation swelled among the widows. The war that had claimed their husbands was now right outside their door. The threat was no longer for other people in another country. It was present, it was real, and it was a serious threat to them.

As the women anxiously deliberated about the problem—each scared to go home that night—Aneeth sat in silence, wondering what to do.

"I need a moment to pray," Pastor Manoj quietly said to the group. "Excuse me." He then slowly retreated to the prayer room behind his office with his bible, the anxious chatter fading as he closed the door behind him.

Pastor Manoj set his bible on the old pulpit that stood on one side of the prayer room, gripping its sides with trembling hands.

"Oh, Lord." He began. "What do I do for these women? And the church? How can I know that my flock will be safe tonight? Or tomorrow even?"

Tears began falling down his cheeks and onto the pulpit as he continued. "These women, Father. They cannot go home. They are young and beautiful, and they would not be safe from those monsters outside. Please, Lord. There is much to attend to for those in the church, but what of these in my office right now?"

The pastor shook his arms with emotion. "Show me the way!" He pleaded. His hands dropped down on the top of the pulpit, inadvertently knocking his bible to the floor.

When he picked up the open bible and set it on the pulpit, he paused as he noticed the passage it was open to. His eyes slowly scanned the text, his worry and fear slowly morphing into a grin. Looking up from the passage, he raised his eyes toward heaven with a smile. "Oh, Lord. There is no sense of humor as great as Yours in all the universe," he said as he playfully pointed upwards and shook his finger. Snickering to himself, he took the bible and returned to the office.

He found the scene he'd expected. Worried women, and Aneeth at a loss for words.

"What are we going to do, pastor?" Sonali anxiously voiced.

Anjali was perched on the edge of her seat. "We can't go back to our homes in the city. It's not safe."

"Especially with no husbands to protect us," Payal added, her usual confidence revealing its vulnerability in light of such terrifying force.

Their questions and concerns were fired at Pastor Manoj in a cacophony of worry as he returned to his desk. Without speaking, he placed his open bible in front of him as he sat, which caused the group to inquisitively quiet down.

"I would like to read you all a portion of scripture," the pastor said with a well-hidden grin.

The widows returned to their seats to listen, curiosity piqued, Aneeth's especially.

Pastor Manoj began, "I'm reading from Isaiah 3:25 to 4:2." He cleared his throat and began reading.

"Your men will fall by the sword and your mighty ones in battle. And her gates will lament and mourn, and deserted she will sit on the ground. For seven women will take hold of one man in that day, saying, 'We will eat our own bread and wear our own clothes, only let us be called by your name; take away our reproach!' In that day, the branch of the Lord will be beautiful and glorious, and the fruit of the earth will be the pride and the adornment of the survivors of Israel."

Having finished the passage, he looked up to assess the group's reaction. He said nothing, hoping that the widows—more than Aneeth—would catch on without help. The widows looked back at him blankly, initially oblivious to the passage's relevance to their situation.

"What exactly is that supposed to mean, pastor?" Ishika asked, breaking the confusing silence.

Pastor Manoj shrugged. "You tell me."

"Well," Ankita said, "it says that men had died in battle, just like our husbands..."

"And that mourning would follow," Anjali pointed out, "just like it has for us..."

"And what was the next part?" Ruhi asked.

"It was something about seven women—" Sonali innocently began and then paused.

Payal cleared her throat, her eyes going wide. "*How* many women?" she loudly asked, walking over to the pastor's desk to double-check the verse. She looked down to scan it, then looked up in shock. "It's seven..." she said in a hushed tone.

"And those seven women..." Anjali said, her eyes widening in revelation.

"All marry one man..." Bhumika quietly muttered, breaking her own silence.

With that, the widows, all in perfect unison, slowly turned their heads toward the smiling pastor. At this point, Aneeth had also realized what was going on, but didn't dare interject.

"Pastor Manoj?" Ankita prompted hesitantly. "Are you suggesting that we... that all of us..."—she gestured with her hand to the rest of the widows—"marry Aneeth?"

"Well?" The almost snickering pastor said. "You said it yourselves. Where will you go? Aneeth has a house outside of the city, money enough to provide for you all in the struggling economy, and apparently,"—the pastor said playfully, trying to keep himself from laughing—"he has room in his heart for all of you..."

Aneeth's eyes went wide as the widows looked at each other, and then him, stunned.

Anjali broke the silence that seemed to last for hours. "But pastor..." she said softly. "That is no longer legal in India. Even if we wanted to, how would it work?"

The pastor let out a lighthearted huff. "Legal. Illegal. One wife. Seven wives. Who cares at a time like this? Certainly not the Indian government. They've got bigger fish to fry." He looked around the room. "You all wanted to marry Aneeth... Go ahead and marry Aneeth," he said as he gestured to a very blushed and nervous Aneeth. "He's a new Christian, yes." A smile played on his lips... "But what could sanctify a man faster than having seven wives all at once?"

He laughed at his own joke, but only received quiet chuckles from his nervous audience.

Sobering up a bit, the pastor sat up straight, seriously addressing the women. "Look. If you seven women can live together in harmony in that big mansion of his, this would solve all of your problems. The safety, the money, the husband—all of it. Paul told younger widows to get married and keep house. Well? Get married and keep house. Who's stopping you?"

The women looked at each other and Aneeth, their eyes darting back and forth in bewilderment. Aneeth remained frozen in place, still too scared to speak.

Finally, Bhumika spoke up. "Why don't we take the night to think about this. And maybe meet again in the morning."

The other widows slowly voiced their agreement.

With that, Pastor Manoj addressed the women. "It's not safe to return home tonight, for any of you. Why don't you stay at the church? Aneeth can go home and return in the morning."

Everyone agreed and Aneeth left for home, his head spinning from the events of the evening. In less than an hour, he'd gone from being these women's worst enemy to their prospective husband. As he drove home, passing by police barricades being set up along the way, he couldn't stop thinking about the pastor's suggestion. Could this really be God's plan for him? To marry seven women whom he had wronged? He felt hopelessly unworthy of such a task, yet the appeal of such an arrangement couldn't escape him either.

Back at his home, he slowly moved about the mansion, as if in a daze, getting ready for bed. When he finally settled into bed for the night, his mind raced as he opened his bible and attempted to pray. What should he even say?

At the church, the widows spread out old pillows and blankets on the floor of the larger meeting room, discussing the situation as they prepared for bed. The conversation went as one would expect. They weighed the pros and cons of such a large household, grappled with any conflicts they felt it presented in light of their faith, and—sometimes humorously—imagined what day-to-day life with Aneeth in his mansion would look like. The very real threat of both war and poverty was at the forefront of the women's discussion as they considered their options. They talked and prayed together late into the night, hoping that God would guide them toward the right decision.

On the other side of town, Aneeth had drifted off to sleep and found himself in a vivid dream...

***

Aneeth stood on a paved road with nothing but white on either side. As he struggled to see in front of him because of the light, a tall man in a white robe approached him on the road.

"Aneeth!" The man called out.

"Yes? I am Aneeth."

The figure stopped just a few feet in front of him. "Aneeth, you have lived your entire life serving yourself. Now, for the glory of God, you will give up all that you have gained."

"But what about the women?" Aneeth asked. "What do I do about the women?"

The angel ignored his question and continued. "Sell all that is within your house—though not your house itself—and give what you receive to the cause of the gospel. Your riches will be used to bring many souls to Christ in Asia and the Middle East."

Aneeth hesitated, momentarily doubting whether selling his goods was worth it.

Seeing his hesitation, the angel inquired, "Have you forgotten already? **What does it profit a man to gain the whole world and forfeit his own soul?**"

***

Before Aneeth could respond, he awoke from his dream, sweat dripping down his head and his heart racing inside his chest. He knew what he had to do, but he was given no answer about the widows. What did that mean? Was he told to keep his house so that he'd have enough room for them? Would the women not want to marry him if he sold his luxurious belongings? He decided to leave those answers in the hands of the widows. For his part, he would do what he was told.

He glanced over at his alarm clock. 4:27 AM. With everything going on, there was no chance of going back to sleep, so he showered and started packing up his belongings, room by room. When the sun had risen, and the widows had plenty of time to wake up and gather their thoughts, Aneeth drove to the church. The drive across the city was ominous. Police checks and barricades were everywhere as they attempted to thwart the plans of the invading terrorists. The difficulties plaguing his country—and now his city—weighed heavily on him as the events of yesterday swirled around in his mind. He prayed for strength, for wisdom, and for guidance.

When he arrived at the church, he slowly exited his Lamborghini, taking in the fact that it would soon be sold and replaced with something far more modest.

When he entered the building, the women were already waiting in Pastor Manoj's office, though the pastor had not arrived yet. Aneeth made his way down the hallway and turned into the office of waiting widows.

"Good morning, Aneeth," Bhumika greeted, followed by soft greetings from the others.

"Please, sit," Anjali said as she gestured toward the empty chair.

Aneeth sat down, partly nervous about the answer that awaited him but partly nervous about informing the widows that his life of luxury was a thing of the past.

"Aneeth," Payal said, "we—"

"Wait." Aneeth interrupted, holding his hand up. "Before you say anything, I need to tell you all something."

The women nodded, prompting him to say what he had to say.

"I had a dream last night," Aneeth began. He proceeded to tell them all that transpired in his dream, and how the angel commanded him to sell his goods—all except his house—for the cause of the gospel.

The women listened attentively, deep in thought about the implications of Aneeth's drastic lifestyle change. When he finished, some of the women looked confused, some concerned.

"I think we need time to talk about this, Aneeth," Ishika said, the rest of the widows voicing their agreement. With that, Aneeth headed home to continue his packing, leaving the widows to deliberate amongst themselves.

Anjali was the first to speak after he left. "What will we do?" she asked the group.

Ruhi added, "When we decided to marry him, we had no idea he would sell his belongings."

Payal thought for a moment with a serious look on her face, then spoke. "Before we consider what we'd lose, why don't we consider what Aneeth has gained?"

The others looked at her, some tilting their heads in confusion.

"What do you mean, Payal?" Sonali voiced.

"Look at what's become of him," Payal reasoned. "A changed man, overnight. He's gotten right with God and man all in one day, he's clearly sorry for the way he treated us, and now he is willing to give up his riches for the sake of the gospel? Is this not the kind of man we'd want to be with? Even if it meant our lives were less luxurious?"

The women murmured and nodded, looking at each other for signs of agreement.

"It's hard to say, after all those nights on the town, that I wouldn't miss the rich life," Ishika said with a reminiscent smile.

"He did say he would keep the house.." Bhumika pointed out.

"An empty house..." Ruhi solemnly added.

They all paused for a moment as they considered the change.

"Why should the house be empty?" Ankita reasoned, drawing everyone's attention. "He said he would sell his possessions. But what would keep us from bringing our own?"

Some of the women tilted their heads, seeming to get her point right away. Ankita continued, "Think about that property, how many rooms he has in that house. I could bring my books and have a library. Anjali could easily find room in that massive kitchen..."

Anjali's eyes widened. "There's certainly plenty of room," she conceded.

"And Bhumika," Ankita continued, drawing Bhumika's attentive gaze. "He has almost an acre of grass outside. That's ten times the room you've had before to garden."

Bhumika nodded in agreement. "That's very true. I could grow a lot out there."

More of the women started joining in, following Ankita's lead. As they reviewed their options and what they'd bring with them to his home, they began to realize... They wouldn't lose that much after all!

"Here's what I say," Payal declared with a sense of finality in her voice. "If Aneeth has become the kind of man who would give up his riches for Christ, then he's the kind of man I want to marry, especially in uncertain times like these." She looked around the room with purpose. "Who's with me?"

"His house has plenty of room for us all," Sonali asserted. "Besides, where else will we go? This may be the only safe option we have."

The seven widows looked at each other, all of them realizing they had come to the same conclusion...

They would marry Aneeth.

With a nod from Payal, they all stood up and made their way down the hallway and out the church's front door. As they turned toward the church van, Pastor Manoj was just getting out of his car. "Where are you going?" He called over.

"No time to talk, pastor!" Ishika called back. "We're getting married today!"

Several of the women looked back at him and smiled before getting in the van. As they drove off, Pastor Manoj grinned, slowly shook his head back and forth in amazement, then looked up towards heaven with his arms out wide. "Only you, Lord," he said with a chuckle. "Only you..."

Meanwhile, back at the mansion, Aneeth was praying as he continued to pack his belongings in cardboard boxes. The situation weighed heavily on him, and he found it difficult to wait any longer for the widows' answer. About the time that the widows had begun driving to his house to inform him of their decision, Aneeth had made a decision of his own.

"I just can't do it," he said as he exited his house and walked to his car. "Lord, I'm a Christian now. And I can't imagine marrying seven beautiful women for any other reason than my own personal gain. How could I have even considered this?" He sat down in his sports car and started the throaty engine. "I'm a fool for ever thinking they'd say yes," he concluded, as he drove away from his home.

The widows hurried through the tension-filled city, excitement starting to build about their new lives, even amidst the nervous feelings the hardening city induced. In fact, they were so busy talking about what their new lives would be like that they completely missed the black Lamborghini passing them on the other side of the road...

Aneeth sped past, himself not noticing the church van heading for his house.

When the widows arrived at Aneeth's mansion, they saw themselves in and took in the scene. The walls were empty of art and decorations, fancy furniture was stacked in corners, and cardboard boxes lined the floors, filled with technology and other things Aneeth didn't need. The women stood in the living room, processing what they were seeing. Then, as if the same idea settled over all of them at once, they looked at each other and, without a word, knew what they should do...

Aneeth pulled into the church in a hurry, expecting to interrupt a room full of debating widows, but all he found in the office was Pastor Manoj, who was busy fielding calls about other members who needed help.

Aneeth knocked gently on the open door. Pastor Manoj, phone pressed to his ear, motioned for him to come in. Aneeth slowly walked in and sat down as the pastor hung up the phone.

"So," the pastor said with a sigh and a smile, "what can I do for you, my friend?"

"Well," Aneeth said hesitantly, "I had come to tell the women that I wouldn't marry them. It's just too much for—"

"You're a bit late for that!" Pastor Manoj interrupted, as he laughed at Aneeth.

"What do you mean?" Aneeth asked, confused at the pastor's response.

"Well," the amused pastor continued, "seeing as they're already on their way to your house to marry you, I'd say you're a bit late to cancel things."

The pastor continued chuckling as Aneeth sat back in his chair, a look of shock crossing his face. "They really said yes?" Aneeth asked the pastor, completely overwhelmed by their faith in him.

"Yes, yes!" Pastor Manoj said with a smile as he gestured with his hand for Aneeth to leave his office. "Now, *you're* problem is solved. The city is on fire and I have other members to attend to. Go enjoy your life, your wives, and your salvation!"

He rose from his desk chair and walked towards the still-seated Aneeth, motioning for him to get up. Aneeth stood up as the pastor nearly pushed him out of his office. "God bless, beta!" He shouted at Aneeth as the thoroughly shocked new convert made his way down the hall.

As Aneeth made his way to his car, he found his steps lightening with each one he took, a smile even emerging on his face. "Maybe I *can* do this," he said out loud as he strapped himself into his car. "Maybe I *can* do this!" he repeated with confidence as he sped off.

When he reached his house, he found the front door ajar. He walked inside and headed for the living room. When he arrived, he saw the most peculiar sight... There they were. Seven beautiful women. Three were packing, two were cleaning, and two were cooking lunch in the kitchen. None of them noticed Aneeth's arrival.

Frozen and staring at the scene in his home, Aneeth found his thoughts inadvertently drifting to a familiar dream... As his favorite dance tune began playing in his head, a goofy grin formed on his face. The women's outfits slowly morphed into exotic dresses in his mind. Before he knew it, he was sitting on a throne in the center of his living room, the women dancing to the music as they rhythmically completed their work and showered him with affection. "Aneeth!" They playfully sang. "Aneeth... Aneeth!!"

"Huh?" Aneeth was snapped back to the present, Ishika standing in front of him, waving her hand to get his attention.

"Are you okay?" she prodded with a playful smirk.

"Yes. I... uh... what's all this?" Aneeth asked with a nervous smile, alerting the rest to his presence.

The chatter and the movement stopped as the women made their way over to him.

"Welcome home, Aneeth," Anjali warmly greeted, embracing him with a hug. The other women followed suit, greeting him and then inviting him to sit down.

The eight of them sat down on the floor, as all of the sitting furniture had been stacked against walls.

"I don't understand," Aneeth began. "You all decided to say yes, even though you knew I was giving up my stuff?"

"We talked it about all night," Bhumika said with a pleasant smile.

"And all morning, too," Sonali eagerly clarified.

Payal was sitting next to him and put a hand on his, looking into his eyes with warmth. "We decided that the kind of man you've become is the kind of man we want to love."

"Especially in times like these," Ishika added, pulling her heels off of her feet. Holding them in front of her, she smirked at them and then threw them behind her with a playful smile. The entire group laughed at her antics.

"I guess we're getting rid of weapons as well..." Ruhi teased, causing the laughter to continue.

Is this really happening? Aneeth thought to himself, looking around at the laughing women in amazement.

As the group settled down, Sonali lifted her hand, pointing her finger upwards. "I... uh... made something for our house last night. After you all went to sleep."

As she rose to go get it, the others whispered about what it could be.

She promptly returned with a brown paper bag and handed it to Aneeth with a smile. "I thought, in light of all the decorations you're losing, this would be the perfect one to start over with..."

The six other women gathered around Aneeth to watch him open it. He reached his hand in and pulled out a wooden sign with hand-drawn white lettering on it. At first, he was stunned. Tears welled up in his eyes as he hovered over the lettering with his fingers. Then, as others began to tear up alongside him, he abruptly stood up and walked over to the most prominent wall in the living room.

"Where are going?" Bhumika asked with a curious smile.

"Yeah, where are you going, Aneeth?" Anjali pressed with a smile of her own.

Saying nothing, Aneeth picked up a hammer and nail, and promptly mounted the sign he was given to the center of the wall. After he hung it, he took a few steps backwards and admired the sign, his soon-to-be wives gathering round and admiring it with him. It was the first piece they had put in their home as a family, and they all clearly loved it.

"So you like it?" Sonali asked with a smile and tears in her eyes.

"Like it?" Aneeth said through tears of his own. "I don't think I've ever loved anything more..."

"Read it out loud!" Ishika insisted, giving a loving nudge to his side.

Aneeth stared for a few more moments, then read the hand-crafted sign out loud...

"Husbands, Love Your Wives,

Just As Christ Loved The Church..."

Ephesians 5:25

Story 5 - Better To Marry Than To Burn

Setting – Greece, Modern Day

This story depicts an attractive, passionately-in-love married couple and centers around a man's struggle with sexual temptation. While there are no specific descriptions of intimacy, some may feel that the slightly more mature theme is not suitable for younger audiences.

The plane descended through wispy clouds, revealing the familiar landscape of Greece below. Candice pressed her face to the window, tracing with her eyes the coastline where the waves crashed against weathered cliffs.

Beside her, Paul fidgeted with his seat belt, his knee bouncing nervously.

"Look at that view," Candice murmured, her voice full of awe despite having seen it countless times before.

Paul leaned over, his broad shoulder brushing against hers as he peered out. "Never gets old, does it?"

As the wheels touched down, Candice felt a familiar flutter in her stomach—part excitement, part lingering disbelief that this was now their home. They'd spent years dreaming of Greece from their kitchen table, but when they'd finally sold their house and booked those one-way tickets, his hands had trembled as he signed the papers, grinning like a madman..

The cabin filled with the sounds of seatbelts unclicking and overhead compartments being wrenched open. Paul stood, his tall frame towering over the seats. He reached up to grab their carry-ons, muscles in his arms flexing beneath his tan skin.

"Still thinking about that gelato in Rome?" he asked, glancing at his wife over his shoulder.

Candice turned to him with a grin. "You know me too well. I think if we lived in Italy, I'd gain a hundred pounds."

Paul chuckled, reaching over to squeeze her hand. "Then I guess it's a good thing we chose Greece, huh?"

"Absolutely," Candice agreed, standing up before joining her husband.

They shuffled down the aisle, joining the throng of passengers eager to alight. As they stepped into the jet bridge, the stuffy airplane air gave way to the crisp scent of the Mediterranean.

"I can't believe it's been a year," Candice mused as they made their way through the terminal, her long wavy blonde hair rippling behind her back.

Paul nodded, his dark eyes scanning the signs overhead. "A year since we packed up our lives in Boston and decided to become olive-oil-guzzling, ouzo-sipping Greeks."

Candice laughed, the sound echoing off the polished floors. "I'm pretty sure that's not how the locals would describe themselves."

"No? Dang, I've been doing it all wrong then."

They bantered back and forth as they went through customs and collected their luggage. It wasn't until they left the terminal and the Greek heat pressed against their skin that reality began to sink in. Their anniversary trip was over. It was time to return to their new normal.

Paul fished the car keys from his pocket as they approached the parking garage. "You want to drive?" he offered.

Candice shook her head. "Not unless you want to end up in Athens instead of home."

"Fair point," Paul conceded, unlocking their modest sedan. As he loaded their suitcases into the trunk, Candice leaned against the car, observing the din of the airport. Travelers rushed past them, dragging suitcases and calling out in various languages.

"Hey," Paul said softly, closing the trunk and moving to stand in front of her. "You okay?"

Candice smiled, reaching up to brush a lock of his thick black hair from his forehead. "Just... processing, I guess. Leaving Greece, even temporarily, it stirred up a lot of memories."

Paul's brow furrowed. "Good ones, I hope?"

"Mostly," Candice assured him. "But it also made me realize how much our life has changed. How much *we've* changed."

Paul nodded slowly, understanding dawning in his eyes. He took her hands in his, his thumb tracing circles on her skin. "Change isn't always bad, though, right?"

Candice squeezed his hands. "No, it's not. This past year... it's been challenging, but I wouldn't trade it for anything."

They stood there for a moment, the din of the airport fading into the background. Then Paul grinned, breaking the spell. "Come on, let's go home. I'm dying for some real Greek coffee after that swill they served on the plane."

The drive home passed mostly in comfortable silence, except when they made idle chatter about their trip. As Paul drove through the winding roads, Candice found herself admiring the landscape. The rugged cliffs, the sprawling olive groves, the glimpses of sparkling sea between hills—it was a view that never failed to take her breath away.

"Remember when we first drove this road?" she asked, a smile tugging at her lips.

Paul groaned. "How could I forget? I was convinced we were going to drive off a cliff at every turn."

"And now look at you, zipping around like a local."

"I wouldn't go that far," Paul chuckled. "I still get honked at for driving too slow."

As they climbed higher into the hills, their neighborhood came into view. Whitewashed houses clung to the slopes, their blue-domed roofs a stark contrast against the earthy tones of the landscape.

Paul pulled up to the house, which was nestled in a miniature cul-de-sac with one other house next to theirs, killing the engine. For a moment, they both sat in silence, taking in the sight of their home. It wasn't grand—a modest two-story house with a small balcony overlooking the bay—but to Candice, it was perfect. Even though her home was modest, it was charming, and the patio and pool outback was all the space she needed to breathe.

"Home sweet—" Paul began, then caught himself with a sheepish grin. "I mean, good to be back."

Candice rolled her eyes affectionately. "Come on, you big dork. Let's unpack before jet lag hits us like a truck."

Paul nodded, reaching over to tuck a strand of hair behind her ear. His touch lingered, tracing the line of her jaw. "You know, as amazing as Italy was, I think I missed this place."

Candice leaned into his touch, her eyes meeting his. Even after a year together, the intensity of his gaze still sent a thrill through her.

At six-foot-three, Paul cut an impressive figure. The Mediterranean sun had darkened his short hair to pitch black and bronzed his once-pale skin golden.

Candice knew she turned heads too, standing at five-foot-ten with a fit physique and sun-kissed blonde hair, but it was moments like these, quiet and intimate, that reminded her of the depth of their connection.

As they lugged their suitcases inside, Candice noticed something different about the house next door. "Paul," she called, "look at the 'For Sale' sign."

Paul glanced over, his eyebrows rising. "Well, what do you know? Looks like we're finally getting new neighbors."

The 'SOLD' sticker plastered across the sign was impossible to miss. Candice's stomach fluttered as she fidgeted with her keys, hesitating at the threshold. They'd grown used to having no one next door. What would their new neighbors be like?

"I hope they're not the party-all-night type," she mused.

Paul snorted. "In this neighborhood? More likely to be retirees looking for a quiet place to enjoy their twilight years."

They spent the rest of the evening unpacking and settling back into their space. As night fell, they found themselves on their small balcony, glasses of local wine in hand, gazing out at the twinkling lights of the town below.

"I've missed this view," Candice sighed, leaning into Paul's side.

He wrapped an arm around her shoulders, pulling her close. "It's good to be home," he murmured into her hair.

The following morning, the first light spilling across the sky chased away every wisp of cloud. It was the perfect day for their usual run. As they stepped outside, stretching in preparation, the rumble of an engine caught their attention.

A large moving truck was pulling up to the house next door, followed closely by a sleek black car. As they watched, a woman emerged from the vehicle, moving gracefully and with purpose.

Even from a distance, her beauty was striking. She was tall and slim, with long wavy dark hair that covered half of her back, and catlike eyes of emerald green without a touch of hazel. Her skin was a rich olive tone and her features hinted at Middle Eastern heritage.

"Well," Paul said, his voice low, "I guess we can rule out retirees..."

Candice elbowed him gently. "Should we go say hello?"

Paul hesitated, then shrugged. "Might as well. Establish ourselves as the friendly neighbors before she realizes how nosy we are."

They made their way over to the neighbouring property, where the woman was directing movers quietly but efficiently. As they approached, she turned, standing only an inch shorter than Candice.

"Hi there," Candice called out with a friendly wave. "We're your next-door neighbors. I'm Candice, and this is my husband, Paul."

The woman's face lit up with a warm smile. "It's wonderful to meet you both," she said, her voice carrying a slight accent that was hard to place. "I'm Miranda. I just moved here from London."

As they chatted, Candice couldn't help but notice a familiar book sitting atop one of the nearby moving boxes. "Is that a Bible?" she asked, gesturing towards it.

Miranda's smile widened. "Yes, it is. I'm a Christian. It's the first thing I always unpack in a new place."

Paul and Candice exchanged a surprised and delighted glance. "We're Christians too," Paul said, his tone warm. "We actually attend a church not far from here. You're welcome to join us sometime, if you'd like."

Miranda's eyes lit up at the invitation. "I'd love that," she said, her voice filled with genuine enthusiasm. "I was worried about finding a church community here. This feels like a bit of a God-moment."

They chatted for a few more minutes, learning that Miranda was a student who had decided to go to school in Greece after falling in love with the country during a vacation the previous year.

"Well, we won't keep you from your unpacking," Candice said finally, noticing the movers starting to bring boxes into the house. "But please, don't hesitate to come over if you need anything at all."

Miranda thanked them warmly, and as Paul and Candice turned to leave, she called out, "Maybe once I'm settled, we could have dinner together? I'd love to get to know you both better."

"That sounds great," Candice replied, feeling a jolt of excitement at the prospect of a new friendship. "Just let us know when you're ready."

As they jogged down the familiar path that wound through their neighborhood, Candice found her thoughts drifting back to Miranda. "She seems nice," she commented between breaths.

Paul nodded, his breathing steady despite the incline. "It'll be good to have someone living there again. The empty house was starting to feel a bit… I don't know, ominous?"

Candice laughed, the sound slightly breathless. "Only you would find an empty house ominous in broad daylight."

Their conversation lulled as they focused on their run, their feet pounding steadily against the pavement. The route took them past other hillside homes, each one a variation on the classic white Mediterranean style that had initially drawn them to the area.

As they rounded a bend, the bay came into view, sunlight glinting off the water. Candice felt a familiar surge of emotion go through her—gratitude, wonder, and a lingering disbelief that this was now their home.

They finished their run and circled back to their house, both pleasantly winded. As they cooled down in their front yard, Candice noticed Miranda waving at them from her driveway. They waved back and Candice smiled at their new neighbour.

"You know," she said to Paul as they headed inside, "I have a good feeling about her. I think she'll fit in well here."

Paul nodded, wiping sweat from his brow. "Yeah, she seems great. It'll be nice to have someone our age in the neighborhood."

As they stepped into the coolness of their home, Candice found herself overcome with contentment. Their life here wasn't perfect—there were still moments of homesickness, cultural misunderstandings, and the occasional bout of doubt, but standing there, with the man she loved, in the home they'd chosen together, in a country that continued to captivate them… it felt right.

"Shower, then breakfast?" Paul suggested, already heading for the stairs.

Candice nodded, already thinking of what they'd do on their first day home. There was work to catch up on, groceries to buy, a house to clean after their absence, but there was also the hope of new friendships, of continued discoveries in their adopted home, of a life they were building together.

As the fishing boats began returning to the harbor, holds full from the day's catch, Paul's car crunched up the gravel driveway. He stepped out, briefcase in hand, expecting to be greeted by Candice's warm smile. Instead, the house stood silent, without the smell of food that he'd been expecting to waft from the kitchen windows.

"Candice?" he called, pushing open the front door. His voice echoed through empty rooms.

Frowning, Paul set down his briefcase and stepped back outside. A burst of laughter from next door caught his attention. There, amid a sea of cardboard boxes, stood Candice and their new neighbor, Miranda.

Paul made his way over, taking in the chaos of moving day. "Ladies," he greeted, a questioning look directed at his wife.

Candice turned, her face flushed with exertion. "Oh, Paul! I lost track of time. Miranda needed help unpacking, and well…" She gestured at the mess around them.

Miranda stepped forward, putting her hand on Paul's forearm in a friendly manner, still catching her breath from her recent laugh. "I'm so grateful for your wife's help. She's been a lifesaver."

Paul noticed the softness of her hand against his arm. "Happy to help," he said, then turned to Candice. "Dinner plans?"

Candice's eyes widened. "Oh, shoot! I completely forgot. I should get started on that."

"Why don't you go ahead?" Paul suggested. "I can stay and help with some of the heavier items."

Candice hesitated, glancing between Paul and Miranda. "Are you sure?"

Paul nodded, already rolling up his sleeves. "Of course. I got it from here. Go do your thing."

With a grateful smile, Candice headed home, leaving Paul alone with Miranda. He turned to find her appraising him, those striking green eyes taking his measure.

"So," Miranda said, clapping her hands together. "Ready for some heavy lifting?"

For the next hour, Paul found himself going up and down narrow staircases with bulky furniture, muscles straining as he put dressers and bed frames into place. Miranda directed operations with mixed authority and charm that left him both impressed and slightly off-balance.

"Just a bit to the left," Miranda instructed as they wrestled with a particularly unwieldy bookcase. Stepping back to get a better view, her foot caught on a stray power cord.

Time seemed to slow as Miranda teetered backward, arms windmilling. Without thinking, Paul lunged forward, catching her against his chest. For a heartbeat, they stood frozen, Miranda's emerald eyes wide with surprise.

Then, as if shocked, they sprang apart. "I'm so sorry," Miranda stammered, smoothing down her shirt.

Paul ran a hand through his hair, forcing a laugh. "No harm done. Hazards of moving day, right?"

They shared an awkward chuckle before turning back to the task at hand, both seemingly eager to move past the moment.

As they continued working, Paul found himself curious about their new neighbor, whose enigmatic quality seemed to be steadily increasing. "So, Miranda," he began, hefting a box labeled 'Kitchen', "Remind me again; what brought you to Greece? It's quite a change from London."

Miranda paused, her hand hovering over a vase she'd been unwrapping. "Oh, it's a bit of a story," she said, her tone light but seeming to hint at something Paul couldn't quite place. "I'm actually originally from Canada."

Paul's eyebrows rose. "Canada to Greece? That's quite a journey."

Miranda nodded, resuming her unpacking with a forced casualness. "I've always dreamed of studying here. There's this amazing school... well, when my father passed, he left me enough to make that dream a reality."

As Miranda continued her tale, Paul found himself listening with growing puzzlement. Something about her story didn't quite add up. She mentioned details about Greek education that he, after a year of living here, knew to be incorrect, but each time he considered pressing for clarification, Miranda would smoothly change the subject or ask for help with another piece of furniture.

By the time they finished, the sun had long since set, and Paul's muscles ached pleasantly from the exertion. "Well," he said, surveying the now-organised living room, "I'd say that's a job well done."

Miranda beamed at him, her earlier awkwardness seemingly forgotten. "I can't thank you enough, Paul. I don't know how I would have managed without you and Candice."

"It's our pleasure," Paul replied, then added on impulse, "Why don't you join us for dinner? I'm sure Candice made enough for three."

A flicker of something resembling hesitation crossed Miranda's face before she smiled apologetically. "That's so kind of you, but I actually have plans tonight. Rain check?"

Paul nodded, tamping down an inexplicable sense of disappointment. "Of course. Anytime."

As he made his way home, the savory scent of Candice's cooking greeted him, making his stomach growl with hunger he'd thus far ignored. He found her in the kitchen, humming softly as she stirred a pot of what smelled like her famous beef stew.

"There you are," she said, offering her cheek for a kiss. "I was beginning to think Miranda had kidnapped you."

Paul chuckled, wrapping his arms around her waist. "Nearly. That woman has an endless supply of heavy furniture."

They settled into dinner, but while Candice chatted about her latest art project, Paul found his mind drifting back to Miranda's disjointed story.

Later, as Candice cleared the dishes, Paul opened his laptop. He told himself he was just being thorough, looking out for their new neighbor, but as he delved deeper into his research, a knot formed in his stomach.

"Candice," he called, "come look at this."

She appeared at his shoulder, drying her hands on a dish towel. "What is it?"

Paul pointed to the screen. "Miranda mentioned a school. She said she came here to attend it." At Candice's nod, he continued, "It closed down last year. And some of the other details she gave about the Greek education system... they're just not right."

Candice frowned, leaning in to scan the web page. "Are you sure? Maybe you misunderstood."

Paul shook his head. "I don't think so. It's like... like her whole story doesn't add up."

To his surprise, Candice laughed, ruffling his hair affectionately. "Oh, Sweetie. She's probably just flustered from the move. You know how stressful that can be. Remember how many times we got Greek customs wrong when we first arrived?"

Paul opened his mouth to argue, but Candice was already moving away, a mischievous glint in her eye. "Now," she said, her voice dropping to a sultry whisper as she dropped the dish towel and untied her apron, "I can think of much more interesting things to do than worry about our new neighbor's academic choices..."

She trailed her fingers along his arm, raising goosebumps in their wake. Paul felt his concerns about Miranda begin to fade as Candice leaned in, her lips brushing his ear. "Come to bed?"

As he followed Candice upstairs—often his favorite part of the day—Paul easily pushed all thoughts of Miranda out of his head as his eyes followed the backs of his wife's long legs up the stairs. Before long, they were lost in each other's passionate embrace, any cares of the day being lost in their love.

In the quiet hours of the night, as Candice slept peacefully beside him, Paul found himself staring at the ceiling. He couldn't shake the nagging feeling that something was off about Miranda's story. The inconsistencies, the way she'd deftly avoided certain questions—it all added up to a picture that didn't quite fit.

But then, hadn't he and Candice fumbled their way through countless cultural misunderstandings when they'd first arrived in Greece? He could still recall the embarrassment of confidently ordering what he thought was a coffee, only to be served a plate of grilled meat. Perhaps Miranda was simply overwhelmed, her story muddled by the stress of relocation and the desire to make a good impression.

Paul turned on his side, studying Candice's face in the dim light filtering through the curtains. Her features were relaxed in sleep, a small smile playing at the corners of her mouth. He felt a surge of love for her, this woman who had uprooted her entire life to chase a dream with him. She'd always been the optimistic one, quick to see the best in people and situations. Maybe he needed to take a page from her book and give Miranda the benefit of the doubt.

The next day was a Saturday. As Paul and Candice went about their usual routine—a quick run, followed by breakfast on their small balcony—they found their conversation drifting back to their new neighbor.

"I was thinking," Candice said, stirring her coffee thoughtfully, "we should invite Miranda over for dinner properly. You know, officially welcome her to the neighborhood."

Paul nodded, his gaze drifting to the house next door. "Sounds good. Though I have to admit, I'm still a bit... curious about her story."

Candice rolled her eyes good-naturedly. "Sweetie, let it go. Not everyone has their life perfectly sorted out when they move to a new country. Give her time to settle in."

Paul nodded slowly, letting out a breath he hadn't realized he'd been holding. "You're right, as usual," he added with a small smile.

Candice grinned, reaching up to plant a quick kiss on his lips. "That's why you married me, remember? Now, why don't you work on the back yard while I go to the breakfast I promised Eleni and Niko Papadopoulos?"

An hour later, Paul wrestled with an overgrown hedge in their backyard. Sweat beaded on his brow, muscles straining against the resistance of stubborn branches. He paused, wiping his forehead with the back of his hand, and surveyed his progress. The yard was slowly coming back to life after their absence, but there was still work to be done.

A thud from next door caught his attention. Paul glanced over the fence, curiosity piqued. Miranda had emerged from her back door, arms laden with what looked like patio furniture. She set down her burden with a soft grunt, then straightened, pushing a stray lock of hair from her face.

Paul's breath caught in his throat. Miranda was clad in a dark green bikini that matched her eyes and a wispy white cover-up doing little to conceal her slender frame. He knew swimsuits were as common as souvlaki around here, but something about Miranda in hers made his heart skip a beat.

Shaking his head to clear it, as was his typical re-direction custom, Paul called out, "Need a hand with that?"

Miranda turned, her face lighting up with a smile that could rival the Grecian sun. "Paul! I'd love some help, if you don't mind."

Without hesitation, Paul vaulted over the low fence separating their properties. As he approached, he couldn't help but notice the way Miranda's green eyes sparkled with amusement.

"You're a hero," she teased, gesturing to the pile of furniture. "I may have been a bit ambitious in my decorating plans."

Paul chuckled, already bending to lift a heavy wrought-iron table. "Well, that's what neighbors are for, right? To save you from your own ambition."

They quickly found their groove with the heavy lifting—when he tilted, she steadied; when she pushed, he pulled, making the furniture seem lighter than it was. They arranged chairs and tables around Miranda's pool area. The work was punctuated by bursts of laughter and playful banter, making the time fly by.

As Paul set down a particularly cumbersome lounge chair, he decided to satisfy his lingering curiosity. "So, Miranda," he began, trying to keep his tone casual, "when you inherited the money, did you know right away that Greece was the destination?"

She nervously chuckled. "My grandfather had always known how much I wanted to live here. I loved and studied the Classics so much. That's why he left me all of the money instead of donating some."

"Your grandfather?"

Miranda froze for a split second, her hand hovering over a potted plant she'd been adjusting. "I'm sorry, what?"

Paul frowned, a growing sense of unease creeping up his spine. "The money your grandfather left you... But yesterday you mentioned it was your father who left you the money."

"Oh!" Miranda's laugh sounded forced to Paul's ears. "I meant my father, of course. I used to call them both Dad. It's been such a long week, my brain's a bit scrambled. Yes, my father left me the money."

Paul nodded slowly, not entirely convinced. "Right, of course. Must be quite an adjustment, moving to a new country."

Miranda seemed eager to change the subject, launching into a story about her misadventures in Greek grocery stores. Yet, as they continued working, Paul couldn't shake the feeling that something was off. Miranda's tale seemed to shift with each retelling, small details changing or being omitted entirely.

At one point, she mentioned growing up in the States, only to backtrack moments later and claim she was Canadian, as she had mentioned earlier. When Paul gently pressed for clarification, Miranda's eyes darted away, her fingers twisting nervously in the fabric of her cover-up.

Despite the growing list of inconsistencies, Paul found himself drawn to Miranda's vivacity. Her laughter was infectious, her wit sharp and engaging. He told himself he was being paranoid, that the discrepancies in her story were likely just the result of stress or jet lag.

As they finished arranging the last of the furniture, Paul made a split-second decision. "Hey, Candice and I were planning on whipping up some authentic Greek food tonight. Would you like to join us?"

Miranda's face lit up, all traces of her earlier nervousness vanishing. "I'd love to! What time should I come over?"

They settled on eight o'clock, and Paul made his way back to his own yard, his mind racing with conflicting thoughts. He hoped that spending more time with Miranda would help Candice form a friendship with their increasingly mysterious new neighbor. Perhaps his wife's easygoing nature would help smooth over any lingering awkwardness.

As he resumed working on the hedges, Paul couldn't shake the image of Miranda in her swimsuit from his mind. He felt a twinge of guilt, quickly suppressed. It was natural to notice an attractive woman, he reasoned. It didn't mean anything.

Hours slipped away between weeding the garden and dicing vegetables in the kitchen. When Candice returned from her breakfast with friends, she was thrilled at the prospect of hosting Miranda for dinner.

"Oh, Paul, that's perfect!" she exclaimed, already mentally revising the menu. "I picked up some fresh seafood at the market yesterday. We can grill it with lemon and herbs."

Paul smiled, pulling her in for a quick kiss. "Sounds delicious. I'm sure Miranda will love it."

As he worked in the kitchen—the familiar dance of chopping, stirring, and seasoning—Paul found himself relaxing, taking in the scent of sautéing garlic and herbs that filled the kitchen as he stirred the simmering pot of seafood paella. It was Saturday night, and his cooking dinner had become their cherished weekend tradition.

Candice sat at the kitchen island, sipping a glass of white wine and watching her husband put to work his amazing culinary skills. This was what he loved about their life here in Greece—the simple pleasures of good food, good company, and the woman he loved by his side.

"You know," Candice mused, twirling the stem of her glass between her fingers, "I still can't believe you kept this talent hidden for the first year we dated. I thought I'd be the one doing all the cooking."

Paul chuckled, adding a pinch of saffron to the pot. "Well, I had to make sure you weren't just after me for my paella skills."

Their laughter was interrupted by the chiming of the doorbell. Candice set down her glass, a puzzled expression crossing her face. "Is it eight o'clock already?"

Paul shrugged, wiping his hands on a dishtowel. "I think so. Go check. It must be Miranda."

Candice's face lit up at the mention of their new neighbor. She hurried to the door, smoothing her sundress as she went. When she opened it, Miranda stood there, looking slightly sheepish, but undeniably stunning in a pair of jean shorts and a flowing blouse that emphasized her lithe figure. She held a bottle of wine in one hand, a shy smile playing on her lips.

Candice gave a periphery glance to the clock. Indeed, the doorbell had chimed at precisely eight o'clock. "Miranda!" she exclaimed, pulling her into a warm hug. "Welcome to our home!"

"I hope I'm not early," Miranda said, her voice tinged with uncertainty. "I just… well, I smelled something amazing and couldn't wait. I hope this pairs well with whatever you're serving," she said, offering the bottle to Candice.

She took it. "I'm sure it'll be perfect," she said, stepping aside to let her in.

She ushered Miranda inside, leading her to the kitchen where Paul was stirring the paella. "You're just in time. Paul's making his famous seafood paella."

Miranda's eyes lit up as she took in the scene. Without hesitation, she walked over to Paul and wrapped him in a hug. "Thank you again for your help this morning," she said, her voice warm against his ear. "I don't know what I would've done without you."

Paul stiffened slightly, caught off guard by the embrace. He patted her back awkwardly, his eyes meeting Candice's over Miranda's shoulder. "It was no trouble at all," he managed, gently extricating himself from her arms.

Candice's brow furrowed slightly. "Help? What help?"

Miranda turned to her, a bright smile on her face. "Oh, nothing worth mentioning. He saw me struggling with some outdoor furniture this morning and came over to lend a hand. Good thing, too. My arms are still sore from moving day."

"Is that so?" Candice raised an eyebrow at her husband, amusement and curiosity mingled in her widened eyes. "Well, that was certainly kind of him."

Paul busied himself with the paella, avoiding Candice's gaze. "It was nothing, really. Just being neighborly."

As they settled around the dining table, the conversation flowed easily. Miranda seemed particularly interested in their church, peppering them with questions about the denomination, the programs they offered, and the community.

"It sounds wonderful," Miranda said, her eyes bright with enthusiasm. "It'd be quite a blessing to not have to hunt for a church. Maybe I could join you next Sunday?"

Before Candice could respond, the shrill ring of a cell phone cut through the air. Miranda's face fell as she glanced at the screen, her earlier enthusiasm replaced by a flicker of apprehension.

"I'm so sorry," she said, rising from her seat. "I have to take this. Excuse me for a moment."

As Miranda walked out onto the patio, Candice couldn't help but notice Paul's gaze going up and down her long, slender legs in her shorts. She gave him a playful elbow to the side. "They're legs, honey. You okay?"

Paul started, his face flushing as he realized he'd been caught staring. "I'm sorry," he mumbled, looking genuinely ashamed. "I didn't mean to..."

Candice chuckled, the sound light and free of judgment. "They are *nice* legs. I'll give you that..." A mischievous glint appeared in her eye as she propped her bare feet up on the table, showing off her own legs as her short sundress slid to reveal them. "How about mine?" she asked flirtatiously. "Are *mine* worth a stare?"

Paul's embarrassment melted away as he took in the sight of his wife. He reached out, running a hand along her calf. "Always," he murmured, his voice low and intimate.

Their moment was interrupted by Miranda's return. She paused in the doorway, taking in the scene before her. "Should I leave you two alone?" she teased, though there was something tight in her smile that hadn't been there before.

Candice quickly put her feet back under the table, laughing as she gestured for Miranda to sit. "Not at all. Come, finish your paella. It's far too good to let it go cold."

As Miranda settled back into her seat, Paul couldn't help but notice the tension in her shoulders. "Everything all right?" he asked, nodding towards the patio where she'd taken the call.

Miranda's smile didn't quite reach her eyes. "Oh, yes. Just... family stuff, you know how it is." She quickly steered the conversation back to the topic of church, her earlier enthusiasm seeming somewhat forced now.

Later that night, as Candice loaded the dishwasher, she remarked, "Well, that was lovely. Miranda's quite the character, isn't she?"

Paul hummed noncommittally, focusing on scrubbing a particularly stubborn spot on a plate.

Candice paused, turning to look at him. "Is everything okay, Sweetie?"

He forced a smile, meeting her concerned gaze. "Of course. Just tired, I guess. It was a long day of yard work."

Candice stepped closer, wrapping her arms around his waist. "Well, how about we call it a night then? I can think of a few ways to help you relax," she added with a suggestive wink.

While Paul and Candice prepared for bed, the conversation inevitably turned to their new neighbor.

"Did you notice how she dodged the question about the phone call?" Paul said suddenly, pulling back the covers on their bed. "And earlier, when she was talking about why she moved here... some of the details seemed off again."

Candice sighed, beginning to turn off the lights. "Yeah, I noticed that too. Maybe she got some details mixed up. It happens."

"But it's not just that. There's something... off about her whole story. Don't you feel it?"

Candice fell on their bed with more force than necessary, turning to face him. "What I feel is that we have a new neighbor who's trying to make friends. Why are you so determined to find something wrong with her?" Candice paused, then smirked. "You know, if you found her story as perfect as you find her legs, you wouldn't be having this problem..."

She raised an eyebrow in an expression of playful vengeance with regard to Paul's earlier blunder.

He froze for a moment and then apologized again for the incident, to which Candice rolled her eyes. "Just don't make a habit of it, Romeo... But really, why so hard on Miranda?"

Paul shuffled around to get comfortable, a slight look of worry appearing on his face. "I... I don't know," he admitted finally. "I just want to make sure we're being careful, I guess."

Candice's expression softened. She crept closer, wrapping her arms around his waist. "You're not completely off, you know. Sometimes it does feel like her story changes a little each time she tells it. But Paul, we can't let fear or suspicion keep us from making connections. Isn't that why we came here? To experience new things, to meet new people?"

Paul nodded. "Of course. You're right."

Remembering the seemingly tense phone call, Candice asked, "What do you think her phone call was about?"

"I don't know, probably something personal? She said family matters."

"She seemed bothered by it. I hope nothing's wrong."

Paul nodded before pulling Candice even closer and running his fingers through her soft blonde waves. His expression was serious now, although she didn't see it. "I need to apologize to you about something."

Candice pulled herself out of his grasp and propped herself up on one elbow, giving him her full attention. "What is it, love?"

Paul took a deep breath, his words coming out in a rush. "I've been looking at Miranda a little too much. I feel… guilty. Like I'm being tempted to lust or something, and I hate it."

To his surprise, Candice's expression softened. She reached out, cupping his face in her hand. "Thank you for being honest with me. Miranda is a beautiful woman, and it's natural to notice that. What matters is what you do with those thoughts."

Paul leaned into her touch, relief washing over him. "You're not angry?"

Candice shook her head, a small smile playing on her lips. "No, I'm not angry. I trust you, but if you're really struggling with this, maybe you should talk to Pastor Alex about it?"

He pulled her back to him. "You're amazing, you know that?" he murmured into her hair.

The next morning found them pulling into their driveway after church, both feeling refreshed by the service.

"I really thought Miranda might show up today," Candice said as they walked towards their front door. "She seemed so interested last night."

Paul was about to respond when movement in Miranda's living room window caught his eye. He nudged Candice, gesturing towards the house next door. Through the window, they could see Miranda pacing back and forth, her phone pressed to her ear. Even from a distance, the tension in her body was obvious.

"I hope everything's okay," Candice murmured, concern etching her features.

Paul squeezed her hand. "Why don't you go over and check on her? She might need a friend right now."

Candice nodded and made her way over to Miranda's house, smoothing down her church dress before ringing the doorbell.

When Miranda answered, the contrast between her appearance now and the night before was stark. Her hair was disheveled, dark circles under her eyes suggesting a sleepless night.

"Candice," Miranda said, her voice flat. "What can I do for you?"

Candice's concern deepened at Miranda's tone. "We saw you through the window and thought you might be upset. Is everything all right?"

Miranda's gaze darted over Candice's shoulder, as if checking to see if anyone else was there. "I'm fine," she said, her words clipped. "Just... dealing with some personal matters."

"We missed you at church today," Candice pressed gently. "We were looking forward to introducing you to our friends."

Something akin to guilt or fear flashed in Miranda's eyes before she schooled her features into a neutral expression. "I'm sorry. I should have let you know I couldn't make it. I've been... preoccupied."

Candice took a step forward, reaching out to touch Miranda's arm. "Miranda, if you need help with anything—"

Miranda flinched away from the touch, her body language suddenly closed off. "I appreciate your concern, but I really need to be alone right now. Please."

Before Candice could respond, Miranda had already stepped back, closing the door with a soft but final click.

Candice stood there for a moment, stunned by the abrupt dismissal. As she made her way back to her own house, her thoughts tumbled over themselves as questions piled up without answers.

Paul was waiting for her in the living room, his expression expectant. "How did it go?"

Candice sank onto the couch beside him, shaking her head. "Not well. She practically slammed the door in my face. Paul, something's not right. The way she looked, how she was acting... it's like she's a completely different person from the woman we had dinner with last night."

Paul wrapped an arm around her shoulders, pulling her close. "What do you think is going on?"

Candice leaned into him, finding comfort in his solid presence. "I don't know, but I'm worried about her. The phone calls, the inconsistencies in her story, now this… It feels like she's hiding something."

Paul nodded, his brow furrowed in thought. "I agree, but we can't jump to conclusions, right? Just like you said, we barely know her."

"I know," Candice sighed. "But I can't shake the feeling that she's in some kind of trouble. I… I can't stop thinking about her," Candice admitted as Paul took her hand in his. "What if she's in some kind of danger, Paul? What if she needs help but is too afraid to ask for it?"

Paul squeezed her hand, his thumb familiarly tracing soothing circles on her skin. "I understand your concern, love, but we have to be careful. We don't know Miranda's situation, and getting involved without knowing all the facts could potentially make things worse."

Candice nodded, knowing he was right but still feeling torn. "I know. It's just… when we first moved here, remember how overwhelmed we felt? How much it meant to have neighbors who looked out for us?"

Paul's expression softened at the memory. "Of course. Mrs. Papadopoulos and her endless supply of moussaka."

A small smile tugged at Candice's lips. "Exactly. I want to be that for Miranda. A friend she can count on, especially if she's going through something difficult."

They sat in silence for a few moments, their gentle breaths and the beating of their hearts punctuating their thoughts. Finally, Paul spoke, his voice thoughtful. "How about this—we'll continue to be friendly and available, but we won't push. If she needs help, we'll make sure she knows she can come to us, but we have to respect her boundaries too."

Candice leaned into him. "You're right. Good job taking a turn as the voice of reason."

He smiled, and then, considering, added, "Let's give her some space for now. If she's going through something personal, the last thing she needs is nosy neighbors prying into her business, but we'll keep an eye out, okay? If it seems like she's in real trouble, we'll find a way to help."

Candice nodded, but her gaze drifted to the window, towards Miranda's house. As much as she wanted to respect Miranda's privacy, she couldn't shake the nagging feeling that their new neighbor was carrying a burden far heavier than she let on.

The week crawled by with an unsettling silence from next door. Miranda's car remained absent from the driveway, and her house stood dark and still. Candice found herself glancing out the window more often than she cared to admit, hoping to catch a glimpse of their now-elusive neighbour.

"Still no sign of her?" Paul asked one evening, finding Candice peering through the curtains.

She shook her head, worry etching lines on her forehead. "Nothing. I've sent a couple of texts, but no response. Paul, what if something's happened to her?"

Paul wrapped his arms around his wife, offering comfort even as his own unease grew. "Let's not jump to conclusions. She might just need some space."

Candice leaned into his embrace, drawing strength from his steady presence. "I know, I know. It's just... after how upset she seemed that day, I can't help but worry."

Paul pressed a gentle kiss to her temple. "I understand, but remember what we talked about? We can't force our help on her. All we can do is be here if she needs us."

Candice nodded, but her gaze drifted back to the window. The silence from Miranda's house seemed to grow more oppressive with each passing day.

With no news of Miranda even on the fifth day since they'd seen her last, their concern deepened. Paul found himself distracted during his work calls, his thoughts constantly drifting to their missing neighbor. Candice caught herself glancing at Miranda's driveway every time she left for shopping or returned home, hoping to see her car in its usual spot.

On the seventh day of Miranda's absence, as they sat on their balcony enjoying their morning coffee, Candice broached the subject again.

"Paul," she began, her fingers tapping nervously on her mug, "do you think we should call someone? The police, maybe?"

Paul frowned, considering. "I'm not sure that's necessary yet. We don't really know her well enough to say if this is unusual for her. Maybe she just took an impromptu trip."

Candice bit her lip, unconvinced. "But what about that phone call? How upset she was? It just doesn't feel right."

Paul reached across the table, taking her hand in his. "I know you're worried, love. I am too, but we have to be careful about overstepping. Let's give it one more day, okay? If we still haven't heard from her by tomorrow, we can consider our options."

Candice nodded reluctantly, squeezing his hand in return. "You're right. One more day."

That night, as they prepared for bed, the worry that had been simmering all week seemed to reach a boiling point. Candice found herself unable to settle, tossing and turning as scenarios of what might have happened to Miranda played out in her mind.

Paul, attuned to his wife's restlessness, pulled her close. "Try to sleep, love.."

Candice nestled into his embrace, grateful for his unwavering support. As she finally drifted off, her last thoughts were of Miranda, hoping that wherever she was, she was safe.

In the depths of the night, a flicker of movement jolted Paul from his sleep. He blinked, disoriented, before realizing a faint light was dancing across their bedroom wall. Carefully extracting himself from Candice's embrace, he padded to the window.

The light vanished as suddenly as it had appeared. Paul squinted into the darkness, trying to make out any shapes in Miranda's yard, but saw nothing. As he turned back to bed, the light reappeared, more frantic this time.

"Sweetie?" Candice's sleepy voice called out. "What's wrong?"

"There's something like a flashlight moving around at Miranda's house," he whispered, reaching for his robe. "I'm going to check it out."

Candice sat up, suddenly alert. "Be careful. Do you want me to come with you?"

Paul shook his head. "No, stay here. It's probably nothing, but just in case… keep your phone handy."

The cool night air raised goosebumps on Paul's skin as he stepped outside. The silence seemed to press in on him, broken only by the distant sound of waves and the occasional rustle of leaves. He moved cautiously across the yard, his heart pounding in his chest.

As he neared Miranda's property, the light darted wildly before winking out, accompanied by a rustling sound, like something fleeing into the shadows. Paul's breath caught in his throat as he swept his own flashlight across the yard, half expecting to see a figure darting away.

But there was nothing. No movement, no sound, just the empty darkness of the Greek night.

"Hello?" Paul called out, his voice sounding unnaturally loud in the stillness. "Is anyone there?"

Silence answered him. He stood for a moment longer, straining his ears for any sound, but heard nothing beyond the usual nighttime noises.

"Probably just some kids playing pranks," he muttered, trying to convince himself as he hurried back inside.

Candice was waiting for him, worry etched on her pretty face. "What was it? Did you see anything?"

Paul shook his head, sliding back into bed beside her. "Nothing. Whatever it was, it's gone now."

Candice curled into his side, her voice muffled against his chest. "Do you think it could have been Miranda?"

Paul wrapped an arm around her, his mind turning over the possibilities. "I don't know. It seemed… furtive. Like whoever it was didn't want to be seen."

They lay in silence for a while, both lost in thought. Finally, Candice spoke again, her voice small in the darkness. "Paul, I'm scared."

Paul tightened his hold on her, wishing he had answers to give. "You have nothing to fear, my love."

Candice nodded against his chest, and gradually, they both drifted back to sleep, but their dreams were uneasy.

The next day when the rays of morning light illuminated the peaceful Greek hills, yesterday's chaos felt like a distant nightmare. As Paul and Candice laced up their running shoes for their usual morning jog, the crunch of tires on gravel caught their attention.

Miranda's car pulled into her driveway, and she emerged looking utterly exhausted. Her usually vibrant face was drawn and pale, dark circles still shadowing her eyes.

"Miranda!" Candice called out, taking a step towards their neighbor's house. "Are you okay?"

Miranda looked up, startled, as if she hadn't noticed them standing there. She managed a weak smile and a small wave before hurrying inside, the door closing firmly behind her.

Candice turned to Paul, her eyes wide with concern. "Did you see how she looked? Something's wrong, Paul. We need to go talk to her."

Paul gently caught her arm as she started towards Miranda's house. "Let's give her some time to rest. We can check on her later. She looked like she hasn't slept in days."

Candice hesitated, clearly torn between her desire to help and the need to respect Miranda's privacy. Finally, she nodded. "You're right. We'll give her a little time, but I'm worried. Did you see how she rushed inside? It's like she couldn't get away from us fast enough."

As they jogged away, Paul couldn't shake the memory of the strange lights from the night before. Had that been Miranda, sneaking back home in the middle of the night? And if so, why the secrecy?

Their feet that morning hit the pavement harder than usual, shoulders tense, barely speaking. Both Paul and Candice were lost in thought, their minds upset with questions and concerns about their neighbor.

As they rounded the final corner back to their street, Candice broke the silence. "Do you think we should tell her about the lights last night?"

Paul considered for a moment before shaking his head. "Not yet. Let's see how she is when we check on her later. No need to add to her stress if she's already dealing with something."

Hours blurred together as they moved through the day, their minds elsewhere. Candice found herself unable to focus on the housework, her eyes constantly drifting to the window that faced Miranda's house. Paul, at his office in town, caught himself checking his phone more often than usual, half expecting a message from Candice about some new development.

As evening approached, Paul's car pulled into their driveway. He sat for a moment, gathering his thoughts, before stepping out. As he did, movement caught his eye. Miranda was at her car, rummaging in the trunk.

Taking a deep breath, Paul approached, calling out a friendly greeting that made her jump.

"Oh, Paul!" Miranda laughed, her hand flying to her chest. "You startled me."

"Sorry about that," Paul chuckled, then his tone softened. "How are you doing? We've been worried—you've been gone all week."

Miranda's smile faltered for a moment as she curiously tugged a blanket over something in her trunk behind her back. "I'm so sorry for worrying you. I got news that my mother had passed away, and I had to go home for the funeral."

Paul's heart sank. "Miranda, I'm so sorry for your loss. Is there anything we can do?"

She shook her head, her smile returning with surprising brightness. "That's very kind, but I'm all right. Could you please pass along my apologies to Candice for my behavior the other day? I was just totally in shock from the news."

Before Paul could respond, Miranda stepped forward and enveloped him in a hug, pressing a quick, chaste kiss to his cheek. "Candice is lucky to have a husband like you," she murmured as she pulled away.

Paul stood rooted to the spot, watching as Miranda disappeared into her house. His cheek tingled where her lips had touched, and he felt a surge of guilt at the warmth spreading through his chest. He knew Miranda's gesture had been purely platonic, a symbol of gratitude and nothing more, yet he couldn't deny the growing attraction he felt towards her, an attraction he desperately wished he could ignore, especially in light of her interesting behavior.

As Paul finally turned to head home, his mind raced with conflicting emotions. He loved Candice deeply and would never do anything to jeopardize their marriage, but Miranda's presence in their lives was stirring up feelings he hadn't experienced in years. He silently prayed for strength, determined to honor his commitment to his wife while dealing with this unexpected temptation.

Inside, Candice was waiting, her expression a mix of curiosity and concern. "Well? How is she?"

Paul recounted his conversation with Miranda, watching as relief washed over Candice's features. "Oh, thank goodness," she breathed. "I mean, it's terrible about her mother, but at least we know she's okay."

Paul nodded, pushing aside his lingering doubts. Something about Miranda's story still felt off, but he couldn't put his finger on why. "Yeah, it's good to know she's back safely."

As they prepared dinner together, falling into their usual comfortable routine, Paul found his thoughts drifting back to Miranda. The warmth of her hug, the softness of her lips on his cheek... He shook his head, trying to dispel the images.

"Paul?" Candice's voice broke through his reverie. "Are you okay? You seem distracted."

He forced a smile, focusing on the vegetables he was chopping. "Just thinking about Miranda. It must be hard, losing a parent."

Candice's expression softened. "You're right. Maybe we should do something for her. Bring over a meal or something?"

Paul nodded, grateful for his wife's compassionate nature. "That's a great idea. I'm sure she'd appreciate it."

As they sat down to eat, Paul found himself struggling to maintain his usual easy conversation with Candice. Guilt gnawed at him—not for any action he'd taken, but for the thoughts he couldn't seem to shake.

Candice, perceptive as always, reached across the table to take his hand. "Are you sure you're okay? You seem... I don't know, distant tonight."

Paul squeezed her hand, forcing himself to meet her eyes. "I'm fine, love. Just tired, I guess. It's been a long week of worrying."

Candice nodded, but Paul could see the flicker of doubt in her eyes. He hated himself for putting it there, for allowing his inappropriate attraction to Miranda to create even the slightest wedge between them.

Later that night, as they lay in bed, Paul stared at the ceiling, sleep eluding him. Beside him, Candice's breathing had evened out and her chest rose and fell softly against the pillows, her face peaceful in sleep. He turned to look at her, drinking in the sight of her peaceful face, the gentle curve of her cheek, the way her hair fanned out on the pillow.

He loved this woman with every fiber of his being. She was his partner, his best friend, the one person he could always count on. The thought of doing anything to hurt her made him physically ill.

And yet... the memory of Miranda's touch lingered, seeming to haunt his skin and his mind alike. Paul squeezed his eyes shut, willing the thoughts away. This was just a test, he told himself. A momentary weakness that he would overcome.

As he finally drifted off to sleep, Paul made a silent vow. He would distance himself from Miranda, limit their interactions to polite neighbourly exchanges. He would focus on his wife and on the beautiful life they'd built together here in Greece.

But even as he made this promise to himself, a small part of him wondered if it would be enough. The seed of attraction had been planted, and Paul feared it might have taken root more deeply than he cared to admit.

The following morning, Paul found himself alone in their bedroom, kneeling beside the bed. His hands were clasped tightly, knuckles white with tension as he bowed his head in prayer.

"Lord," he whispered, his voice barely audible, "please give me strength. Help me to honor my wife, to keep my thoughts pure. I don't want to lust after anyone but Candice. Guide me, Father."

As he finished his prayer, Paul felt a sense of resolve settle over him. He stood, straightening his shoulders, silently rehearsing his vow to avoid spending any more time alone with Miranda.

Downstairs, he found Candice preparing breakfast, the scent of freshly brewed coffee filling the kitchen. She looked up as he entered, a warm smile spreading across her face.

"Good morning, love," she said, sliding a mug of coffee towards him.

Paul returned her smile, though it didn't quite reach his eyes. "Morning," he replied, taking a sip of the rich, dark liquid. He hesitated for a moment before continuing, "You know, I've been thinking... Maybe you should spend more time with Miranda. I think she could use a friend right now."

Candice raised an eyebrow, studying her husband's face. "Oh? And does this sudden interest in my social life have anything to do with how attractive you find her?"

Paul choked on his coffee, nearly dropping the mug due to being so caught off guard by his wife's directness. He set the mug down, running a hand through his hair as he considered his response. "I... yes," he finally admitted, meeting Candice's gaze. "I won't lie to you. I'm struggling with this, and I thought if you two spent more time together, I'd be less likely to run into her alone."

Candice's expression softened, and she reached out to take Paul's hand. "I appreciate your honesty, Paul. Have you considered talking to Pastor Alex about this?"

Paul nodded slowly. "I have. Maybe I'll stop by after work tomorrow."

"I think that's a good idea," Candice replied, giving his hand a gentle squeeze. "And don't worry, I'll reach out to Miranda. It'll be nice to have one more girlfriend to hang with."

As they finished their breakfast, Paul felt a weight lift from his shoulders. He was grateful for Candice's understanding and support, even in the face of his confession.

Later that day, Candice found herself standing on Miranda's doorstep, her heart beating a little faster than usual. She took a deep breath and rang the doorbell, adjusting her hair in the window's reflection as she waited.

The door swung open, revealing Miranda looking far more relaxed than she had the day before. Her green eyes lit up with surprise and pleasure at the sight of Candice.

"Candice! What a lovely surprise," Miranda exclaimed, stepping back to invite her in.

Candice smiled, crossing the threshold into Miranda's cool, airy living room. "I hope I'm not interrupting anything," she began, "but I was wondering if you'd like to hang out today? I really want us to be friends, and I thought maybe we could spend some time together."

Miranda's previous hesitation seemed to have vanished entirely. She clapped her hands together, a bright smile spreading across her face. "I'd love that! What did you have in mind?"

And so began a day of female bonding that neither woman had realized how much they needed. They started with a shopping trip to the local markets, arms linked as they wandered through stalls filled with vibrant fruits, vegetables, and handcrafted goods.

"Oh, look at these olives!" Miranda exclaimed, her eyes wide with delight as she sampled one from a vendor's tray. "I've never tasted anything like them."

Candice laughed, the sound light and carefree. "Welcome to Greece, my friend. The olives here will spoil you for life."

As they meandered through the market, their conversation flowed easily from topic to topic. They discussed their favorite Greek dishes, shared stories of cultural misunderstandings they'd experienced since moving to the country, and giggled over the charming attempts of local men to flirt with them.

"So," Miranda said as they settled into a quaint café for lunch, "how did you and Paul end up in Greece? It's quite a change from Boston, I imagine."

Candice's eyes sparkled as she launched into the tale of their decision to uproot their lives and move across the world. "It was a leap of faith, really," she admitted. "We'd always dreamed of living somewhere with history, culture, and incredible food. When Paul got the opportunity to transfer here with his company, we couldn't resist."

Miranda leaned forward, her chin resting on her hand as she listened intently. "That's so brave of you both. I can't imagine making such a big move with a partner. It must have brought you even closer together."

A shadow flickered across Candice's face for a moment, so brief that Miranda might have imagined it. "It hasn't always been easy," Candice said softly, "but yes, I think it has made us stronger as a couple."

As the day wore on, the two women found themselves growing closer, sharing hopes, fears, and dreams. By the time they returned to Candice and Paul's house, they felt like old friends rather than new acquaintances.

"Oh, I have an idea!" Candice exclaimed as they approached the house. "Why don't we relax in the jacuzzi? We've got one out back. It'd be the perfect way to end the day."

Miranda's eyes lit up. "That sounds heavenly, but the only swimsuit I have right now is dirty."

Candice waved away her concern. "I'm sure I have one that'll fit you. Come on, let's go find something."

Soon, the two women were settled in the bubbling waters of the jacuzzi, the stress of the past week melting away in the warm jets. Candice couldn't help but notice how stunning Miranda looked in the borrowed bikini, her olive skin glowing in the early evening light, providing a striking contrast to the light blue color of the swimsuit.

"This was exactly what I needed," Miranda sighed, tilting her head back to rest against the edge of the tub. "Thank you for today, Candice. I didn't realize how lonely I've been feeling."

Candice reached out to squeeze Miranda's hand. "That's what friends are for. I'm just glad we finally got to spend some time together."

As the sky began to darken, they reluctantly climbed out of the jacuzzi. "We should probably think about dinner," Candice mused as they made their way into the kitchen.

They were standing side by side at the counter, still in their swimsuits, when the front door opened. Paul walked in, his briefcase in hand, and comically froze at the sight of the two beautiful women in his kitchen.

Candice and Miranda exchanged a glance before bursting into laughter at Paul's deer-in-the-headlights expression.

"Paul?" Candice managed between giggles. "Are you all right?"

Paul blinked rapidly, his gaze darting between his wife and their neighbor. "Uhm... I have a meeting at church..." he stammered, already backing towards the door.

"Now?" Miranda asked, amusement clear in her voice.

Paul nodded vigorously, his hand fumbling for the doorknob behind him. "Yes, now. Very important. Can't be late. Bye!"

And with that, he was gone, the door slamming shut behind him.

Candice and Miranda looked at each other for a moment before dissolving into another fit of laughter.

"Oh my," Miranda gasped, wiping tears from her eyes. "Is he always like that?"

Candice shook her head, still chuckling. "No, that was... new. I think we might have short-circuited his brain."

The women, almost perfectly in sync, looked each other up and down with sassy expressions. Then Candice affirmed, "Mm! We *do* look good!" as she raised her hand for a victorious high five, which Miranda heartily responded to, adding, "Good enough to keep 'em comin'!"

As the 'clap' of their hands sounded, Candice gestured to the front door with her head, "Or keep 'em *runnin'*..." They once again laughed at their own wit and Paul's nervous exit out of the house.

As their laughter subsided, Candice couldn't help but feel a twinge of concern. She knew Paul had been struggling with his attraction to Miranda, and seeing them both together like this must have been overwhelming for him. She made a mental note to talk to him later, to make sure he was okay.

Meanwhile, Paul found himself practically sprinting towards the church, his heart pounding in his chest. The image of Candice and

Miranda, both stunning in their swimsuits, seemed burned into his retinas. He knew he needed help, and he needed it now.

Pastor Alex was just locking up his office when Paul arrived, out of breath and looking decidedly flustered.

"Paul?" the pastor said, concern evident in his voice. "Is everything all right?"

Paul shook his head, trying to catch his breath. "That's the problem, Pastor. *Every*thing is most certainly all right. In fact, it's so all right that I'm losing my mind!"

A hint of amusement appeared on the lively Pastor's face. "Help me understand. Everything is all right, yet you sprinted here like your life depended on it?"

Paul forced a small smile as his heart rate began to lessen and breathing became easier. "If you were in my kitchen tonight, you'd know exactly what I'm talking about..."

Pastor Alex studied Paul's face for a moment before nodding, unlocking his office door. "Come on in, my friend. Let's talk."

Once inside, Paul sank into a chair across from the pastor's desk, running his hands through his hair. "I'm struggling, Pastor," he began, his voice low and filled with shame. "It's our new neighbor, Miranda. I... I'm attracted to her, and I don't know what to do. I'm praying. I'm trying to keep my distance. But nothing is working." He went on to explain the physical affection he'd been shown and the amusing run-in with the women at his home that evening.

Pastor Alex leaned back in his chair, a thoughtful expression on his face. After a moment, he chuckled softly, almost to himself. "If only it were the old days..."

Paul looked up, confusion replacing the guilt on his face. "I'm sorry, what did you say?"

The pastor's chuckle grew louder. "I just said this would be easier if it were the old days. You know, before Greece and Rome and all of these modern places came to be." He arose from his chair, revealing the hand-woven Israeli jacket wrapped around its back, the Pastor himself being from Israel. He meandered over to his window and looked outside.

"Marriage was so much simpler back then. There wasn't all of this complication and confusion about the matter. It was better to marry than to burn. So we married."

Paul felt a smile tugging at the corners of his mouth despite his distress. "How does that apply to me? I'm already married."

"Never stopped the Israelites," Pastor Alex said with a grin, still looking outside.

Paul's eyes widened as he realized what the pastor was implying. "You're talking about polygamy," he said slowly. "You're joking, right?"

Pastor Alex turned around and held up his hands in a placating manner. "Of course, of course. I'm not seriously recommending something like that for you. Not yet anyway..." The animated Pastor smiled as he returned to his desk chair. "It's just that I've been reading this fascinating book about the history of marriage, and the idea was fresh in my mind."

Paul's gaze fell on a book lying on the pastor's desk. Its title jumped out at him: *Marriage, Sex, & Polygamy—It's about to get Biblical up in here by J.D. Langton.*

"May I?" Paul asked, gesturing towards the book.

Pastor Alex nodded, and Paul picked up the volume, flipping through its pages with growing interest. After a few moments, he looked up at the pastor. "So what does the book say would happen in a situation like mine?"

The pastor leaned forward, his expression becoming more matter-of-fact. "Well, the book shows that for most of the world's history and in most of the world's cultures, polygamy was commonplace and expected. If a married man liked a woman, he made a deal with her father and took her as a wife, and that was that."

Paul nodded slowly, trying to wrap his mind around the concept. It seemed so foreign to his modern sensibilities, yet there was a part of him that couldn't help but be intrigued by the idea.

Pastor Alex continued, his voice taking on a more practical tone. "But Paul, that's not the world we live in now. What you're feeling is natural, but acting on it would be a betrayal of your precious Candice. The key is to keep your thoughts in check, to focus on the love and commitment you share with your wife. God can help you, and your efforts to avoid lust are necessary, but more than anything, you need to make up your mind that you're simply not going to go there. The more you entertain lust, the stronger its hold will become."

Paul sighed, setting the book back on the desk. "You're right, of course. It's just... hard sometimes."

The pastor reached out, placing a comforting hand on Paul's shoulder. "I know it is, my friend, but remember, God doesn't allow more temptation than we can bear. There is always a way of escape. This is a test of your faith and your commitment. Stay strong, stay honest with Candice, and keep praying for guidance."

As Paul stood to leave, he hesitated for a moment. "Pastor, would it be all right if I borrowed that book? I've never read much about marriage."

Pastor Alex raised an eyebrow, then nodded, handing over the volume. "Of course. Just remember, it's an academic study, not a how-to guide," he added with a wink.

Paul laughed, some of the tension finally leaving his body. "Don't worry. I'm not planning on starting a harem anytime soon."

As he left the church, book tucked under his arm, Paul's insides twisted themselves into knots. He was grateful for the pastor's understanding and advice, but he couldn't shake the fascination he felt with the historical perspective on marriage and attraction.

Walking home in the gathering twilight, Paul tried to sort through his jumbled thoughts. He loved Candice deeply, and he knew he would never do anything to jeopardize their marriage, but the idea that, in another time and place, his attraction to Miranda might not have been seen as a threat to his relationship with Candice... it was a provocative thought.

He shook his head, trying to clear it of such dangerous musings. What mattered was the here and now, the vows he had made to Candice, the life they had built together in this beautiful country.

As he approached their house, Paul took a deep breath, steeling himself for what awaited him inside. He knew he needed to talk to Candice about what happened earlier, to reassure her of his love and commitment.

But first, he decided, he would spend some time with the book Pastor Alex had lent him. Perhaps understanding the historical context of marriage and attraction would help him deal with his current struggles.

With that thought in mind, Paul crossed the threshold of his home. It was clear that Candice had already gone to bed. After getting some water and washing his face, he sat down with the book in the living room.

As the night deepened, Paul found himself engrossed in the book. The living room was quiet, save for the occasional rustle of pages and the soft ticking of the antique clock on the mantle. Candice had long since fallen asleep, leaving Paul alone with his thoughts and this unexpected exploration of marital history.

The book lay open on his lap, its pages illuminated by the warm glow of the reading lamp. Beside him, his well-worn Bible sat at the ready, its familiar presence a comforting anchor as he delved into unfamiliar theological territory. Paul's eyes darted between the two texts, cross-referencing passages and mulling over interpretations he'd never considered before.

"'For it is better to marry than to burn with passion,'" Paul murmured, quoting from 1 Corinthians. He'd read that verse countless times before, but now, in light of the historical context provided by the book, it took on new layers of meaning.

As the clock struck midnight, a sudden loud thud from next door jolted Paul from his contemplative state. He froze, listening intently. The sound had come from Miranda's house, eerily reminiscent of the strange occurrence from the other night.

Paul set the book aside, his brow furrowed with concern. He moved to the window, peering out into the darkness. What appeared to be the faint shadow of a person was moving along the smooth side of Miranda's home, but he couldn't tell for sure.

Driven by mingled curiosity and neighborly concern, Paul slipped out the front door and made his way towards Miranda's property. As he neared her house, a faint rustling sound caught his attention—like someone trying to move stealthily through the backyard. While looking in that direction, he heard the sound of wrought iron scrape against concrete for a moment, a sound very familiar to him after helping Miranda move her furniture outside.

Without hesitation, Paul hopped the low fence separating their properties. His heart raced as he crept along the side of the house, straining his ears for any further sounds. As he rounded the corner to the back patio, a figure suddenly loomed before him.

A piercing scream shattered the night's silence, causing Paul to stumble backward in shock. It took a moment for his eyes to adjust, to recognize the trembling form before him.

"Miranda?" he gasped, his voice barely above a whisper.

Miranda's eyes were wide with fear, her chest heaving as she tried to catch her breath. Recognition dawned on her face, quickly followed by a wave of relief so palpable it seemed to physically move through her.

Before Paul could react, Miranda threw herself into his arms, her body wracked with sobs. "Oh, Paul," she choked out between tears, "I was so scared."

Paul stood frozen, acutely aware of Miranda's warm body pressed against his. His arms hung awkwardly at his sides as he struggled with the urge to comfort her and the need to maintain appropriate boundaries.

"It's okay," he managed, gently trying to extricate himself from her embrace. "You're safe... What happened? Did you hear something too?"

Miranda pulled back slightly, wiping at her tear-stained cheeks. "I... I heard a noise, like a slam or something, outside. I thought someone might be trying to break in."

As quickly as she had embraced him, Miranda suddenly stepped away, wrapping her arms around herself, shivering a little in her robe. "I'm sorry," she said, her voice still slightly shaky from the fright and the cold. "I didn't mean to... I just panicked. I think I'd like to be alone now."

Before Paul could respond, Miranda had turned and was hurrying back towards her house. He stood there, bewildered by her sudden change in demeanor, when movement from his own house caught his eye.

Candice stood on their bedroom balcony, her silhouette unmistakable in the moonlight. "Paul?" she called down, her voice tinged with confusion and concern. "What's going on? I heard a scream."

Paul felt a flash of guilt, though he knew he'd done nothing wrong. "I'll be right up," he called back. "I'll explain everything."

As he made his way back inside and up the stairs, Paul's mind raced. How could he explain this situation without raising suspicions? He loved Candice, trusted her completely, but he knew how this might look.

Entering their bedroom, Paul found Candice sitting on the edge of the bed, her eyes questioning. He took a deep breath and launched into an explanation, detailing the thud he'd heard, his decision to investigate, and the confusing encounter with Miranda.

"She just seemed so frightened," Paul concluded, shrugging his shoulders in something akin to exasperation. "I didn't know what to do."

Candice listened quietly, her expression unreadable. When Paul finished, she nodded slowly. "That must have been scary for her," she said softly. "I'm glad you were there to help."

Paul felt a wave of relief wash over him at Candice's understanding response. He climbed into bed beside her, pulling her close. "I love you," he murmured into her hair.

"I love you too," Candice replied, her voice muffled against his chest.

As Paul drifted off to sleep, exhausted by the night's events, Candice lay awake. Despite her outward calm, a seed of unease had taken root in her mind. She trusted Paul implicitly, but the situation with Miranda was becoming increasingly complex. Between the repeated oddities at her house in the middle of the night and Paul's apparent struggle, her confidence that everything was okay was beginning to lessen.

Unable to shake her disquiet, Candice carefully extricated herself from Paul's embrace once his breathing had evened out into sleep. She padded softly downstairs, retrieving her phone from where she'd left it charging in the kitchen.

Back in bed, Candice opened the app for their Ring cameras. The soft glow of the screen illuminated her face as she scrolled through the night's footage. She watched as Paul exited the house and saw his encounter with Miranda play out exactly as he'd described.

A plethora of emotions seemed to overcome Candice as she set her phone aside. Relief that Paul had been entirely truthful, concern for Miranda's apparent distress, and a lingering worry about the strange occurrences that seemed to be plaguing their neighbor.

As she snuggled back into Paul's warmth, Candice made a mental note to check in on Miranda the next day. Whatever was going on, it was clear their new neighbor could use a friend. And perhaps, Candice mused as sleep began to claim her again, by strengthening her own friendship with Miranda, she could help ease the tension that seemed to be building between the three of them.

The next morning, as sunlight stabbed through the gaps in the curtains, Candice rolled over. The warm beams crisscrossed the bed, making her squint and reach for a pillow to block her face, before she gave in and finally stirred from her slumber. She woke up to an empty bed.

She had slept in that day, so she stretched languidly, savoring the luxury of it. Paul had already left for work, his side of the bed cool to the touch. With a contented sigh, she swung her legs over the side of the bed and padded downstairs, the hardwood floor cool beneath her bare feet.

As she entered the living room on her way to the kitchen, something caught her eye. A book lay on the coffee table. Its cover looked intriguing. Candice paused, her brow furrowing as she tried to recall if she'd seen it before.

Curiosity piqued, she picked up the volume, running her fingers over the embossed title: *Marriage, Sex, & Polygamy—It's about to get Biblical up in here*. Her eyebrows shot up in surprise. This certainly wasn't their usual bedtime reading.

Flipping open to a random page, Candice began to read, her eyes widening as she absorbed the content. Before she knew it, she was engrossed, barely noticing as her stomach grumbled in protest of its neglect.

With the book in one hand, Candice made her way to the kitchen, absentmindedly preparing a simple breakfast of Greek yogurt and honey. She perched on a stool at the kitchen island, spooning yogurt into her mouth as her eyes remained glued to the pages before her.

"For most of human history," she read aloud, her voice barely above a whisper, "systemic monogamy was the exception rather than the rule. Many cultures embraced polygamy as a normal and even preferred form of marriage. God's people, especially, viewed more wives as a blessing from God, rather than what the modern West deems a perversion of that same God's blessing."

Candice's mind whirled with this new information. She'd always thought of polygamy as something exotic and foreign, relegated to the pages of the Old Testament or remote tribal societies, but here it was, presented as a common thread throughout human history.

As she finished her breakfast, Candice found herself unable to put the book down. She moved to the couch, curling up with a throw blanket as she delved deeper into the historical and theological perspectives on marriage and sexual morality.

Hours ticked by unnoticed as Candice lost herself in the book's pages. She read about dozens of polygamous families in the Bible and about the cultural and economic factors that influenced marriage practices throughout history. She found herself fascinated by the different perspectives presented, challenging her long-held assumptions about relationships and commitment.

"In many ancient cultures," one passage read, "the majority of women preferred having co-wives, as it demonstrated their husband's honorable leadership and significantly lessened their workload at home. In even some modern polygamous societies, such as those in Africa, women are actually the biggest proponents of polygamy, and have been known to bring a friend to their husband in an attempt to increase their household's efficiency."

Candice paused, her mind drifting to Paul and their life together. She loved him deeply, their bond strengthened by the challenges they'd faced in moving to Greece, but she couldn't help but wonder—if they'd been born in a different time, a different culture, how might their relationship have looked?

The thought of Paul with another wife should have repulsed her, she knew. Yet, as she read on, she found herself oddly intrigued by the concept. The idea of expanding their family unit, of bringing in new love and companionship, held an unexpected appeal.

Her thoughts drifted to Miranda, their beautiful and enigmatic neighbor—the woman who had so clearly caught Paul's eye, despite his best efforts to hide it. In another time, another place, might she have been welcomed into their family rather than seen as a threat?

Candice shook her head, trying to clear it of these strange musings. She was being ridiculous, surely. This was just academic curiosity, nothing more.

Yet as she continued to read, she couldn't shake the feeling that something was imposingly challenging her worldview. The certainties she'd always held about marriage and monogamy were being pressed for explanation, and she wasn't entirely sure how to feel about it.

It wasn't until she glanced up and noticed the lengthening shadows in the room that she realized how much time had passed. With a start, she saw that it was nearly 5 o'clock. Paul would be home soon, and she hadn't even thought about dinner.

"Oh, shoot," she muttered, hastily marking her place in the book and setting it back on the coffee table. As she rushed to the kitchen to start preparing a meal, she didn't notice that she'd placed the book in exactly the same position Paul had left it in.

As she grabbed the knives and cutting boards she needed for dinner, she made herself chuckle, saying out loud to herself, "Maybe if I had a co-wife, she could've made dinner while I read my book..." Amused at her quip, she popped a cherry tomato in her mouth then started working.

Her mind was on another planet as she chopped vegetables and seasoned chicken for a quick stir-fry. What would Paul think if he knew she'd been reading that book? Should she tell him? Or wait for him to bring it up?

The sound of a key in the lock interrupted her thoughts. Paul's familiar footsteps echoed in the living room, and Candice felt a flutter of nerves in her stomach. She turned to greet him with a smile, deciding to act as if nothing had changed.

But something had changed. As she watched Paul enter the kitchen, his face lighting up at the sight of her, Candice knew that the ideas she'd encountered that day had planted a seed in her mind. A seed that, for better or worse, might grow into something that would change their lives forever.

"Hey, love," Paul said, leaning in to kiss her cheek. "Something smells good."

Candice smiled, pushing her tumultuous thoughts aside for the moment. "Just a quick stir-fry. How was your day?"

As Paul launched into a story about his workday, Candice noticed him glancing towards the living room. She saw the moment he spotted the book, then saw a flicker of relief, and then guilt cross his face. Silently, she watched as he casually made his way to the coffee table, picked up the book, and slipped it into his pocket.

Candice turned back to the stove, hiding her knowing smile. It seemed she and Paul had some interesting conversations ahead of them, but until then, she would keep her new knowledge to herself, letting it simmer like the thoughts and questions bubbling just beneath the surface of their seemingly ordinary evening.

Paul ascended the stairs to their bedroom, his heart beating against his chest. How could he be so careless as to leave the book behind? It was a miracle Candice hadn't noticed it. He found himself alone with his thoughts. The ideas the book presented both intrigued and unsettled him. He knew he loved Candice, knew their marriage was strong. And yet…

For a moment, Paul allowed himself to imagine a world where his attraction to Miranda wasn't a source of guilt and confusion. A world where, perhaps, there was room in his heart—and his life—for both women.

But that world wasn't this one.

So, the weight of the book in his pocket felt like a secret he wasn't quite ready to share. As he descended the stairs, Candice's voice called out from the kitchen, pulling him back to the present moment.

"Paul, honey? Can you come here for a sec?"

He made his way to the kitchen, where Candice was scurrying about, pulling ingredients from the fridge. Her blonde hair was tied back in a messy bun, and a smudge of flour adorned her cheek. Paul felt a surge of affection for his wife, pushing aside the complicated emotions that had been plaguing him lately.

"What's up?" he asked, leaning against the door frame, with one hand hanging on the frame above—a pose that always got Candice going.

Candice turned, a bunch of cilantro in one hand and a tomato in the other, completely oblivious to Paul's smooth move. "Just wanted to remind you that we're hosting Bible study tonight. Can you believe I almost forgot?"

Paul's eyes widened. "That's tonight? Shoot, I completely lost track of the days."

Candice laughed, setting the vegetables on the counter. "Well, lucky for you, I remembered just in time. Mind giving me a hand with the snacks?"

As Paul moved to help, the doorbell chimed. They exchanged a glance, eyebrows raised in mutual surprise.

"I'll get it," Paul offered, wiping his hands on a dish towel.

He opened the front door to find Miranda standing there, looking uncharacteristically nervous. Her usual confident demeanor was replaced by a hesitant smile and fidgeting hands. Paul felt his heart skip a beat, memories of the previous night flooding back.

"Miranda," Paul greeted, trying to keep his voice steady. "This is unexpected."

"I hope I'm not interrupting," Miranda said, her green eyes darting past him into the house. "I just... I wanted to apologize for last night. My behavior was... well, it was embarrassing."

Paul felt a surge of empathy take precedent over any conflicting feelings. "No need to apologize. Come in, please."

As Miranda stepped inside, Candice emerged from the kitchen, her face lighting up at the sight of their neighbor. "Miranda! What a lovely surprise."

Paul watched as the two women embraced, feeling a mix of warmth and unease at their easy affection. He cleared his throat. "Miranda was just about to explain last night."

The three of them settled in the living room, Miranda perched on the edge of the sofa, her posture tense. Paul couldn't help but notice how the afternoon light seemed to make her olive skin shine. He forced himself to look away, focusing on Miranda's words.

"I feel like I owe you both an explanation," she began, her voice soft. "Back in Canada, my house was robbed in the middle of the night. I was home alone, and... well, I guess you could say it left me somewhat traumatized."

Candice reached out, placing a comforting hand on Miranda's knee. "That must have been terrifying."

Miranda nodded, her eyes glistening. "It was. And last night, when I heard that noise... I just panicked. I'm so sorry for dragging you into it, Paul."

Paul shook his head, his voice gentle. "There's no need to apologize. We're just glad you're okay."

A moment of understanding passed between the three of them, the previous night's events finally being settled. Candice suddenly brightened. "Say, Miranda, why don't you join us for Bible study tonight? We're hosting a small group from church."

Miranda's face lit up, her earlier nervousness melting away. "Really? I'd love that. Are you sure I wouldn't be intruding?"

"Not at all," Paul assured her, surprising himself with his sincerity. "In fact, why don't you help Candice with the food prep? I can handle the cleaning."

As Paul busied himself tidying the living room, he could hear Candice and Miranda chatting and laughing in the kitchen. The sound filled him with a confusing blend of joy and longing. He found himself pausing in his work, straining to catch snippets of their conversation.

Then, feeling a pang of guilt for eavesdropping, he resumed his cleaning vigorously, trying to drown out his conflicting emotions in the mundane task of dusting shelves. Making sure that nobody saw him, he quietly took the book out of his pocket and hid it in a closet. He didn't want Candice—or worse, Miranda—to get the wrong ideas about his reasons for reading it.

Before long, the doorbell rang again, signaling the arrival of their Bible study group. Paul opened the door to greet their friends: Niko and Eleni Papadopoulos, the Greek couple; Hans and Gretl Schmidt, the German pair; and Kwesi and Anastasia, the Ghanaian-Greek couple.

As greetings were exchanged and everyone settled into the living room, Paul couldn't help but notice the easy way Miranda fit into their group. She sat between Eleni and Gretl on a couch opposite to where Candace was sitting, Paul having sat down on a chair to the side.

Niko, a bespeckled stocky man with a neatly trimmed beard, cleared his throat. "So, shall we begin? I believe we were discussing the qualifications for church overseers in First Timothy."

Paul nodded, reaching for his Bible. "That's right. Chapter 3, verses 2 through 12."

As they read through the passage, Paul found his mind wandering, hyper-aware of Miranda's presence across the room. He forced himself to focus as they reached verse 2: "An overseer, then, must be above reproach, the husband of one wife..."

Niko, pushing his wire-rimmed glasses up his nose, spoke up. "Now, why would Paul say this—that an overseer must be the husband of one wife?"

"Isn't it obvious?" Eleni somewhat abruptly replied with a proud huff. "Many of Israel's leaders indulged in the grotesque sin of polygamy and Paul was ensuring that church leaders didn't do the same."

Her husband, Niko, nodded in agreement. "That's exactly right. Many Jews—"

"Wait, wait, wait," Kwesi light-heartedly but firmly interrupted in his thick Ghanaian accent, his dark black hands lifted up as if to suggest everyone not move forward so hastily.

Everyone, especially Paul and Candice, looked at him in anticipation of what would come next, genuinely intrigued as to what he might have to say.

Kwesi slowly put his hands down with a smile on his face. Through a few chuckles, he asked, "How exactly did we come to the conclusion that what modern people call 'polygamy' is a grotesque sin?"

Eleni let out another proud and nervous huff. "I don't know. Maybe because it's obvious? It's absolutely disgusting and it's the most degrading thing to women I've ever heard of."

Kwesi took in her emphatic comments with all too familiar ease, his relaxed facial expression indicating he'd been down this road before.

"I'm not sure it's quite that simple," Hans responded in his thick German accent. God regulated having multiple wives in the Levitical Law, and in some cases even commanded it. While it may not be ideal, I don't think we can just jump to that conclusion when God didn't seem to have much of a problem with it. If you ask me, it's certainly not ideal for most people, but clearly some women wanted it. If I remember correctly, in both Abraham's and Jacob's cases, it was the wives who gave their husbands more wives."

Hans' wife, Gretl, chimed in, her face full of inquisitiveness. "But those families had many problems. If anything, wouldn't the bible be showing us that polygamy causes more problems than monogamy?"

Miranda, much to Paul's surprise, offered her thoughts. "Well, the strife in the patriarchs' families was centered around the shame associated with bareness and their children's inheritance. We're not told that having more wives was the cause of the issues.

"But it did cause issues," Eleni said with a slightly raised voice, clearly somewhat irritated that people in the group were not condemning the practice as quickly as her. "If they didn't have multiple wives, those problems surrounding their children couldn't have happened."

Candice started to recall some relevant information from the book she'd been reading. "Not necessarily. Isaac was monogamous, yet his wife still caused problems by favoring one child over the other. It seems that in both kinds of families, Hebrew women sometimes went to sinful extents to ensure certain things for their children. If we're going to blame polygamy for that, then we'd have to blame monogamy too."

Paul looked at Candice in silent awe while Kwesi and his wife, Anastasia, glanced at each other with amused smiles, clearly enjoying the intelligent responses.

Gretl added more thoughts. "I have mixed feelings about the issue. In some ways, I do believe it is harmful for women, but I can also see the benefits. Back home in Germany, polygamy was an accepted practice for some time even after Jesus' time on earth. It helped ensure a strong population and made housework easier for women, especially in difficult times and bad winters. I agree with Niko. I don't believe it is God's ideal, and I certainly wouldn't want it for myself, but there are real reasons why some people would."

Niko, having flipped to Matthew 19, kept a neutral expression for the time being. "Interesting. I don't think I've ever heard a woman argue the benefits of something like that."

"Because it's gross," Eleni abrasively interjected.

Niko put his head down for a moment, seemingly ashamed of his wife's attitude, but then continued. "A couple of people have said that it's not ideal, rather than calling it sin. How do we reconcile that with Jesus' words, 'The two shall become one flesh?' Wouldn't we all agree that marriage, by definition, is between one man and one woman?"

Miranda answered with confidence, almost as if she'd considered this topic before. "That's actually an irrelevant point—" She caught herself and shrunk back a little, apologizing for her straightforwardness, but Niko smiled and encouraged her to go on. "That objection assumes that polygamous families are some kind of corporate marriage, as if the man has one marriage with multiple wives in it."

"That's exactly what it is," Eleni pushed. "I mean, isn't that the definition of polygamy?"

Miranda was already prepared with an answer. "Well, polygamy isn't a biblical term, so I don't think we need to worry about defining it. But, when it comes to marriage, a man with multiple wives doesn't have multiple wives in one marriage; he has multiple marriages, each between him and one wife."

Niko piggy-backed off Miranda's response. "And the Bible technically never says that a man can only have one marriage at a time. She does have a point. I never quite thought of it that way."

Eleni gave her husband, Niko, a piercing stare. "What are doing?" she said almost under her breath, annoyed. "Since when did I marry a Mormon?"

Most of the group succumbed to tense silence in light of Eleni's aggravation, but Kwesi felt it was his turn to chime in. "Now hold on," he said with a confident smile. "Why are we bringing a modern cult into the equation? Was King David a Mormon? Josiah? Moses? We cannot define marriage in reaction to some modern cult's behavior. We must get our definitions from the Scripture. The Law prescribed it, God never forbid it, and many of His people practiced it. In fact, there are more polygamous marriages named in Scripture than monogamous ones. If anything, that would make monogamy the odd one out, wouldn't you say?"

Candace and Paul "hmm'd" in thoughtful agreement, Paul still taking a listening role.

Eleni sarcastically quipped at Kwesi. "What are you, some kind of expert? Name one reputable woman who—"

"My mother," Kwesi interrupted with a more serious tone than he'd had up to that point. Eleni was stopped in her tracks as all eyes moved to Kwesi. "My mother," he continued, "was one of three wives. She became sick a long time ago and could no longer care for me and my sister, so she encouraged my father to take another wife. When he did, her burden was lifted. A couple of years later, my father came across a young woman whose father was going to sell her into slavery because he desperately needed money. My father offered the man double the money to take the woman for himself so that she didn't end up in the hands of cruel men. She stayed with us for a few months as no more than a friend, but then she gave her heart to Jesus, at which point my father took her as a wife."

The whole room listened quietly, sincerely absorbing the realities within Kwesi's story.

Kwesi continued, a genuine care shining through his eyes. "People tell me it is oppressive and dishonoring to women to have more than one wife, yet which part of my parent's story is dishonoring and oppressive to women? My mother was relieved and had more time for us, the second wife was blessed with a good husband and six children, and the third escaped the very fires of Hell. Me and my siblings always had a loving mother figure present. When I fell and scraped my knee, someone was always there to take the pain away. Please tell me, how did my father oppress his wives in all of this?"

While everyone else in the room thoughtfully pondered Kwesi's story, Eleni became more and more visibly uncomfortable, barely being able to keep herself still in her seat, though she bit her tongue for the moment.

Kwesi lightened up again and chuckled. "But that is, of course, just a story. What truly matters is what the Scriptures have to say about it."

Hans muffled, "Amen. That's true, brother." Then, looking over to Niko. "Niko?"

Niko cleared his throat and flipped back to where they had started. "If we focus back on our passage for the night, the issue is about the church. Let's, for a moment, assume polygamy is moral."—Eleni could be seen rolling her eyes at her husband's neutral language—"Why, then, would God forbid it for church leaders and not anyone else?"

Anastasia, not wanting to let Kwesi have all the fun, finally chimed in. "Well," she said with a bit of a confident smirk, "the first thing we'd want to note is that if Paul is truly forbidding it for leaders, that means he's, by default, permitting it for everyone else."

Gretl perked up at the point she made. "Interesting..."

Some of the others nodded in agreement.

Paul finally broke his own silence. "I think there's a more fundamental question to ask, actually."

"What's that?" Niko asked, as Kwesi wore a big smile, presuming where Paul was going with this.

"I think—" Paul cleared his throat, shaking off any nerves. "I think the first thing to determine is whether or not this passage is really forbidding church leaders from having multiple wives in the first place."

Miranda tilted her head in confusion. "But Paul, it says 'one.' I'm open to new ideas and all"—she continued with a light-hearted smile—"but I'm pretty sure 'one' means 'one.'"

The group—all except Eleni—chuckled at her comment.

Paul, chuckling at himself along with them, finished his thought. "Right, but track with me here. Let's say your kid wants to play on my baseball team. If I tell your kid he needs a good attitude and one baseball glove to play on the team, would he be disqualified if he had *two* baseball gloves?"

Paul paused for a moment, as the analogy curiously settled in everyone's minds, some even making a small vocal murmur to suggest they'd never thought of it like that. Kwesi, meanwhile, was thoroughly impressed by the progress.

Paul continued, "What if Paul isn't saying that a husband can *only* have one wife? What if he's saying that a husband needs *at least* one wife to qualify for the position? I mean, the whole point of the condition has to do with him proving he can manage his household, right? Wouldn't a guy with more wives prove his management skills better than a guy with one?

Kwesi clapped his hands together once in excitement. "He's got it!"

What followed was a mixture of laughter and serious consideration. Some members of the group were sincerely intaking the information, Niko even voicing his desire to study this more later.

Eleni, however, upon her husband's stated intent to study it more, seemed to have reached her breaking point. Her voice cut through the room, sharp and frustrated. "What is happening here? Isn't this supposed to be a *Christian* Bible study!?"

Niko motioned with his hand to settle her down. "Honey—"

Eleni cut him off. "No!"

She then turned toward Kwesi. "Look Kwesi, I get your parents' situation, but this isn't Ghana, or wherever you're from. This is the modern, real world—"

With that, everyone froze as she caught herself, realizing that her frustration had led her to say something almost racist. She back-peddled, but not by much.

Now speaking to the entire room, Eleni sighed in exasperation. "Sorry. Look, all I'm saying is it's not natural, it's not normal, and it's not right." She stammered for a moment while throwing her arms up as if in disbelief she was having to say these things. "At the end of the day, what's clear is clear."—the side of her open palm hit the top of the other with each mention of 'clear.' Then, with a raised voice, her frustration peaked. "What woman in her right mind would ever be okay with her husband having other wives?!"

The room fell silent, the tension palpable. Then, to everyone's shock, two feminine voices spoke in matter-of-fact unison:

"I would."

Paul's head snapped up, his eyes darting between Candice and Miranda. The two women stared at each other from across the room, both looking equally surprised at their synchronized response.

Nobody spoke, but their answer seemed to pulse in the room like a living creature. Paul felt his heart racing, his mind reeling as he tried to process what had just happened. He caught Kwesi's eye, noting the thoroughly amused grin on his face.

Time seemed to stand still as the weight of those two words settled over the room. Paul found himself studying the faces of everyone present, trying to gauge their reactions. Hans looked mildly amused, while Gretl seemed more intrigued than shocked. Niko appeared uncomfortable, shifting in his seat and avoiding eye contact with everyone.

Anastasia was the first to break the silence, her voice gentle but firm. "I think we need to remember that marriage customs vary greatly across cultures and throughout history. What seems unthinkable to one person might be perfectly normal to another."

Her words seemed to break the spell that had fallen over the group. Conversation sparked around the room as Paul found himself in a daze, barely registering the discussion happening around him.

He couldn't stop his gaze from darting between Candice and Miranda. His wife sat with her back straight, a slight flush on her cheeks but her eyes clear and unashamed. Miranda, on the other hand, looked almost as shocked by her own words as everyone else, her hand covering her mouth as if she could take back what she'd just said.

Clearing his throat, Paul managed to find his voice. "Well, uh… perhaps this is a good place to stop for tonight. It's getting late, and we've certainly given ourselves a lot to think about."

As the group began to disperse, an awkward pressure lingered. Goodbyes were exchanged with forced casualness, everyone pointedly avoiding mention of the evening's unexpected revelation.

Eleni practically dragged Niko out the door, not even bothering to hide the disapproval she felt. Hans and Gretl left more slowly, engaged in a lively whispered discussion. Kwesi and Anastasia were the last couple to leave, with Kwesi pausing to give Paul a hearty pat on the back.

"Interesting evening, my friend," Kwesi said, his eyes still twinkling with amusement. "I look forward to continuing this discussion next time."

After they left, Paul found himself alone with Candice and Miranda. The three of them stood in the entryway, an uncomfortable silence stretching between them. The air felt thick with unspoken words and hidden emotions.

Miranda was the first to speak, her voice unnaturally high. "Thank you both for having me. It was… illuminating."

Candice nodded, her cheeks still flushed. "Yes, it certainly was. Goodnight, Miranda."

As Miranda slipped out the door, Paul turned to his wife, a thousand questions on the tip of his tongue, but Candice simply shook her head, her eyes pleading for time.

"Not tonight, honey," she said softly. "Let's just... sleep on it, okay?"

Paul nodded, watching as Candice made her way upstairs. He stood there for a long moment, his mind replaying the events of the evening. The synchronized "I would" echoed in his ears, a phrase that seemed to have shifted the very foundation of his world.

As he finally moved to follow his wife, Paul couldn't shake the feeling that something remarkable had happened. He paused at the foot of the stairs, his hand resting on the banister. Through the window, he could see Miranda's house, a warm light glowing in her living room window. For a moment, he once again allowed himself to imagine a different life, one where the boundaries between neighbor and family weren't so clearly defined.

Shaking his head to clear it of what still seemed like dangerous thoughts, Paul climbed the stairs.

As he shifted into bed, his mind still reeling from the events of the Bible study, Candice sat on the edge, her fingers tracing patterns on the duvet. The silence between them felt unwontedly uncomfortable, almost awkward.

"Paul," Candice began, her voice soft but steady, "I need to tell you something. I read some of that book. The one about marriage and polygamy."

Paul felt his heart skip a beat. So she had found it after all. He swallowed hard, trying to find his voice. "You did? I... How did you...?"

Candice turned to face him, her expression open and calm. "I found it on the coffee table. At first, I was just curious, but then I couldn't put it down." She paused for a moment. "Why didn't you tell me about it?"

Paul ran a hand through his hair, feeling relieved yet anxious. "Honestly? I was afraid of what you might think. I borrowed it from Pastor Alex. After... after I started noticing Miranda, I went to him for advice like you told me to. He lent me the book as a sort of historical perspective. It wasn't his idea. I saw it on his desk and asked to borrow it."

Candice nodded, processing this information. "And what did you think of it?"

Paul hesitated, choosing his words carefully. "I'm not sure I have a fully formed opinion yet. I want to finish reading it first, but it's... eye-opening, to say the least. What about you? What did you think?"

Candice's gaze grew distant, thoughtful. "You know, it's strange. Everything I read in that book... it made sense to me. I've never had a problem with the polygamy in the Bible. I'd never really thought about it much, but it never troubled me either."

Paul felt a surge of surprise. This wasn't the reaction he'd expected. "Really? You've never found it... I don't know, morally questionable?"

Candice shook her head, retaining a somewhat neutral expression. "No, not really. I mean, I can see the benefits and the difficulties, but it's clearly not something God condemns. It's just... normal in His eyes, from what I can tell."

Paul nodded slowly, absorbing her words. He felt a weight lifting from his shoulders, replaced by a growing sense of curiosity. He responded, "I think I need to finish the book before I can really say where I stand, but I'm glad we can talk about it."

Candice reached out, taking his hand in hers. "Me too. It's important that we can discuss these things, even if they're hard to get through."

As their eyes met, Paul felt a familiar warmth spreading through him. The stress of the evening seemed to melt away, replaced by a deep appreciation for his wife's open-mindedness and understanding. He tugged gently on her hand, pulling her closer.

"You know," he murmured, his voice taking on a playfully seductive tone, "all this serious talk has me thinking we could use a little fun before bed..."

Candice's eyebrows rose, a mischievous glint appearing in her eye. "Oh really? What kind of fun did you have in mind?"

Paul wrapped an arm around her waist, drawing her against him. "Well, Mrs. Thompson, I was thinking we could start with this..." He leaned in, capturing her lips in a deep, passionate kiss.

Candice responded eagerly, her fingers threading through his hair. As they fell back onto the bed, their laughter mingling with soft sighs of pleasure, the complicated emotions of the day faded into the background. In that moment, there was only Paul and Candice, their love for each other as strong and vibrant as ever.

Over the next month, their days fell into a pattern that felt both comfortable and somehow different. Candice and Miranda began spending more time together, almost daily cultivating their friendship while Paul mostly focused on work. His routine remained largely the same—early mornings at the office, meetings with clients, and the satisfying challenge of navigating the intricacies of international business in Greece. Yet, as he moved through his days, he found his thoughts often drifting to the conversations of that night, to the book waiting for him at home, and to the complicated feelings that came forward through Miranda's presence in their lives.

One afternoon, as Paul was wrapping up a conference call, his phone buzzed with a text from Candice. It was a photo of her and Miranda, grinning widely as they held up fresh produce from the local market. The caption read, "Heading to cooking class!"

Paul found himself smiling at the image, even as a familiar twinge of conflicted emotions tugged at his heart. He was glad Candice had found a close friend in Miranda, but the memory of their synchronized "I would" from the Bible study still echoed in his mind.

As the weeks went on, it became clear that Candice and Miranda's friendship was blossoming rapidly. Paul would come home to find them chatting animatedly in the kitchen, or hear Candice's laughter floating through an open window as they worked in Miranda's garden.

One evening, as Paul was settling in to read more of the book on polygamy, Candice burst through the front door, her cheeks flushed with excitement.

"Paul, you won't believe what happened today!" she exclaimed, dropping her bag and flopping onto the couch beside him.

Paul set the book aside, giving her his full attention. "What's got you so worked up?"

Candice's eyes sparkled as she launched into her story. "So, Miranda and I were at this little café in town, right? And this group of Greek men started chatting us up. At first, it was just friendly, but then one of them got a bit… pushy."

Paul felt a flare of protective anger. "Did he bother you? Are you okay?"

Candice waved off his concern, beginning to laugh as she recounted the events in her mind. "Oh, we're fine. That's the best part. Miranda…" Candice snorted and slapped Paul's leg as she tried to speak through her laughter, "she handled it beautifully. She told the guy off in perfect Greek—I didn't even know she knew any! And then…" Candace took a breath and put her hand up to her chest to try and calm her laughter long enough to finish, "then she took the guy's smoothie and dumped it on his head!"

Paul's defenses fell as a smile began to emerge.

"You should have seen his face!" Candice continued. "He looked like a scolded puppy!"

Paul couldn't help but laugh at the image. "Sounds like Miranda's quite the firecracker."

"She really is," Candice agreed, her voice warm with admiration as her laughter died down. "You know, I'm so glad she moved in next door. It's nice having someone to spend time with during the day while you're at work, especially since Eleni's been avoiding me ever since that Bible Study."

"I'm glad you two are getting along so well," he said, enjoying Candice's all-too-familiar bubbling personality.

Candice tilted her head, studying his face. "You know, you should join us sometime. Miranda's always asking about you. I think she feels bad about how things ended that fateful night…"

Paul felt a flutter in his stomach at the mention of that night. "Maybe I will," he said, trying to keep his voice neutral. "It would be nice to get to know her better."

Another week passed with not much changing. One afternoon, as Paul was leaving the office early, he decided to take a detour through the local park. As he rounded a bend in the path, he spotted two familiar figures seated on a bench by the fountain. Candice and Miranda were deep in conversation, their body language intimate and relaxed.

Paul slowed his pace, observing them from a distance. He watched as Miranda said something that made Candice throw her head back in laughter, her hand coming to rest on Miranda's arm. There was an ease between them, a natural chemistry that was both beautiful and unsettling to witness in light of his inner conflict.

Just as he was about to turn and leave, not wanting to intrude on their moment, Candice looked up and spotted him. Her face lit up with a smile that never failed to make his heart skip a beat.

"Paul!" she called out, waving him over. "Come join us!"

As Paul made his way to the bench, he saw Miranda turn to look at him. For a moment, he caught an expression on her face that he couldn't quite decipher—warmth, nervousness, and something else, something that made his pulse quicken.

"Well, if it isn't the man of the hour," Miranda said as he approached, her tone light and teasing. "We were just talking about you."

Paul raised an eyebrow, settling onto the bench beside Candice. "Oh really? Should I be worried?"

Candice laughed, leaning into him affectionately. "Not at all. We were just saying how nice it would be if we could all have dinner together sometime this week. What do you think? Maybe Friday night at our place?"

Paul looked between the two women, feeling the weight of their expectant gazes. He felt that, somehow, accepting this invitation would be more than just a simple dinner. It would be a step into uncharted territory, an acknowledgment of the changing dynamics between the three of them.

Taking a deep breath, Paul made his decision. "Friday sounds great," he said, surprised by the steadiness in his voice. "I'm looking forward to it."

As Candice beamed at him and Miranda's eyes sparkled with something that looked like eagerness, he said his goodbyes and took off for home.

Paul spent the rest of the week in anticipation, but he also couldn't shake the nervousness he felt. He found himself both looking forward to and dreading Friday night. He threw himself into his work, trying to distract himself from the constant thoughts of what this dinner might mean, what conversations might arise.

At home, he noticed Candice seemed more affectionate than usual, often reaching out to touch him as she passed by, or curling up next to him on the couch in the evenings. It was as if she sensed his inner turmoil and was trying to reassure him of her love and commitment.

The book on polygamy sat on his nightstand, nearly finished now, its contents swirling in his mind alongside memories of Bible study conversations and glimpses of Candice and Miranda's growing closeness.

On Thursday night, Paul's key turned in the lock, the familiar click echoing in the quiet living room. He stepped into the house, his briefcase heavy with the weight of a long day at the office. The house seemed unusually still, no sign of Candice in the kitchen or living room.

"Candice?" he called out, loosening his tie as he moved through the house.

That's when he heard it—the unmistakable sound of their laughter floating in from the backyard. Curious, Paul made his way to the back door and stepped out onto the patio.

The sight that greeted him made his breath catch in his throat. There, in the softly lit pool, were Candice and Miranda, each lounging on a large inflatable float, their faces flushed with laughter and the warm evening air. Paul couldn't help but notice how the water glistened on their skin, how their swimsuits clung to their curves.

"Paul!" Candice exclaimed, her face lighting up at the sight of him. "You're home!"

Miranda turned, her green eyes sparkling as they met his. "Hey there, stranger. Long day at the office?"

Paul nodded, trying to keep his eyes from wandering. "Yeah, pretty intense. What's all this?"

Candice was already paddling to the edge of the pool. "Just a little impromptu girls' night. Come here, you."

She hoisted herself out of the pool, water cascading off her body as she approached Paul. He felt a familiar warmth spread through him as she wrapped her arms around him, her wet skin soaking his work shirt.

"Missed you," she murmured, pressing a soft kiss to his lips.

As Candice pulled away, Paul saw Miranda approaching. She'd gotten out of the pool too, and was now standing just a few feet away, droplets of water trailing down her tanned skin.

"Can I get one?" Miranda asked with a friendly grin, stepping forward to hug Paul. "Don't worry, I'll skip the kiss."

They all laughed, but Paul felt his heart racing as Miranda's arms encircled him. The hug lasted only a moment, but the feeling of her body against his, the scent of her perfume mixed with chlorine, it was almost overwhelmingly intoxicating.

"I, uh, I should probably head in," Paul said, taking a step back. "Pretty wiped out from the day."

Candice nodded understandingly. "Of course, honey. We'll try to keep it down out here."

As Paul retreated into the house, he could hear the women's conversation resuming behind him. He climbed the stairs to the bedroom, his mind a mess.

Closing the bedroom door behind him, Paul sank to his knees beside the bed. He clasped his hands together, bowing his head in prayer.

"Lord," he whispered, his voice trembling slightly. "I'm really struggling here. I can't seem to get Miranda out of my head. These feelings, they're so strong. I'm not sure I can handle another hug like that, but I don't want to make things awkward by saying anything. Please, give me strength, show me the way forward—"

As Paul said those words, an image suddenly popped into his mind—Kwesi, his Ghanaian friend from Bible study. The memory of their conversation about polygamy floated to the surface of his thoughts. With a start, Paul realized what he needed to do.

"Thank you, Lord," he murmured, rising to his feet. He'd call Kwesi in the morning to see if they could meet for lunch. Maybe his friend could offer some perspective on this whole situation.

The next day, Paul found himself sitting across from Kwesi in a small café near his office. The rich smell of Greek coffee pervaded the air as Paul poured out his heart to his friend.

"I don't know what to do, Kwesi," Paul said, running a hand through his hair. "These feelings for Miranda, they're getting really intense. And she's so physically affectionate, it's driving me crazy. I swear, if I have to see her in a swimsuit one more time…"

Kwesi listened intently, his dark eyes filled with understanding. When Paul finished, Kwesi leaned forward, his expression serious.

"Brother," he said, his deep voice low and measured. "I have a question for you. Do you want Western advice, or African advice?"

Paul couldn't help but chuckle at the unexpected query. "African advice, I suppose," he replied, curious to see where this was going.

Kwesi's face broke into a wide grin. "Excellent choice, my friend. For you see, the African advice is actually the Biblical advice."

Paul raised an eyebrow, intrigued. "Go on…"

Kwesi took a sip of his coffee before continuing. Then, gesturing to the Mediterranean bay outside with a wave of his hand, looking at it with a shake of his head and a small hint of indignation; he spoke slowly and clearly in his still-retained African accent. "You know, it was Greece and Rome that first made polygamy socially unacceptable and then illegal. Before that, it was normal in almost every part of the world. Even today, it's still practiced in almost 30% of cultures around the globe."

Paul nodded slowly, recalling similar information from the book he'd been reading.

Kwesi, still looking out at the bay, proceeded with what seemed like bewilderment in his voice. "The West has made marriage so complicated. Love has to feel a certain way, weddings have to look a certain way. Monogamy. Polygamy. Modern concepts that cannot be found in Scripture. We craft all these regulations when God simply said that a man would join to his wife. It makes one wonder, who gave Europe the right to define marriage in ways that God has not done so?"

Paul, noting the mindful reflection in both Kwesi's tone and his face, gently interrupted. "Your parents' story isn't the only one that makes this personal, is it?"

Kwesi looked back at Paul. "I have a brother-in-law who lives just outside of Kenya. His name is Jabari. He is a godly man, a righteous man. He and his wife were unable to bear children, so they assumed she was barren. Because they wanted children, Jabari took a second wife, my sister, Imani. At the time, Imani was going to a school in Kenya and attending a church started by American missionaries. When the elders at her church learned of her plans to quit school to become a man's second wife, they treated her harshly for this decision. They accused her of not being a Christian and excommunicated her from fellowship. I was here in Greece already and could not help her."

Paul quietly listened with interest.

"When she moved in with Jabari and his wife, the church left her alone, but after a few months of trying to conceive a child, the family started to realize that the problem of fertility was Jabari's, not his wife's. Although this was a difficult realization, Imani was happy to be his wife because she loved them very much, but people from her old church began reaching out to her behind Jabari's back, encouraging her to abandon her husband in light of his inability to give her children. While she did not entertain their temptations—she is a rather quiet and humble soul—she feared telling her husband about the situation. But one day, Jabari found out," Kwesi said as his eyes went wide and a grin finally emerged from his lips.

"What happened?" Paul inquired, clearly anxious to hear how the story ended.

"Well," Kwesi continued, now in a more light-hearted manner. "Jabari invited the elders of Imani's old church and their wives to his home for dinner. They all spoke about the issue of multiple wives in his back yard while he grilled steaks. Finally, the moment came that Jabari was waiting for... One of the elders demanded that Imani leave him to fix the 'sin of polygamy.' Now, you must understand that Jabari is a big man with a big personality." Kwesi let out a chuckle as he took a sip of coffee.

Looking back at Paul, who was on the edge of his seat, he smiled in amusement. "Do you want to know what he did?"

Paul nodded, smiling in anticipation of a comical outcome.

"With spatula in hand, he raised his arms and his eyes toward heaven, and said, 'O great King of the universe, they wish me to solve the sin of polygamy by committing the sin of divorce. I ask you, Father—which is worse?' As the elders started making excuses for their suggestion, Jabari said to them, 'I have a Bible verse for you elders.' Then, as he picked up some raw steaks, he quoted to them, 'For though by this time you ought to be teachers, you have need again for someone to teach you the elementary principles of the oracles of God, and you have come to need milk, not solid food.' So the elders asked him what this meant, and I'm sure they regret their inquiry to this very day... Jabari turned around, with steaks in hand, and yelled, 'It means you're in need of solid food! You need MEAT!!!' He then roared like a lion and began throwing the raw steaks at the elders and their wives!"

Kwesi let out a laugh that he could barely contain, a wide-eyed Paul joining him.

"You've got to be kidding me!" Paul said in-between breaths.

Kwesi rowdily shook his head side to side, stomping the marble floor with one foot as he tried to keep himself from laughing too hard. Trying to compose himself, he continued, "The elders and their wives were terrified. They ran for their lives off his property and into their cars, all the while Jabari still yelling with his big smile and throwing steaks at them!"

The two shared the rest of a hearty laugh at the picture this painted in their minds. When they finally brought themselves to stop, Kwesi finished the story with a more even-keeled tone. "You see, brother. They couldn't see what was best for everyone involved, but more important than that, they couldn't see the Scriptures. God hates divorce, yet they encourage it. God prescribed multiple wives to one man on many occasions, yet they forbid it. It's all backwards."

Paul listened, his original intensity somewhat returning. "I get it. I really do. I've actually been reading a book about all this, and it all makes sense. But how does this specifically apply to my situation? Not just practically, but biblically? I don't want to do what seems right in my own eyes, even if it makes sense on the surface. I want to do what the bible tells me to do."

Kwesi fixed Paul with a now-serious, penetrating gaze. "Let me ask you this, my brother. Are you burning?"

Paul felt his face flush. He looked at Kwesi, who widened his eyes, silently urging him to answer. Paul nodded. "Yeah, I guess you could say that..."

"Well then," Kwesi said, leaning back in his chair. "Paul—the apostle, not you—didn't say it's better to pray against lust than to burn. He said it's better to *marry* than to burn."

Paul seemed stunned, not because he hadn't thought of this before, but because for the first time, someone actually went deeper than theology or theorizing and made the exhortation personal. "Are you really suggesting what I think you're suggesting?"

Kwesi smiled, then glanced at his watch and stood up. "I've got to get back to work, my friend, but think about it. Pray about it." He gave Paul a reassuring pat on the shoulder. "And keep reading that book of yours."

As Kwesi walked away, Paul sat there, stunned. The thought of having two wives, especially two women like Candice and Miranda, seemed more like some fantasy world than God's will for real life...

Paul gathered his things and headed back to the office, his mind racing. He thought about Kwesi's words, about the book he'd borrowed from Pastor Alex, about the way Candice and Miranda had looked last night in the pool. It all blurred together in his mind, a confusing feeling of desire, guilt, and the faintest glimmer of hope.

As he settled back at his desk, he found himself reaching for his phone. He pulled up the photos Candice had sent him over the past few weeks—snapshots of her and Miranda at the market, in the garden, laughing together over coffee, etc. He studied their faces, noting the easy affection between them, the way they seemed to fit so naturally into each other's lives.

What if, he wondered, not for the first time, there was room in their lives for something more? What if this wasn't temptation to be resisted, but an opportunity to obey?

Paul shook his head, trying to clear it of what he still deemed questionable thoughts. He had work to do, clients to call, reports to finish, but as he turned his attention to his computer screen, he couldn't quite shake the feeling that something fundamental was shifting in his life.

That evening, as Paul drove home, his mind kept drifting back to his conversation with Kwesi. The idea of polygamy, of actually considering it as a real possibility in his life, both terrified and exhilarated him. He thought about Candice, about the strength of their marriage, about the deep love and trust they shared. Could that love possibly expand to include Miranda?

As he pulled into the driveway, Paul saw Miranda's car parked in front of her house. A light was on in her living room, and he could just make out her silhouette moving behind the curtains. His heart rate picked up at the sight, and he had to take a deep breath to steady himself before getting out of the car.

Inside, he found Candice in the kitchen, humming softly as she prepared dinner. The familiar domestic scene, including no one but his wife, brought a feeling of relief to his hectic day and his similarly hectic thoughts. He wrapped his arms around her from behind, pressing a kiss to her neck.

"Mmm, hello to you too," Candice said, leaning back into his embrace. "How was your day?"

Paul hesitated for a moment, wondering if he should tell her about his lunch with Kwesi, about the thoughts that had been consuming him, but the moment passed, and he simply said, "It was… interesting. How about yours?"

As Candice launched into a story about her day, Paul half-listened, his mind elsewhere. He watched her as she talked, gesturing animatedly with a wooden spoon, her face alight with enthusiasm. His love for her welled up inside him, strong and sure as ever.

As they sat down to dinner, Paul made a decision. He wouldn't act on anything, not yet, but he would finish reading that book. He would pray, earnestly and openly, for guidance. And he would watch, carefully, to see if maybe—just maybe—God was opening a door he'd never even known existed.

At dinner, Paul studied Candice as she told a story, most of it being told with her mouth half full, typical for Candice when she was in a chatty mood. Her eyes lit up the way they always did when she was excited, and he remembered how she'd quit her stable job back home, sold her car, and learned basic Greek just to live here with him. She could have chosen an easier life, but she'd chosen this one—chosen him.

Another month passed, and Candice and Miranda seemed to have become the best of friends. They spent their mornings doing housework together, afternoons cooking in each other's kitchens, and evenings sharing wine on one of their patios until Paul got home from work. Yet, amidst their flourishing friendship, Candice couldn't help noticing the moments when Miranda's phone would buzz and her friend's face would cloud over.

"Just family stuff," Miranda would say with a tight smile, stepping away to take calls, "drama over my parents' estate." But her voice would carry notes of tension that didn't match such a mundane explanation. She clearly trusted Candice, but something was still preoccupying her on occasion that she wasn't ready to divulge.

One afternoon, while they were preparing spanakopita in Miranda's kitchen, Miranda excused herself to use the bathroom. Her phone buzzed on the counter—the third time that hour. Candice hesitated, guilt warring with concern. Finally, worry for her friend won out. She picked up the phone, her heart pounding.

The message preview showed texts from an unknown number:

"He's asking questions again."

"Getting closer. Be careful."

"Don't trust anyone new."

Candice set the phone down, her hands trembling slightly. The bathroom door opened, and she busied herself with the phyllo dough as Miranda returned.

"Everything okay?" Miranda asked, noticing Candice's distraction.

"Of course," Candice replied, forcing a smile. She watched as Miranda checked her phone and saw the slight tightening around her friend's eyes as she read the messages.

Later that night, lying in bed beside Paul, Candice wrestled with what she'd seen. Part of her wanted to confront Miranda, to demand the truth, but she thought about how Miranda had finally begun to relax and trust them.

Whatever trouble followed Miranda, whatever secrets she kept, Candice decided the best thing she could do was simply be present. Be the friend Miranda clearly needed. The truth would emerge when it needed to.

A couple of months having passed since Miranda moved next door, with Paul seeing her in small spurts but mostly focused on his work, he finally finished the lengthy book about marriage Pastor Alex had lent him. As he drove home from work that day, the book sat heavy in his lap, a constant reminder of the tumultuous thoughts that had been plaguing him for weeks. He glanced at the clock on the dashboard—still plenty of time to drop by Pastor Alex's office to return it before heading home.

As he pulled into the driveway, Candice emerged from the house, a large leftover dish in her hands. Her face lit up at the sight of him, and Paul felt a familiar warmth spread through his chest. No matter what confusing emotions he'd been grappling with lately, his love for Candice remained a steadfast anchor.

"Perfect timing!" Candice called out as Paul stepped from the car. "Can you do me a favor?"

Paul raised an eyebrow, a small smile playing on his lips. "Oh? What kind of favor?"

Oblivious to his playful suspicion and his puckered lips for a kiss, Candice held out the dish. "Could you drop this off at Miranda's on your way to see Pastor Alex? I told her I'd return it right now, but I just got a call I need to take."

Paul hesitated for a moment. "Sure, no problem. Should I knock, or…?"

"No, just go on in," Candice said with a wave of her hand. "She said to just walk in."

Paul nodded, taking the dish from Candice. As he turned to leave, she caught his arm, phone now pressed between her ear and shoulder, pulling him in for a quick kiss. "Love you," she murmured against his lips.

"Love you too," Paul replied, his voice slightly husky. He cleared his throat. "I won't be long at the church."

With the book tucked under one arm and the dish balanced in his hands, Paul made his way next door. He paused for a moment on Miranda's front step, taking a deep breath to steady himself. It was just a quick errand, he told himself. Drop off the food, say a quick hello, and be on his way.

Paul pushed open the front door, calling out as he stepped inside. "Miranda? I've got your leftover dish."

"Is that you, Candice?" Miranda's voice floated from another room. "One sec. I'll come grab it."

Before Paul could respond, Miranda emerged from her bedroom. Time seemed to slow as his brain processed the sight before him. Miranda stood there, clad only in a pair of shorts, her top half completely bare. For a split second, Paul's eyes took in the sight—before his brain caught up with what he was seeing.

A strangled gasp escaped Miranda's lips as she realized it wasn't Candice standing in her entryway. In a flash, she grabbed a towel hanging nearby, clutching it to her chest. At the same moment, Paul's hand flew up to cover his eyes, the sudden movement causing him to lose his grip on both the book and the dish.

The sound of shattering ceramic filled the air, punctuated by Miranda's startled yelp and Paul's stammered apologies.

"Miranda, I'm so sorry," Paul babbled, his eyes still tightly shut. "I didn't mean to—Candice said—I thought you knew I was coming—the bowl, I'm sorry about the bowl—"

"Paul, it's okay," Miranda's voice cut through his rambling, a mix of embarrassment and concern evident in her tone. "It was just an accident. I thought Candice was bringing the dish, I didn't realize—"

But Paul was already backing towards the door, his face burning with shame and guilt. "I'm so sorry," he repeated, fumbling for the doorknob. "I'll replace the dish, I'll—I have to go."

He practically stumbled out of the house, Miranda's voice calling after him, but he couldn't bring himself to look back. Paul all but ran to his car, his heart pounding in his chest. As he slid behind the wheel, he caught a glimpse of his reflection in the rearview mirror—his face was flushed, his eyes wide with panic.

Candice watched Paul's car peel out of their driveway. His tires screeched against the pavement, a sound as jarring as the distress etched on his face moments before. Concern bloomed in her chest as she hung up the phone and made her way next door, determined to unravel the mystery of what had transpired.

Candice knocked gently on Miranda's front door, calling out, "Miranda? It's Candice. Is everything okay?"

The door creaked open, revealing Miranda's flushed face as she was slipping a tank top on. Her eyes were wide, a mixture of embarrassment and worry clouding her usually confident demeanor. "Oh, Candice," she breathed, "I'm so glad you're here. Come in."

As Candice stepped inside, she noticed the shattered remains of the leftover dish scattered across the floor. "What in the world happened? Paul looked really upset."

Miranda sank onto the couch, burying her face in her hands. "It was a horrible misunderstanding. I thought you were bringing the dish over, so I... well, I wasn't exactly dressed... When Paul walked in, I didn't have a shirt on, and—" Miranda took a deep breath to calm herself. "This is so embarrassing. I'm so sorry."

Understanding dawned on Candice's face. "Oh, Miranda," she said softly, sitting beside her friend and placing a comforting hand on hers. "It was just an accident. There's nothing to apologize for."

Miranda looked up, her eyes glistening with unshed tears. "Paul seemed so upset. I feel terrible."

Candice wrapped her arm over Miranda's shoulders and squeezed reassuringly. "He'll be okay. He's just... sensitive about these things. I'll talk to him when he gets home."

As she spoke, Candice's eyes landed on a familiar book lying amidst the broken ceramic. She reached down to pick it up, brushing off a few stray pieces of the shattered dish. "Oh, Paul must have dropped this too."

Miranda's gaze focused on the book in Candice's hands. "What is it?" she asked, curiosity momentarily overriding her distress.

Candice hesitated for a moment before responding. "It's a book Paul borrowed from our pastor." She walked over and picked it up. "We've both been reading it. It's about... well, it's about marriage and polygamy in the Bible."

Miranda's eyebrows shot up. "Polygamy? That's... unexpected. Did the bible study last month inspire you to read it?"

Candice shook her head. "Nope. By chance, Paul borrowed it a couple of days *before* that fateful study." Both of them smiled, Miranda rolling her eyes as they recalled the difficult evening in their minds. "But we certainly started reading it more after that," Candice clarified.

Miranda walked over to take a closer look. "Have you been enjoying it?"

Candice nodded, trying to keep her expression neutral. "We have. It's honestly been really eye-opening." She set the book down on Miranda's coffee table. "There's so much in the Scripture about marriage that we never really noticed before."

Miranda took another deep breath, momentarily chasing away the lingering embarrassment. "Well," she said, her tone light—but not at all mischievous—"I guess if I was married to Paul, tonight wouldn't have been a problem."

Time seemed to pause, holding those words suspended between them before both women succumbed to nervous laughter. The sound was tinged with an undercurrent of something else—a tension, an unspoken possibility that neither was quite ready to acknowledge.

As their laughter faded, an awkward silence settled between them. Candice cleared her throat and stepped away from Miranda, suddenly needing space from whatever was happening in that moment.

"I should probably head home," she said, taking a cautious step toward the front door. "Paul will be back soon, and I want to make sure he's okay."

Miranda nodded, walking Candice to the door. "Of course. And Candice? Thank you. For understanding, and for being such a good friend."

Candice smiled warmly at Miranda before stepping out into the cool evening air.

Miranda closed her door and turned around, realizing Candice had left the book on her coffee table. Curiosity piqued, she quickly cleaned up the floor, then settled on her couch to peruse the book.

As Candice made her way back to her own house, her mind was occupied with thoughts of the book, of Paul's reaction, and of the joke Miranda had made. There was a shift happening, subtle but undeniable, in the dynamics between the three of them. Candice wasn't sure where it would lead, but she felt expectant, and hopeful.

Back in her own home, Candice settled onto the couch with her phone, composing a text to Paul: "Everything's okay, sweetie. It was just a misunderstanding. Take all the time you need to pray, but know that there's nothing to feel guilty about. I love you."

As she hit send, Candice let out a long breath. She knew Paul would need time to process what had happened, to reconcile his feelings of guilt and attraction, but she also knew the strength of their marriage, the depth of their love.

During his drive to the church, houses and streets whipped past in a green-gold blur. Paul's mind replayed the incident over and over. He could still see Miranda standing there, vulnerable and exposed, the look of shock on her face etched into his memory. Guilt gnawed at him—guilt for seeing her like that, guilt for the thoughts that had flashed through his mind in that split second before propriety kicked in, and guilt for the way his body had responded to the sight of her.

By the time Paul pulled into the church parking lot, tears were streaming down his face. He sat in the car for a long moment, trying to compose himself, but the flood of emotions was too strong to contain. With shaking hands, he got out of the car and made his way to Pastor Alex's office.

The pastor looked up in surprise as Paul burst through the door, his face a mask of distress. "Paul? What's wrong?"

Paul collapsed into a chair, burying his face in his hands. "Pastor, I've done something terrible," he choked out.

Pastor Alex leaned forward, concern etched on his features. "Take a deep breath, Paul. Tell me what happened."

Slowly, haltingly, Paul recounted the incident at Miranda's house. As he spoke, he felt the weight of his struggle with lust, the constant battle he'd been fighting for weeks, come crashing down on him. He told Pastor Alex everything—his growing attraction to Miranda, the conversations with Kwesi, the book on polygamy, and now this accidental intrusion on Miranda's privacy.

"I don't know what to do," Paul finished, his voice barely above a whisper. "I love Candice more than anything, but these feelings for Miranda... they're tearing me apart. It's exactly what I felt for Candice when I first met her—what I still feel for her now! And now, after what just happened... I feel like I've betrayed them both."

Pastor Alex was silent for a long moment, his fingers steepled under his chin as he considered Paul's words. When he finally spoke, his voice was gentle but firm.

"Paul, first of all, I want you to understand that what happened at Miranda's house was an accident. You didn't intend to violate her privacy, and from what you've told me, she understands that too. Forgive yourself for that."

Paul nodded, wiping at his eyes with the back of his hand.

"As for the rest," Pastor Alex continued, "I can see you're really struggling with this. You love your wife. Candice knows that. I know that. God knows that. But you love your neighbor too. If you're being honest with yourself, that's the truth of the matter."

Paul hesitated to respond.

Pastor Alex took a deep breath, compassion evident in his face. "I've been praying for you a lot, Paul."

"Thanks," Paul muttered.

"Let me ask you something," the caring pastor continued. "What if you're not 'struggling' with lust at all?"

Paul looked up, confusion evident on his face. "What do you mean?"

Pastor Alex leaned back in his chair, his expression thoughtful. "You've been reading that book you borrowed, yes? And you've had conversations with Kwesi about it. Then you should know at this point— the very fact that you're running from sexual temptation means you're *not* struggling with lust. Not once have you communicated to me that you're interested in being inappropriate with Miranda. In fact, it would appear that you desire the very opposite. You've spent the last two months praying for help, seeking wise counsel, and keeping a safe distance from this woman so as not to give temptation any room. That's not lust, Paul. That's holiness."

Paul's jaw remained tight. "But the feelings for her are so strong, I—"

Pastor Alex interrupted. "Indeed they are, but lust isn't the firing of chemicals in your brain that you never asked for. Lust is a purposeful desire to do something sinful, but you have done the opposite of that. The question you'll have to answer is, 'What does a man do who's burning with passion yet will not sin?'"

Paul threw his hands up and let them drop on his knees in frustration. "According to Kwesi, I'm supposed to become a polygamist because 'It's better to marry than to burn.' But—"

Pastor Alex—just as Paul had done—threw his own hands up and let them slap down on his knees, causing Paul to stop mid-sentence. He looked into Paul's eyes and shrugged. "It's better to marry than to burn. Was the apostle right or was he wrong?"

Paul sat back, stunned. Of all the responses he'd expected from his pastor, this certainly wasn't one of them. "But… but polygamy?"

"You mean marriage?" Pastor Alex interjected. "There are no monogamists or polygamists in God's eyes, Paul. There are only husbands." The pastor leaned forward over his desk. "Tell me something, my friend. Pretend you're a Hebrew, living 4,000 years ago off the coast of the Jordan, enjoying your inheritance with the rest of Reuben and Gad. You're married to this beautiful woman whom you love passionately, just as you are now. While taking a boat out to fish, you spot a man with his daughter—our Miranda, if you will. More than half the households in your community have more than one wife in them, some, as a direct result of God's very Law through Moses, so it's all quite normal. You see this woman, you approach them and introduce yourself, and you begin to burn. Tell me, what would you do?"

Paul paused for a moment, then took a deep breath to relax his nerves. "Page 47."

The Pastor looked at him in confusion.

"The book," Paul clarified. "It's right there on Page 47. I would run home, inform my wife of the good news, make sure she didn't object, then I'd go make a deal with her father, and if he was willing, I'd be given a wife. Simple as that."

"And if she had no father?" Pastor Alex pressed.

"Then I'd just ask her and hope she said yes," Paul said with rising confidence as he looked his pastor in the eyes.

Pastor Alex reached for his Bible, flipping it open with practiced ease to a now-very familiar passage to Paul in 1 Corinthians. He turned the Bible around and plopped it on his desk in front of Paul. "Do you want to obey the Scriptures, Paul?"

"Yes," Paul said resolutely.

"Are you burning?" Pastor Alex continued bluntly.

Paul glanced at the Bible then back up at the Pastor, the fact that he was again being asked this question beginning to bring clarity to his mind, almost as if God was asking it—through people—over and over again until he got the point. "Yes," he again replied.

"And it's better to pray really hard than to burn, right?" Pastor Alex retained his matter-of-fact attitude while questioning Paul. "It's better to hide in your room and avoid the woman than to burn, right? It's better to will yourself to not burn than to burn, right? You are commanded to flee unlawful lust, yes. But that is not what's happening here. Did you run from Candice when you first burned with passion for her? Did you try to pray it away? Did you lament your burning to your pastor in his office? Or did you embrace that burning passion and take her to be your wife?"

"I took her to be my wife," Paul answered, understanding beginning to dawn in his eyes.

"Then—and I'm not telling you what to do—but I'm asking you: Why are you trying to solve the same puzzle with a different solution when the first solution is the one that worked?"

Paul shook his head back and forth a bit. "It just doesn't feel right.."

"And this does?" A hint of surprising indignation rose up in Pastor Alex's typically calm voice, catching Paul off guard. "Losing sleep over the guilt you feel, tip-toeing around your own wife in fear of your feelings, failing to focus on anything besides this 'struggle?' You honestly believe that this is God's will? This *feels* right to you?"

Paul lowered his head, unsure of how to respond.

Pastor Alex reached his hand out and roughly put his pointer finger down on the applicable verse in his open Bible. "One day, you are going to stand before God in judgment, Paul. And you are going to give an account for how you handled this situation. He won't be interested in your feelings on that day. He'll only be interested in one thing. Only one question will be asked of you—'Did you keep My word?' Now, when you stand before the God of this Scripture, and He demands an account of your actions, what is the one thing you can answer Him in confidence? What is it you could say that would tell the Almighty, 'Regardless of what seemed right to me, I kept Your word?'"

After a few seconds of taking in the challenging exhortation, Paul finally answered. "It's better to marry than to burn."

Seeing that Paul had gotten the point, Pastor Alex lifted his finger—which looked to weigh a ton to Paul in that moment—off of his bible and compassionately smiled at the conflicted man sitting before him. "I'm not saying this is definitely what God wants for you, but I am saying that perhaps you need to be open to the possibility. Pray about it. Talk to Candice. See where the Holy Spirit leads you. Because one thing's for sure, you can't go on like you are now. There has to be an answer, my friend."

Paul left Pastor Alex's office that evening with his head spinning. The pastor's words echoed in his mind, challenging everything he'd ever believed about marriage and relationships. As he drove home, he found himself wondering—could this really be a viable option? Could God really be calling him to consider a path he'd never even imagined before?

The house was quiet when Paul arrived home. He found Candice asleep in their bedroom, and he still felt terrible about the events of the evening. He longed to tell her everything, but it wouldn't do to wake her, not when she looked so peaceful in her sleep.

The next morning was a Friday. Paul woke up alone, blinking groggily. He was surprised to find Candice's side of the bed empty and cold. Memories of the previous night came flooding back, and he quickly dressed for the day, eager to check on his wife.

As Paul descended the stairs, he found Candice in the kitchen, her back to him as she flipped pancakes on the griddle. She turned to him as he entered, her smile faltering as she took in his red-rimmed eyes and disheveled appearance.

"Good morning," she said softly, not wanting to startle him.

Paul stepped closer, a sheepish smile on his face. "Morning, love. I sure am starving."

Candice crossed the kitchen, wrapping her arms around Paul's waist and pressing a kiss to his cheek. "Starving, eh? But first, you must tell me what's wrong. I was so worried about you last night, and now you look like you've barely slept. When did you get back?"

Paul took a deep breath, steeling himself for what he was about to say. "I'm okay. Better than last night, at least. Candice, we need to talk. Something... something happened yesterday, and... and... well, there's a lot we need to discuss."

Candice's brow furrowed with concern. She turned off the stove and gave Paul her full attention. "Okay. What's going on? I'm all ears."

Paul led her to the living room, where they sat side by side on the couch. Slowly, carefully, he began to recount the events of yesterday afternoon—the incident at Miranda's, his conversation with Pastor Alex, and the tumultuous emotions he'd been grappling with for weeks.

As he spoke, Paul watched Candice's face carefully, searching for signs of anger or betrayal, but to his surprise, her expression remained open and attentive, even as he confessed the intensity of his growing attraction to Miranda, of how he was *burning*.

When he finally finished speaking, silence fell between them. Paul held his breath, waiting for Candice's reaction. After what felt like an eternity, she spoke.

"Paul," she said softly, reaching out to take his hand, "thank you for being honest with me. I have to admit, I'm not really... displeased."

Paul blinked in confusion. "You're not?" he sighed. "Candice, I'm so sorry. For what happened, for how I reacted... all of it."

Candice shook her head, her hands coming up to cup Paul's face, and her expression free of concern but also quite neutral. "There's nothing to apologize for, sweetie. It was an accident, plain and simple. Plus, I visited Miranda after you left and she filled me in. I even sent you a text saying everything was okay."

Paul felt as if the world had tilted on its axis. Here he'd been, torturing himself with guilt over his feelings for Miranda, and all along, Candice had known what happened and forgiven him already?

"My phone was off. Oh, Candice..." Paul leaned into her touch, his eyes closing briefly. When he opened them again, Candice saw a mixture of gratitude and lingering guilt. "I just... I don't want you to think that I... that my feelings for Miranda... I just don't want to sin, and I definitely don't want to betray you in any way. You know how much I love you, right?"

Candice nodded, reaching across her lap to take Paul's hand. "I do know that. And I love you too. So much. I'm praying for you, sweetie. For all of us, really."

A comfortable silence fell between them as they moved to the kitchen table and began to eat. Candice watched Paul, noting how he seemed to relax more with each passing moment. As he took a bite of toast, Candice decided to lighten the mood.

"You know," she said, with a hesitant but light-hearted tone, "Miranda made the funniest comment last night."

Paul looked up, curiosity piqued. "Oh?"

Candice grinned. "She said that if she was married to you, last night wouldn't have been a problem."

As was becoming Paul's custom when Candice said something shocking in the kitchen, he choked on his breakfast, his face turning a deep shade of red as he coughed and sputtered. Candice couldn't help but snicker at his reaction, even as she stood up to get him a glass of water.

Once Paul regained his composure, Candice leaned in over the table, her voice low and teasing. "Why did you choke, sweetie? You wouldn't... like that, would you?"

Paul's blush deepened, his eyes wide as he stammered, "I... Candice, I don't... that's not..."

Candice sensually chuckled, cutely patting Paul's head as she grabbed her keys and started walking toward the front door. "Relax, honey. I'm just teasing you," she said as she opened the door. Then, standing in the open doorway, she looked back at Paul with a flirtatious smile. "Sort of..."

As Paul continued to sputter and blush, Candice reverted to the matter-of-factness of the moment. "I've got some errands to run this morning. Why don't you tackle some yard work while I'm gone?"

Paul nodded, still looking a bit shell-shocked. "Yeah, that... that sounds good. I have some things to take care of too."

Paul watched Candice's car pull out of the driveway, his mind still reeling from their conversation. The memory of last night's incident with Miranda was fresh in his mind, mingling with Candice's teasing words about polygamy. He ran a hand through his hair, feeling overwhelmed by the conflicting emotions within him. Was Candice trying to hint at certain possibilities? Why else would she think it a good idea to tease at a time like this, given everything that's happened?

Deciding he needed some air, Paul stepped out onto the back porch. The Greek morning was already warm, the scent of blooming flowers carrying on the gentle breeze. As he leaned against the railing, his gaze inevitably drifted to Miranda's house next door.

As he stood there, lost in thought, he heard the sound of a door opening. Paul's eyes snapped open to see Miranda stepping out onto her own back porch, a mug of coffee in her hands. Their eyes met across the space between their houses, and for a moment, neither moved.

Miranda was the first to break the silence. "Good morning, Paul," she called, her voice carrying a note of hesitation. "I hope you're feeling better today."

Paul swallowed hard, willing his voice to remain steady. "Good morning, Miranda. I am, thank you. Listen, I'm truly sorry about last night. My reaction was... well, it was uncalled for."

Miranda shook her head, a small smile playing on her lips. "No need to apologize. It was an honest mistake. I'm just glad we're past it."

Paul was quiet for a few seconds as Miranda shifted her chair to where she wanted it.

"I like your top," Paul sheepishly complimented, clearly in reference to last night.

Miranda, immediately getting the joke, was relieved of all tension and let out a small, comfortable laugh.

Looking to capitalize on the humorous relief, Paul followed up, "To be honest, I think I'll like *all* of your tops from now on.."

With a shared laugh and another assurance that all was forgiven, Miranda settled into her chair with her coffee. Paul headed back inside to get ready for the day. He had a lot to think about, a lot to pray about, but for the first time in weeks, he felt a feeling of peace settling over him that God's plan, whatever it was, was going to reveal itself soon. His car ride into town was finally reminiscent of the peaceful morning drives he used to enjoy so much.

Later that afternoon, as Candice pulled into the driveway, her arms laden with groceries, she noticed an unfamiliar figure standing in Miranda's front yard. The man stood motionless, his gaze fixed on Miranda's house with an intensity that sent a chill down Candice's spine. Miranda's car was nowhere to be seen, which only added to the strangeness of the situation.

Setting her grocery bags on the hood of her car, Candice approached the stranger cautiously. "Excuse me," she called out, her voice steady despite the unease growing in her chest. "Can I help you with something?"

The man turned to face her, his expression blank and unreadable. His eyes, cold and grey, seemed to look through her rather than at her.

Neither spoke, and the quiet between them felt thick enough to cut with a knife.

Finally, the man spoke, his voice flat and emotionless. "I'm fine."

Those two words did nothing to alleviate Candice's growing sense of unease. If anything, they intensified it. She nodded slowly, backing away towards her house. "All right then. Have a good day."

Once inside, Candice immediately locked the door behind her, her heart pounding in her chest. Something was definitely off about that man. His presence, coupled with Miranda's occasional secretive behavior and the two strange occurrences at night a couple of months ago, painted a worrying picture in Candice's mind.

She fumbled for her phone, dialing Paul's number with shaking fingers. The call went straight to voicemail. "Paul," she said, trying to keep her voice calm, "I need you to come home right away. There's a strange man outside Miranda's house, and I've got a really bad feeling about him. Please call me back as soon as you get this."

As she ended the call, the doorbell rang, causing Candice to jump. She approached the door cautiously, peering through the peephole. Her breath caught in her throat as she recognized the stranger from Miranda's yard.

Taking a deep breath to steady herself, Candice opened the door slightly, keeping one hand firmly on the doorknob in case she needed to slam it shut quickly. "Yes?" she asked, her voice wavering slightly. "Can I help you?"

The man's eyes bore into hers, his expression still unnervingly blank. "I have some questions about the neighboring house," he said, his tone flat. "Who bought it?"

Candice hesitated, her mind racing. Should she answer? Was this man dangerous? She gripped the doorknob tighter, her heart hammering against her ribs. "The house next door? It was sold recently, yes."

"When exactly?" His grey eyes never blinked, like a snake watching its prey.

"About a month ago, I think." Candice kept her voice steady despite her growing unease. "Why do you ask?"

"And the buyer—was it a woman? Alone?" He took a small step forward, making Candice instinctively lean back.

"I... yes, a single woman moved in." The words tumbled out before she could stop them. Something in his demeanor made her skin crawl.

"What's her name?" His question came quick and sharp.

The intensity of his interest set off alarm bells in Candice's mind. She straightened her spine, finding her courage. "I'm sorry, but I don't want to share any more information about my neighbors with strangers. My husband will be home soon—perhaps you could come back then."

Without waiting for his response, she stepped back and firmly closed the door, engaging both locks with trembling fingers. Through the window, she watched him retreat down the driveway and disappear around the corner, his unhurried pace somehow more unsettling than if he had run.

Her phone buzzed with a text from Paul: "On my way. 30 minutes out. Everything okay?"

Candice typed back a quick reply, her hands still shaking slightly: "Hurry. I'll explain when you get here."

The next half hour felt like an eternity. Candice paced the living room, alternating between peeking out the window and checking her phone. When she finally heard Paul's car pull into the driveway, she rushed to meet him at the door.

Paul's face was etched with concern as he took in Candice's shaken appearance. "What happened?" he asked, pulling her into a tight embrace.

Candice recounted the events of the afternoon, her words tumbling out in a rush. Paul listened intently, his brow furrowing with each new detail. As Candice finished her story, a movement outside caught their attention.

Miranda's car was pulling into her driveway, followed closely by a sleek black vehicle with tinted windows. They watched as Miranda stepped out, her body language tense and defensive. Two men emerged from the black car, their demeanor screaming 'federal agents,' even from a distance.

Paul and Candice moved closer to the window, straining to hear the conversation taking place in Miranda's driveway. Miranda's voice was raised, her hands gesticulating wildly, but the words were indistinct. The two men remained impassive, occasionally interjecting with what appeared to be calm, measured responses.

After several minutes of heated discussion, the men returned to their vehicle and drove away. Miranda stood in her driveway for a long moment, her shoulders slumped in what looked like defeat.

Paul turned to Candice, his expression grim. "We need to talk to her. Now. This has gone on long enough."

Candice nodded in agreement, her earlier fear now replaced with determination to uncover the truth. They made their way next door, Paul's protective arm around Candice's waist.

As they approached Miranda's front door, they could hear muffled sounds of movement inside. Paul knocked firmly, calling out, "Miranda? It's Paul and Candice. We need to talk."

There was a pause, then the sound of the lock turning. The door opened a crack, revealing Miranda's face, her eyes red-rimmed and puffy. "Now's not a good time," she said, her voice hoarse. The whole scene was eerily reminiscent of her strange behavior when she first moved in.

Paul shook his head, his jaw set. "I'm sorry, Miranda, but we can't wait any longer. There was a strange man here earlier, asking questions about you. Candice was frightened. And now these men in suits... What's going on?"

Miranda's face crumpled, tears welling up in her eyes. "It's... it's just family stuff. Please, I can't... I can't talk about this right now."

Paul's patience, already stretched thin by worry for Candice and the stress of the past few weeks, finally snapped. "Family stuff? Miranda, come on. The inconsistencies in your stories, the strange noises and lights at night, and now federal agents? This is more than just 'family stuff.'" Paul's frustration with the re-emergence of bizarre events suddenly overshadowed any affection that had been growing for Miranda. "You know, things had been going so well that I thought we were past all this cryptic behavior. Who even are you? Did your mother even die last month, or was that another one of your inconsistencies?"

Candice squeezed Paul's arm, as if to communicate he'd gone too far. "Sweetie.."

"No," Paul insisted. "Not 'sweetie.' How about explaining the fact that the school you claimed to have moved here for closed down over a year ago. I don't know what's going on, but whatever it is put Candice in danger today, so now I've got a problem."

Miranda flinched at Paul's words, shock at her friend's anger evident in her face, her grip on the door tightening. "You don't understand," she whispered, her voice breaking. "You can't understand. Please, just… leave me alone."

Before either Paul or Candice could respond, Miranda slammed the door shut. The sound of multiple locks engaging echoed in the sudden silence.

Paul and Candice stood there for a moment, stunned by the abrupt dismissal. Finally, Candice tugged gently on Paul's arm. "Come on," she said softly. "Let's go home."

As they made their way back to their house, both of them were stricken with concern. Was Miranda some kind of criminal? A fugitive? Or was she the victim in all this, running from something or someone?

Once inside, Paul began to pace the living room, his agitation palpable. "I don't like this, Candice. Any of it. What if we're in danger? What if she's brought some kind of trouble to our neighborhood?"

Candice sank onto the couch, feeling drained. "I don't know, Paul, but I can't believe Miranda would intentionally put us in harm's way. Whatever's going on, I think she's scared. Call it women's intuition, I guess."

Paul stopped pacing, turning to face his wife. The worry etched on her face tugged at his heart, momentarily overshadowing his anger and fear. He sat down beside her, pulling her close.

"You're right," he said with forced calmness. "We don't know the whole story."

Candice nestled into Paul's embrace, drawing comfort from his solid presence. "What should we do?"

Paul was quiet for a moment, considering. Finally, he said, "I think we should pray. For Miranda, for guidance, for protection. Whatever's going on, we need God's help."

Candice nodded, a small smile tugging at her lips despite the tension of the day. "You're right. That's exactly what we need to do."

They bowed their heads together, their voices joining in quiet supplication. As they prayed, they felt peace gradually settle over them, easing the fear and confusion that had gripped them earlier.

The evening settled around them like a heavy blanket, the usual laughter and chatter giving way to contemplative silence. Candice moved through the kitchen with practiced ease, chopping vegetables while Paul seasoned chicken. Their hands occasionally brushed as they worked, each touch a small comfort in the midst of their troubled thoughts.

Over dinner, they exchanged glances that hinted at their unspoken concerns. Paul pushed his food around his plate, his appetite diminished as he watched and re-watched the Ring camera footage of the strange man who'd appeared at their door. Candice noticed but said nothing, understanding his distraction all too well.

"I keep thinking about her, all alone in that house," she finally murmured, setting down her fork. "Should we have invited her to stay with us?"

Paul reached across the table, taking her hand in his. "I thought about that too. I'm honestly not sure."

After dinner, they moved through their evening routine in sync, a little over a year of marriage making their movements synchronized. As Candice loaded the dishwasher, Paul found himself pausing at the window, his eyes drawn to Miranda's darkened house next door.

Later, as they prepared for bed, the familiar comfort of their bedroom felt different somehow. Candice emerged from the bathroom in her softest fuzzy robe, her face free of makeup, vulnerability written in the slight furrow of her brow.

Paul was already in bed, the sheets pulled back invitingly. As Candice slipped under the covers, he drew her close, breathing in the familiar scent of her strawberry shampoo. Her body molded against his, fitting perfectly as it always had.

"You know I love you, right?" he murmured. "I'll never leave your side. Ever."

Candice nodded, snuggling deeper into Paul's embrace. Despite the lingering questions and concerns in her mind, she felt safe and loved. "I know," she whispered. "I love you too."

As sleep began to claim them, both Paul and Candice's thoughts drifted to Miranda. In the quiet of the night, they each sent up silent prayers for their troubled neighbor, hoping that somehow, some way, she would find a path forward through this unexpected turmoil.

The house creaked and settled around them. Paul's mind drifted in that hazy space between wake and sleep, fragments of the day replaying behind his closed eyes. He shifted slightly, his thoughts growing more disjointed as sleep pulled at him.

Oddly—given the lateness of the hour—a car drove past, its headlights sweeping across their bedroom ceiling. In the distance, a dog barked twice, then fell silent. Paul was nearly gone now, sinking deeper into sleep, when something registered—the soft but distinct sound of footsteps on gravel. His eyes opened, focusing in the dark. The steps paused, followed by what might have been the sound of a door handle being tested.

Suddenly, after an uneasy minute of silence, the stillness of the midnight shattered with a resounding crash, followed by a blood-curdling scream. Paul bolted upright in bed, his heart pounding in his chest. Beside him, Candice stirred, her eyes wide with fear.

"That came from Miranda's house," Paul said, already swinging his legs over the side of the bed.

Candice grabbed his arm, her voice trembling. "Paul, what are you doing?"

He turned to her, his face reflecting worry and protectiveness. "I'm going over to check on her. You stay here and pray. Lock the doors behind me."

Candice nodded, her lips pressed into a thin line of worry. As Paul stood, she couldn't help but notice how vulnerable he looked in just his athletic shorts. "Be careful," she whispered.

Paul paused at the bedroom door, grabbing the old baseball bat they kept for emergencies. With a final nod to Candice, he descended the stairs and headed out into the night.

He sprinted across the lawn to Miranda's house. As he approached, he could see the front door hanging askew, splintered wood evidence of a forced entry. His grip tightened on the bat as he called out, "Miranda? Are you okay?"

No response came, but another crash echoed from inside the house, followed by Miranda's terrified scream. Paul's protective instincts kicked into overdrive. He rushed through the broken door, his eyes straining to adjust to the darkness inside.

"Miranda!" he shouted again, his voice echoing in the eerily quiet house.

A muffled sob from upstairs caught his attention. Paul took the stairs two at a time, his bare feet silent on the carpeted steps. As he reached the top, he saw Miranda crumpled on the floor of the hallway, her body shaking with silent tears.

Relief flooded through Paul as he approached her. "Miranda, it's okay. I'm—"

"Watch out!" Miranda's scream came a second too late.

Strong arms wrapped around Paul from behind, lifting him off his feet. The bat clattered to the floor as Paul struggled against his unseen attacker. They stumbled backwards, teetering at the top of the stairs for a heart-stopping moment before tumbling down in a tangle of limbs.

Pain exploded through Paul's body as they crashed onto the landing. He barely had time to catch his breath before a fist connected with his jaw, stars exploding behind his eyes. Instinct took over as Paul fought back, years of high school wrestling coming to his aid as he grappled with the assailant.

They rolled across the floor, trading blows, neither able to gain the upper hand. Paul could taste blood in his mouth and feel the sting of split skin on his knuckles, but beneath the pain and fear, he felt more courageous and energetic than ever. He had to protect Miranda, had to get back to Candice.

The fight spilled into the kitchen, both men gasping for breath. Paul's back slammed against the counter, knocking the wind out of him. His attacker seized the opportunity, wrapping his arms around Paul's neck in a vicious choke hold.

Black spots danced at the edges of Paul's vision as he struggled to breathe. His fingers scrabbled desperately against the counter, searching for anything he could use as a weapon. Just as his consciousness began to fade, his hand closed around the handle of a knife.

Without hesitation, Paul plunged the blade backwards into the man's side. He felt it sink into flesh and heard the shocked gasp of his attacker. The arms around his neck loosened, and Paul stumbled forward, gulping in precious air.

With a horrifying look in his enemy's eyes, the man pulled the knife from his side with a yell, then held it up to attack Paul. Having barely enough breath to move, Paul seized his arm, causing the knife to fall on the floor. He pushed the invader away, picked up the knife, then as the man charged at him with a determined scream, Paul plunged the bloody knife straight into his chest.

The intruder collapsed to the floor, the knife still protruding from his torso. Paul stared in horror at the growing pool of blood, the reality of what he'd done crashing over him like a tidal wave.

A whimper from upstairs snapped Paul back to the present. Miranda. He had to make sure she was okay.

Taking the stairs, off-balance and disoriented, Paul rushed back to where he'd last seen Miranda. She was still huddled on the hallway floor, her eyes wide with fear as she looked up at him.

"It's over," Paul said, his voice hoarse. "You're safe now."

Miranda's face crumpled, tears streaming down her cheeks as she reached for him. Paul dropped to his knees beside her, gathering her trembling form into his arms. She clung to him desperately, her sobs muffled against his bare chest.

"I'm so sorry," Miranda choked out between gasps. "I never meant for any of this to happen. I never wanted to put you in danger."

Paul stroked her hair, murmuring soothing words even as his own heart raced with the aftermath of adrenaline. "Shh, it's okay. You're safe now. That's all that matters."

They stayed like that for what felt like hours, Miranda's tears gradually subsiding into hiccuping breaths. Paul had a lot of questions he wanted to ask, but he pushed them aside. There would be time for answers later.

The sound of the front door opening sent a jolt of panic through Paul until he heard Candice's voice calling out. "Paul? Miranda? Are you okay?"

"We're up here," Paul called back, his voice cracking with emotion. "We're okay."

Candace followed the sound of his voice to the stairs. When she reached the first step, she looked over towards the kitchen and saw the dead body on the floor. Putting her hands to her mouth, she gasped and got closer to see who it was. She soon realized that it was the man who had come to her door earlier that day. Tears began welling up in her eyes as she pieced together the events of the night.

She hurried upstairs, her face pale with worry. She took in the scene before her—Paul's battered form, Miranda curled against him—and immediately moved to embrace them both.

"Oh my gosh," Candice breathed, her arms encircling Miranda and Paul, seemingly oblivious to the tears and blood soaking her robe. "I was so worried. I heard the fighting, and then it got quiet, and I couldn't stand not knowing anymore."

Miranda lifted her tear-stained face, looking between Paul and Candice with both gratitude and shame. "I'm so sorry," she whispered again. "I never meant for any of this to happen."

Candice smoothed Miranda's hair back from her face, her touch gentle. "It's okay. You're safe now. That's all that matters."

Paul managed a very small chuckle, though it hurt his side. "Hey, that's exactly what *I* said."

As the three of them huddled together on the floor, the sound of sirens pierced the night. Someone—likely a neighbor awakened by the commotion—had called the police.

Paul felt Miranda stiffen in his arms at the sound. He pulled back slightly, meeting her eyes. "Miranda, I know you're scared, but we need to know what's going on. Who was that man? Why was he after you?"

Miranda took a shuddering breath, her eyes darting between Paul and Candice. "I… I'm in witness protection," she finally admitted, her voice barely above a whisper. "That man… he was my ex-husband."

The revelation was shocking enough that they both went still, trying to take in what Miranda had confessed. Candice gasped softly, her hand gently resting on Paul's arm. Paul felt a wave of understanding wash over him, pieces of the puzzle suddenly falling into place—Miranda's secretive behavior, the inconsistencies in her story, the mysterious phone calls.

"The men in suits…" Candice said slowly. "They were your handlers, weren't they?"

Miranda nodded, fresh tears spilling down her cheeks. "I thought I was safe here. I thought… I thought I could start over, have a normal life, but he found me."

Paul tightened his arms around Miranda, his protective instincts flaring. "You're safe now," he said firmly. "We won't let anything happen to you."

Candice nodded in agreement, her hand finding Miranda's and squeezing gently. "We're here for you. Whatever you need."

The sound of car doors slamming outside signaled the arrival of the police. Miranda tensed again, fear flickering across her face.

"It's okay," Paul reassured her. "We'll explain everything to them. You're not alone in this anymore."

As they waited for the police to enter, Paul found his mind drifting to the man lying dead in the kitchen below. The weight of what he'd done settled heavily on his shoulders. He had taken a life tonight, had crossed a line he never thought he'd cross. The knowledge of it sat uneasily in his gut, a turbulent mess of regret and the grim satisfaction of having protected those he cared about.

Candice seemed to sense his inner turmoil. She reached out, her hand finding his, her touch grounding him in the moment. Their eyes met over Miranda's head, a wordless communication passing between them. They were there for each other. No matter what.

The sound of heavy footsteps ascending the stairs broke the moment. Paul took a deep breath, preparing himself for the questioning that was sure to come. He caught Candice's eye one last time, saw the love and support shining there, and felt a wave of calm wash over him.

As the first police officer appeared at the top of the stairs, Paul straightened his shoulders, his arms still protectively around Miranda. He may not have all the answers, may not know what the future held, but he knew one thing for certain: their lives had changed irrevocably tonight. The simple life they had sought in Greece had become infinitely more complicated, but also, somehow, richer.

The officer approached, his expression indicating professional concern. "Is everyone all right here?" he asked in accented English.

Paul nodded, his voice steady as he replied, "We're okay, but there's a lot we need to tell you."

As the officer began to take their statement, Paul's voice wavered through the report details while his fingers dug half-moons into his palms. Each word felt like walking on glass, but his spine stayed straight as steel—he had two people counting on him to get this right. The officer's pen scratched against paper in the silence between sentences.

Soon, a team of paramedics rushed up the stairs, their faces concerned and serious. "Is anyone injured?" one of them asked, kneeling beside the trio.

Paul shook his head, his voice hoarse. "We're okay, but there's… there's a man downstairs. In the kitchen. He's dead."

The paramedic's eyes widened slightly, but he maintained his composure. "All right, we'll take care of that. For now, let's get you all checked out."

As the paramedics began their assessment, police officers swarmed the house. One approached the group, notepad in hand. "I'm Officer Kostas. I need to speak with each of you separately about what happened here tonight."

They spent the next hour busy with answering questions, medical examinations, and barely contained anxiety. Paul found himself recounting the night's events over and over, each retelling making the reality of what had transpired sink in deeper.

Miranda, looking small and vulnerable on a gurney, was whispered to by men in dark suits—her handlers, Paul now realized. She caught his eye as they wheeled her towards an ambulance, mouthing a silent "Thank you" before she was whisked away.

A young doctor approached Paul and Candice as the commotion began to die down. "We're taking your friend to the hospital for observation," he explained. "Standard procedure after a traumatic event. We'll keep her overnight and release her in the morning if everything looks good."

Paul nodded, feeling the weight of exhaustion settling over him. "Thank you, doctor. We appreciate everything you've done."

"What about you, sir?" the Doctor asked. "You seem pretty beat up."

"I'll be fine," Paul responded. "Nothing a few band-aids"—he looked at Candice—"and kisses can't fix."

The doctor smiled and let them be. As the emergency services began to clear out, leaving behind only a few police officers to secure the scene, Paul and Candice made their way back to their own house. The familiar surroundings felt surreal after the chaos of the night.

"We should try to get some sleep," Candice murmured, though her eyes were wide and alert.

Paul agreed, but as they lay in bed, sleep eluded them both. They tossed and turned, battling unanswered questions and lingering adrenaline. Paul kept replaying the fight in his mind, feeling the knife in his hand, seeing the shocked expression on the intruder's face as he fell.

Candice's voice broke through his thoughts. "Sweetie? Are you okay?"

He turned to face her, seeing the concern in her eyes. "I don't know," he admitted. "I killed a man tonight. I know I had to, to protect Miranda, to protect us, but... I never thought I'd be capable of something like that."

Candice reached out, her hand finding his in the darkness. "You did what you had to do. You saved Miranda's life. You're a hero, Paul."

Paul squeezed her hand, grateful for her unwavering support. "Well," Paul said as he winced in pain, "you might need to save the hero's reward until after my ribs heal..."

The small laugh was exactly what they needed before trying to doze off. They fell into silence after that, each lost in their own thoughts. It wasn't until the first hints of dawn began to creep through the curtains that they finally drifted off into a fitful slumber.

The insistent buzz of a phone jolted them awake. Paul fumbled for his device, squinting at the bright screen. It was already 10 AM—they had slept far later than usual.

"It's from Miranda," he said, his voice thick with sleep. "She says she's okay and wants to explain everything. She's asking if we can meet her at the hospital cafeteria before she's released."

Candice hopped out of bed and started rummaging through their closet. "Tell her we'll be there as soon as we can."

They dressed quickly, the events of the previous night hanging heavy between them. As they drove to the hospital, Paul found himself gripping the steering wheel tightly, his mind replaying the fight in Miranda's kitchen.

The hospital cafeteria was quiet when they arrived, most of the morning rush having passed. They spotted Miranda at a corner table, looking pale but composed in a hospital gown and robe.

"Thank you for coming," Miranda said as they approached, her voice soft. "I... I owe you both so much. An explanation, at the very least."

Paul and Candice sat across from her, their faces a mixture of concern and curiosity. "We're just glad you're okay," Candice said, reaching out to squeeze Miranda's hand.

Miranda took a deep breath, her eyes focusing on a point in the distance. "I was married, back in the States," she began. "But only for a few months... He seemed like a good man at first. Charming, successful, supposedly a Christian, but it was all a lie."

She paused, her hands trembling slightly as she continued. "He was a criminal. Not just petty crimes, but... he had killed people. Three that I knew of. When I found out, I went to the police immediately."

Paul felt a chill run down his spine as Miranda's story unfolded. The seemingly idyllic life in Greece, the mysterious phone calls, the odd behavior—it all made more and more sense as she spoke.

"About a year ago," Miranda continued, "they arrested him and I testified against him in court, but before they could transfer him to a high-security prison, he escaped. He vowed to find me, to kill me for betraying him."

Candice gasped softly, her hand flying to her mouth. "Oh, Miranda..."

Miranda's eyes filled with tears. "That's how I ended up here. The witness protection program sent me to Greece. I thought... I thought I could start over, have a normal life, but I was never really free. The secretive behavior, the phone calls—it was all because I couldn't tell anyone why I was really here. And then we started getting reports that he might have figured out where I was."

Paul's mind flashed back to the men in suits they had seen at Miranda's house. "The federal agents," he said, "they were warning you?"

Miranda nodded. "They told me they thought he'd found out where I was living. They were going to set up protection in the morning, but..." She trailed off, her voice breaking.

"But he got there first," Paul finished, the weight of what could have happened settling heavily on his shoulders.

"I'm so sorry," Miranda whispered, tears spilling down her cheeks. "For all the secrecy, for the crazy behavior, for putting you both in danger. I never meant for any of this to happen."

Candice moved to Miranda's side of the table, wrapping her in a tight embrace. "You have nothing to apologize for," she said fiercely. "We're just grateful you're safe now."

Paul nodded in agreement, reaching out to clasp Miranda's hand. "It's over now. You're free of him, truly free."

As the weight of Miranda's confession settled over them, a nurse approached their table. "Miranda? The doctor says you're clear to be discharged. I have your paperwork ready whenever you're set to go."

Miranda wiped at her eyes, managing a small smile. "Thank you. I'll be there in just a moment."

As the nurse walked away, Paul was struck by a sudden thought. "Miranda," he said, "have you considered sharing your story at church? Not the details, of course, but... your testimony of God's protection?"

Miranda looked surprised. "I hadn't thought about it. I've been avoiding your church because I was trying to maintain my cover."

Candice's face lit up. "Oh, you should! It would be so powerful. And it might help you process everything that's happened."

For the first time since they'd arrived, a genuine smile spread across Miranda's face. "You know what? I think I'd like that. It feels right, somehow."

As they stood to leave, Paul couldn't help but chuckle. "You know, all this talk of testimonies and God's protection... it's making me feel a bit like a bible hero." He straightened up, putting his fists on his waist in a superhero pose. "Paul the Mighty, defender of damsels in distress!"

Miranda let out a startled laugh, the sound brightening the sterile hospital cafeteria. "Oh yes, very heroic. Especially the part where you fought a trained killer in nothing but your pajama shorts."

Candice joined in the laughter, the tension of the past day finally beginning to dissipate. "Yeah, more like Paul the Naked," she teased, linking her arm through his.

As they made their way out of the hospital, the mood had lightened considerably. The trauma of the night before was still there, lingering beneath the surface, but it was tempered now by relief, understanding, and the beginnings of healing.

Paul helped Miranda into the back seat of their car, catching her eye in the rearview mirror as he started the engine. "So," he said, a mischievous glint in his eye, "does this mean I get to add 'vanquisher of evil ex-husbands' to my resume?"

Miranda rolled her eyes, but her smile was warm. "Only if I get to add 'creepy new neighbor' to mine..."

Candice lifted her hands up in playful indignation. "Hey, what do I get to add to *my* resume?"

Miranda thought for a second, then smiled. "Well, since you practically told my killer ex-husband where to find me, how about 'spiller of beans?'"

They finally got a solid group laugh, Paul adding, "How about 'eye candy?' Are you allowed to put *that* on a resume?"

Candace whacked him in jest, then Paul winced in pain from the damage done last night.

"Not so hard," He joked. "I'm only indestructible in my super-suit."

Miranda snickered. "No problem. There's boxers in the trunk..."

The car filled with laughter as they drove home, the Greek countryside stretching out before them, Paul felt peace and relief wash over him. The past twenty-four hours had been chaotic, terrifying, and life-changing, but no more.

Miranda leaned forward, her hand resting lightly on Paul's shoulder. "I don't know how I can ever thank you both enough. You've given me my life back."

As they pulled into their driveway, Paul felt a sense of completion, as if a door in their lives was closing even as a new one opened. As Paul sat thinking about the future, he found himself surprisingly calm despite all the uncertainty. Maybe Miranda would become just another close friend who shared their morning runs and evening meals. Maybe their relationship would evolve into something none of them had anticipated yet. Or perhaps everything would settle back into their previous routine.

The church bells chimed melodiously as the congregation of about fifty people filed into the small, charming Greek chapel. Paul, Candice, and Miranda found seats near the front, the lingering weight of the past week evident in their tired eyes but tempered by a shared sense of relief and a new feeling of closeness. The wooden pews creaked softly as they settled in, the familiar scent of old hymnals and polished wood filling the air.

As the service began, Pastor Alex stepped up to the pulpit, his kind eyes scanning the familiar faces before him. "Brothers and sisters," he began, his voice warm and inviting, "we have a special guest with us today. Miranda Hurley, our new neighbor, has a powerful testimony to share."

Miranda stood, her legs slightly shaky as she made her way to the front. She gripped the edges of the pulpit, her knuckles white with tension. Taking a deep breath, her eyes scanned the faces of her potential new community before landing on Paul and Candice. Their encouraging smiles gave her the strength to begin.

"Good morning," she said, her voice soft but steady. "I'm Miranda and for those who weren't aware, I moved next door to Paul and Candice almost three months ago.."

Miranda gripped the pulpit, looking down at her trembling hands before raising her eyes to meet the congregation.

"Just under a year ago, I had what looked like the perfect life," she began, her voice soft but clear in the hushed church. "A successful husband. A beautiful home, but it all quickly unraveled. I found out my husband wasn't who he said he was. One day, while using his computer to look something up, I stumbled across files that I shouldn't have seen. That day, I found out my husband was not only a criminal, but a killer."

As collective gasps could be heard around the sanctuary, Paul watched as Miranda's fingers traced the edge of the pulpit, steadying herself. The morning light filtered through the stained glass windows, casting colored shadows across her face.

"The witness protection program sent me here, to Greece. New life. New start." Her voice cracked slightly. "But he found me. Last week, my ex-husband came to finish what he'd started."

Miranda's gaze found Paul in the congregation. "I heard the door splinter. I heard his footsteps on the stairs. I thought…" Her voice dropped to almost a whisper. "I thought that was the end."

She straightened her shoulders, strength returning to her voice. "But God had other plans. He placed next door not just neighbors, but guardians. Paul…" She paused, a soft smile touching her lips. "Paul ran into danger wearing nothing but his sleep shorts and carrying a baseball bat."

Quiet laughter rippled through the church, breaking the tension. Paul felt Candice's hand tighten around his.

"You might laugh," Miranda continued, her eyes bright with unshed tears, "but in that moment, he was God's warrior. When my would-be killer had me cornered, when I thought all hope was lost, Paul fought for my life with every literal breath in his body. He fought for me without knowing my story, and without knowing why I needed saving. He just knew someone needed help."

She gripped the pulpit again, but this time from emotion rather than fear. "I've spent at least six months looking over my shoulder, jumping at shadows, trusting no one, but here, in this beautiful country… here I found not just safety, but family. In Paul and Candice Thompson, I found people who took me in without knowing my past. People who protected me without asking why."

Miranda wiped a tear from her cheek. "I don't know what tomorrow holds. But I know that yesterday's chains are broken. I'm free—truly free—for the first time in a long time. And I'm exactly where God wants me to be."

The silence in the church was absolute, heavy with shared emotion. Paul noticed several people wiping their eyes, and even Pastor Alex seemed moved. Beside him, Candice's shoulders shook with silent tears.

"Thank you," Miranda finished simply.

As Miranda returned to her seat, Pastor Alex stepped forward, his face beaming with warmth. "Miranda, on behalf of our entire congregation, I want to say welcome. You're not just our neighbor anymore—you're family."

The rest of the service passed as church services do, hymns and prayers echoing in the room. The crowd stood shoulder to shoulder, their unity visible in their matching determined expressions. As the congregation filed out, many stopped to embrace Miranda, offering words of support and friendship. Paul and Candice stood nearby, watching with pride as their friend was enveloped in the love of their church family.

"That was beautiful," Candice murmured to Paul, her eyes misty with emotion. "I'm so glad she felt comfortable sharing her story."

Paul nodded, his arm wrapped around Candice's waist. "It's amazing how God works. Who would have thought that all this would happen to people like us?"

As the last of the well-wishers drifted away, Miranda rejoined Paul and Candice, her face glowing with relief and happiness. "Thank you both so much for encouraging me to do this," she said, pulling them into a group hug. "I couldn't have done it without you."

The trio decided to celebrate at their favorite outdoor café, just down the road from their homes. As they settled into their seats at the table, a comfortable silence fell over them. The events of the past few days had forged a bond between them that went beyond mere friendship, but none of them seemed quite sure how to deal with the unspoken dynamic. Candice, for some reason, suddenly seemed decidedly bubbly and even... was it nervous?

The waiter came and took their orders—a Greek salad for Candice, moussaka for Paul, and souvlaki for Miranda. As they waited for their food, Miranda broke the silence, reaching into her bag.

"Oh, I almost forgot," she said, pulling out a familiar book. "I still have this. I hope you don't mind, but I read some of it while I was in the hospital."

Paul took the book on polygamy, his fingers tracing the cover. He held the book carefully, as if its words might rearrange themselves under his fingers. "What did you think?" he asked, his voice carefully neutral.

Miranda's eyes sparkled with interest. "It was... enlightening. I learned a lot, actually. I had no idea that polygamy was so prevalent in biblical times, or modern times for that matter." Miranda leaned in as if to tell them a secret and whispered, "Just don't tell Eleni I liked it..."

Cheeky laughter turned into an awkward silence that descended upon the table, each of them acutely aware of the unspoken implications of all of them having enjoyed the book. Every word now felt like it might tip the delicate balance of the moment.

Paul's mind suddenly reverted back to the racing it had been doing for most of the last few months. In all the commotion and recovery of the past week, he had almost completely forgotten about the struggle. Once again torn between his growing feelings for Miranda and his deep love for Candice, he glanced at his wife, trying to gauge her reaction.

Candice purposefully met his gaze, a peculiarly cheerful sparkle in her eye. She cleared her throat as their waiter put her salad down in front of her. She took her first bite eagerly, overemphasizing how good it tasted. Her sudden bubbly behavior drew the curious attention of both Paul and Miranda. They watched her take a second bite, as if waiting for her to explain her sudden playful demeanour. With her mouth half full, as was her typical table etiquette, she casually blurted out a shocking string of words. "You know, Miranda, my husband's crazy about you..."

Paul froze, his fork suspended halfway to his mouth. A piece of moussaka slid off, landing with a soft plop back on his plate. Miranda went saucer-eyed in shock, her emerald orbs darting between Paul and Candice. The nervousness at the table was palpable. Two people's forks clinked against plates in the silence, but Candice continued eating her salad as if nothing had happened, barely holding back a mischievous smile. Her eyes resonated the pride she took in disrupting the sensibilities of her lunch dates.

In-between bites, Candace looked at Miranda, silently coaxing her to follow along. Miranda's expression of shock slowly turned into a grin, eventually creating a devious stare between the two women that nearly made Paul's heart beat clear out of his chest.

Candice continued, her tone deceptively casual as she took another bite of salad. "Miranda and I have become such good friends. I was really looking forward to her sticking around, but I guess she can't, you know, with all that lust you're"—Candice held up her fingers to make air quotes—"'struggling' with..."

Miranda's lips curved into a cute pout, her eyes twinkling with mischief. "Too bad," she murmured, her voice soft and tinged with mock regret.

Paul sat motionless, acutely aware of the sweat beading on his forehead. His mind raced, unable to process the turn the conversation had taken. Was this really happening? He glanced around the café, half-expecting to see shocked faces staring at them, but everyone else seemed oblivious to the drama unfolding at their table.

Miranda's eyes flicked to the book on the table, then back to Paul. Her gaze was sharp with an intensity that made his breath catch. "So," she purred, leaning forward slightly as she interlaced her fingers under her chin, "what are we going to do about this?"

Candice set down her fork with a soft clink, fixing Paul with a steady look. "Yes, my love, what *are* we going to do about this?"

The strain at the table ratcheted up another notch as the women looked back and forth between each other and Paul. Miranda reached out, her fingers brushing against Paul's as she flipped the book open to a specific page and slid it in front of him.

Candice nodded towards the book, her eyebrows raised expectantly. "What does it say we should do about it, sweetie?"

Paul's eyes dropped to the page, his heart pounding so loudly in his chest, he was sure the others could hear it. Candice, his rock, his partner in all things, was not just accepting of his feelings for Miranda but was now unashamedly encouraging them. And Miranda, the woman who had unexpectedly entered their lives and turned everything upside down, was openly reciprocating those feelings.

The section title at the top of the page seemed to leap out at him, the familiar words burning into his retinas. He read it aloud, his voice barely above a whisper. "It's better to marry than to burn."

"It's what?" Candice prompted, leaning in, her eyes dancing with amusement and anticipation."

Something shifted in Paul's demeanor. The nervousness melted away, replaced by a sudden, confident realization. He looked up, meeting their expectant gazes. "It's better to marry than to burn," he repeated, his voice strong and clear.

Candice—mouth half full again—threw her hands up, a large, playful smile dancing on her lips. "It's better to marry than to burn!" she exclaimed, drawing curious glances from nearby tables.

Paul's gaze shifted to Miranda. She was intensely staring at him, her eyes saturated in affection and desire. Looking directly into his eyes, she repeated the phrase, her voice low and determined. "It's better to marry than to burn."

The most passionately charged smile Paul had ever seen began to spread across Miranda's face as she teasingly bit her lower lip, silently begging for a spontaneous proposal...

...Let them marry; for it is better to marry than to burn with passion.

1 Corinthians 7:9

Story 6 - A Brother's Duty

Setting – Kenya, Modern Day

This story was written in such a way as to account for slower, more pronounced speech typical of East Africa. The African dialogue is meant be read as they speak—thickly accented and clearly enunciated. Reading in "speedy" English will rob the story of much of its dramatic effect and emotional impact. (If you need a reference, look up Kenyans speaking on Youtube, or, if you saw Black Panther, the Wakandans are close enough...)

In a makeshift soccer field in Kiambu, Kenya, two teams battled for dominance. No stadium lights illuminated the patchy grass, no rows of benches lined the sidelines. Instead, a motley assortment of folding chairs, blankets, and eager spectators ringed the field, their excited chatter filling the warm evening air.

Kiano Mutua, a lean man in his mid-thirties with laugh lines etched around his eyes, paced the sideline. His gaze darted between the players on the field and the scoreboard, which showed a precarious 2-2 tie with only minutes left in the game. Across the field, his older brother Jabari prowled like a lion, barking instructions to his own team.

"Come on, Malik!" Kiano shouted, his voice carrying over the din of the crowd. "Push up! Create space!"

Twelve-year-old Malik Mutua, a gangly boy with his father's determined set to his jaw, nodded sharply. He darted between two defenders, his cleats kicking up small puffs of dust as he maneuvered for position.

On the sidelines, Kiano's wife Amani sat on a colorful woven blanket, their five-year-old daughter Zuri nestled in her lap. Next to them, Jabari's two wives, Safiya and Imani, leaned forward with identical expressions of concentration.

"Your boy's got speed," Safiya remarked, her eyes never leaving the field. "Takes after his father, I'd say."

Amani smiled, her face prideful and alit. "That he does," she agreed. "Though sometimes I wonder if that's entirely a blessing."

Safiya glanced at her, curiosity piqued, but a roar from the crowd drew their attention back to the game. Malik had the ball again, weaving through the opposition with a grace that belied his age.

Kiano felt his heart racing, a mixture of parental pride and coaching anxiety churning in his stomach. He'd seen Malik's potential from the moment his son first kicked a ball, but moments like these still took his breath away.

"That's it, Malik!" he shouted, clapping his hands. "Look for the pass!"

Across the field, Jabari's voice boomed out, a counterpoint to his brother's encouragement. "Press him! Don't let him through!"

The brothers' eyes met for a brief moment, a flicker of understanding passing between them. It was mutually understood that whichever brother's team won, the other would never hear the end of it. The two brothers had always been playfully competitive, never turning down a chance to beat the other. But beneath the competition lay a deep well of love and respect, which was only made stronger by their keenness towards healthy rivalry.

On the field, Malik feinted left, then right, leaving a defender wrong-footed. The crowd held its collective breath as he approached the goal, the keeper crouched and ready.

Time seemed to slow. Kiano could hear his own heartbeat thundering in his ears. Beside him, his assistant coach muttered a prayer. In the stands, Amani clutched Zuri closer, while Safiya and Imani leaned forward, fixing their eyes on their nephew's final play.

Malik drew back his leg, every muscle coiled with potential energy. The keeper shifted his weight, preparing to spring. And then, in a move that drew gasps from the crowd, Malik didn't shoot. Instead, he flicked the ball to his left, where his teammate Denis had materialized, unguarded and perfectly positioned.

Denis didn't hesitate. His foot connected with the ball, sending it arcing over the keeper's outstretched hands and into the back of the net.

The explosion of sound was deafening. Kiano found himself engulfed by his celebrating players, their joy infectious. Through the sea of bodies, he caught sight of Malik, grinning from ear to ear as his teammates rubbed his head and pounded his back.

As the final whistle blew, cementing their 3-2 victory, Kiano felt a swell of emotion that threatened to overwhelm him. Pride in his son and his team mingled with a bittersweet awareness of the weight of expectations that came with such talent.

He made his way across the field to where Jabari stood, his brother's expression a mix of disappointment for his own team yet pure admiration and pride for his nephew's skills.

"Well played," Jabari said, defeated, extending his hand. "That boy of yours..." his inner defeat quickly being overshadowed by his big smile, "I can't help but cheer him on even when I'm losing to him!"

Kiano clasped his brother's hand, feeling the familiar calluses, the strength that mirrored his own. "Thank you, brother," he said gratefully. "I'm sure he gets at least some of it from his uncle. Your team gave us a real fight out there. Keep your chin up!"

Malik bounded up, invading their exchange, his face flushed with exertion and triumph. "Did you see, Dad? Did you see the pass?"

Kiano offered his son a high-five with an ear-to-ear smile, which Malik reached up to hit. "I saw, my son. You made us all proud today."

Jabari crouched down to Malik's eye level, his expression loving. "That was excellent vision, Malik. You saw the whole field, not just the goal. Keep playing like that, and you'll go far."

Malik's eyes widened at the praise from his uncle, a man he greatly admired. "Thank you, Uncle Jabari," he said solemnly.

As the families began to gather their belongings, preparing to head home for the evening, Kiano found himself lost in thought. The joy of victory was sweet, but he couldn't shake a nagging sense of unease. He watched as Jabari made his way to where Safiya and Imani waited, the three of them forming a unit that was joyously solidified just over a year ago. The only thing missing was the conception of a child, something Kiano thought might be due to some kind of health problem, as neither of the wives had gotten pregnant. Jabari never told his friends and family why, specifically, he had taken Imani as his second wife, the only reason he ever cited being love. Kiano began wondering if he should ask his brother about it.

Amani appeared at his side, Zuri drowsy in her arms. "Everything alright?" she asked softly, noticing his pensive expression.

Kiano nodded, forcing a smile. "Just thinking," he said, wrapping an arm around her shoulders. "It was a good game."

As they made their way off the field, the first stars beginning to twinkle in the darkening sky, Kiano glanced back, catching sight of Jabari deep in conversation with his wives. His brother looked up, their eyes meeting across the emptying field. For a moment, Kiano saw a flicker of something in Jabari's expression—longing, perhaps, or regret. Then it was gone, replaced by his usual confident smile.

Turning back to his own family, Kiano took a deep breath of the cooling evening air, and with one last look at the field where so much had transpired, Kiano guided his family towards home, the echoes of the game's excitement still ringing in his ears.

Two cars wound their way through the streets of Kiambu. Kiano followed his brother Jabari's vehicle, the excitement of the afternoon's victory still thrumming through his veins. As they pulled into Jabari's driveway, the modest but well-maintained house came into view, its warm yellow exterior a beacon of welcome in the gathering twilight. It was here that family dinner had taken place every Friday night for the past year. They had a large back yard with a neat patio for their grill and an eight-seat table, with hung up lights that illuminated the whole patio area with ease.

Malik was the first to tumble out of the car, his energy seemingly undiminished by the intense soccer match. "Uncle Jabari, can I help with the grill?" he called out, bouncing on the balls of his feet.

Jabari chuckled, the earlier disappointment of defeat softening in the face of his nephew's enthusiasm. "Of course, Malik! But first, let's get everything inside."

As the two families filed into the house, the familiar scents of home enveloped them—a mixture of spices, polished wood, and the faint aroma of evening jasmine wafting through an open window. The living room, with its well-worn but comfortable furniture, spoke of a life lived fully, if not lavishly.

Kiano's eyes swept across the room, taking in the details that made Jabari's house a home. Family photos adorned the walls, capturing moments of joy and celebration. A bookshelf in the corner held a mix of religious texts, soccer manuals, and well-thumbed novels. It was a space that reflected Jabari's faith, intelligence, and favorite pastime.

Safiya, the livelier of the two wives, shouted loud enough for all to hear, with her thick and melodic African accent, "Let's make dinner! Starving should never be done while looking at food!"

Amani laughed, handing a sleepy Zuri to Kiano. "Be good for Baba," she murmured, pressing a kiss to her daughter's forehead before following Safiya and Imani into the kitchen.

Kiano watched as the women disappeared into the kitchen, a slight frown creasing his brow. He'd noticed a tension in Safiya's shoulders, a tightness around Imani's eyes that hadn't been there before. He made a mental note to ask Amani about it later.

"Come on, brother," Jabari's voice broke through his thoughts. "Let's get that meat on the grill. Malik, you can help by bringing out the plates and utensils."

As they stepped out onto the patio, the cooler evening air was a welcome relief after the day's heat. Jabari busied himself with the grill, the familiar ritual of preparing the coals a soothing counterpoint to the day's excitement.

"You did well today, little brother," Jabari said, arranging the charcoal with practiced ease. "Your team has improved greatly."

Kiano nodded, accepting the compliment with a small smile. "They've worked hard. Malik especially."

At the sound of his name, Malik perked up, returning from the kitchen with an armful of traditional bowls. "Do you think I could play for your team someday, Uncle Jabari?"

Jabari laughed, a rich, warm sound that seemed to fill the gathering darkness. "Play for me? Boy, if you keep improving like this, you'll be coaching me before long."

As Malik beamed under the praise, displaying what was possibly a hint of arrogance on his face, Kiano felt a familiar mixture of pride and unease settle in his chest. He loved seeing his son excel, but the weight of expectation—from family, from the community—sometimes felt overwhelming.

"You know, Malik," Kiano said, trying to temper the boy's excitement with a dose of reality, "being a great player isn't just about skill. It's about discipline, teamwork, and balancing soccer with your other responsibilities."

Jabari nodded approvingly. "Your father's right. And speaking of balance..." He trailed off, a mischievous glint in his eye. "When are you going to come back to a proper church, brother? All those wazungu at your place..."

Kiano rolled his eyes good-naturedly, recognizing the nagging look in his brother's eyes, and let out a groan. "Oh no! When will you let me go to church in peace, brother?" He gently shook his head and chuckled at their age-old church feud.

"I'm just saying," Jabari continued, "all those Americans coming in and telling everyone what to do and how do it. It can have the Michael Jackson effect if you're not careful."

Kiano smiled a confused smile, knowing his brother was baiting him for a joke. "The Michael Jackson effect? What is that?"

"You don't know?" Jabari said as he turned around with comical surprise on his face. "It's when so many mzungus teach you that your skin actually turns white!" He burst out with a boisterous laugh, thoroughly entertained by his own joke, while Kiano laughed and shook his head, regretting having taken the bait.

"How are they so different?" Malik interjected, enjoying the usual sound of his father and uncle's teasing.

Kiano raised his eyebrows, as this was the first time his twelve-year-old son had seriously inquired about church life.

But before he could respond, Jabari answered, half serious, half continuing to tease his brother. "Let's just say your Uncle Jabari couldn't come to church with you, at least not with his whole family."

"Why not?" Malik curiously asked.

Jabari, potentially pushing the limits of appropriate prodding, said to Kiano, "Go ahead, brother. Tell him why you can't invite your own family to church."

"Alright, alright," Kiano said with a smile, his open palms motioning down to suggest that Jabari let him answer the question.

As Jabari shoved a piece of food in his mouth and returned to grilling, Kiano turned to Malik. "Son." He then paused and took a deep breath, retaining his smile in the midst of Jabari's teasing. "Our church believes that a man can only have one wife."

"They also don't dance enough," Jabari playfully interjected, relieving any tension and causing the others to laugh.

Kiano then continued. "They think the Bible teaches that God's plan is for a man to have only one wife. It's something that most of the Western world believes, and they have sent their missionaries here to preach the gospel, but those missionaries have also taught this doctrine about marriage."

Malik was clearly trying to rationalize the idea in his mind, having grown up with plenty of friends who had more than one wife in their families. "But there are so many more women than men here. What will they do for husbands if men can only have one wife?"

Jabari, with eyes toward the sky and his arms spread out, exuberantly let out a sigh of vindication. "Ahh!"

Kiano immediately started laughing. "Alright, brother. I know. I know. There's no need to—"

"God be praised!" Jabari interrupted, eyes and hands still lifted toward the sky. "It's so easy, even a child can know it!" he continued as he laughed and returned to the meat.

The other two laughed at Jabari's typical enthusiasm and larger-than-life personality.

Kiano turned to his son with a little more seriousness in his tone. "Malik. It's something they are wrong about, but the church still does many good things and I have been attending since I was your age. I do my best to understand that many people from other cultures have become part of our church's leadership. I pray for them and serve, even in the midst of differences. You know, the Bible says that the outside world will know we are Christians by our love, not by our arguments over doctrine. There is certainly a time to leave a church when something is really wrong, but this is something that we can disagree on and still stay."

Malik genuinely took in his father's words, then asked, "But what if you wanted to take another wife, Baba? Would we have to leave our church?"

"IF"—Amani yelled with a smile on her face as she emerged from the kitchen with pans of food in her hands—"your father FINALLY"—she dragged out that word as she paused and sternly looked at Kiano, then returned to placing food on the table—"took another wife, maybe cooking and cleanup would be as nice for me at home as it is here," she snarkily continued while gesturing with her head to the two wives entering the backyard with more food.

"Yes. Yes, I get it." Kiano chuckled as he held up his hands to temper more inevitable teasing. "Just don't call me a 'poor man' again. I can only take so much."

Malik and his mother snickered. "Look how happy we all are" Amani light-heartedly continued, while gesturing again to the other wives setting the table, "having each other to do all this work. But no.. My husband makes me do it all alone."

"Mmm-hm. Like those lonely white women in American suburbs," Safiya butted in with a big, mischievous smile on her face, clearly keeping the friendly mockery of Kiano alive.

"I'm just saying," Amani more seriously added as she sat down opposite her husband, "the more hands to help, the easier th—"

"God be praised!" Jabari loudly interrupted, causing all to freeze and look his way. His eyes and hands (one of which was holding a spatula) were once again lifted toward heaven, an enormous smile on his face. "The women know it too!"

His arms shook with humorous enthusiasm while everyone laughed at his antics.

Hearing the laughter, he went on. "O, great ruler of heaven and earth! Bless my brother and his church with the ability to read a Bible." The laughter deepened. "That they would learn of Abraham, Jacob, and David, who—"

"Alright! Alright, Jabari!" Kiano yelled out as he nearly fell off his chair in laughter, the others laughing just as hard. Jabari took a deep breath as he waited for the laughter to subside, his arms having returned to his side, but his head still tilted upward. When the last laugh died out, he waited another moment then let out a quick, matter-of-fact "Amen" as he put his head back down to tend the grill. This resulted in another round of laughter as Jabari took the meat off the grill and set it on the table.

Everyone sat down and Jabari thanked God for the food. The reverence and seriousness with which he prayed was a striking contrast to his humorous outbursts, signifying his strength as a man of God.

When he finished praying, the family members each started reaching for food with their hands and putting some in their bowls, the men complimenting their wives on the food. After a few bites, Kiano looked at his wife, Amani. "You know. I thought you liked being the queen of your castle."

They then heard an elderly, female voice come from the neighboring yard. It resonated almost a hundred years of heavy accent and a deep well of motherly wisdom. "Wamagharibi wanataka mrahaba. Waafrika wanataka dada."

Jabari chuckled, being the only one who heard her clearly. Then Malik shouted over, "What does that mean?"

They all looked over and smiled at the woman as she answered in English, wearing a smile herself. "Westerners want royalty. Africans want sisters."

The women and Jabari collectively shouted "Amen" and joyfully called over a uniform greeting in Swahili to their neighbor while Kiano and Malik just looked at each other and laughed.

As the laughter subsided, Kiano whispered to Amani, "Thank you for not calling me 'poor man.'"

Amani smiled with love at her husband. "You are rich to me," she said sincerely. With that, the joke was put to rest for the evening.

The meal progressed, filled with animated discussion about the day's match, local news, and playful debates about everything from politics to the best way to prepare ugali. Kiano watched as Malik regaled the table with a play-by-play of his assist in the winning goal, noting the pride that swelled in Jabari's eyes even as a shadow of something else—envy? regret?—passed across his face. Kiano found himself once again thinking about how Jabari had not yet had children, wondering if he should ask him about it.

"You know," Jabari said, leaning back in his chair with a satisfied sigh, "there's something to be said for these family gatherings. It's good to remember what's truly important."

Safiya nodded, her hand resting lightly on Jabari's arm. "Family is everything," she agreed, her eyes meeting Imani's across the table. Something unspoken passed between the two women, a shared understanding that Kiano couldn't quite decipher.

"Speaking of family," Amani interjected, her tone carefully light, "have you thought about expanding yours, Jabari? Surely there's room in your heart for a few little ones running around."

The question, innocent as it seemed, landed like a stone in a still pond. Ripples of tension spread across the table, visible in the sudden stiffening of Jabari's shoulders, the way Safiya's hand tightened on his arm, and the way Imani, the quietest of the three women, looked down in concern.

"Children are a blessing from God," Jabari said after a moment, his voice carefully neutral. "When He sees fit to grant us that blessing, we will be grateful."

Kiano watched his brother closely, noting the strain behind his smile and the way Imani's eyes dropped to her plate. There was a story here, he realized, one that ran deeper than the surface pleasantries of their dinner conversation.

"And what about you, Kiano?" Jabari asked, clearly eager to shift the focus. "Will you and Amani be giving Malik and Zuri any more siblings?"

Kiano chuckled, wrapping an arm around Amani's shoulders. "Two is plenty for now, I think. Though if Amani had her way, we'd make more kids than I could name." The group chuckled, somewhat breaking up the tension caused by Amani's question.

As the night drew to a close and they began to gather their things to leave, Kiano found himself lingering. He watched as Jabari helped clear the table, noticing the gentle touches exchanged between him and his wives and the looks of deep affection that passed between all three.

"It's been a good evening," he said to Jabari as they stood by the cars, the women inside saying their final goodbyes. "See you next Friday, brother."

Jabari nodded, clapping a hand on Kiano's shoulder. "Of course, my brother. If the Lord wills."

As they embraced, Kiano felt the strength in his brother's arms, the shared history that bound them together no matter the circumstances. He felt determined to help his family with whatever they were going through, no matter how hard it was.

The drive home was quiet, Malik and Zuri dozing in the backseat, Amani lost in her own thoughts beside him. Kiano's mind raced, replaying both the jokes and the more serious moments from the evening.

He glanced at Amani, her profile silvered by the moonlight streaming through the car window. She was everything he'd ever wanted in a wife—smart, kind, and a wonderful mother. For the first time, he wondered if he should really let her pick out another wife for him. Her teasing him about this was steadily increasing over the last few months. But their church. He knew expanding their family would mean being at odds with the church he had served in his whole life. He silently pondered these things as they arrived at home and settled in for the night, the sound of Amani singing the children to sleep soothing his anxious thoughts for now.

Kiano stood before the mirror in the bedroom, adjusting his tie with practiced fingers. The crisp white shirt and dark suit felt almost ceremonial, an armor of sorts for the spiritual battle he always felt he was fighting. In the reflection, he could see Amani behind him, smoothing down Zuri's unruly curls.

"Malik!" Amani called out, her voice carrying through the house. "Have you found your Bible yet?"

A muffled response came from the direction of Malik's room, followed by the sound of drawers being hastily opened and closed. Kiano shook his head, a small smile playing on his lips. Some things never changed, no matter how many times they went through this routine.

"I'll go help him," Kiano said, turning away from the mirror. As he passed Amani, he placed a gentle hand on her shoulder. "You look beautiful, by the way."

Amani's eyes met his in the mirror, a flicker of warmth passing between them. "Thank you," she said softly. Then, with a loving smirk, "You clean up pretty well yourself."

Kiano placed a kiss on the side of her forehead as they smiled at each other. "For a poor man..." she continued with a snarky tone as she returned to her daughter's hair.

Kiano chuckled as he left to help Malik, calling back as he fast-walked away in the hall, "You know, if we weren't going to church, I'd be offended."

Amani snickered at Zuri, prompting her to laugh before giving her a mother-daughter high-five in celebration of her joke.

As Kiano stepped into the hallway, a sharp knock at the front door cut through the domestic cacophony. Kiano frowned, glancing at his watch. They weren't expecting anyone, and it was nearly time to leave for the church service.

"I'll get it," he called out, changing direction and heading for the door. The knocking came again, more insistent this time. A prickle of unease ran down Kiano's spine.

He opened the door to find his parents—his Mama and Baba—standing on the threshold. The sight of them was shocking enough—they rarely visited unannounced—but it was their expressions that made Kiano's blood run cold. His mother's face was streaked with tears, her usual composure shattered. His father stood rigid, his eyes haunted.

"What's happened?" Kiano asked, the words tumbling out before he could even invite them in.

Mama let out a choked sob. "It's Jabari," she managed, her voice breaking on her son's name. "There's been an accident."

The world seemed to tilt beneath Kiano's feet. He gripped the doorframe, steadying himself. "An accident? What kind of accident? Is he alright?"

Baba placed a steadying hand on his wife's shoulder. When he spoke, his voice was low and strained. "A car hit him. He's in the hospital. They... they don't know if he's going to make it."

The words hung in the air, heavy and terrible. Kiano felt as if all the oxygen had been sucked out of the room. Jabari, his strong, vital brother... how could this be happening?

"Kiano? Who is it?" Amani's voice floated down the hallway, followed by the sound of her approaching footsteps.

Kiano turned, meeting his wife's questioning gaze. He saw the moment she registered the scene at the door, watching her playful attitude suddenly turn to deep concern.

"Amani," he said, his voice sounding strange and distant to his own ears, "we need to go to the hospital. Now."

The next few minutes passed in a blur of hurried explanations and frantic activity. Amani, her face set in lines of worry, ran to call their neighbor. Kiano found Malik, explanations tumbling out in a rush as he sent the confused boy to gather his sister.

"But what about church?" Malik asked, his young face creased with concern.

Kiano placed his hands on his son's shoulders, forcing himself to speak calmly. "Sometimes, Malik, family has to come first. Even before church. Can you understand that?"

Malik nodded solemnly, his eyes wide. "Is Uncle Jabari going to be okay?"

The question pierced Kiano's heart. He swallowed hard, fighting back the tide of fear threatening to overwhelm him. "I don't know, son. But we're going to pray for him, alright? We're going to pray very hard."

Within minutes, the children were settled with the neighbor, and Kiano found himself behind the wheel of the car, Amani beside him, and his parents in the back seat. The familiar streets of their neighborhood blurred past as Kiano navigated through traffic, his knuckles white on the steering wheel.

The drive to the hospital felt interminable, each red light an agony of impatience. Kiano's mind raced, memories of Jabari flashing through his thoughts. Their childhood games, their rivalry on the soccer field, the proud look on Jabari's face at Kiano's wedding. How could all of that be threatened, teetering on the brink of extinction?

As they pulled into the hospital parking lot, Kiano spotted Safiya and Imani hurrying towards the entrance. The sight of Jabari's wives, their faces etched with fear and grief, made the situation suddenly, terribly real.

The group converged at the hospital doors, a flurry of embraces and tearful greetings. Kiano found himself holding Safiya as she sobbed into his shoulder, while Amani wrapped her arms around a shell-shocked Imani.

"Have you heard anything?" Kiano asked, his voice rough with emotion.

Safiya shook her head, pulling back to wipe at her eyes. "Nothing yet. They just told us to wait."

Together, they made their way to the waiting area, a sterile space of uncomfortable chairs and outdated magazines. The fluorescent lights cast a harsh glow, emphasizing the pallor of their faces, their red-rimmed eyes and trembling hands.

Time seemed to stretch and warp, minutes feeling like hours. Kiano found himself pacing, unable to sit still, his prayers a constant litany in his mind. He watched as Amani sat with Safiya and Imani, their heads bent together, offering what comfort she could.

When the doctor finally appeared, his face grave and posture rigid, Kiano felt his heart plummet. He knew, with a certainty that shook him to his core, what the man was about to say.

"Family of Jabari Mutua?" the doctor asked, his eyes scanning the group.

They clustered around him, a united front against the news they all dreaded. Kiano felt Amani's hand slip into his, squeezing tightly.

The doctor's words washed over them, clinical terms barely registering. "Severe trauma... internal bleeding... did everything we could..." But it all boiled down to one devastating truth: Jabari was gone.

The wail that tore from Mama's throat would haunt Kiano for years to come. He watched, feeling oddly detached, as Safiya crumpled to the floor, Imani falling with her, the two women clinging to each other in their shared grief.

Baba stood rigid, his face a mask of disbelief and anguish. Kiano moved to him, wrapping his arms around his father, feeling the older man's body shake with silent sobs.

Amani moved among them all, offering touches of comfort, murmuring soothing words that seemed to float in the air, meaningless in the face of their loss.

Kiano felt numb, his mind unable to fully grasp the reality of what had happened. Jabari, his brother, his rival, his friend... gone. Just like that. No chance to say goodbye, no opportunity to resolve the lingering tension from their last conversation.

As the initial shock began to ebb, practical matters intruded. There were forms to be signed, decisions to be made. Kiano found himself stepping into the role of family spokesperson, his voice steady even as his heart ached.

"We'd like to see him," he said to the doctor, the words feeling strange in his mouth. "To say goodbye."

The doctor nodded, his face softening with sympathy. "Of course. I'll have a nurse show you to the room."

They moved as a group, supporting each other down the long hospital corridor. The nurse's soft voice and gentle demeanor were a balm, but nothing could prepare them for the sight of Jabari's still form on the hospital bed.

He looked peaceful, Kiano thought numbly. As if he were merely sleeping. But the unnatural stillness, the absence of Jabari's larger-than-life presence, was unmistakable.

They gathered around the bed, each lost in their own memories and regrets. Kiano watched as Safiya and Imani each took one of Jabari's hands, their tears falling silently. Mama and Baba stood at the foot of the bed, their grief a palpable force.

Amani's hand found Kiano's again, anchoring him in the storm of emotions threatening to overwhelm him. He looked at her, saw the tears streaming down her face, and felt his own eyes begin to burn.

"He was a good man," Amani said softly, her voice thick with emotion. "A good brother, a good husband, a good son."

Kiano nodded, unable to speak past the lump in his throat. He thought of all the things left unsaid between them, the competition and the laughter, the shared history and the unspoken respect. Now, it all seemed so insignificant in the face of this final, irrevocable separation.

They stayed there, a family united in grief, until the nurse gently suggested it was time to leave. As they filed out of the room, Kiano was the last to go. He paused at the door, looking back at his brother's still form.

"Goodbye, Jabari," he whispered, his voice barely audible. "Rest easy, brother."

The journey home was subdued, the car filled with the heavy silence of shared sorrow. Plans were made in hushed tones. Safiya and Imani would stay with Mama and Baba and arrangements would need to be made for the funeral.

As they pulled up to their house, Kiano felt a wave of exhaustion wash over him. The events of the evening seemed surreal, as if he might wake up at any moment to find it had all been a terrible dream.

But the weight of grief in his chest, the tear stains on Amani's cheeks, the memory of Jabari's still form—these were all too real. As they walked towards their front door, Kiano knew that nothing would ever be quite the same again.

The loss of his brother had left a void, one that would reshape their lives in ways he couldn't yet fathom.

The gentle patter of rain against the windows provided a somber backdrop to the gathering in Mama and Baba's modest living room. A week had passed since Jabari's funeral, but the weight of loss still hung heavy in the air, palpable in every sigh and downcast glance.

Kiano sat on the well-worn sofa, Amani a comforting presence beside him. Across from them, Safiya and Imani perched on the edge of their seats, their faces etched with grief and uncertainty. The parents of both widows occupied chairs brought in from the dining room, their expressions a mix of sorrow and grim determination.

Mama bustled in, carrying a tray laden with steaming cups of chai. The familiar aroma of spices wafted through the room, a small comfort in the face of their shared loss. As she distributed the cups, her hands trembled slightly, betraying the emotional toll of the past week.

"Thank you, Mama," Kiano said softly, accepting a cup. He watched as she made her way around the room, noting how she lingered near Safiya and Imani, her motherly instincts evident in the gentle touch on their shoulders and the extra sugar she added to their tea.

Baba cleared his throat, drawing everyone's attention. "We have gathered today," he began, his voice rough with emotion though still carrying its rich, local accent, "to remember our beloved Jabari and to discuss... what comes next."

A heavy silence fell over the room. Kiano's eyes met Amani's as they instinctively joined hands, seeing their own grief reflected in each other's eyes.

"Jabari was a good man," Safiya's father spoke up in a determined, serious tone, his eyes fixed on Kiano. "A good husband, a good son. But now..." he paused, his gaze sweeping the room before settling back on Kiano. "Now we must address the matter of his widows."

Kiano felt a knot form in his stomach. He had known this moment was coming, had spent sleepless nights turning it over in his mind, but now that it was here, he felt woefully unprepared.

"Kiano," Imani's father said, a less intimidating presence than Safiya's, leaning forward in his chair, "I know your modern church doesn't take kindly to it, but you know what you must do."

The room seemed to hold its breath, all eyes on Kiano. He swallowed hard, feeling the weight of tradition and expectation pressing down on him.

"Since your brother had no children," Safiya's father continued, his tone brooking no argument, "it's your duty to inherit his wives, provide for them, and raise up children in your brother's name. This is the way it has always been among our people and even your foreign pastors cannot deny that this is what is written in the Law of Moses."

Murmurs of agreement rippled through the room. Kiano glanced at Safiya and Imani, noting the mix of hope and fear in their eyes. They had lost not just a husband, but their entire way of life. In the eyes of their community, they were now his responsibility.

Kiano's mind raced. He thought of his church, of the teachings he had let roll off his shoulders over the past fifteen years, the Western preachers who condemned polygamy, and the church leaders who refused membership to multi-wife families. He thought of the sermons he had heard on God's supposed will for monogamy and remembered a few families who were hurt along the way, split apart at the church's recommendation.

Then he thought of Jabari. Of the countless times his brother had challenged him on these very issues, arguing for the wisdom in their traditional ways. He remembered the easy companionship between Safiya and Imani, the way they had worked together to create a harmonious home.

"Kiano?" Amani's soft voice broke through his thoughts. He turned to her, searching her face for any sign of hesitation or disapproval. But all he saw was understanding, and a quiet resolve that seemed to echo what he knew to be right.

Taking a deep breath, Kiano addressed the room. "You're right," he said, his voice steady despite the turmoil in his heart. "This is what must be done. It's the only honorable—and Biblical—thing to do."

A collective sigh of relief seemed to pass through the gathering. Mama dabbed at her eyes with a handkerchief, while Baba nodded approvingly.

"But," Kiano continued, holding up a hand, "I won't pretend this will be easy. My church..." he trailed off, the magnitude of what he was about to do finally hitting him.

"Your church," Baba said, his tone gentle but firm, "is not your family. We are your family." He pointed to the two widows. *"They* are your family."

Kiano nodded, feeling a strange mix of trepidation and resolve. He disagreed that the church was not family, but it was not the time to argue. He did heartily agree that taking care of the women was more important than staying at a certain church, no matter how much he loved it. He looked at Safiya and Imani, really looked at them for the first time since Jabari's death. They were his family now, for better or worse.

"We'll help you move tomorrow," he said, addressing the widows directly. "If... if that's alright with you both?"

Safiya and Imani exchanged a glance, familiar unspoken communication passing between them in an instant. It was Imani who spoke, her voice soft but clear. "Thank you, Kiano. We... we are grateful."

Safiya nodded in agreement. "Yes. Thank you, brother."

As the meeting wound down, plans were made for the move. Kiano found himself in a daze, nodding along as logistics were discussed, trying to wrap his mind around how drastically his life was about to change.

Later, as they prepared to leave, Kiano found himself alone with Baba in the hallway. The older man placed a hand on Kiano's shoulder, his grip firm and reassuring.

"You're doing the right thing, my son," he said, his eyes shining with unshed tears. "Jabari would be proud."

Kiano felt his throat tighten. "I hope so," he managed. "I just... I don't know how to go with all this. The church, the community..."

Baba squeezed his shoulder. "You have your family behind you, Kiano. Remember that. And I will support you always."

The drive home was quiet, the rain having eased to a gentle mist. Kiano's mind whirled with the enormity of what lay ahead. He glanced at Amani, marveling at her calm demeanor.

"Are you really okay with this?" he asked softly, not wanting to wake Malik and Zuri sleeping in the back seat.

Amani was quiet for a long moment, her gaze fixed on the road ahead. When she spoke, her voice was thoughtful. "It's not what I pictured for us," she admitted. "But it's the right thing to do." She looked at him reassuringly. "I will always be content if we are doing the will of God, and that is exactly what we are doing."

Kiano felt a rush of love and gratitude for his wife. Her strength, her wisdom, her ability to see the bigger picture—these were the qualities that had first drawn him to her, and they continued to amaze him.

As they pulled into their driveway, the reality of their situation hit Kiano anew. Their modest three-bedroom house suddenly seemed impossibly small. Where would everyone sleep? How would they manage meals, schedules, the day-to-day logistics of a suddenly expanded family?

But as he helped a sleepy Zuri out of the car, her small arms wrapping trustingly around his neck, Kiano realized that if God had called him to lead this family, *all* of this family, that's exactly what God would give him the strength to do.

Inside, as Amani tucked the children into bed, Kiano found himself standing in the doorway of their spare room. It had been used for storage, filled with boxes of old clothes and forgotten hobbies. Now, it would need to be cleared out, transformed into a bedroom for Safiya and Imani.

The task ahead was daunting, but as Kiano began to move boxes, he felt something dawn upon him. This wasn't just about fulfilling a cultural obligation or following a biblical mandate. It was about honoring his brother's memory, about taking care of family in the truest sense of the word.

Amani appeared in the doorway, watching him work. Without a word, she stepped in and began helping, the two of them working in comfortable silence. As they cleared the room, Kiano felt as if they were clearing space in their lives, making room for the new family dynamic that awaited them.

Later, as they lay in bed, the house quiet around them, Kiano turned to Amani. "Thank you," he said softly. "For understanding. For supporting this."

Amani propped herself up on one elbow, her eyes serious in the dim light. "We're in this together, Kiano. Always have been, always will be. It might not be easy at first, but we'll figure it out. They lost their husband. They are what's important."

Kiano nodded, feeling a lump form in his throat. He thought of Jabari, of the conversations they'd had about family and tradition. He thought of Safiya and Imani, of the uncertainty they must be feeling. And he thought of his own children, of the example he wanted to set for them about love, duty, and family.

As sleep finally claimed him, Kiano's last conscious thought was a prayer—for strength, for wisdom, and for the grace to keep his head above water.

It was morning when Kiano and Amani pulled up to Jabari's house. The modest two-story building stood silent, a stark reminder of the life that had been abruptly cut short. As Kiano stepped out of the car, memories of countless visits and shared laughter flooded his mind.

Safiya and Imani emerged from the front door, their faces a mix of sorrow and nervous anticipation. Despite the circumstances, Kiano couldn't help but notice how they moved in sync, a testament to their bond of friendship that had strengthened in their short time as co-wives.

"Good morning," Kiano said softly, approaching the women. "Are you... ready for this?"

Safiya nodded, her eyes bright with unshed tears. "As ready as we'll ever be, I suppose."

Imani reached out, squeezing Safiya's hand. "We're together," she said with a little more confidence than usually befell her. "That's what matters."

Amani stepped forward, enveloping both women in a warm embrace. "And now you have us too," she said, her voice filled with genuine affection. "We are family."

As they began the process of packing and moving, the house came alive with activity. Boxes were filled, furniture was wrapped, and memories were unearthed with each opened drawer and emptied shelf.

Kiano found himself in Jabari's study, carefully wrapping his brother's prized soccer trophies. He picked up a framed photo of the two of them, arms slung around each other's shoulders after a particularly intense match. Jabari's grin was wide and infectious, his eyes sparkling with joy.

"I miss you, brother," Kiano murmured, running his thumb over the glass. "I hope I'm doing right by you."

"He'd be proud of you, you know."

Kiano turned to find Safiya standing in the doorway, a cardboard box in her arms. Her eyes were fixed on the photo in Kiano's hands, a wistful smile playing on her lips.

"Jabari always spoke so highly of you," she continued, stepping into the room. "He admired your faith, your dedication to your family. He would be grateful to know you're taking care of us."

Kiano felt his throat tighten with emotion. "Jabari was the best of us," he said softly. "I just hope I can live up to his example."

Safiya set down her box and placed a gentle hand on Kiano's arm. "You already are," she said, her eyes meeting his with a warmth that made his heart skip a beat.

The moment was interrupted by a peal of laughter from downstairs. Kiano and Safiya exchanged a surprised look before heading down to investigate.

In the kitchen, they found Amani and Imani doubled over with laughter, tears streaming down their faces. Between them on the counter sat a ridiculously gaudy ceramic rooster, its colors so bright they almost hurt to look at.

"What on earth is that?" Kiano asked, unable to keep the amusement from his voice.

Imani wiped her eyes, still giggling. "It was a wedding gift," she explained. "From Jabari's aunt. He hated it, but he didn't have the heart to get rid of it."

"Every time she visited," Safiya added, joining in the laughter, "he'd dig it out of the back of the cupboard and put it on display. Then it would disappear again the moment she left."

As the laughter subsided, Amani picked up the rooster, turning it over in her hands. "Well," she said with a mischievous grin, "I think this fine specimen deserves a place of honor in our new home. Don't you agree?"

Imani, who wasn't usually the one to crack jokes, added with a held-in laugh, "Perhaps it will keep robbers away. They will think it is an evil apparition guarding the house."

The kitchen erupted in laughter once more, the sound filling the house with a warmth it hadn't known in weeks. For a moment, the grief and uncertainty of their situation faded, replaced by the simple joy of shared memories and newfound connections.

As the day wore on, the house slowly emptied, each box and piece of furniture a step towards their new life together. Kiano found himself marveling at the easy camaraderie that had developed between the three women. They worked together seamlessly, just like they did when preparing dinner and cleaning at Jabari's house, anticipating each other's needs and offering support without a word being spoken.

By late afternoon, the last box had been loaded into the moving truck. Kiano stood in the empty living room, a bittersweet ache in his chest. This house had been more than just Jabari's home; it had been a second home to Kiano and his family, a place of countless shared meals, lively debates, and loving embraces.

"It feels strange, doesn't it?" Imani's soft voice broke through his reverie. She stood beside him, her eyes scanning the bare walls and empty spaces. "Leaving it all behind."

Kiano nodded, unable to find the right words. He felt the weight of responsibility settle more firmly on his shoulders. These women had lost not just a husband, but a home, a life they had only just begun to build.

"We're not leaving it all behind," he said finally, turning to face Imani. "We're taking the most important parts with us. The memories, the love... Jabari will always be a part of our family."

Imani's eyes welled with tears, but she managed a small smile. "Thank you, Kiano. For everything."

She was interrupted by her cell phone, and lifted it up to see who was calling. On her screen appeared a Greek phone number and a picture of her brother, Kwesi.

Imani excused herself and stepped off to the side, answering the phone. "Habari ndugu (Hello, brother)," she greeted him with weary warmth, knowing he was calling in light of their loss. Even in sadness, Kwesi's animated voice brought cheer to her heart.

"I have heard about Jabari. How are doing, sister?"

"I am well. Safiya also. We are mourning his loss, but God has been good to us."

Kwesi's empathy was evident through the phone. "Ah, my sister. He was a good man. It breaks my heart to hear of what you are going through. I wish I could be there for you. Who is taking care of you now?"

Imani glanced at Kiano and smiled. "Another good man," she answered her brother. "Jabari's brother, Kiano, has agreed to take us in and provide for us, even though his church does not approve of such actions. We are very grateful for his kindness."

Kwesi sighed in relief when he heard that his sister would continue to be cared for. "You know, if he needs help fighting the church over this, Jabari always kept some steaks in the freezer..."

Imani laughed, wiping a tear from one of her eyes as she recalled the time her husband chased away ornery elders in their backyard.

Kwesi followed with laughter of his own. "Can you see it, sister? Jabari is probably throwing steaks at heretics in the afterlife! As we speak!"

The two of them shared a joyful, hearty laugh in fond memory of the exuberant Jabari.

When they collected themselves, Kwesi said to her, "I just wanted to call to see how you were doing. If you need anything at all, let me know."

"I will," Imani responded. "Thank you, brother."

"Now," Kwesi sighed, as if to wrap up the call, "I see my friend Paul walking over to me to have lunch. He has something important to talk to me about."

"What sort of problem does this Paul have?" Imani inquired.

Kwesi paused for a moment. Imani could feel his smile emerge from the other side of the phone. He answered, snickering. "Let's just say I'm ordering steak..."

Imani laughed, getting the joke that their lunch had something to do with marriage. "I love you, Kwesi," she affectionately concluded.

"I love you, Imani. God bless."

With that, they hung up the phone, and Imani's heart was warmly reminded of the man she loved so much. The next step in her life wouldn't be easy, but somehow the call gave her more strength to take it with.

The drive to Kiano's house—the widows' house now—was filled with a somewhat nervous energy. Safiya and Imani sat in the backseat, their hands clasped tightly together. Amani kept up a steady stream of chatter, pointing out landmarks and sharing stories about the neighborhood.

As they pulled into the driveway, Kiano felt a sudden surge of anxiety. This was it. There was no going back now. He glanced at Amani, drawing strength from her steady presence.

Once the truck was unloaded and the last box placed in the spare room—now Safiya and Imani's room—Kiano found himself standing on the back porch with the two women.

Taking a deep breath, Kiano turned to Safiya. He looked into her eyes, seeing the mixture of hope and uncertainty there. With a voice filled with emotion, he said, "Safiya, I will be a good husband to you and I will love you till the day I die."

Safiya's eyes widened with confidence as she replied, "I will be a faithful wife, and will love you as long as you live."

Kiano then turned to Imani, repeating the same heartfelt promise. "Imani, I will be a good husband to you and will love you till the day I die."

Imani's voice trembled slightly as she responded, "I will be a faithful wife, and will love you as long as you live."

The weight of the moment hung in the air, the magnitude of the commitment they had just made settling over them like a warm blanket. Kiano looked at both women, his heart full of a complex mix of emotions—love, responsibility, and a fierce determination to honor the trust they had placed in him.

"Everything will be okay," he said softly, his voice filled with reassurance. "This is your home now, and you are most welcome."

This wasn't the life he had envisioned, but it was the life that had been entrusted to him. With Amani's strength, Safiya and Imani's trust, and the memory of Jabari to guide him, he knew they would face whatever came their way as a family.

The porch door creaked open, and Amani stepped out, a tray of steaming chai in her hands. "I thought we could use a little celebration before Baba brings the kids back," she said, her smile warm and welcoming.

As they sipped their tea, the stars beginning to twinkle in the darkening sky, Kiano looked at the three women who now made up his family. Each unique, each bringing their own strengths and perspectives. He thought of Malik and Zuri, of the example of love and commitment they would grow up witnessing.

The morning sun filtered through the stained glass windows of the church office and Kiano sat beside Amani, their hands intertwined, drawing strength from each other as they faced Pastor David, one of several white elders at their church. The American missionary's face was etched with concern, his blue eyes filled with genuine sympathy.

"I'm so sorry for your loss," Pastor David said, leaning forward in his chair. "Jabari was a pillar of the community. How are you both holding up?"

Kiano nodded in agreement, the pain of his brother's absence still felt. "It's been... difficult," he managed, his voice rough with emotion. "But we're taking it one day at a time."

Amani rested her hand on his, offering silent support. "The church community has been very kind," she added, her smile tinged with sadness. "The meals, the prayers... it's all meant so much."

Pastor David nodded, his expression warm. "That's what family in Christ is for. We're here to support each other through the good times and the bad." He paused, his brow furrowing slightly. "I've been meaning to ask... what will become of Jabari's wives? Safiya and Imani, right? Do they have family to stay with? The church can certainly help if they need it."

Kiano felt a flicker of nervousness in his stomach. This was the moment he'd been dreading. He glanced at Amani, seeing the encouragement in her eyes, and took a deep breath.

"Actually, Pastor," he began, his voice steady despite his racing heart, "Safiya and Imani are already taken care of... the traditional way."

Pastor David's eyebrows rose, confusion evident on his face. "Traditional way? What do you mean by that, Kiano?"

Kiano straightened in his chair, drawing on the conviction that had led him to this decision. "As Jabari's brother, it was my duty—my Biblical duty—to take in his widows. To provide for them, to... to marry them."

The silence that followed was deafening. Pastor David's face went through a range of emotions—confusion, disbelief, and finally, dismay. "Kiano," he said slowly, his voice tight with controlled emotion, "are you telling me that you've taken Safiya and Imani as your wives?"

Kiano nodded, his jaw set. "Yes, Pastor. I have."

Pastor David leaned back in his chair, stressfully running a hand from the top to the bottom of his face. When he spoke again, his voice was filled with disappointment and barely contained anger. "Kiano, you know this is contrary to God's word. Polygamy is not God's plan for marriage. It's sin, plain and simple."

Kiano felt a surge of frustration rise within him. He'd expected this reaction, but it still stung to hear his own decision—a decision made out of obedience to the Scriptures—dismissed so easily.

"With all due respect, Pastor," Kiano said, his voice calm but firm, "I disagree. The Bible doesn't condemn what you call polygamy. In fact, the majority of God's people had multiple wives for thousands of years."

Pastor David shook his head, his face reddening. "Those were different times, Kiano. God allowed certain practices in the Old Testament that we now know are not His ideal. Jesus made it clear that marriage is between one man and one woman."

Kiano leaned forward, his eyes intense. "Did He? Where exactly did Jesus say this? Where, in all the gospels, did Jesus repeal His own laws, which prescribed multiple wives in certain situations? He spoke against divorce, yes, but not once did He speak against having multiple wives."

"That's because it was understood!" Pastor David's voice rose slightly. "God's design for marriage is clear from the beginning – Adam and Eve, not Adam and Eve and Sarah and Rachel."

Amani, who had been silent until now, spoke up. "But Pastor, what about Levirate marriage? God commanded that a man should marry his brother's widow if she had no children. Isn't that exactly what Kiano is doing?"

Pastor David turned to Amani, his expression softening slightly. "Amani, I understand this is a difficult situation. But that was an Old Testament law, specific to the Israelites. We are under a new covenant now."

Kiano felt his frustration growing. "A new covenant that doesn't negate God's character or His concern for widows and orphans. Pastor, what would you have me do? Cast Safiya and Imani out? Leave them without protection or provision?"

"Of course not," Pastor David said, more exasperation creeping into his voice. "The church can help them. There are other ways to provide for widows without resorting to—"

"To what?" Amani interrupted, her own voice now showing a hint of indignation. "To marriage? Since when is marriage some kind of last resort? Isn't marriage the whole reason those women were created? Why, then, do we treat it like it's last on a list of man-made alternatives? They have a right to a good husband as much as any other—"

Kiano placed a hand on his wife's arm, seeing that she was becoming upset. Amani, suddenly aware of her louder tone, went quiet to leave room for the men to respond. Kiano shook his head and looked at the pastor, his voice filled with quiet intensity. "This isn't just about provision, Pastor. It's about family and the will of God as revealed in the Scriptures. It's about honoring my brother's memory and fulfilling my duty both as a Kikuyu man and as a Christian."

Pastor David's face hardened. "Kiano, I'm sorry, but I can't condone this. These new marriages are not valid in the eyes of God or the church. You need to send these women away and repent."

Kiano felt as if he'd been slapped. He stood up slowly, his body tense with barely contained emotion. "Send them away?" he repeated, his voice low and dangerous. "Pastor, with all due respect, that is not going to happen. Safiya and Imani are my wives now, as much as this woman is." He gestured to Amani sitting next to him. "I made a commitment before God to love and protect them, and I intend to honor that commitment. The Lord hates divorce. Nowhere are we told that the Lord hates marriage. I will not send them away."

Amani stood as well. "Pastor David," she said, her voice calm but firm, "we came here out of respect, to inform you of our decision. But we did not come seeking your permission or approval. This is our family now, and we will not abandon it."

Pastor David's face was a mask of disappointment and anger. "I'm sorry you feel that way," he said stiffly. "But I cannot allow this in our church. If you persist in this... arrangement, I'll have no choice but to bring it before the elders for disciplinary action."

Kiano felt a wave of sadness wash over him. This church had been his spiritual home for over a decade. The thought of leaving it behind was painful, but not as painful as the thought of betraying his family.

"Then we'll save you the trouble," Kiano said, his voice heavy with emotion. "We'll find a church that believes the Scriptures."

Without waiting for a response, Kiano turned and walked out of the office, Amani by his side. As they stepped into the warm Kenyan sunlight, Kiano felt a mix of emotions swirling within him—anger, sadness, disappointment, but also a deep sense of conviction that he was doing the right thing.

Amani squeezed his hand, drawing his attention. Her eyes were filled with a mixture of concern and pride. "Are you okay?" she asked softly.

Kiano took a deep breath, feeling the tension slowly leave his body. "I will be," he said, managing a small smile. "It's not easy, leaving behind what we've known for so long. But we're doing the right thing, Amani. I know we are."

As they walked to their car, Kiano's mind raced with thoughts of the future. Finding a new church, explaining the situation to Malik and Zuri, and navigating the complexities of their new family dynamic. It would not be easy, but as he looked at Amani, her unwavering support evident in every line of her face, he knew they would face it together.

The drive home was quiet, each lost in their own thoughts. As they pulled into their driveway, Kiano saw Safiya and Imani in the front yard, playing with Zuri. The little girl's laughter floated through the air, a joyous counterpoint to the heaviness in Kiano's heart.

Imani looked up as they parked, her face breaking into a warm smile. But as Kiano and Amani approached, her expression changed to one of concern. "Is everything alright?" she asked, her eyes darting between them.

Kiano forced a smile, not wanting to burden them with the details of the confrontation just yet. "Everything's fine," he said, reaching out to ruffle Zuri's hair. "Just a... challenging meeting."

Safiya, never one to leave matters unattended to, raised an eyebrow. "The pastor didn't take it well, did he?"

Amani sighed, shaking her head. "No, he didn't. But that's a conversation for later. Right now, I think we could all use some lunch. Who's hungry?"

"All of us," Safiya said with a confident smile. "Why do you think we made it?"

"Made it? Already? There's nothing to do?" Amani asked in surprise.

Imani grabbed Amani's arm and began to lead her inside as she chuckled. "Welcome to sisterhood, my queen."

Safiya grabbed her other arm and joined in the reassuring laughter as they went inside to eat. Kiano heard her tease Amani from outside. "Tell me. When you were queen of this castle, did anyone make you food?" He smiled as the women laughed together, his heart warmed by how blessed the whole transition seemed to feel.

As they sat down to eat, Malik burst through the front door, his soccer uniform covered in dust and grass stains. "Dad!" he called out, his face flushed with excitement. "Coach says they want to move me up to play on the high school team!"

Kiano's jaw dropped as he slapped the table with pride. "That's amazing news, son!" he said, gesturing for Malik to join them at the table. "Come, sit down and tell us all about it."

As Malik regaled them with tales of his soccer exploits, Kiano looked around the table. Amani, her eyes shining with love and pride. Safiya and Imani, listening intently to Malik's story, genuine interest on their faces. Zuri, giggling at her brother's animated gestures. This was his family, his home, and nothing could take away the satisfaction of getting to be a part of it.

The pastor's words echoed in his mind – "These new marriages are not valid in the eyes of God or the church." But looking at the scene before him, Kiano knew in his heart that this was exactly what God intended. Love, support, family—these were the things that truly mattered.

As the meal wound down, Kiano cleared his throat, drawing everyone's attention. "There's something we need to discuss," he said, his eyes meeting each of theirs in turn. "Our meeting with Pastor David... it didn't go well. We may need to find a new church."

A hush fell over the table. Malik's eyes widened in surprise, while Safiya and Imani exchanged worried glances. It was Amani who broke the silence, her voice calm and reassuring.

"We knew this might happen," she said, reaching out to squeeze Kiano's hand. "But we're a family. We'll face this together, just like everything else."

Safiya nodded, her eyes filled with determination. "We will find a church that understands. Perhaps we should talk to Pastor Muthomi?"

Pastor Muthomi was the leader of the more traditional church they had attended with Jabari for the last year. Kiano knew him, though not as well as Jabari.

After thinking for a moment, Kiano looked at everyone. "Yes. I think we should talk to Pastor Muthomi."

As they all nodded and murmured in agreement, Malik interjected. "I would like to go to Uncle Jabari's church!"

Kiano looked at him curiously. "Why is that, my son?"

"Well," Malik answered with the corner of his mouth beginning to stretch into a smile, "they wear African clothing, and the tie I have to wear to ours is very uncomfortable."

Everyone laughed and began settling in for the day, having resolved to invite Pastor Muthomi over to talk.

Kiano sat surrounded by his family and their expected guest. Pastor Muthomi, a man in his sixties with salt-and-pepper hair and kind eyes crinkled by years of laughter, leaned forward in his chair; his long, colorful shirt, made by locals, strikingly contrasting his skin.

"So, they just dismissed you like that?" Pastor Muthomi asked in his unmistakably deep voice, which was tinged with a mixture of disbelief and sympathy. "After all your years of faithful service?"

Kiano nodded, feeling the familiar twinge of hurt and anger that had been his constant companion since that fateful meeting with Pastor David. "They didn't even try to understand," he said, his voice low but intense. "It was as if everything we'd shared over the years meant nothing in the face of this one decision."

Amani, seated beside Kiano on the couch, reached out and squeezed his hand. Safiya and Imani, perched on the adjacent loveseat, exchanged worried glances. The weight of their shared struggle hung heavy in the air.

Pastor Muthomi shook his head, a rueful smile playing on his lips. "I'm sorry you've had to go through this, my brother," he said. "But I want you to know that you'd be more than welcome at our church. We actually believe the Bible, you know." His eyes twinkled with good-natured humor, drawing a chuckle from the group.

Kiano felt a surge of gratitude for the older man's understanding and acceptance. The offer was tempting—a chance to be part of a community that wouldn't make an issue of their decision, that would even embrace and honor it.

But something stirred within Kiano's spirit, a restlessness that he couldn't quite name. He stood up abruptly, pacing the length of the living room as his mind raced. The others watched him, concern etched on their faces.

"Kiano?" Amani's voice was soft, questioning. "What is it?"

Pastor Muthomi smiled. "Oh, I've seen this before. His spirit is roused within him!"

He turned to face them, his eyes blazing with a sudden intensity. "How many?" he asked, his voice barely above a whisper.

"How many what?" Imani asked, leaning forward.

"How many African families have been damaged by this... this monogamy-onlyism taught by the Westerners?" Kiano's voice rose with each word, filled with a passion that surprised even him. "How many brothers and sisters have been forced to choose between their faith and their family?"

The room fell silent, the weight of his words settling over them like a heavy blanket. Pastor Muthomi nodded slowly, understanding dawning in his eyes that perhaps God was calling Kiano in this moment.

"You want to fight this," he said. It wasn't a question.

Kiano nodded, his jaw set with determination. "I can't just leave quietly, Pastor. Not when I know we're doing the right thing. Not when I think about all the others who might be facing the same struggle."

Safiya stood up as well. "I heard one pastor say that this is the single biggest issue in the church in Kenya," she said while moving to stand beside Kiano. "Why shouldn't someone do something about it?" She clasped her husband's hand and looked in his eyes with a beaming pride.

Amani and Imani joined them, forming a circle of unity and strength. Kiano felt a wave of love and gratitude wash over him, bolstering his resolve.

Pastor Muthomi watched them, a mixture of admiration and concern on his face. "I admire your conviction, Kiano," he said carefully. "And I believe you're right to want to stand up for what you believe in. But..." He paused, choosing his words carefully. "While you're a wonderful Christian and you know your Bible well, I wonder if you're prepared for the theological defenses the church will mount." He set his tea down and waved his finger up and down at Kiano. "Their American theologians can be very convincing." He took a breath and slapped his waving hand down onto his leg. "And not only that, but they think their culture is superior to ours. It's not just about besting them in Scripture. It's about them knowing that African Christianity is not lesser than European Christianity. Part of the problem is they don't take us Africans seriously. They think they have everything to teach us and nothing to learn. I fear they would not listen to you with their whole heart."

Kiano felt a flicker of doubt, but it was quickly extinguished by a spark of inspiration. A slow smile spread across his face as an idea began to take shape.

"Then maybe," he said, looking back at Pastor Muthomi, "what we need is an American of our own."

The room fell silent as the implications of Kiano's words sank in, but Amani instantly wore a large smile, knowing exactly who Kiano had in mind.

Pastor Muthomi was the first to speak, his voice and facial expression saturated with piqued curiosity. "You're talking about a mzungu who supports multiple wives? And from America, no less?"

Kiano nodded, his mind already racing with possibilities. "Exactly! Someone who can speak their language, who values our culture, and can best even the best in Scripture."

He turned and looked at Amani to gauge her reaction.

She wore a smile that seemed ready to burst with anticipation. "Do you really think he'd come all that way for us?"

"I believe he will," Kiano answered excitedly, as he grabbed and squeezed Amani's hands, then released them to go find his contacts book.

Pastor Muthomi and the other two wives were left looking back and forth at each other, shrugging in light of the curious development.

"Found it!" Kiano yelled from another room, causing his guests to jolt.

He ran back in with a business card in hand. Nothing was written on it except a U.S. phone number and the name "Jack Hall," with a Bible logo on the back.

"So, your plan is to have a white man from America come and save us Africans? To fight our battles for us?" Pastor Muthomi said this partly in jest, but also acknowledging that Africans didn't need a foreign 'savior' to fight their battles for them.

"Not to fight our battles," Kiano said as he pointed the card in the astonished pastor's direction. "But to teach *me* to fight them."

Pastor Muthomi's expression softened, returning to its former curiosity.

Kiano continued. "You're right, Pastor. They will have crafty arguments used by centuries of European theologians. I know my Bible, yes, but I'm afraid not as well as some of them. My friend Jack is mighty in the Scriptures. He can help me prepare so that I can fight with the whole counsel of God's word."

The pastor smiled and gave one last shrug to Safiya and Imani, who were still having a hard time believing this character existed. With that, he laughed and stood up, looking at Kiano in amazement. "You never know, I guess. God does work in mysterious ways. I suppose I'll leave you to your mission for now."

He smiled as he took a few steps toward the door, but paused before he reached it, turning back to face the family. His eyes were warm with affection and respect. "You know," he said, his voice gentle, "when I came here today, I thought I was coming to offer comfort and support. But you've reminded me of something important, Kiano. Sometimes, God calls us not just to refuse injustice, but to stand against it. To be a voice for those who cannot speak for themselves."

He reached out, clasping Kiano's hand firmly. "Whatever you need, my brother, my church and I will support you. This fight is not just yours—it's ours. It's for all those who believe in a God big enough to be Lord of the African as well as Lord of the American."

As the door closed behind Pastor Muthomi, Kiano turned to face his family. Their eyes shone with a mixture of determination and love, reflecting the emotions swirling in his own heart. Kiano looked at each of them in turn, drawing strength from their support for the journey that lay ahead.

The small Kenyan airport was busy as Kiano, Amani, Safiya, and Imani stood near the arrivals gate. The afternoon sun beat down on the tarmac, causing heat waves to shimmer in the distance. Kiano's eyes were fixed on the small plane that had just touched down, its propellers slowing to a stop.

Amani squeezed Kiano's arm, her voice filled with excitement to see their old friends. "It's been so long since we've seen them. Do you think they've changed much?"

Kiano shook his head, a small smile playing on his lips. "Who? Jack and Sarah? I doubt it. I can't see him becoming anything other than a wilder version of himself."

As the plane's door opened and passengers began to disembark, Kiano felt a flutter of anticipation in his chest. Safiya and Imani exchanged glances, their trepidation evident in the way they adjusted and smoothed their dresses. Despite Kiano's confidence, they were clearly unsure how the American couple would react to their situation, even though Kiano had already explained it to them over the phone.

Finally, the last two passengers appeared at the top of the stairs—a white American couple in their mid-30s, dressed casually in jeans and t-shirts. The man, tall with short, brown hair, spotted Kiano and his family immediately. His face broke into a wide grin as he nudged his wife, a petite woman with curly brown hair and sparkling brown eyes.

"Jambo, rafiki!" (Hello, friends!) Jack's voice boomed across the tarmac in accented Swahili, drawing curious glances from nearby travelers.

Sarah joined in, her laughter ringing out as she excitedly waved to their friends on the ground. "Habari za asubuhi marafiki zangui!" (Good morning, my friends!)

Kiano felt a wave of warmth wash over him at the sound of their voices. It had been years since they'd last seen each other in person, but in that moment, it felt like no time had passed at all.

Jack and Sarah practically bounded down the stairs, their excitement palpable. They reached Kiano and Amani in a flurry of hugs and exclamations.

"Look at you two!" Sarah beamed, holding Amani at arm's length. "You haven't aged a day!"

Jack clasped Kiano's shoulder, his expression softening. "Kiano, my friend. I'm so sorry about Jabari. I can't imagine how hard that must have been."

Kiano nodded, feeling the familiar ache of loss. "Thank you, Jack. It's been... difficult. But God has been good to us, even in our grief."

Jack's gaze shifted to Safiya and Imani, who stood slightly apart, watching the reunion with a mixture of curiosity and apprehension. "And who are these beautiful ladies?" he asked, his tone light and his smile large.

Kiano may have had good reason to be nervous around other Americans, given his situation—but not this time. "Jack, Sarah... I'd like you to meet Safiya and Imani. These are my wives who I inherited from Jabari."

Jack and Sarah didn't miss a beat. Their smiles, if anything, grew wider.

"Well, praise God!" Jack exclaimed, stepping forward to embrace Safiya and Imani in turn. "What a blessing to meet you both!"

Sarah followed suit, her eyes shining with genuine warmth. "Welcome to the family! I can't wait to get to know you both!"

Safiya and Imani exchanged bewildered glances amidst the hugs, clearly taken back by the Americans' enthusiastic response. Safiya, always the more outspoken of the two, couldn't contain her surprise.

"Kiano," she said, her tone sharp and playful. "What kind of mzungu are these? Did they drink on the plane?"

Jack threw his head back and laughed, a deep, rumbling sound that seemed to come from his very soul. "We're a special kind of mzungu, my sister," he said, his eyes twinkling with mischief, "a rare breed that was assigned the wrong skin color at birth."

The tension that had been building in Safiya and Imani's shoulders instantly melted away as they glanced at each other. Both of them burst into laughter, the sound mingling with Jack and Sarah's chuckles to create a symphony of joy and relief.

Kiano felt his heart swell with gratitude. He'd known Jack and Sarah would be understanding—it was why he'd reached out to them in the first place—but their immediate and unequivocal acceptance made him more grateful than he'd expected.

As they made their way to baggage claim, the conversation flowed easily. Jack and Sarah peppered Safiya and Imani with questions about their lives, their interests, their dreams. There was no hint of judgment or discomfort, just genuine curiosity and warmth. Jack and Safiya quickly settled into trading sarcastic quips throughout their conversation, something both of them were much accustomed to. Imani very naturally joined Sarah in playful eye-rolling and behind-their-back jokes of their own.

"Jack," Kiano said as they waited for the luggage carousel to start. "I am glad people like you exist in this world. I'm looking forward to you helping me fight for truth."

Jack's expression grew almost serious for a moment. "Kiano, my friend, the West is convinced that the Bible was written by wig-toting Europeans a few hundred years ago. They don't say it, but it's exactly how they behave. They seem to forget that we didn't bring Christianity to Africa; Africa brought Christianity to us. They also seem to forget that more than half the information about marriage in their Bibles was put there by men with multiple wives. I was happy to come. Besides, I'm heading to the Philippines to preach in a couple of weeks, and this meant I got to take the scenic route."

Sarah smiled in agreement. "If anyone can help you fight this fight, it's Jack."

As they loaded the luggage into Kiano's van, the conversation turned to lighter topics—catching up on old times, sharing stories of their children, laughing over shared memories. But beneath the easy camaraderie, there was an undercurrent of excitement and anticipation.

The drive back to Kiano's home was filled with the sounds of laughter and animated conversation. Jack regaled them with tales of his and Sarah's adventures in various parts of the world, his storytelling punctuated by Sarah's witty asides and gentle corrections.

"Remember that time in Yorubaland," Jack began, his eyes dancing with mirth, "when we accidentally wandered into that village elder's compound?"

Sarah smiled and let out an exaggerated groan. "Oh, don't remind me. I've never been so afraid of being executed in my life! We are never getting *that* greeting wrong again!"

With everyone's curiosity piqued, Safira just had to know. "Well, what did you say?!"

Sarah tried to hold in her laugh as her cheeks got red. "I don't remember the words at this point." She put her hand up to her mouth to contain her laughter but snorted and began laughing through the rest of her story, only getting it out in bits. "We had learned some Yoruba greetings and basic phrases of the gospel. We walked in somewhere we weren't supposed to be and this powerful chief guy had us brought to him. When we got there..." Her laughter was almost so uncontainable that she could barely breathe enough to get the rest out. "When we got there, he asked us to introduce ourselves, and after telling him our names, we tried to say, 'We mean peace,' but what we actually said was, 'Your sister is pig food.'"

At this point, she completely lost it and was falling over Imani's lap in the back seat of the van, Jack and the others unable to help themselves from joining her.

As Kiano navigated the busy Kiambu streets, he found himself marveling at how easily Jack and Sarah fit into their family dynamic. There was no awkwardness, no sense of them being outsiders. It was as if they had always been a part of this tapestry of love and connection.

When they finally arrived at the house, Malik and Zuri burst out the front door, their faces alight with excitement. "Uncle Jack! Aunt Sarah!" they cried in unison, launching themselves at the Americans.

Jack scooped Zuri up in his arms, spinning her around as she giggled uncontrollably. "Look at you, little one!" he exclaimed. "You've grown so much since we last saw you!"

Sarah hugged Malik tightly, then held him at arm's length to examine him. "And you, young man, I hear you've become quite the soccer player! We heard about your game-winning pass last season. Way to go!" She raised her hand, which Malik met with a fervent high-five.

Later that evening, after a lively dinner filled with more storytelling and laughter, Kiano found himself sitting on the back porch with Jack. The night air was cool and fragrant with the scent of blooming jasmine.

"You know," Jack said, his voice thoughtful, "when you first reached out to us about your situation, I was frustrated. Not at you, of course, but at the narrow-mindedness that led to this."

Kiano nodded, understanding all too well. "It's been... challenging. Trying to reconcile our faith with the teachings we've been given. So many churches here have been influenced by Western missionaries for so long... It's as if they've bought the lie that Western culture is Christian culture. I don't know how to undo that on my own."

Jack turned to face him, his expression serious. "Kiano, what you're doing—standing up for your family, for your culture, for a faithful interpretation of scripture—it's important. More important than you might realize."

"What do you mean?" Kiano asked, intrigued.

"Think about it," Jack said, leaning forward. "How many African Christians have been told that their traditional family structures are sinful? And not just in Africa. The Middle East, Asia, the South Sea islands. How many have been forced to choose between their faith and their family in the name of 'monogamy?' How many Africans sit bored in their own local churches because Wesley's hymns are the 'right' way to worship? Listen. I love Wesley as much as the next guy, but sometimes a brotha's gotta dance before the Lord."

Kiano nodded his head up and down several times, chuckling in agreement.

"The thing is," Jack continued, "this isn't just about Biblical marriage. It's about Biblical everything. So many people are letting the West tell them how to interpret the Bible—which, there's no two ways about it, the West has produced some incredible preachers and theologians—but they lack cultural perspective. America is the newest culture in the world, yet it claims to have carte blanche on interpreting the marriage customs of the oldest cultures in the world. It's arrogant, it's ignorant, and it's a mishandling of God's word. God wasn't confused when He let His people marry freely for thousands of years. Moses, a man who had three wives himself, wasn't confused when he wrote the creation account. We simply need to take the Scripture as it is, not how it has to be to conform to Disney fairy tales. That's what's at stake here. Scripture Alone."

Kiano felt a spark of recognition ignite within him. This was exactly what he'd been feeling, but hadn't been able to articulate.

Jack continued, his voice growing passionate. "By challenging this interpretation, you're not just fighting for your own family. You're fighting for the right of African Christians everywhere to obey the Word and marry as God intended, whether they take one wife or more. Not to mention all of the families you could save. I'm all too familiar with modern churches here forcing men to divorce all their wives but the first. It's an abomination, Kiano. And I believe God has put this fight within you to save lives."

As Jack's words sank in, Kiano felt a weight lift from his shoulders. This wasn't just about him, or even just about his family. It was about something much bigger—a chance to bridge the gap between faith and culture, to challenge harmful misconceptions, to pave the way for a stronger, more Biblical Christianity in East Africa.

Inside the house, he could hear the sounds of laughter and conversation. Amani's melodic voice mingled with Sarah's American accent, while Safiya and Imani's gentle teasing of Malik drifted through the open windows.

This, Kiano realized, was what they were fighting for. Not just the right to live as they chose, but the right for all families like theirs to exist without shame or condemnation. To be recognized as valid expressions of love and commitment, blessed by God and accepted by their communities.

As he and Jack rejoined the others inside, Kiano felt a surge of determination. With Jack and Sarah's help, with the strength of his family behind him, he was ready to take on this challenge. Not just for themselves, but for all those who had been silenced, shamed, or forced to choose between their faith and their family.

At midday, the air of Kiano's home was filled with the lingering aroma of a hearty lunch and the soft clink of dishes being cleared away. Kiano leaned back in his chair, his eyes following Amani as she gathered plates with practiced efficiency.

"You know," Amani said, a mischievous glint in her eye, knowing her husband was listening, "I could get used to this, having a rich man. Cleanup has never been easier." She winked at Safiya and Imani, who chuckled as they helped her carry dishes to the kitchen.

Kiano shook his head, a smile playing on his lips. He marveled at how seamlessly his wives had adapted to their new family dynamic, finding joy and camaraderie in the shared responsibilities of running their household.

As the women disappeared into the kitchen, their laughter and chatter fading into a pleasant background hum, Kiano turned his attention to Jack. The American sat across from him, his posture relaxed but his eyes alert and focused.

"Jack," Kiano began, his voice low and earnest, "I can't thank you enough for coming. I know it's a lot to ask, especially on such short notice."

Jack waved off the gratitude with a gentle hand gesture. "Kiano, my friend, you don't need to thank me. When you reached out, Sarah and I knew we had to come. We couldn't be happier that we're here."

Kiano nodded, feeling a mix of relief and anticipation settle in his chest. He leaned forward, resting his elbows on the table. "I've been trying to prepare, to gather my thoughts and arguments, but..." He trailed off, searching for the right words.

Jack's eyes softened with understanding. "But it's hard when it's so personal, isn't it? When it's your family, your life on the line?"

"Exactly," Kiano sighed. "Every time I try to approach it logically, I find myself getting angry or frustrated. How can they not see it? How can they dismiss millennia of tradition just because some foreign missionaries told them to?"

Jack nodded, his expression thoughtful. "It's a serious issue, no doubt about it. But that's why I'm here, brother. To help you navigate these waters, to help you find the Biblical ammo you need to fight this battle."

Kiano felt a surge of gratitude for his friend's presence and expertise. "Where do we start?" he asked, eager to begin.

Jack leaned back, his fingers drumming lightly on the table. "First, we need to understand their arguments inside and out. What specific verses are they using to condemn polygamy? What historical and Biblical context are they ignoring? They always begin with Jesus' words to the Pharisees about divorce..."

As Jack spoke, Kiano found himself reaching for a notepad and pen. He began jotting down points, his handwriting quick and decisive. Jack's words flowed smoothly, years of study and passion evident in every sentence.

"We'll need to address the common misconceptions," Jack continued. "The idea that monogamy was God's only plan from the beginning, the assumption that Jesus or Paul condemned polygamy, the conflation of Western cultural norms with Biblical mandates. The biggest out-of-context line they'll hit us with is 'The two shall become one flesh.' Next will come the bit about being joined to his 'wife,' not 'wives.'"

Kiano's pen flew across the page, capturing key points and questions. As he wrote, he felt a sense of clarity beginning to form. The jumble of emotions and arguments in his mind started to arrange themselves into a coherent structure.

"But it's not just about winning a theological debate," Jack added, his voice softening. "It's about helping them see the real-life implications of their stance. Families are being torn apart. We're not trying to win an argument so we can feel good about ourselves. We're trying to save lives."

Kiano paused in his writing, looking up at Jack. "How do we do that without coming across as confrontational?"

Jack smiled, a mix of humor and determination in his eyes. "Who, my friend, said anything about not being confrontational?"

Kiano chuckled, basking in the constant reassurances that his friend was the same as he'd always been.

Jack continued, "Do you really think I flew halfway around the world just to tip-toe? Not a chance. I'm not leaving here until a Caucasian board member is storming out of a church redder than a tomato."

They both shared a good laugh over the fruitful analogy. As they prepared to return to their studies, the sound of laughter suddenly erupted from the kitchen, punctuated by Malik's voice protesting some friendly teasing. Kiano and Jack paused, sharing a smile at the joyful noise.

"That's what we're fighting for," Kiano said softly, gesturing towards the kitchen. "That laughter, that love, that sense of belonging."

"Then let's make sure they hear it, my friend. Let's make sure they see the glory of God in this truth."

With that, they finished their studying for the night and the house quieted down for bed. Jack and Sarah slept on the couches in the living room, enjoying their usual goofing off before going to sleep, trying to keep things quiet so as not to wake anyone. Tomorrow was Sunday and a big day for Kiano, as it was the day he would publicly confront his pastor about the issue.

The Sunday morning sun blazed through the stained-glass windows of the church. The senior pastor, Pastor Kwamin, spoke with determination. His voice resonated through the sanctuary, his words falling on attentive ears as he expounded on the virtues of Christian love.

Kiano stood at the back of the church, his heart pounding in his chest. Jack stood beside him, a steadying presence in the storm of emotions threatening to overwhelm him. They'd arrived late, slipping in unnoticed as the sermon reached its crescendo.

"Remember," Jack whispered, his voice barely audible above the pastor's impassioned speech, "the Lord is with you."

Kiano nodded, his jaw set with determination. He took a deep breath, feeling the weight of his decision pressing down on him. This was it. There was no turning back now.

As Pastor Kwamin's voice swelled, building towards his conclusion, Kiano walked halfway up the center aisle. His voice, clear and strong, cut through the air like a knife.

"What you are doing to families is wrong!"

The effect was immediate. A collective gasp rippled through the congregation as heads whipped around to find the source of the interruption. Pastor Kwamin froze mid-sentence, his eyes widening as he spotted Kiano standing in the center aisle.

Kiano felt hundreds of eyes on him, but he kept his gaze locked on Pastor Kwamin. "I will not quietly accept the church's ruling on having multiple wives," he continued, his voice gaining strength with each word. "I challenge you to a public debate next week, in front of the whole church, to settle this matter once and for all."

A murmur swept through the congregation, growing louder with each passing second. Pastor Kwamin's face flushed red, a mix of anger and shock etched across his features.

"Kiano," he said, his voice strained as he tried to maintain composure, "this is not the time or place for such... disruptions. Please, let's discuss this privately after the service."

But Kiano stood his ground, emboldened by the whispers of support he heard from the congregation. "No! Things have been done in private too long. It is time this destructive doctrine was dealt with in the open."

Two associate pastors hurried down from the stage, their faces tight with concern. They flanked Pastor Kwamin, speaking to him in hushed, urgent tones. Kiano could see the conflict playing out on the lead pastor's face—the desire to shut down this challenge warring with the fear of appearing unreasonable in front of his flock.

As the whispers grew louder, fragments of conversation reached Kiano's ears.

"...about time someone spoke up..."

"...my cousin had to leave his wives..."

"...tore my parents apart..."

The realization hit Kiano like a thunderbolt. He wasn't alone in this struggle. His story was just one among many, a single thread in a tapestry of pain and confusion woven by well-meaning but misguided teachings.

Pastor Kwamin raised his hands, attempting to quiet the growing hubbub. "Brothers and sisters, please. This is not the way we conduct ourselves in God's house." Turning to Kiano, his voice began to patronize as an arrogant smile emerged. "Kiano, I understand you're upset, but—"

Jack, sensing the pastor's trivializing the situation, stepped forward, his tall frame drawing all eyes to him. His voice was strong as steel and bore the marks of godly authority, cutting through the chaos.

"You know what I think your pastor's problem is?" he said, his gaze sweeping across the congregation before settling on Pastor Kwamin. He pointed a finger at the shocked pastor—"Once a slave to the white man, always a slave to the white man!"

The sanctuary fell silent, the weight of Jack's words hanging heavy in the air. Pastor Kwamin's face darkened, his eyes flashing with indignation.

"How dare you," he sputtered, his composure cracking as he hit the pulpit with the side of his fist. "I am a slave to no one but Christ!"

Jack didn't back down. He took another step forward, his voice carrying to every corner of the church. "Yet here you are, oppressing African women and destroying African families because the **white** man told you that ***their*** tradition is holier than yours. Sure sounds like slavery to me!"

The words hit their mark. Kiano could see the impact rippling through the congregation, faces clouding with doubt, brows furrowing in thought. Even some of the church elders shifted uncomfortably in their seats.

Pastor Kwamin's knuckles turned white as he gripped the pulpit. His eyes darted from face to face, seeking support but finding only confusion and growing discontent. Kiano felt a pang of sympathy for the man, even as he stood firm in his conviction.

"This... this is outrageous," Pastor Kwamin said, his voice wavering slightly. "We cannot entertain such baseless accusations and challenges. This service is over. Please, everyone, go home and—"

But his words were drowned out by a swell of voices from the congregation. People stood up, calling out for the debate to be held, demanding answers to questions long suppressed.

"Let them speak!"

"We deserve to hear both sides!"

"What if they're right?"

Kiano watched as the carefully maintained order of the church service dissolved into a cacophony of voices and emotions. He hadn't expected this level of support, this hunger for answers that had clearly been simmering beneath the surface for far too long.

Pastor Kwamin conferred hurriedly with his associate pastors, their faces drawn with worry. Kiano could see the moment the fight left the lead pastor's eyes. With a defeated slump of his shoulders, Pastor Kwamin turned back to face the congregation.

"Very well," he said, his voice barely audible above the din. He cleared his throat and tried again. "Very well! If this is what the congregation wants, then we will have this debate. Next Friday evening, here in the sanctuary."

A cheer and applause went up from many in the crowd, while others sat in stunned silence. A visiting American journalist sat there wide-eyed, taking her phone out to note something down. Kiano felt a hand on his shoulder and turned to find Jack grinning at him.

"Couldn't let you have *all* the fun," Jack said playfully. "But the hard part's just beginning. We've got work to do."

As the congregation began to file out, a mix of excited chatter and worried whispers filling the air, Kiano found himself surrounded by people. Some offered words of encouragement, while others asked questions or shared their own stories of struggle with the church's teachings.

In the midst of it all, Kiano caught sight of Pastor David, the elder who originally condemned his marriages in the church office, making his way towards them. The older man's face was a mask of conflicting emotions—anger, fear, and something that looked almost like curiosity.

"Kiano," Pastor David said as he reached them, his voice low and tightly controlled. "I hope you understand what you've done here today. The disruption you've caused..."

Kiano met his pastor's gaze steadily. "I understand, Pastor. And I'm sorry for the disruption. But this is long overdue. Too many families have suffered in silence. It's time we addressed this issue openly and honestly."

Pastor David's eyes flickered to Jack, a hint of resentment and fear flashing across his face. "And you... You've got some nerve to do what you did here today young man."

Jack smiled, the strength in his countenance thoroughly intimidating the unsure elder. "Yeah, well. That's what separates the men of God from the boys playing church. Nerve."

Jack turned to Kinao. "I'll wait outside." He tapped him on the back then turned to head out the lobby doors.

Before Kiano could leave, Pastor Kwamin called his name. "Brother Kiano." He walked all the way up to him. "Are you sure you want to do this, my old friend?"

Kiano remained steady, even though some doubt remained inside of him regarding his own capability. "I am."

"Friday evening, then," the pastor said, his voice gruff but no longer hostile. "I hope you're prepared."

As Pastor Kwamin walked away, Kiano felt the weight of what they'd just set in motion settle over him. He turned to catch up with Jack in the parking lot.

As they walked to the car, Kiano found himself eager to get home, to share the news with Amani, Safiya, and Imani. Whatever the outcome of Friday's debate, they had already achieved something monumental—they had broken the silence, challenged the status quo, and opened the door for a conversation that was long overdue.

With his family's love, Jack's expertise, and the unexpected support of many in the congregation, Kiano dared to hope that real change might be possible. Not just for his family, but for countless others who had been caught between their faith and their cultural heritage.

In the week following the church confrontation, Kiano and Jack's days were filled with intense study sessions, poring over biblical texts and historical documents, crafting arguments, and anticipating counterpoints. The living room of Kiano's home had transformed into a makeshift war room, with books, papers, and laptops strewn across every available surface.

On Wednesday's particularly warm afternoon, Kiano leaned back in his chair on their back patio, rubbing his eyes wearily. "I never thought I'd be spending my days debating the finer points of ancient Hebrew marriage customs," he said with a wry smile.

Jack looked up from the thick volume he was studying, his eyes twinkling. "Welcome to my world, brother. But you're catching on quick. You've got the advantage of having this truth in your blood. Americans... All they have in their blood is Hallmark movies. Talking about this with them is like telling a monkey he shouldn't eat bananas. It goes completely against their cultural instincts, but you have thousands of years of tradition on your side. And not just tradition, but need. Genuine, real, life-preserving need. What does America know besides luxury? The West is too accustomed to food banks and homeless shelters. They've completely lost touch with the reality that, one day, women might lose access to those things, and then who will help them? The feminist movement only survives as long as the government is on its side. What if Russia invades next week and all that crumbles? I hate to say it this way, but when things go down, the women of the West will suddenly remember why they need men. Real men. Not men who look good in Instagram photos, but men who can lead their family through war and protect their children from Satan. It's as Isaiah prophesied. When everything starts to come to a head, "Seven women will take hold of one man in that day." Why? Because suddenly, having a man to provide for them and their children will be the only thing left. Monogamy. Polygamy. All Greco-Roman constructs that don't exist in Scripture. The West can't tell the difference between a man and a woman yet they want to teach the rest of the world how marriage should work. The irony is mesmerizing."

Jack took a deep breath, his frustration at the West's extra-Biblical ideals and self-proclaimed social superiority evident in his face. Then he looked back at Kiano. "But you're standing up for truth and righteousness here, and that's an incredible thing to do."

Kiano shrugged, a hint of pride coloring his voice. "It's my heritage, after all. I just never realized how much of it had been... overshadowed by foreign missions."

As they worked, the women of the household moved around them, a constant source of support and encouragement. Amani would appear with steaming mugs of coffee just when they needed it most. They all took turns entertaining the children, keeping the house running smoothly so Kiano could focus on the task at hand.

As the sun dipped below the horizon, Jack sat back, stretching his arms above his head. "You know," he said, his voice thoughtful, "I think we've covered just about every angle. But there's one perspective we haven't really tapped into yet."

Kiano raised an eyebrow, intrigued. "Oh? What's that?"

Jack grinned, gesturing towards the kitchen where the women's voices could be heard, punctuated by occasional laughter. "The female perspective. After all, they're the ones most affected by these teachings, aren't they?"

Kiano nodded slowly, realization dawning. "You're right. We've been so focused on the theological arguments, I'd almost forgotten the human element."

As if on cue, Sarah appeared in the doorway, a knowing smile on her face. "I couldn't help overhearing. Why don't you boys take a break? We'll send the kids out with a deck of Uno."

The men exchanged amused glances before acquiescing, welcoming the kids to the back patio. Safiya gathered the other women in the living room, their excited chatter filling the space previously occupied by notepads and books.

Amani settled onto the couch, tucking her legs beneath her. "So, Sarah," she said, her eyes bright with curiosity, "what's it like being married to a man who spends his life getting in international trouble?"

Sarah laughed, a warm, rich sound that filled the room. "Oh, it's never boring, that's for sure. Jack's passion for truth and justice... it's one of the things I love most about him. And while so many people only see the bold exterior, I get to see the tender moments. Just a few weeks ago, I walked into his office and saw him crying over his Bible because a local church mistreated a single mother. He loves people, especially those who can't defend themselves. But because the world only sees the waving Bible and hears the scathing sermons, a lot of them don't know that side of him exists." She let out a satisfied sigh. "I'll tell you this, I'll never regret the day Miss Sarah Holm became Mrs. Jack Hall."

Imani leaned forward, her voice soft but earnest. "We can't thank you enough for coming all this way to help us. It means more than you know."

Sarah reached out, squeezing her hand. "We wouldn't dream of being anywhere else. What's happening here... it's important. Not just for your family, but for so many others."

Safiya, whose rambunctiousness often mingled with nosiness, couldn't contain her curiosity any longer. "So, Sarah," she said, a mischievous glint in her eye, "don't you ever get tired of doing everything on your own? Tell me, how easy was dinner tonight?"

Amani and Imani humorously shushed her. "Stop that, Safiya," Amani said with a chuckle.

"I'm just saying," Safiya playfully continued, pushing Imani's hand away before it reached her mouth. "My sister Njeri is single and Jack clearly loves Africans—"

"Safiya!" The other two wives yelled in harmony as the room erupted in laughter, the women's faces alight with amusement. Sarah shook her head, grinning. "Oh, believe me, the thought has crossed my mind. Jack has ministered in several places where having multiple wives is still normal. Sometimes I daydream about getting home from the kid's soccer practice, walking into a clean house, with no hungry husband asking 'What's for dinner' because my co-wife has already made it."

Safiya put her hand up and closed her eyes playfully. "Amen, dada (sister). Amen."

After another shared laugh over Safiya's antics, Imani turned to Sarah. "How many children do you have?"

"We have two," Sarah answered. "They're back home with their grandparents. Unfortunately, I can't have any more. The last pregnancy was really hard."

The other women sighed with sympathy as Sarah continued. "I've sometimes thought about how, for most of the world's history, if a family wanted more children, they simply added more wives. And we've thought about adoption but it's just so expensive. I don't think we could ever afford it."

A comfortable silence fell over the room as the women considered Sarah's words. It was Safiya who broke it, her resolve providing ongoing entertainment. "You could move to Africa," she animatedly suggested. "Njeri is *very* excited to start having children—"

She was interrupted by a couch pillow hurled across the room by Amani, resulting in another uproar of laughter. Even Imani, who didn't laugh this hard very often, was holding her stomach and wiping tears from her eyes, a sight that seemed to make everyone aware of God's blessing on their time together.

As the laughter subsided, the conversation flowed on, and as they touched on everything from the challenges of raising children to the joys of shared sisterhood, a deep bond began to form between the women. They shared stories, laughed over common experiences, and offered words of encouragement and support.

Outside on the porch, Kiano and Jack sat in stunned silence as the kids beat them at eight rounds of UNO in a row. The evening air carried the sound of the women's laughter through the open windows, warming their hearts as they enjoyed their respite.

"You hear that, Jack?" Kiano said softly. "That's what we're fighting for. That laughter, that love, that sense of family."

Jack nodded, his eyes distant. "It's beautiful, isn't it? That kind of joy after such a great loss... It's a testament to the strength of your family." He smiled and pointed at Kiano. "And the strength of its leader."

Kiano turned to his friend, his expression humble but serious. "Jack, I can't thank you enough for everything you're doing. For being here, for standing with us."

Jack waved off the gratitude with a smile. "Kiano, my friend, you don't need to thank me. This is what I do. Though I usually do it without going through five shirts a day..." He pointed to his shirt, which was drenched in sweat, as Kiano laughed at him. "Perhaps," Jack continued, "the next time you want to take a stand, we could do it farther away from the equator..." The kids joined in on the laughter as Kiano sent them off to bed.

As the night deepened around them, the two men fell into a companionable silence, each lost in their own thoughts. The weight of the coming debate hung over them, but it was tempered by the sounds of joy and love emanating from the house behind them.

When they finally came inside, they found the women huddled together on the couch, laughing over something Sarah was showing them on her phone. The sight warmed Kiano's heart, reminding him once again of what they were fighting for.

As they prepared for bed that night, Kiano found himself filled with a quiet determination. The coming debate would be challenging, no doubt, but he felt more prepared than ever. Not just because of the hours of study and preparation, but because of the love and support surrounding him.

Lying in bed, Amani curled up beside him, Kiano stared at the ceiling, his mind racing with arguments and counterarguments. Amani seemed to sense his restlessness, propping herself up on one elbow to look at him.

"You're going to do great," she said softly, her voice filled with conviction. "We all believe in you."

Kiano turned to her, drinking in the love and support shining in her eyes. "I couldn't do this without you," he said. "Without all of you."

Amani smiled, leaning down to kiss him gently. "You don't have to. We're in this together. Don't forget that."

As sleep finally claimed him, Kiano's last thoughts were of his family—Amani, Safiya, Imani, the children, and even Jack and Sarah. They were more than just a collection of individuals; they were a unit, bound together by love, faith, and a shared commitment to truth.

The sun had barely risen over Kiambu when Kiano awoke, his heart already racing with anticipation. He lay still for a moment, listening to the gentle breathing of Amani beside him, gathering his thoughts for the day ahead. Today was the day—the debate that could change everything.

As he made his way downstairs, the house was already buzzing with activity. Safiya and Imani were in the kitchen, preparing a hearty breakfast for everyone. The aroma of freshly brewed coffee and sizzling bacon filled the air, a comforting contrast to the tension that hung over the household.

Jack sat at the dining table, seemingly unfazed by the impending conflict. He looked up as Kiano entered, offering a reassuring smile. "Ready for the big day?"

Kiano nodded, pouring himself a cup of coffee. "As ready as I'll ever be," he replied, his voice steady despite the butterflies in his stomach.

Both the morning and afternoon passed in a blur of last-minute preparations and pep talks. As they piled into the car to head to the church, Kiano felt a hand slip into his. He turned to see Imani looking at him, her eyes shining with pride and love.

"You've got this," she whispered, squeezing his hand. "We're all with you."

The drive to Calvary Community Church was silent, each person lost in their own thoughts. As they pulled into the parking lot, Kiano's eyes widened in surprise. The lot was packed, with cars spilling out onto the street.

"Looks like word got out," Jack happily murmured, surveying the crowd gathering outside the church.

As they made their way through the throng of people, Kiano could feel the weight of hundreds of eyes on him. He heard snippets of conversation, his name mentioned in hushed tones. Some faces were curious, others skeptical, while many offered encouraging smiles.

Inside the church, the atmosphere was electric. The pews were filled to capacity, with people standing in the aisles and at the back. Kiano spotted familiar faces from the congregation, but also many he didn't recognize. It seemed the entire community had turned out for this event.

As they made their way to the front, Kiano's eyes fell on a familiar face in the front row. Pastor Muthomi, Jabari's old pastor, sat there, his eyes twinkling with encouragement. Beside him were empty seats, clearly reserved for Kiano and his family.

Pastor Muthomi stood as they approached, enveloping Kiano in a warm embrace. "I wouldn't have missed this for the world, my brother," he said, his voice low and filled with pride.

When he saw Jack and Sarah approach behind Kiano, his eyes lit up. "So.. This is the crazy mzungu who came all the way from America to help you?"

"I know no other way!" Jack said as he joyfully reached out his hand to shake the pastor's.

Muthomi also greeted Sarah, and as they settled into their seats, Kiano scanned the crowd. He saw faces filled with curiosity, skepticism, and even a few with open hostility. But he also saw hope—in the eyes of other polygamous families who had come to support him, in the faces of those who had been hurt by the church's stance on traditional African family structures.

Pastor Kwamin took the stage, his face a mask of calm determination. The room fell silent as he began to speak. "Brothers and sisters. Why we are here today needs no explanation. Today, it is my duty to present to you God's design for marriage, as it is taught in the Scriptures. I will waste no time and begin my lesson."

After praying for the meeting, he laid out his case against polygamy with practiced ease. He cited scripture, quoted European theologians, and spoke of the sanctity of monogamous marriage as God's will in his thick, slow, and commanding accent.

A few excerpts from his presentation included—"You see, brethren. In the beginning, God made Adam and Eve. He did not make two or three women for Adam; but one. He also said, when He instituted marriage, that the man would be joined to his wife, not wives. In Matthew 19:5, Jesus supports this definition of marriage by saying to the religious leaders of His day, 'The two,' not three for four, 'shall become one flesh.'"—"When we examine the Old Testament, we can see that every time a man had multiple wives, it ended in disaster. Lamech, the first polygamist in the world, was a murderer. Abraham, Jacob, and Samuel's families experienced constant discord because they had multiple wives, revealing that their wives did not want this arrangement."—"And what of adultery? Have we forgotten that for a married man to desire another wife is adultery, for he is being unfaithful to his first wife? The Scripture is clear. 'No adulterer shall inherit the Kingdom of heaven.'"—"Another thing to note is that this system of having multiple wives is dishonoring and oppressive to women. Just look at the Mormons or Islam for all the example you need. Women are treated as sex objects to be collected and used rather than human beings. What Christian, in good conscience, could endorse such a tyrannical system, in which women are regarded as cattle, rather than human beings?"—"And finally, in closing, I leave you with the exhortation of Proverbs 5; 'Drink water from your own cistern and fresh water from your own well. Should your springs be dispersed abroad, streams of water in the streets? Let your fountain be blessed, and rejoice in the wife,' not wives"—he added with a confident smile—"'of your youth.'"

Kiano listened intently, his mind racing as he noted points to address and arguments to counter. He could feel Jack beside him, relaxed but focused, occasionally trying to hide his rolling eyes in response to arguments he'd heard a thousand times.

As Pastor Kwamin's speech drew to a close, there was a smattering of applause, mostly from the church leadership and a few devoted members. But the response was tepid at best. It was clear that most of the audience was reserving judgment, waiting to hear Kiano's side.

When Pastor Kwamin finally stepped down from the pulpit, Kiano felt a moment of panic. This was it. Everything they had worked for, everything they had fought for, came down to this moment.

Kiano's heart pounded in his chest, about to burst out at any moment. Before he could stop himself, he fast-walked out of the sanctuary into an empty side hallway, desperate to calm himself. Meanwhile, Jack reassured the hosts that he just needed a minute.

As Kiano breathed in and then out, he heard an unfamiliar voice calling to him from the hallway door, "Brother Kiano!"

An African man in traditional dress, seeming to be in his 40s, with what appeared to be his wife and son, slowly walked towards him. "We wanted to thank you for your bravery in this matter and came to support you as you fight for marriage."

Kiano nodded and gently reached out his hand to shake the man's, still trying to calm his nerves.

"What you are doing means more than you know," the man said, his wife smiling and wiping a single tear away from her cheek beside him.

Seeing her emotion, Kiano postured himself to listen intently to what the man had to say.

"I, too, served in a church like this for many years," the man continued. "I had one wife but she was barren. We tried for many years to have children but we could not." His wife, becoming a little more emotional, nodded in agreement as if to confirm herself as the barren wife.

The man soothingly touched her shoulder and then looked back at Kiano. "After some time, my wife suggested that I marry a friend of hers. This woman's parents had passed away and was struggling to make a living on her own. She had no living family to speak of, and so we talked with her and I believed it was the right thing for me to take her to be my wife."

Kiano's eyebrows raised slightly as his interest in the story piqued.

"We attended a church that believed a man could only have one wife, so we hid the other wife from them for fear of discipline. In only two months, we discovered that she was pregnant. We successfully hid her and the baby that was to be born for one year, but then the elders found out when the baby was just a couple of months old."

Kiano listened intently as tears began to well up in the man's eyes, as well as his son's, who appeared to be around eight years old.

"The elders rebuked me for taking a second wife. They told me that it was God's design for one man and one woman, and that I had sinned in doing this. And then they commanded me to send my second wife and my son away. I fought them at first, but soon, I let them convince me that this was God's desire. So, to avoid the discipline of the church, I sent her away."

The man's tears began to flow as he tried to keep his composure for the rest of the story. His wife held his arm reassuringly.

"I sent her away with a two-month-old baby. We did not live in a very nice part of the city. I knew she would be unprotected and have little hope of provision, but I sent her away anyway because the church told me to."

He paused for a moment as his eyes became red and he sniffed in to prevent his nose from running. After taking a deep breath, he continued, barely able to keep his frame from trembling as he went on.

"A few months later, we got word that she had been approached by a gang, and they convinced her to become..."

His chest started to rise and fall with his heavy breathing, as the weight of the events began to overwhelm him. But he pressed on.

"They made her a prostitute in exchange for providing her food, enough to sustain her and the baby. When I heard this news, I knew that I had sinned, so I fell to my knees in my home and repented. And then I went to go find her and bring her home, but..."

His wife began crying almost as much as he was, which led to Kiano's eyes brimming with tears as he awaited what he knew would be a tragic outcome.

"I looked all over the city that night, and then I found her lying in an alley, her clothes ripped with blood around her waist. There was a drug syringe near her arm and"—he took a deep breath to get it out—"and the baby was in a box on the side of the road. I went and got the baby and came back to pick her up, but she was not moving and barely breathing. When I lifted her skirt, I realized..."

He let out a moan of pain that shook Kiano to his core, as he could no longer contain his emotion, causing Kiano to nearly burst into tears himself.

"I realized that someone had raped her. So I grabbed her and held her, but she was not responding. And I repented, brother Kiano! I yelled that I was sorry and that I had sinned and that I would take her home, but then... then..." The man began weeping profusely and shaking almost uncontrollably. "She died right there in my arms!"

The floodgates of Kiano's eyes burst open as he tightly embraced the man, his wife also weeping and holding their crying son close to herself.

The man shook violently in Kiano's arms, their tears staining each other's clothes. "I sent my own wife to her death!" The man yelled into Kiano's shoulder. "It was my fault! It was my fault!" The man pulled himself off of Kiano to look at him. "And now I look my son in the eyes, knowing his father is his mother's killer!"

Followed by another heart-wrenching groan, the man embraced Kiano again. The weeping continued for a couple of minutes as Kiano realized that this was God telling him he was doing the right thing. This was the motivation he needed to gather his strength and fight this fight. Still in tears, the two men let go of each other, and Kiano, with striking resolve in his eyes and voice, looked the man in the eye. "I will fight for your wife, my brother. In the name of Jesus, her death will not be for nothing."

The man nodded with gratitude, not yet able to fully steady himself, as Kiano re-entered the sanctuary.

All eyes were on him, wondering where he had been. Jack stood up, with a set to his face that revealed his knowledge that God did something to Kiano in that hallway. He approached Kiano, put a hand on his shoulder, and whispered in his ear, "However God spoke to you personally, fight with Scripture, not with stories."

As Jack backed up, Kiano looked at him with a bold determination that surprised even Jack. Jack knew, in this moment, that God had empowered Kiano for the task at hand. He took his seat next to Sarah and Pastor Muthomi as Kiano walked up to the pulpit and set his notepad on top of it.

The room fell silent, the tension palpable. He looked out over the sea of faces, all waiting, all watching. In that moment, he felt the weight of not just his own family's future, but the futures of countless other families who had been torn apart by destructive doctrine and cultural imperialism.

"Brothers and sisters," he began, his voice strong and clear. "I find it interesting that Pastor Kwamin ended his defense of monogamy by quoting from Proverbs. He seems to have forgotten that its author had a thousand wives..."

Half the audience broke out in laughter, while the other half's laughter gradually swelled, understanding dawning as to what Kiano just said.

The positive response from the crowd set any nerves remaining in Kiano completely at ease. Pastor Muthomi and Jack also looked at each other and laughed. Jack shook his head in amazement while leaning into Pastor Muthomi. "That wasn't planned at all."

The two of them exchanged a glance that silently spoke of their confidence in Kiano's calling.

Kiano then began his discourse, meticulously disproving the previous speaker's points.

"Some will tell you that God only made Adam and Eve in the beginning, and that is true. But what does that teach us about marriage? Claiming that God limited all men to one wife because he gave only one to Adam is nothing more than historical inference. And we do not establish doctrine by historical inference, but by Biblical teaching. What next? They will tell you that man would be joined to his wife, not wives, but isn't the former what happens with each marriage a man contracts?

When a man takes his first wife, he is joined to his wife. When that man takes a second wife, he is joined to his wife. What about God's statement here prevents this from happening? Polygamy's opponents will tell you that marriage is between one man and one woman, and indeed it is! But no one is suggesting that a polygamous man is corporately married to multiple women. Such a man does not have one marriage with multiple wives, but rather multiple marriages, each to one wife; and so, in each of his unique marriages, the two certainly do become one flesh. Jesus was not addressing polygamy in any way when speaking to the Pharisees in Matthew 19. He was addressing divorce. And while we are in Matthew 19, I should note that divorce was commonly used in their day for a man to discard one wife in favor of another. If anything, what Jesus said here *supports* polygamy, as He would have clearly preferred it to divorcing one wife for another. God never said, 'I hate the taking of multiple wives,' but He did say, 'I hate divorce.'"

Pastor Muthomi and Jack nodded in agreement to everything Kiano was saying, proud of the way he was presenting his case. The rest of the audience was completely silent. Some were shocked, some thrilled, and others nervous that Kiano would succeed in his mission. He continued, unfazed by the crowd's silence.

"When we turn to the Old Testament, many claim that polygamy always ends in disaster, citing Abraham, Jacob, and Elkanah as examples. But have you ever noticed, these are the only examples given? That is because they are the only examples available. There are nearly forty polygamous husbands mentioned by name in the Old Testament, and only three of them are reported as having conflict between their co-wives. For two of them, Abraham and Elkanah's, the conflict is exclusively with regard to the shame of barrenness. Not once is conflict recorded outside of their attempts to bear children. Not that we should, but if we were to judge polygamy's merit on the problems it caused in Scripture, it would emerge overwhelmingly triumphant over monogamy. And on top of this, while many claim the patriarchs' wives didn't want this arrangement, in most cases, it was the *wives* who suggested that their husbands take more wives! And another point I must make—With regard to the bad behavior of people like Lamech; why do we attribute the bad behavior of polygamists to their family structure but not the bad behavior of monogamists? If how many wives one marries is responsible for their bad behavior or indicative of their sinfulness, then it must be concluded that we can only marry *more* than one wife, for Adam, in his monogamy, doomed the entire human race, and Cain, who seemed to be single at this point, was the world's first murderer! If *their* family structures have nothing to do with their sin—and we all agree that they don't—then neither does the polygamist's."

At this point, Kiano started getting faint "Amens" and agreeable murmuring from the crowd as the host leaders became more and more nervous. Safiya nudged Amani with her arm and leaned over closer to her head. "I am so hot for our husband right now," she whispered, causing Amani to hold in a laugh.

Kiano continued, "And what of adultery? Pastor Kwamin asked... This argument stems from an erroneous definition of adultery. According to Scripture, adultery is only committed when a married woman is defiled by a man who is not her husband. The Bible never once indicates that a married man commits adultery by sleeping with another woman. It is a sin to have sex without marriage, yes, but it is not adultery unless a married woman is defiled. A man no more commits adultery when desiring his second wife than he does when desiring his first wife. Now, for the matter of Mormons and Muslims and other false religions. What do they matter to us? God's people took multiple wives thousands of years before either of those religions existed. We cannot interpret the Scriptures in reaction to what false religions are doing. We must interpret them as sufficient within themselves, regardless of how people abuse them. Do the Mormons abuse marriage? Yes. Should that stop us from marrying? I ask you this. Does the Catholic Church abuse the gospel? Yes. Should that stop us from preaching the gospel? So you see that the abuses of false religions should not impact how we interpret Scripture or how we obey it. And for my last rebuttal to the Pastor's arguments, I will address his charge that having multiple wives in one family dishonors and oppresses women. Here, I remind the Pastor and all listening that it is God Himself who not only regulated, but commanded polygamy in the Law of Moses under certain circumstances. It is God Himself who, in Exodus 21, told men with additional wives to love and provide for them, not cast them out! And it is God Himself who said to David, '*I* gave you your master's wives into your care.' If one lays charge against polygamy for dishonoring and oppressing women, then that one also lays charge against God Almighty for dishonoring and oppressing women—and such a charge is blasphemy!"

As the passion began to swell in Kiano's voice, the applauses and verbal affirmations from the crowd began to swell in tandem. Jack and Pastor Muthomi, however, sat in stunned, wide-eyed silence at the boldness and eloquence emanating from Kiano's speech.

He went on to highlight the various Mosaic laws that encouraged polygamy, Paul's exhortation for younger widows to marry being impossible to broadly obey without polygamy, the polygamous bridegroom returning in Jesus' parable of the ten virgins, and the complete lack of any correction, rebuke, punishment, or even negative statement whatsoever in the entire Bible with regard to having multiple wives.

The audience remained on the edge of their seats, listening in amazement as Kiano logically dismantled every possible objection to polygamy. He left no stone unturned, handling the Word of God with astonishing clarity and never once resorting to cultural or historical arguments. After thirty minutes, he brought his defense to a close.

"And so, brothers and sisters, when all is said and done, the truth of the matter is this. *We* are the ones who differentiate between a man with one wife and a man with more, but God calls each man the same— 'husband.' I rest my case here... 'Monogamy' and 'polygamy' do not exist in the Scriptures, nor in the mind of God. In His eyes, there is only marriage. And God permits a man to have more than one marriage at a time for the holy benefit of all."

Kiano slowly looked up from his notes at the attentive crowd and after a moment of silence, he took a deep breath. "Amen."

With that, the crowd of over a thousand instantly lept to their feet to cheer and applaud. Lively shouts of "Hallelujah" and "Amen" showered the teary-eyed Kiano as he descended the steps of the altar. His family ran to him and enveloped him in a group embrace, with Jack, Sarah, and Pastor Muthomi waiting next in line to congratulate him. The only people not on their feet were Pastor Kwamin and most of his half-white staff, who sat in their seats in humiliation as the crowd had plainly determined that Kiano was the debate's winner. Two of the host elders, one African and one American, joined the audience in applauding Kiano, having been persuaded by his arguments that they were wrong.

As Kiano emerged from his family and friends' embrace, he was engulfed in a sea of hugs and handshakes. People reached out to touch him, to offer words of support and gratitude. He saw families who had been torn apart by the church's stance on polygamy, tears streaming down their faces as they thanked him for speaking out.

Amani, Safiya, and Imani observed the scene, their faces glowing with pride and love. Jack playfully held out his fist to Pastor Muthomi off to the side. "Mzungu for the win?" Pastor Muthomi let out a bombastic, satisfied laugh as he connected with Jack's fist for a fist-bump. "Mzungu for the win!" The pastor declared. They laughed together and hugged in celebration of Kiano's victory.

As the crowd began to head outside, still buzzing with excitement and discussion, Pastor Kwamin approached Kiano. His face was a study in conflicting emotions—surprise, respect, and a hint of uncertainty.

"Kiano," he said, extending his hand, "I must admit, you've given us all a lot to think about. Your arguments were compelling, and your ability to handle the Word is evident."

Kiano shook the pastor's hand, feeling a glimmer of hope. "Thank you, Pastor," he said. "I hope this can be the beginning of a dialogue, not the end of one."

Pastor Kwamin nodded slowly. "Perhaps you are right."

With that, the respectably defeated pastor retired to his office as Kiano, along with his family and friends, made their way outside. As they crossed through the front door and into the parking lot, the remaining crowd of hundreds repeated their cheers and applause for Kiano. Jack put his arm around him as they walked through the crowd, once again congratulating him for a job well done. Kiano likewise swung his arm around Jack's shoulders in brotherly affection. "I can't thank you enough for coming here, brother. Where are you off to next?"

"The Philippines," Jack yelled over the noise. "I'm scheduled to preach a series of revival meetings in Manila."

"When do you leave?" Kiano shouted back.

"We're flying out today after lunch," Jack answered.

Kiano smiled and shook his head in delight. "Well, my brother, may God be as good to you there as He was to us here."

Jack looked back at Sarah and Kiano's family following them to their cars, and then turned his head to face in front of them again with a huge smile on his face. "God is good all the time, my friend."

Kiano heartily nodded in agreement. "And all the time, God is good!"

Be diligent to present yourself approved to God as a workman who does not need to be ashamed, accurately handling the word of truth.

2 Timothy 2:15

Epilogue

Henry Green gripped the steering wheel as he drove through the busy Manila streets. He glanced occasionally at Lily and Lola in his rearview mirror, and his heart swelled with a love that still amazed him daily.

Lola shifted uncomfortably in her seat, her eight-months-pregnant belly making it difficult to find a comfortable position. She'd been having contractions all day, though she'd insisted on coming to the service anyway. The doctor had assured them everything was progressing normally, but Henry couldn't help worrying.

"Almost there," Henry said softly, catching Lola's eye in the mirror. Though they'd only been married eight months, he'd grown attuned to her needs, just as he had with Lily over their years together. He could read the discomfort in the slight furrow of her brow and the way she pressed one hand against her lower back.

Lily reached back to squeeze Lola's hand, their sisterly bond evident in the wordless gesture of support. The sight warmed Henry's heart—how far they'd all come from those first awkward days of their arrangement.

"I still can't believe how many cars are headed to the church," Lily marveled, peering through the window at the stream of vehicles all seeming to flow in the same direction. The traffic had grown notably worse as they approached Faith Assembly. "Have you ever seen a service this big before?"

Henry shook his head. Their own church gatherings, while vibrant and full of life, rarely topped a hundred people. But this—this was something else entirely. Cars filled every side street, with volunteers in reflective vests directing traffic. He'd heard the visiting American preacher could draw thousands, but seeing the reality of it was overwhelming.

"It reminds me of the crusades they used to have at Luneta Park when I was a child," Lola commented, momentarily forgetting her discomfort as she remembered. "Mama would take us early in the morning to get good seats. The whole place would be packed with people bringing the sick, hoping for miracles."

"Did you ever see any?" Lily asked, turning in her seat to face her co-wife.

Lola's eyes grew distant with memory. "I'm sure I saw many, but I really only remember one. A little blind girl. When they prayed for her..." She trailed off, one hand absently stroking her belly. "I'll never forget her mother's face when she saw her for the first time."

As they pulled into the sprawling parking lot of Faith Assembly, Henry felt a familiar flutter of anticipation in his chest. He couldn't explain it, but something about tonight felt significant. The same unexplainable urge that had drawn him to attend this service seemed to be stronger now that they were here.

"There's Papa and Mama!" Lola called out, pointing to where her parents stood with Pastor Alon near the church's entrance. The older couple had arrived early to help with set up, as they often did for special services.

Henry made his way through the crowded lot, finally finding a spot in the far corner. He hurried around to help his wives out of the car, one hand supporting Lola's back as she eased herself up. The early evening air was humid and they could hear the mingled sounds of car doors slamming, children calling to each other, and the distant worship music coming from inside the building as the band warmed up.

Streams of people flowed toward the building's grand entrance, its modern architecture a stark contrast to their own modest church building. The glass doors stood wide open, welcoming the crowd, while ushers in crisp white shirts directed the people inside.

"My daughter!" Lola's mother rushed toward them, her colorful dress billowing in the evening breeze as she embraced Lola carefully around her swollen belly. "How are you feeling?"

"Like I'm carrying a watermelon," Lola laughed, returning her mother's hug. "But the doctor says everything's perfect. I wouldn't miss this for anything."

"Come, let's get you both seated before the crowds get worse," Lola's mother said, ushering Lily and Lola toward the entrance. Her maternal instincts extended naturally to both young women, another blessing Henry never took for granted. "We have spots saved near the front," she told the women as they entered the crowded sanctuary.

As they walked, Lily leaned close to Maria, her eyes sparkling. "Actually... there's some news we just found out." She glanced back at Henry, seeking his permission to share. At his encouraging nod, she continued, "I'm expecting too."

The older woman stopped in her tracks, joy blooming across her face like a sunrise. "Two grandchildren? Oh, praise God!" She pulled Lily into a tight embrace, tears welling up in her eyes. "When did you find out? How far along are you?"

"Just yesterday," Lily replied, her own eyes growing misty. "The doctor says about eight weeks. We wanted to wait until we were sure before telling everyone."

"Two babies," Lola's mother marveled, looking between the two women. "Oh, what a blessing! They'll be so close in age—like twins!"

Henry watched them disappear into the building, his heart so full it felt like it might burst. A year ago, he never could have imagined his life taking such a turn—two loving wives, two babies on the way. The path hadn't been easy, and there had been plenty of raised eyebrows and whispered judgments, but God's grace had seen them through.

"You look happy, my friend." Pastor Alon's voice drew Henry from his thoughts. The older man's kind face creased with genuine pleasure as he regarded Henry.

"I am," Henry replied, turning to face the pastor and Lola's father. "And we just found out—Lily's pregnant too."

Both men's faces lit up with genuine joy. "God is good!" Pastor Alon exclaimed, clapping Henry on the shoulder. His enthusiasm was infectious, his whole body seeming to radiate delight at the news. "Two new lives to celebrate!"

"Two new souls to raise in the faith," Lola's father added, his eyes crinkling with pleasure.

Henry nodded, then hesitated. Something he'd been carrying in his heart pressed forward, demanding to be voiced. The weight of it had been growing for weeks, becoming impossible to ignore. "Pastor, there's something else..." He paused, searching for the right words. "I've been feeling this call lately. Like God wants more from me than just attending church and serving in little ways. It's like He's telling me He wants me to do something... bigger. I'm not sure how to explain it."

Pastor Alon studied him thoughtfully, his expression growing serious. This was not a conversation to be taken lightly. "That's why you wanted to come tonight?"

"Partly," Henry admitted. "I can't explain it, but I felt drawn here. Like something important is going to happen."

A knowing smile crossed Pastor Alon's face. "I've known Brother Jack from his previous visits. You're in the right place tonight, Henry."

The words settled over Henry like a warm blanket, confirming what his heart had been telling him. He thanked them and headed inside to find his family, leaving the two older men in the lobby.

He entered the massive sanctuary, its contemporary design a masterpiece of wood and glass. The professional lighting system cast a glow over everything, while the state-of-the-art sound system carried the worship team's practice throughout the room.

Henry found his wives seated in the third row, center section—prime seats that showed Lola's parents' influence in the church community. The space was already filling rapidly, people flowing into the rows like water finding its level. He settled between Lily and Lola, his hands finding theirs instinctively.

The worship leader took the stage, and the atmosphere shifted palpably. The crowd went silent and attentive as he stepped up to the microphone, his voice carrying clearly through the professional sound system. The first notes rang out—a familiar chorus that had Henry's heart leaping.

Three thousand voices joined together in worship, the sound overwhelming in its intensity. Henry had never experienced anything like it. The harmony of so many believers singing in unity sent chills down his spine. Beside him, Lily's clear soprano lifted above the crowd, while Lola swayed gently, one hand resting on her belly as if inviting their unborn child to join the worship.

Henry tried to focus on the words, on lifting his voice in praise, but his thoughts kept drifting to what lay ahead. The nagging sense of destiny—of something monumental approaching—wouldn't leave him.

"You have no rival. You have no equal. Now and forever God you reign," the worship leader sang, and the crowd responded with such fervor that Henry felt the floor vibrate beneath his feet. Around him, hands lifted in praise while tears streamed down hundreds of faces as God's presence filled the room.

After forty minutes that felt both like an eternity and mere moments, the music faded to a gentle instrumental backing. The host pastor stepped forward, his voice carrying clearly through the sound system. "Brothers and sisters, what a joy to welcome you tonight!" His smile was genuine, his excitement tangible. "Looking out at this crowd, I'm reminded of what the prophet Joel saw—that in the last days, God would pour out His Spirit on all flesh."

The congregation murmured in agreement, scattered "Amens" punctuating his words. The host pastor continued, "We are blessed to have with us a man who needs no introduction—a servant of God who has seen revivals break out across four continents. From the streets of London to the villages of Kenya, from the megachurches of Seoul to the house churches of China, his ministry has touched countless lives. Please welcome Evangelist Jack Hall!"

The crowd erupted in applause as a tall American man bounded onto the stage with infectious charisma. Jack moved with the confidence of someone completely at home in front of large crowds, but there was nothing showy or artificial about him. His wife Sarah beamed from her seat in the front row as he took the microphone, her pride in her husband evident in every line of her face, which was thoroughly tanned from their recent time in Africa.

Jack set his Bible on the pulpit and surveyed the crowd, his eyes bright with holy fire. He said nothing for a long moment, letting the anticipation build. Then, without preamble or introduction, he brought the microphone up to his mouth and yelled, "Does anybody in Manila believe that the blood of Jesus has lost none of its power!?"

The response was immediate and thunderous. Henry found himself on his feet with everyone else, electricity seeming to crackle through the air. He'd heard many preachers before, but something about Jack was different. This man carried an authority, a tangible sense of God's presence that made Henry's spirit stand at attention.

As if to confirm his thoughts, Lily squeezed his hand, whispering, "I've never felt anything like this." Her eyes shone with tears, and Henry could see Lola nodding in agreement on his other side.

Henry nodded, unable to take his eyes off the dynamic preacher. He'd come seeking answers, direction for the stirring in his soul. Now, watching Jack command the stage with Holy Ghost power, Henry felt his heart race. Something was about to break loose—he could feel it in his bones.

Jack prowled the stage like a lion, his voice rising and falling with heartfelt intensity as he laid out the fundamentals of the gospel. His American accent, rather than being a barrier, seemed to add weight to his words. "When Jesus went to that cross," he declared, his voice thick with emotion and his eyes brimming with tears, "He didn't die because God just couldn't help but love you. He didn't die because someone made Him do it. He went to that cross because He *chose* to love you—while you were His enemies, while you were dead in your sins! Behold the mercy of God! Not that something in us deserved saving, but that God Himself is rich in mercy and willing that none perish!"

Many in the crowd responded with shouts of agreement—others seemed to tremble in their seats—as Jack continued. "I'm not asking you if you want to make Jesus Lord of your life. Friend, let me tell you, Jesus doesn't need your consent to be Lord. He's Lord whether you acknowledge it or not! And I'm not asking you if you'd like to slip your hand up and repeat a prayer while no one's watching. What kind of powerless gospel is that? If you won't confess Christ before men, He won't confess you before His Father in heaven!"

Henry leaned forward in his seat, drinking in every word. The preacher's passion was contagious, spreading through the crowd like wildfire.

"I am here to tell you that although the fear of death has haunted you your entire life, God offers you everlasting life through Jesus Christ! He bore the wrath that you deserved on that cross, rose on the third day, ascended to Heaven in front of many witnesses, and is one day returning to judge the world in righteousness! All of us will stand before the judgment seat of Christ and give an account for what we've done. Do not be found wanting on that day! Respond to Him now! Listen to my voice—you who've mocked and ignored the Lamb! You who've turned to that Roman Beast for assurance! And you who've pushed God out of your mind and blasphemed His Name!—You will not escape when the King returns in glory! He will deal out retribution to all those who do not obey the gospel of our Lord and Savior Jesus Christ! There'll be fire in His eyes and a sword that proceeds from His mouth! And the great warriors and kings of the earth will see His fury rise up in His face, and they'll yell to the mountains, 'Fall on us, and save us from the presence of the Lamb!' Time is running out! Jesus has paid the debt you owe! And now, God commands all men everywhere to repent of their sins and believe this gospel!"

People were now standing, shouting, weeping—caught up in the powerful presence of God that seemed to fill every corner of the massive chamber. Henry stayed glued to his seat, almost paralyzed by what felt like divine currents of electricity coursing through his body.

"And as long as this gospel is preached," Jack continued, as he made his way back to the pulpit. "Not the gospel that says you can come and go as you please, not the gospel that says a priest in a fish hat can wash away your sins, and not the gospel that says adulterers and sodomites are fine as they are and can stay as they are..."—His voice took on an edge of authority that seemed to cut through the noise like a sword.—"As long as *this* gospel is preached!" he shouted as he held up his bible over his head, "The lost will be saved! The dead will be raised! And the demon-possessed WILL! GO! FREE!!!"

The crowd roared their approval at seemingly deafening decibels as Jack set his bible back down on the pulpit and waited for the noise to subside. As the noise began to settle, he opened his Bible, then paused. His eyes narrowed, scanning the congregation as if searching for something specific. The sudden shift in his demeanor caused a hush to fall over the crowd.

His gaze settled on the front corner of the room, where a middle-aged woman sat in a wheelchair. Her husband stood protectively behind her, his hands resting on the wheelchair's handles. "And the sick will be healed," Jack added quietly, his tone shifting from bombastic to tender, though still carrying its underlying authority.

The atmosphere in the room changed instantly as Jack descended the stage steps and approached the woman. An usher hurried over with a second microphone, holding it close as Jack knelt before her. The crowd's eyes followed him, some standing and moving up to see what was going on.

Henry's heart began to race faster. The feeling that had been building all evening suddenly intensified, though he couldn't have explained why. He found himself moving forward without conscious thought, drawn by something invisible. He wasn't alone—all around him, people were standing, craning their necks to see what would happen.

Jack's voice carried clearly through the sound system as he spoke to the woman. "How long have you been confined to this chair?" he asked gently.

The woman's voice trembled with emotion as she replied, "Eight years. A car accident..." She paused, fighting back tears. "The doctors said I would never walk again. The nerves in my spine were too damaged."

Her husband squeezed her shoulder in silent support, his own eyes glistening with unshed tears. The entire congregation seemed to hold its breath, waiting to see what would happen next. Jack looked at the host pastor in the front row, himself in tears, clearly signaling that he'd known this woman and her plight.

Henry had made his way to the front by now, stopping just short of the altar area. Something was building in his spirit—a feeling unlike anything he'd ever experienced. He found himself holding his breath, feeling more and more drawn to the scene unfolding in the corner.

Jack's voice carried clearly through the sound system. "God is going to heal you right now—"

He cut off abruptly, spinning around to face the center section. His eyes locked onto Henry with laser focus, and in that moment, time seemed to stop. "You."

Henry glanced behind him, then pointed to himself questioningly. Surely the preacher couldn't mean him?

"Yes, you." Jack's voice carried absolute certainty. "Come here."

Henry's feet felt like lead as he approached, his heart thundering in his chest. Every eye in the building seemed to bore into him. The stares that had been following Jack now encompassed them both.

The woman in the wheelchair looked up at Henry with mixed hope and uncertainty. Her husband's hands tightened slightly on the wheelchair handles, and his expression remained guarded. Henry could read the questions in their eyes—who was this man? Why had the preacher called him forward?

"God wants you to pray for her," Jack said firmly. The microphone picked up his words clearly, broadcasting them throughout the massive room.

"Me?" Henry's voice cracked. He could feel sweat beading on his forehead under the hot lights. "But I'm not... I've never..." The words stuck in his throat. He'd never prayed for healing before, had never considered himself someone God would use in this way.

Suddenly, Jack grabbed Henry's wrist and placed his hand on the woman's head, then looked at him. "The same power that raised Jesus from the dead is at work in you. Tell this woman to get up."

Henry stood frozen, overwhelmed by the pressure of the moment. He could feel Lily and Lola's eyes on him from their seats—the women equally frozen in anticipation—and he could sense the collective expectations of three thousand people holding their breath. The silence in the room was deafening.

The woman's hair was soft under his fingers. He could feel her trembling slightly, whether from fear or hope, he couldn't tell. Her husband watched intently.

Henry closed his eyes, fighting back tears. Images flashed through his mind—Emily's face, his years of anger, the miraculous way God had transformed his life through Lily's faith and Lola's unexpected entry into their family. If God could work those miracles, why not this?

He thought of Lola's story from earlier—the little blind girl she'd seen healed as a child. He thought of the power that accompanied Jack's preaching. The same God who had done those miracles was here now, waiting to work through him.

"In the name of Jesus," Henry said, his voice gaining strength with each word, "get up and walk!"

Nothing happened. Seconds stretched like hours as doubt began to creep in. The woman remained still in her wheelchair, her eyes closed tightly in concentration or prayer. Henry turned toward his family, seeking reassurance—and then it happened.

"I can feel them!" the woman cried out suddenly, her eyes flying open in shock. "I can feel my legs!"

The crowd gasped collectively as she began to move, wiggling her toes inside her shoes. Her husband's face transformed from guarded hope to astonishment as she gripped the arms of the wheelchair.

As she looked up at Jack in disbelief and joy, Jack raised the microphone close to his mouth. "That's right, my sister. You'll never need it again!" Jack then took her hand and pulled her to her feet with one long stroke. She stood shakily for a moment, her legs trembling with disuse. Her husband reached for her instinctively, but Jack held up a hand to stop him. "Let her go—In a moment, you will see the glory of God."

She took one tentative step, then another. Suddenly, strength seemed to flood her body. Her uncertain shuffle transformed into steady steps, and then, to everyone's amazement, she took off running down the center aisle.

The place erupted in chaos—people jumping, shouting, and weeping as the woman ran past them. Her husband followed behind her, tears streaming down his face as he watched his wife of thirty years run for the first time in almost a decade.

Some people were staring in shock, others were on their knees praising God, still others were hugging and crying with perfect strangers. The praise team had begun playing spontaneously, the leader enthusiastically belting, *"Whose report will you believe?"* The crowd erupted in response, *"We shall believe the report of the Lord!"* Half of the building took to the aisles and altar area to dance along with the woman who was healed.

But Henry barely registered the commotion. He stood rooted to the spot, tears streaming down his face as the magnitude of what had just happened sank in. His hand still tingled where it had rested on the woman's head. He felt simultaneously exhausted and energized, emptied and filled.

The commotion lasted about five minutes, the praise team leader eventually bringing things back down. As the crowd regained its composure, Jack cheerfully motioned for the woman to come back to him, Henry still standing there in awe of the events.

The woman jogged back over to Jack with a beaming, glory-filled smile on her face. Jack spoke into the microphone with a smile of his own. "So, what are you going to do now that you've got your legs back?"

The woman turned her head to an usher who was standing by a wide door on the side of the building used for equipment unloading. "Young man, would you mind opening that door for me?" she asked with a smile.

The usher obliged and opened the door, unsure of why he was doing so. The woman then walked over to her wheelchair, picked it up above her head—as the crowd began to cheer—walked it over to the door, and threw it outside with all her might. "Take that devil!!!" she shouted at the tumbling wheelchair while rapidly stomping her feet in victory.

Jack burst into laughter as the crowd applauded the woman's faith-filled antics.

As the noise once again died down and people finally began sitting, the woman having thanked Jack and stood off to the side—she'd sat long enough—Henry still remained frozen in place, unsure of what direction to even move in. The weight of God using him for something so incredible had overwhelmed him. Little did he know, his night was far from over...

"And you!" Jack's amplified voice cut through the still-murmuring crowd. Henry turned to find the preacher pointing at him again, his face alight with prophetic fire.

"This is only the beginning of what you'll see," Jack declared, his voice returning to its sermon-level seriousness.

Henry's legs began to tremble as Jack continued, "This is what the Lord says: 'I have called you out of darkness into marvelous light. You once lived for vengeance, but I have given you peace. As you have been forgiven, so you have forgiven your brother also.'"

Henry's eyes burst forth tears as the reality of God's hand on his life became clearer than ever. He fell to his knees as Jack continued, "'And now, you will preach this gospel of salvation to hundreds and thousands, and many will be added to the Kingdom wherever you go. I will confirm My word with signs, wonders, and miracles, the likes of which you have seen here today. I will never leave you, nor forsake you, and I will be with you until the end of the age.'"

Jack lowered the microphone as Henry fell to his face, sobbing as God's presence overwhelmed him. The hard floor pressed against his forehead, but he barely felt it. Everything—his past, his present, his future—seemed to crystallize in this moment.

Jack returned to the pulpit to deliver his sermon, but Henry remained face-down, lost in his encounter with God. Memories came over him—his arrival in the Philippines bent on revenge, his first meeting with Lily, the unexpected connection with Lola, the grace that had transformed their complicated situation into something beautiful. Each step, even the missteps, had been leading to this moment.

In the third row, Lily and Lola clung to each other, tears streaming down their faces as they watched their husband's transformation.

The service continued around Henry's prone form—Jack preaching with undiminished fire, people responding to altar calls, lives being transformed—but Henry remained where he was, unable and unwilling to move from that holy spot. The cold floor beneath him, the noise of the crowd, the discomfort of his position—none of it mattered compared to the overwhelming presence of God that held him there.

Almost two hours later, the music stopped and the crowd began to thin, voices and footsteps fading as people made their way out into the night. Still, Henry stayed, his face pressed against the floor, his heart too full for words. The worship team had packed up their instruments, their soft conversations and the sound of cables being wrapped providing a gentle backdrop to his continued prayer.

Only when the building had grown nearly silent did he finally push himself to his knees, then to his feet. His legs felt unsteady, and his knees protested from the long contact with the hard floor, but his spirit felt lighter, transformed in a way he couldn't fully explain.

The massive place had emptied except for a few small groups chatting in the aisles. Jack sat on the front row talking with the host pastor, while Lily, Lola, Pastor Alon, and Lola's father waited patiently in their seats. Sarah sat in her original seat, waiting for Jack to be finished for the night, a routine all too familiar to her when she accompanied him to big services.

Henry's legs still felt unsteady as he made his way toward Jack. The host pastor caught his eye and excused himself with a knowing smile, leaving Jack alone on the front pew. The American preacher patted the seat beside him, his face gentle now, all trace of the earlier intensity gone.

"How are you feeling, brother?" Jack asked, his voice warm with genuine excitement.

Henry sank onto the pew, still trembling slightly. The leather was cool beneath him, grounding him in the present moment. "I don't know what to do next," he admitted. "How do I... where do I start?" The enormity of what had happened—what God had declared over his life—felt overwhelming.

Jack reached for his briefcase, a well-worn leather bag that spoke of countless miles traveled. He pulled out a book and a handful of gospel tracts that looked like million-dollar bills. "Start here," he said, pressing them into Henry's hands. "Don't wait for something dramatic to happen. Just start sharing the gospel with people."

Henry traced the title of the book he was given with his tired hand, whispering the information to himself. *"Hell's Best Kept Secret by Ray Comfort."*

"It'll help you learn to present the gospel message Biblically and effectively," Jack said as he watched Henry examine the cover.

Henry nodded, still running his fingers over the book's cover. The simple, practical advice was exactly what he needed—a way to channel the holy fire still burning in his chest into actionable steps.

Behind him, he heard footsteps approaching—his wives coming to meet the man God had used to change their lives. He turned to make introductions, suddenly aware of the potential awkwardness of explaining his unusual family situation to this American preacher. In their own church, people accepted them, but what would an American think?

Before he could speak, Sarah had already joined them, standing next to Jack with the same warmth he exuded. Her eyes sparkled with genuine interest as she looked at the small group approaching.

"And who do we have here?" Jack asked, his smile genuine and welcoming. There wasn't a trace of judgment in his expression, just sincere curiosity.

Henry took a deep breath, steeling himself for a negative reaction. "This is my wife, Lily," he began, watching carefully for any change in Jack's expression. "And this is… this is my wife, Lola."

He waited for the look of shock or disapproval, the subtle stiffening that usually preceded awkward questions or hasty exits—but it never came. Instead, Jack jumped to his feet with surprising agility, pulling both women into enthusiastic hugs while Sarah did the same.

"Look at you both!" Sarah exclaimed, her hands gentle on Lola's pregnant belly. Her face glowed with genuine delight. "When are you due?"

"Next month," Lola answered, relief evident in her voice. She relaxed visibly, the tension leaving her shoulders as she realized there would be no problem here.

Lily leaned in and added, "And I'm due in seven..." sparking a joyful response from Sarah and Jack.

"Two babies!" Jack beamed, looking between them with genuine joy. "God is surely blessing your family."

Henry watched in amazement as Jack and Sarah fussed over his wives, showing nothing but genuine joy and acceptance. Pastor Alon and Lola's father had joined them now, completing their small circle in the nearly empty sanctuary. The huge space felt intimate somehow, like a family gathering rather than a church building.

When Jack finally sat back down next to Henry, his eyes twinkled with curiosity. "So, how did you all come together? I'm guessing it wasn't on Christian Mingle..."

Henry laughed, releasing any leftover tension. "It's kind of a crazy story..." he answered, followed by a deep breath. "Ever dealt with anything like this before?"

Jack looked behind him and exchanged an amused look with Sarah, smiling in light of last week's events in Kenya. He then turned back to Henry, placing a friendly hand on his shoulder. "Brother, you have no idea..."

A few rows back, Sarah and the two women sat down together.

"You two really aren't shocked at all?" Lily questioned Sarah.

Sarah smiled at them both, her face filled with gracious understanding. "Not at all. In fact—" Sarah pulled her wallet out of her purse, flipping it open to a clear sleeve housing an old black and white photo—"My great grandparents' story probably isn't too different from yours."

Sarah removed the photo from her wallet as Lola and Lily listened attentively. "Before I was Sarah Hall, I was Sarah Holm. My grandmother's name was Anna, and she moved from northern Europe to the States for school in the 50's. Her mother—my great grandmother—was a widow for some time, but then a godly couple took her into their home, and she became the second wife of that man."

Sarah paused in a moment of reflection, then smiled at the attentive women. "Without that living faith in action, I never would have existed."

She held out the photo for the other women to look at.

"This is them," Sarah said as she let out an affectionate sigh. "You know, they stayed on that farm 'till the day they died."

Lola and Lily leaned in to see the photo—three elderly people sitting on the porch of a modest, two-story farmhouse—a man in the middle with a woman on each side. Lily squinted to read the weathered inscription on the bottom: "Lars, Elsa, & Hannah Holm, 1942."

Now to Him who is able to do far more abundantly beyond all that we ask or think, according to the power that works within us, to Him be the glory in the church and in Christ Jesus to all generations forever and ever. Amen.

Ephesians 3:20-21

www.ingramcontent.com/pod-product-compliance
Lightning Source LLC
LaVergne TN
LVHW090717080125
800746LV00005B/56